PENGUIN BOOKS

The Cat's Pyjamas

Julia Cresswell studied English at Oxford, specializing in the history of the language and medieval literature. She has worked as a researcher for the Oxford English dictionaries, has taught for several Oxford colleges and written numerous books, mostly on aspects of the English language. She teaches regularly at Oxford University's Department of Continuing Education, and currently splits her time between writing, teaching and looking after a small academic library. She lives in Oxford with her husband, her son Alexander, who is also a published writer, and a pond full of frogs. *The Cat's Pyjamas* is a continuation of the exploration of the history and nature of clichés which she started in *The Penguin Dictionary of Clichés*.

The Cat's Pyjamas

The Penguin Book of Clichés

JULIA CRESSWELL

PENGUIN BOOKS

PENGUIN BOOKS

Published by the Penguin Group
Penguin Books Ltd, 80 Strand, London WC2R ORL, England
Penguin Group (USA) Inc., 375 Hudson Street, New York, New York 10014, USA
Penguin Group (Canada), 90 Eglinton Avenue East, Suite 700, Toronto, Ontario, Canada M4P 2Y3
(a division of Pearson Penguin Canada Inc.)
Penguin Ireland, 25 St Stephen's Green, Dublin 2, Ireland
(a division of Penguin Books Ltd)
Penguin Group (Australia), 250 Camberwell Road, Camberwell, Victoria 3124, Australia
(a division of Pearson Australia Group Pty Ltd)
Penguin Books India Pvt Ltd, 11 Community Centre,
Panchsheel Park, New Delhi – 110 017, India
Penguin Group (NZ), 67 Apollo Drive, Rosedale, North Shore 0632, New Zealand
(a division of Pearson New Zealand Ltd)
Penguin Books (South Africa) (Pty) Ltd, 24 Sturdee Avenue,
Rosebank, Johannesburg 2196, South Africa

Penguin Books Ltd, Registered Offices: 80 Strand, London WC2R ORL, England

www.penguin.com

First published 2007
3

Copyright © Julia Cresswell, 2007
All rights reserved

The moral right of the author has been asserted

Set in 11/13 pt Monotype Bembo
Typeset by Rowland Phototypesetting Ltd, Bury St Edmunds, Suffolk
Printed in England by Clays Ltd, St Ives plc

ISBN: 978-0-141-02516-2

www.greenpenguin.co.uk

With thanks to all the broadcasters, journalists and politicians
who have made this book possible

Contents

Introduction

'Clichés can be quite fun. That's how they got to be clichés'
Alan Bennett, *The History Boys* (2004)

It was depressing, when *The Penguin Dictionary of Clichés* was first published in 2000, to find the first review on Amazon.co.uk read: 'I looked at this book and the first very common cliche [*sic*] that came to mind was "leg pulling". There was not a mention of it nor of any of its alternatives, so I put it back on the shelf and now wait to find another publication.' This sat at the top of the list of reviews for many years, and I feared blighted sales, although I am pleased to note that no one has ever rated the review as useful. However, the person who wrote this does, unwittingly, raise two useful questions: what is a cliché, and what is a cliché's base form? In this case, 'leg pulling' is quite clearly not a cliché. 'To pull someone's leg' is an idiom, a turn of phrase in English with a meaning that is not transparent (a word that itself is growing in clichéd use, but here is used as linguistic jargon) to the non-native user, but which every native speaker understands. The form 'leg pulling' would never appear in a book as a root form. While it is possible to create a sentence that uses it (something on the lines of 'They were indulging in a cruel bout of leg-pulling'), the standard use would be in a sentence such as 'They were pulling her leg', and the term would normally be listed as 'to pull someone's leg'. In this book this problem has largely been avoided. As the clichés are discussed within a narrative, I have used them in whatever form fits most comfortably into the flow. However, this is something the reader might like to keep in mind when using the index. There I have tried to list the clichés discussed under their root forms, but as this form is not always evident, the reader may need to look in more than one place.

A more difficult question is what exactly is a cliché? A flippant answer to this is that for the purposes of this book, it is whatever I say it is. This claim does have a serious point behind it. The usual definition of a cliché is that it is a tired, hackneyed phrase. But however you try to define it, there is no escaping the fact that whatever definition you use, it is still based on subjective judgement. What grates on one person's ear may be perfectly innocuous to another's. It is a matter of personal taste and linguistic sensitivity. There is no doubt that clichés can be an efficient and effective way of getting an idea across quickly. As Terry Pratchett puts it, 'The reason clichés become clichés is that they are the hammers and screwdrivers in the toolbox of communication' (*Guards! Guards!*, 1989, p. 135). This means there is a sliding scale of clichéhood; some terms can be objectionable or not depending how and when they are used. Take the word 'ground-breaking'. This can be a useful bit of journalese, saying something briefly and effectively. But look at how it is used in the following passage from a newspaper: 'A space capsule from the *Stardust* mission, carrying dust and comet fragments that scientists hope will unlock some of the most ancient secrets of the solar system, has landed safely in the Utah desert – the culmination of a hazardous and potentially ground-breaking seven-year mission.' Not only is 'ground-breaking' inappropriately combined with the idea of a mission to space, which is about as far away from the ground as you can get, it also sets up clashing mental images of ground-breaking and 'has landed safely in the Utah desert'. Then what about the journalist who wrote about the discovery of some fossils in Australia of a killer kangaroo that once 'walked the earth'? And am I the only person who responds to the title of the television programme *Who Wants to be a Millionaire?* with the next line of the song the title is taken from – 'I don't'? Actually, given the success of the programme perhaps I am, which is another example of how individual the reaction to language is. In these three cases the writer has simply let the words pour out without thinking of their true meaning. This is, in my view, one of the key ways of telling if something is a cliché: that it can be used thoughtlessly. Language that is carefully considered and backed by clear thought is unlikely to be clichéd.

It is in this ability to blank out clear thought that the danger of clichés is found. Much of what we today call spin and would in the past have called rhetoric is dependent on clichés. Anyone who has listened to a politician or a PR person being interviewed on radio or television will have heard how clichés can be used to obscure or obfuscate. This can be dangerous. There is a saying, attributed to Confucius: 'When words lose their meaning, people lose their freedom' (quoted in John G. Murray's *A Gentleman Publisher's Commonplace Book*, 1996), the truth of which is amply illustrated by the history of twentieth-century dictatorships.

It is not always thoughtlessness that leads to people using clichés. Sometimes it is because the expressions are moving from living metaphor to dead metaphor. It is easy to forget how pervasive metaphor is in language. One of the best recent commentators on the basics of language and how it evolved, Guy Deutscher, has written:

Even in the most commonplace discourse, it is hardly possible to venture a few steps without treading on dozens of metaphors. For metaphors are everywhere, not only in language, but also in our mind. Far from being a rare spark of poetic genius, the marvellous gift of a precious few, metaphor is an indispensable element in the thought process of every one of us . . . We use metaphors not because of any literary leaning or artistic ambitions, but quite simply because metaphor is the chief mechanism through which we can describe and even grasp abstraction.

He goes on to describe:

. . . the stream of metaphors that runs right through language and flows from the concrete to the abstract. In this constant surge, the simplest and sturdiest of words are swept along, one after another, and carried towards abstract meanings. As these words drift downstream, they are bleached of their original vitality and turn into pale lifeless terms for abstract concepts – the substance from which the structure of language is formed. And when at last the river sinks into the sea, these spent metaphors are deposited, layer after layer, and so the structure of language grows, as a reef of dead metaphors. (*The Unfolding of Language*, 2005)

Deutscher is mainly discussing words that have travelled much further down this process than most clichés, although it is worth noting that 'ground-breaking' is the first word he discusses after the quoted passages. This process of being bleached of their original vitality is one of the reasons that we can use phrases as clichés. One of the purposes of this book is to remind readers of the origins of the expressions and of their original vigour.

Where do clichés come from? Some have been in the language since our earliest records, although not necessarily as clichés. Others are new. Fashion plays a role in their use, as do changes in society. While writing this book I have been lucky enough to have been able to observe the development of a new cliché. In Parliament on 23 May 2006, while speaking to the Home Affairs Committee, the recently appointed Home Secretary, John Reid, damned his department's immigration operation as 'not fit for purpose' with 'inadequate' leadership and management systems. The shock that anyone in his position could say such a thing meant that this was quoted in all the papers and other media the next day, and discussed for the next few days. When I heard it, it struck me that it had all the qualities to make a new cliché. It was a new turn of phrase, introduced in striking circumstances with much publicity. It also shared something in common with many other clichés, its rather odd grammar, which helps it stick in people's minds. The natural English would be 'not fit for its purpose' or 'not fit for the purpose', while the use of 'purpose' itself is rather odd. Quite where this comes from, I am not sure. I am assured that the phrasing has nothing to do with Reid's Scottishness. I would guess that it is Civil Service or Government shorthand, using the same sort of elision often found in military jargon. Having noted the birth of the expression, I kept an eye on what happened to it. After the initial fuss died down the term dropped out of use, much to my disappointment. But then after a couple of weeks it began to reappear, and at the time of writing is in daily use, no doubt helped along by further problems at the Home Office. What its future will be is anyone's guess.

Clichés die out as well, or at least become rare enough to cease to be classified as clichés. Take the example of 'prime the pump' as an economic term, which is heard much less often than it used to be. It became a cliché after it was used by President Franklin Delano Roosevelt in speeches describing his government's efforts to stimulate the economy under the New Deal. Two things have affected its use. First, the sort of economics Roosevelt advocated have gone out of fashion. Second, the knowledge of how to prime a pump by filling the chamber with liquid to drive out the air has declined, so the metaphor has become less effective. That this second point does not always mean the decline of a cliché can be seen from a number of clichés in this book, for example under 'done to a turn'.

Much of the material in this book is the same as in my original *Penguin Dictionary of Clichés*. This is inevitable, as the core of clichés in a language does not change. A number of expressions treated in the original have been dropped as I feel that their status has changed, and the overall number of phrases dealt with has been expanded by about a quarter. The way I have treated the material has also changed radically. This book is not a dictionary, but rather an examination of how we use the expressions, and the areas of life we draw them from. This means that I have assumed that the reader is a competent English user, and does not need to have the meaning of common expressions explained as they would be in a dictionary. I am fascinated by what the origins and groupings of these moribund metaphors tell us about the way we think and about our past. I hope others find it as interesting. In my discussion of the clichés I have deliberately used related turns of phrase that come from the same semantic areas and that are often near clichés themselves. The most clear-cut of these have been brought out by the use of italics, while expressions that are used elsewhere in the book are indicated by small capitals. One of the major changes in the material of this book is the dates that have been given to the introduction of the expressions. No one can write on the English language without extensive use of that great national treasure the *Oxford English Dictionary*, shortened to *OED* in the text. While this work is invaluable for dating the introduction of words, it is not infallible, and the date of first use of words is constantly being revised as new discoveries are made. Moreover, it is concerned with individual words and not phrases. In many cases the phrases are either missing from its definitions, or only occur as part of a definition. Even when they are given their own entry, the same attention has not been paid to their dating as to that of individual words. In the last few years so much new material has become available on the Internet that it has become possible for individuals to push these datings back considerably. One of the most important sources for this is *The Times* archive, which I have used extensively as a key to how the English language has been used in the past. For those interested in exploring the history of the language on their own, the good news is that both the *OED* and *The Times* archive are now available for free for most people in the UK via their County Library websites. Another feature of the origins of expressions given in this book is how many of them seem to come from the nineteenth century, and how many from America. This is probably a distortion of the truth caused by the available material, which is why I so often use terms such as 'was in use by . . .' or 'was first recorded in . . .' rather than say when an expression came into use. It is not until the nineteenth century that we find extensive printed material of the type that yields examples of clichés. This means that it is only then that we can confidently say that they are clichés or perhaps even find examples of any use of the cliché. Similarly, it was in the USA that the modern trend to write informally in newspapers and similar material first developed, and so colloquial expressions are likely to be found in written form there first.

Finally, I must thank my editor, Georgina Laycock, for her patience in waiting for the manuscript of the book; express my debt to the many, many other writers on language whose research I have used in this book; and, as ever, thank my family, Philip and Alexander, for their willingness to be used as linguistic sounding-boards, for their general support and for the many cups of tea brought to my desk.

Julia Cresswell

1. Family and Children

We start out by looking at the clichés that have come into the language from the home and the life there. **Family values**, like VICTORIAN VALUES (see Chapter 14), is one of those expressions much loved by modern politicians and moralists, although few venture to define this vague but emotive concept. It probably involves **wedded bliss** (which dates from the nineteenth century) rather than the now rather old-fashioned **living in sin** (from at least 1839). It embraces the idea that married couples should live **happy ever after** – a conscious cliché taken from traditional stories such as fairy tales. The latter has been a cliché since the eighteenth century, and goes with the nineteenth-century clichés of the **happy couple** or **happy pair**. They should live in their **home sweet home** surrounded by their **nearest and dearest**, a phrase that goes back to the sixteenth century, its longevity no doubt helped by its rhyme. The sentimental view of home found in 'home sweet home' comes from the title of a song in the opera *Clari, or The Maid of Milan* of 1823 (words by J. H. Payne, music by Henry R. Bishop). Although the opera has sunk into obscurity, this song is still widely known, along with its line 'Be it never so humble, there's **no place like home**'. 'There's no place like home' is repeated by Dorothy in L. Frank Baum's *The Wonderful Wizard of Oz* (1900) and is widely known from the 1939 film of the book, but both instances merely repeat the words of the Greek poet Hesiod, who said it in his *Works and Days* of about 700 BC.

The ideal family would consist of the **man of the house** alongside **the little woman**. Despite the wincingly un-politically correct connotations this expression now has, it started life as a term of affection (first found in 1765: 'My poor little woman had been in the drooping mood for two or three days') and changed imperceptibly into an affectionate term for 'wife'. In the twentieth century it seemed too condescending and proprietorial to be acceptable to the modern woman, and from around the middle of the century it began to be used to indicate an attitude to the role of woman as a stereotyped homemaker rather than an individual. These developments were no doubt helped by the fame of Louisa M. Alcott's 1868 novel *Little Women*. Much more positive is the masculine cliché of the **man of the world**. This expression originally simply meant a married man, the normal state for someone who was not a man of the church, the latter having rejected the things of this world for those of the next. It seems to have taken on the suggestion of experience and sophistication that it has today some time in the nineteenth century. If things go badly the man may have a **mid-life crisis**, an expression that came into use in the 1960s and was well-established by the 1970s. Mid-life crisis is used more often of men than women (who may suffer from the EMPTY NEST syndrome – see Chapter 22), but exclusively male is the more extreme **male menopause**, a term coined as early as the 1940s, but only recently over-used. This can be balanced by the claim that **life begins at forty**. This was the title of a self-help book written by Walter B. Pitkin in 1932.

After marriage, the traditional, clichéd family can look forward to a **happy event**, a Victorian euphemism-cliché dating from the 1880s for those who do not like to talk about childbirth. Only the most traditional of men would now dare express a wish for a **son and heir**, but in the days when property, and particularly titles, usually passed to the eldest son, as they still do, of course, for the aristocracy, 'son' and 'heir' were distinct ideas, which, combined, usually indicated an eldest son. This use is found from the thirteenth century, but by the nineteenth century the second part of the expression was losing significance, and nowadays it often has little connection with inheritance. When it does we get the conscious cliché, a favourite with cartoonists, that **one day all this will be yours, my son**. It might also be hoped that the child will be a **chip off the old block**. This dates from the sixteenth century, where it was found as either 'a chip *of* the old block' or 'of the same block'. The change from 'of' to 'off' only seems to have happened in the twentieth century. Whichever form is used, the image is of a chip from a block of wood being a smaller version of the original, but made up of exactly the same material. This basic idea goes back even further, for the Greek poet Theocritus, in his *Idylls* written about 270 BC, uses the expression 'a chip of the old flint'. An alternative cliché is **spitting image**. The origin of this term has been much debated, and there is no agreement as to the truth, but some evidence for its history can be found in a book of about 1602 by Nicholas Breton called *Wonders Worth Hearing*, containing a remarkable reference to 'Two girls . . . the one as like an owl, the other as like an urchin, as if they had been spit out of the mouths of them', which suggests that the expression means a child as like his father as if he had been spit out of his father's mouth. In the early nineteenth century it was possible to describe a child as 'the spit' of his father, or for emphasis the 'spit and image'. This could also appear as 'spitten image', which then became 'spitting image'.

Once the child is born, it has to be cared for, although hopefully not from **cradle to grave**. This expression has been in use since the beginning of the eighteenth century. In the eighteenth to nineteenth centuries it was simply a more poetic way of saying the whole of a lifetime – Edward Bulwer Lytton in *Maltravers* (1837) has 'What else have we to do with our mornings, we women? . . . Our life is a lounge from the cradle to the grave', but in the twentieth century the expression has taken on extra resonances. Shortened to 'from cradle to grave' it became strongly associated with the sort of state welfare that looks to the well-being of its people from birth to death, so valued for part of the twentieth century, and so undervalued today. More recently it has come to be used by environmentalists

to mean the environmental effect of the whole cycle of production, use and disposal of an object. One of the first parental
acts is to name the child, possibly with a middle name. The
formula phrase that some quality **is their middle name** is an
American creation from the early years of the twentieth century,
no doubt reflecting the way in which nicknames are sometimes
inserted between a person's given name and surname, as in the
case of Jack 'The Hat' McVitie. The parents, while doing that
fashionable thing, **nurturing** their child, will have to take care
not to **throw the baby out with the bathwater**. This is a
bringing together of two extremes of value – the useless in the
dirty bathwater and the cherished in the baby – to conjure up a
vivid picture of domestic tragedy. It came into use in the later
nineteenth century, and may have been borrowed from an earlier
German proverb used by Thomas Carlyle in 1853 in the form 'you
must empty out the bathing-tub, but not the baby with it'. The
parents will want to give the child **quality time**, which grew up
in the 1980s as a way of justifying parents working long hours, for
they could then argue it was quality not quantity that mattered.
This should not involve too many toyshops with distinctive
names, such as the one that gave rise to the formula 'something
or other **R Us**', a formula that has been grossly overused in
recent years. A quick look at the internet reveals such extreme
uses as Molecules R Us and an amputees' support group called
Stumps R Us. Over-indulgence will just **end in tears** – a
warning endured, and ignored, by generations of children.

The other aspect of traditional family life is **good housekeep-
ing**. This old expression was beginning to be extended in the
1950s to routine business transactions, record keeping and computer maintenance, and was probably much older as a term for
industrial maintenance, although this use is not recorded until
the 1960s. However, its spread to government and other fields
of life must owe much to the policies of Mrs Thatcher and her
government, with their emphasis on running the country as you
would run a household or small shop. Good housewifery was

long associated with moral probity; hence the way in which both slut and slattern started out as terms for a woman who was untidy and dirty, a poor housewife, and then developed the sense of sexually promiscuous. The term 'Goodwife', however, became a term of respect, and was shortened to 'Goody'. This brings us to **Goody Two Shoes**, which comes from an early children's book, *The History of Goody Two-Shoes*, published in 1765 and possibly written by Oliver Goldsmith. It is a story of a pitifully poor child who, through her own efforts, manages to get an education and become the village schoolteacher, before eventually becoming lady of the manor. She is referred to as Goody as a polite term of address, but Goody Two Shoes was also a very good person, and this meaning was implicit from the start. With the loss of the polite form 'Goody' (and the fact that the actual story is now unread except by academics) the term came to be used as an alternative to **goody-goody** (originally the name of a kind of sweet). One job of a good housewife is to keep the house clean and tidy, giving us the overused **sorted** to suggest efficiency, and **done and dusted**. These are both particularly British slang from the 1980s, although it has been suggested that there may be a connection to the 1940s army slang use of sorted to mean ' attacked fiercely'; but the connection may only be that they both go back to 'sorted out'. In such a house there will be no dropped pins. The phrase to **hear a pin drop** is implicit in Fanny Burney's diary entry for 11 June 1775 when she writes, 'Had a *pin* fallen, I suppose we should have taken it at least for a *thunder-clap*'; and must have been well-established by 1816 for Leigh Hunt to refer to it allusively in *The Story of Rimini*, where he writes, 'A pin-drop silence strikes all o'er the place.' In the past another job would have been to **keep the home fires burning**. The importance of keeping a fire lit in the home is both ancient and widespread. There are practical reasons to keep a fire burning at all times. Even today, with all our modern advantages, it is not particularly easy or quick to get a fire started. To cook on a fire it needs to have been burning for some time and be reduced to glowing coals, as any barbecuer knows. Therefore, when fires were the only way of cooking, they were kept burning the whole time, just as with a modern Aga today. However, there seems to be a strong atavistic attachment to the concept of the home fire – after all, both the Greeks and Romans had goddesses particularly associated with it in the form of Hestia and Vesta, each of whom had their temples with their eternal fires. Even today we use an eternal flame to commemorate the war dead who will not be returning to their homes. Given this, it is perhaps surprising that the term 'home-fire' is not recorded before 1892, and did not take off as a cliché until Ivor Novello's 1914 song 'Keep the Home Fires Burning', which became a sentimental anthem (another clichéd use) of the First World War. Previously, the cliché for this idea had been **hearth and home**, which goes back to Anglo-Saxon times. The trouble, of course, with fires is that they can spread. A burning house can get out of control surprisingly quickly, so the image came to be used both for very quickly, and for very well. To **get on like a house on fire** is, if you stop to think about it, in rather bad taste. The first recorded use, by Washington Irving in 1809, suggests from its emphatic exaggeration that it was already well-established: 'At it they went like five hundred houses on fire.' One final cliché of housework involves things being **put through the mangle**. A self-explanatory image, assuming you are old enough to have seen wet washing passed through a mangle to squeeze the water out of it. The image is first recorded in 1924 in the work of John Buchan, with the American equivalent, using 'wringer', twenty years later. Before leaving the household as a source of clichés we should look at **household name**. This term, a compressed way of saying 'a name known in every household', goes back to the nineteenth century. An early use of it, which now sounds rather incongruous, is in Tennyson's dedication of his Arthurian poem sequence *Idylls of the King* to Prince Albert: 'A Prince indeed, / Beyond all titles, and a household name, / Here-after, thro' all times, Albert the Good.'

2. Food and Cooking

Clichés from food and cooking are an interesting collection of both old habits long obsolete and new ones. If we start with basic ingredients we find the **crème de la crème**, which is the French equivalent of the *pick of the crop* (in the US 'the cream of the crop'), the very best. The phrase has been in use in English since the middle of the nineteenth century, but received an added boost, and ironic resonance, when used repeatedly in Muriel Spark's novel *The Prime of Miss Jean Brodie* (1961, filmed 1969). Another ingredient is found in **cut the mustard**, often used in the negative as in 'can't cut the mustard'. There have been numerous attempts to explain the origin of the expression, each wilder than the last and few carrying much conviction. In reality the explanation is probably not anything like as romantic as the stories, but it does illustrate the sort of knock-on effect that the associations words acquire have on the development of new meanings, particularly in slangy English – what the experts call semantic shift. In the early years of the twentieth century, particularly in America, to 'be the mustard' was a term of approval, meaning to be the best of anything, something *hot*, something that adds *zing* to life, just as mustard perks up dull food. For example, the *OED's* first example of this use of mustard is from 1903 in Andy Adams's *Log of a Cowboy*: 'For fear they were not the proper mustard, he had that dog man sue him in court for the balance, so as to make him prove the pedigree.' This use was, in turn, probably a development of expressions such as 'keen as mustard', which goes back to the seventeenth century, the word 'keen' here meaning 'sharp, cutting' so linking the expressions. In the nineteenth century the verb 'to cut' was developing all sorts of new uses, being used in place of common verbs such as 'do' or 'make' or 'go'. In particular it developed the sense of, to quote the *OED*, 'to succeed, to deal with something effectively; to meet an expected or required standard in the performance of a task, to measure up', most often found in the expression 'to cut it' with much the same sense as 'to cut the mustard'. These two trends seems to have come together to produce 'cut the mustard'. The first known example of the use is in the writings of the American writer O. Henry, whose tales of early twentieth-century American low life often provide first citations of unconventional English, as we shall see below. In his 1907 story *The Heart of the West* he writes, 'By nature and doctrines I am addicted to the habit of discovering choice places wherein to feed. So I looked around and found a proposition that exactly cut the mustard. I found a restaurant tent just opened up by an outfit that had drifted in on the tail of the boom.' Here it is tempting to see O. Henry substituting 'cut the mustard' for 'cut it' because of the restaurant connection, and it has been suggested that O. Henry coined the expression and that it spread from this story. While this is possible, for in his day, and for some time after, O. Henry was a popular author, there is no need to argue this. 'Cut it' is an expression that cannot help raising the question of what 'it' is, and there may have been all sorts of variant solutions going round at the time. With 'mustard' being so fashionable at the same time, it may just be that this is the one that won out in the popular imagination. O. Henry features again in the story behind **big cheese**. Etymologists seem to have got themselves in a rather difficult position over its origin. There is an Urdu word *chiz*, meaning 'thing', which was adopted by the British Army in India by the beginning of the nineteenth century in the form 'cheese' as part of their slang, to mean anything particularly good. 'It's the cheese' was used as a term of great praise. The expression 'the big cheese', used initially to mean wealth and fame, then to mean an important person, is often linked to this, but is also recognized as an American usage. How then did it get from India to America? It seems likely that the development of the two terms was largely independent. Certainly the first recorded use of 'big cheese', in the American sense, is clearly using cheese in its usual sense. 'Del had crawled from some Tenth Avenue basement like a lean rat and had bitten his way into the Big Cheese . . . He had danced his way into . . . fame in sixteen minutes.' This comes from a short story by O. Henry, written in the first decade of the twentieth century. Since this author was a master of American street language, it seems best to look to New York slang (compare the Big Apple) for the origin of this. Big cheese has been rather dated, but has recently been revived as City slang. Similar terms include BIG SHOTS, which is again considered mainly American, although it is first recorded in England. It may have developed from the earlier expression BIG GUNS used in the same way, both expressions indicating power. **Big honcho** is by far the most recent of these American expressions, having come into use in the Second World War. Honcho is from *hancho*, a Japanese word for the leader of a small group or squad, and was adopted by American soldiers to mean 'boss'. Cheese appears again in **(different as) chalk and cheese**. To understand this distinction you need to think of a young white cheese rather than a mature yellow one, and freshly gathered chalk, the crumbly type you would use to dress soil, rather than something prepared for the blackboard. They can look very similar, but their taste and value are very different. The image is an old one. In his *Confessio Amantis* of about 1393 John Gower criticizes the Church for teaching one thing and doing another, saying 'Lo, how they feignen chalk for chese' (pretend that chalk is cheese), and again, several thousand lines on in this lengthy book, he writes of the greedy man who does not care what he does as long as he makes money: 'And thus ful ofte chalk for cheese He changeth with ful little cost' ('Thus he frequently swaps chalk for cheese at very little cost'). This sense of comparative worth, not to mention the sharp dealing, has of course now been lost, but the phrase lives on, no doubt kept in use by English speakers' love of alliteration.

The best (or **greatest**) **thing since sliced bread** is a far more recent cliché, having started life in the USA in the 1950s as 'the greatest thing since sliced bread', the alternative 'best' being the British version. Nowadays, with sliced bread often seen not as a convenience, but as an inferior product to 'real' bread, it is usually used ironically. To have **egg on your face** dates from the same period. No one seems quite sure if the original image is of the embarrassment of having been an unconsciously messy eater or of being pelted with eggs. To **spill the beans** is another Americanism, this time from the 1920s. As in the big cheese, it brings together two earlier bits of slang, 'to spill' meaning confess, tell information, and 'beans' for information. An essential ingredient of most food is salt. The idea behind the term **worth his salt** goes back to Roman times, when the soldiers, just as today, were given their food and equipment as part of their wages. There was a special ration of that essential item salt, and at some point this was converted to a cash payment, a *salarium* ('money for salt'), which is the basis of our word 'salary'. As interest in and knowledge of philology grew in the nineteenth century some wit saw the connection and substituted 'salt' for salary, and a cliché was born.

If we now pass from savoury to sweet things, we get **a piece of cake**. This expression passed into general use from Second World War RAF slang, where an easy mission was described as a piece of cake. Its origin is not clear. It has been suggested that it may be linked to 'cakewalk', which dates from the 1870s and was a Black American custom where people would gather to **make their own entertainment**, that ideal of the old-fashioned, with the prize of a cake being given to the best dancers. From that, 'cakewalk' evolved into meaning something pleasurable in general. However, although the first recorded use is from America, there is really no need to suppose this link, as an easy time, rather than a tough one, could readily be compared to something soft, sweet and luxurious without prior inspiration. **Like nailing jelly to the wall** is another Americanism. It was used by President Roosevelt in a letter to William Thayer dated 2 July 1915. He was trying to negotiate terms for building the Panama Canal, and he wrote despairingly, 'You could no more make an agreement with them than you could nail currant jelly to a wall – and the failure to nail currant jelly to a wall is not due to the nail; it is due to the currant jelly.' It passed into the public domain when Thayer, with Roosevelt's permission, used the expression in his biography of the American statesman and author John Hay (1838–1905). The computing world has adopted the form **like nailing jelly to a tree**, particularly for a programming task where the design specifications are inadequate or impossible to implement. The world of computing is particularly rich in such coinages – for example, a particularly slow and difficult process can be described as 'like kicking dead whales down the beach'. The fruit course might contain **peaches and cream**, a description of a woman's complexion in use since the very beginning of the twentieth century, which has also been transferred to conjure up a whole aura of attractiveness (compare ENGLISH ROSE; see Chapter 21). The other clichéd fruit is the pear found in to **go pear-shaped**. A cliché of the 1990s, this was, like a piece of cake, originally RAF slang. Its exact origin is obscure, but it has been claimed that it was used to describe the shape of a plane that has plunged into the ground. Sweets lie behind a common hyperbole of journalism: **handing out pills** or **drugs as if/like they were Smarties**, which became particularly common in the 1990s. Often used to describe doctors' prescribing habits, it picks up on the fact that the brightly coloured chocolate sweets are the same sort of shape and have the same lurid sugar coating as some pills, and the scares there have been of children confusing the two. There is a current trend to use the term **candy** as a combining form. Someone attractive might be **eye-candy** or **arm-candy**, and the word has been particularly lavishly used in product names such as Skull Candy, Nail Candy, Brain Candy, Gadget Candy and Mind Candy. Ice cream gives us **flavour of the month** for something briefly fashionable. This started life in the USA in the middle of the twentieth century, when ice-cream parlours started promoting a different 'flavor of the month' to attract customers. It did not reach the UK until the 1980s.

The opposite of these sweet things is bitter. There are two words regularly coupled to 'bitter' – end and experience. **Bitter experience** – usually 'from bitter experience' – has been in use since the beginning of the nineteenth century, and by 1858 *The Times* could blend two clichés by writing 'Bitter experience has taught us not to cook our hare before we have caught it' (see further FIRST CATCH YOUR HARE, below). But there is much debate about the origin of **bitter end**. In the Bible (Proverbs 4) we find the words 'But her end is bitter as wormwood, sharp as a two-edged sword'. Normally, this would be a perfectly acceptable source, and no one would think about it further. However, there is also a nautical term 'bitter-end', recorded in English from 1627. A bitt on a ship is something that you can wind a rope round; the loops of the rope are bitters, and the bitter end is the end of this rope. As Admiral W. H. Smyth says in his *Sailor's Word-book* of 1867, 'A ship is "brought up to a bitter" when the cable is allowed to run out to that stop . . . When a chain or rope is paid out to the bitter-end, no more remains to be let go.' In other words, you are literally at the END OF YOUR TETHER (see Chapter 22). Whichever of these is the true source of the expression, it was well established by the middle of the nineteenth century.

Cooking

Once you have your ingredients you need to move on to cooking them. We have already mentioned the mid nineteenth-century cliché, supposedly quoting a recipe, **first catch your hare**. This is sometimes erroneously attributed to Mrs Beeton's cookbook, and more often to Hannah Glasse's 1747 cookbook

The Art of Cookery, Made Plain and Easy. It is actually a parody of early cookbooks. Hannah Glasse did write 'First catch your fish', but for hares she wrote 'Take your hare when it is cased', the last word being an old term for 'skinned', and not, as some have thought, a form of 'catched'. Cookbooks give us recipes, and the figurative use of recipe was well established by the seventeenth century, although the clichés **recipe for disaster** and **recipe for success** are much later. The expression 'recipe for success' was in use by the middle of the nineteenth century, but 'recipe for disaster' first occurs in *The Times* in 1957, in a letter from the politician Barbara Castle.

When choosing what to cook, you need to select your ingredients carefully and make sure the meal is balanced. Not enough fat and the food will be dry, giving you something that is **lean, mean** (a recent coinage – the popular quotation from the 1981 film *Stripes*, 'You're a lean, mean, fighting machine', being given massive exposure in the form of George Foreman's much-promoted 'lean, mean . . . grilling machine'). Too much fat, and you have a **fat chance** of success. In societies where food supplies are not reliable, but depend on luck and weather, fatness is a sign of richness and prosperity. Thus in the Bible (Psalm 92:14) we are told that the righteous 'shall be fat and flourishing'. From this idea there developed a wide range of uses of 'fat' to mean great, rich, abundant, and the fat of 'fat chance' belongs with this sense, used ironically. The expression seems to have developed in the USA in the early part of the twentieth century, and to have crossed the Atlantic soon after. If meat is tough, you mince it to make it more easily eaten: so if you decline to **mince words** or **matters** – the expression is always negative – it amounts to *talking tough*. To mince matters dates from the sixteenth century. When cooking you should avoid **over-egging the pudding**. Eggs added to a pudding make it richer, but put too many in and it is spoilt. Dating from the late nineteenth century, this was originally used to mean exaggerate or argue something over-forcefully, but has now been extended to include going too far in general. You also need to make sure that something is not **past** (or has not **passed**) **its sell-by date**. This dates only from the 1980s, when sell-by date labels on food first became common. The opposite cliché, indicating freshness, is **alive and kicking**. A cliché since the nineteenth century, this comes from fishmongers who, to emphasize the freshness of their goods, would claim that they were not just so fresh they were alive, but alive and kicking. If simply reheating something, you must hope it **does what it says on the tin** or **can**, a currently popular term whose American origin is shown by the use of 'can'. If you are distracted from your cooking you can put something **on the back burner**, where the ring or burner is usually smaller, meant for simmering, so something that is on the back burner is left to simmer quietly, nothing being done to it for a while. The expression developed in the USA in the 1950s or 1960s. When it is ready to serve it is **done to a turn**. This cliché for 'perfectly cooked', which has been in use since the eighteenth century, reflects the days when roasting was done on a spit, turned constantly before an open fire. When the roast was perfectly cooked it was 'done to a turn', neither turned too long in front of the fire, nor too little. The tenacity of some phrases in English is well illustrated by this one, used without a second thought well after the oven has replaced the spit in general use. Once the cooking is finished you hope the cook will not **have a finger in every pie**. This image of someone going round a kitchen prodding and poking the pies has been around since at least the 1600s. Shakespeare obviously knew it, for in *Henry VIII* (1613) he has an irritated Duke of Buckingham say of Cardinal Wolsey, 'The devil speed him! No man's pie is freed / From his ambitious finger' (I.1). Nowadays there is sometimes an added implication that to have a finger in too many pies is not necessarily right or honest.

At Table

To do the honours, or to act as host or serve round food or drink, dates from the sixteenth century, and was a cliché by the eighteenth. As a part of this role you might **hand someone something on a plate**. This expression probably arose in the first part of the twentieth century. Someone doing the honours could also be said to **rule the roost**, for this expression was originally 'rule the roast'. It is a curious expression, the exact meaning of which is not clear, although a best guess is that it refers to some sort of custom of being master of a feast. It is first found in the fifteenth century, and was a cliché in the sixteenth. It is not surprising that by the eighteenth century the obscure expression had changed 'to rule the roost', as if referring to a cock dominating the hen house, particularly as it then linked up to other expressions such as **cock of the walk** (chief person in a circle or best person at something – early nineteenth century), the obsolete **cock of the school** for the boy who leads others in games and fights (nineteenth century again) and **dunghill cock** (in use since the fifteenth century for a coward). The guests, it must be hoped, will not **bite the hand that feeds them**. This expression comes from feeding domestic animals such as dogs and is found from the beginning of the eighteenth century. Further bad manners can be found in the vivid **bite off more than you can chew**. The figurative use of the expression developed in the USA, the first recorded use of it being in 1878, in the very American-sounding 'You've bit off more'n you can chaw' (J. Beadle, *Western Wilds*), but it was fully naturalized in the UK by the early twentieth century. Such gluttony leads to the phrase **glutton for punishment**. This expression was in use by the 1930s and seems to be a development of the nineteenth-century 'glutton for work', and indeed glutton for punishment can still have something of the aura of the workaholic about it. It is also found, used in an approving manner, to describe someone or something that keeps coming back for more, or is even DEAD BUT WON'T LIE DOWN. The opposite of gluttony is to **tighten your belt**. Despite the fact that people must have been tightening their belts to ease the pangs of hunger for a very long time, it has not been recorded before the late nineteenth century. It is used frequently both literally and metaphorically in reports from the trenches in the First World War. Another cliché of hunger that is probably not used by parents today, but which drove children of a certain generation wild, was a **starving child in Africa would be glad to have that**, and variations on the expression, used to try to bully children into finishing the food on their plates. As a cliché it probably dates from the second half of the twentieth century. In the first part of the century a child was more likely to be told to think of the starving children in Armenia or China.

A type of meal can be found within the phrase **no picnic**, an understated description of something that is the opposite of a time of relaxed enjoyment in a quiet pastoral setting. 'Picnic' had come to be used as a colloquial term for a treat or lively time by the early years of the nineteenth century (Keats writes, in a letter of 1818, 'you may like a little picnic of scandal'), and by the 1880s 'no picnic' meant the opposite. Lunch also features in three clichés. Around about the 1840s, American bars began advertising 'free lunches' when you bought a drink. These were usually salty snacks put out to encourage you to drink more. John Farmer's *Americanisms* of 1889 contains the entry: 'The free lunch fiend . . . is one who makes a meal off what is really provided as a snack. He pays for a drink, but shamefacedly manages in this way to get something more than his money's worth.' Despite this, the free luncher does not really get his lunch for free – he must not only buy his drink (no doubt priced to cover the cost of food), but if he is really to make a lunch out of it, must pay in subterfuge or embarrassment. The expression **there's no such thing as a free lunch** is sometimes attributed to the American economist Milton Friedman (1912–2006) as it was much used by him and was the title of one of his books, but it antedates this. The expression appears around 1950. As an economic dictum it may have been formulated by a group of economists at the University of Chicago School of Economics, but was probably based on some unrecorded folk saying. Robert Heinlein's 1966 novel *The Moon is a Harsh Mistress* uses a slightly different wording as a repeated motif: 'There ain't no such thing as a free lunch', which could be shortened to the acronym TANSTAAFL, and his popularity as an author no doubt helped spread the expression. The typical **ladies who lunch** probably do not eat much more than the free luncher, but this time in order to preserve their figures. If Stephen Sondheim did not coin this expression for a class of women who have the money and time to meet for leisurely lunches, then he certainly popularized it in his song 'The Ladies Who Lunch', from the 1970 show *Company*. Ladies who lunch may also use the expression **(let's) do lunch**, although it is used by a much wider class of people. A vogue expression starting life on Madison Avenue as an alternative to 'Let's have lunch', this reached Britain in a big way in the 1980s, although few outside the media and advertising dared use it in cold blood.

Finally, meals are traditionally celebrations, but it is very rare, nowadays, for the word 'festive' to signify anything other than 'Christmas'. This restriction seems to have had its birth in the eighteenth century, but not to have become dominant until the twentieth. Almost anything can become 'festive' – decorations, spirit, food – but the commonest phrases are **festive season** and **festive occasion**. The old cliché **festive board**, meaning a richly laden table, is probably the origin of the others but seems to be rare now.

Drink

Is it simply by chance that only one cliché in the book refers specifically to a non-alcoholic drink, or is it a reflection of the English way of life? The only quote that does not involve the **demon drink** (one of the ringing phrases of the nineteenth-century campaign for the abolition of drink, it developed from the expression **demon rum** – for alcoholic drinks in general – which seems to have been in use in the United States twenty to thirty years earlier than demon drink) is **wake up and smell the coffee**, a horribly unthinking way of saying, 'Face facts, think, pay attention'. It was popularized by the American agony aunt Ann Landers in the late 1990s, and used by her as a book title in 1996. There is another cliché that is alcohol neutral – the variable saying about a **glass being half full or half empty**. Terry Pratchett, with his usual wisdom, puts this saying in its place in *The Truth* (2000):

There are, it has been said, two types of people in the world. There are those who, when presented with a glass that is exactly half full, say: this glass is half full. And then there are those who say: this glass is half empty.

The world *belongs*, however, to those who can look at the glass and say: 'What's up with this glass? Excuse me? Excuse *me*? *This* is my glass? I don't *think* so. *My* glass was full! *And* it was a bigger glass!'

And at the other end of the bar the world is full of the other type of person, who has a broken glass, or a glass that has been carelessly knocked over (usually by one of the people calling for a larger glass), or who had no glass at all, because they were at the back of the crowd and had failed to catch the barman's eye.

If something is **meat and drink to** someone, the expression does not demand that we interpret the drink as alcoholic, but somehow the idea of food and drink implies a meal with wine or beer to many. It was in use by 1533, and 'meat' here does not mean 'flesh', but retains its old sense, the more general 'food'.

Otherwise, we are firmly in the realm of the **heady mixture** – in use by 1930 – said of something that is exciting enough to make you act as if intoxicated, to *go to your head* or *turn your head*. It appears to be a modern cliché, but its history is not recorded. This would no doubt be served by **mine host**, a conscious and unnecessary archaism which is still far too common. The facetious use of this term for the person running a place to eat, drink or stay – the temptation is to use the term 'hostelry' to match 'mine host' – probably dates from the early nineteenth century, although it is recorded from the early fourteenth century when it would have been natural English. If you are cautious you will stick to **small beer**. Small beer was weak beer, suitable for quenching thirst, but not for getting drunk. Before the introduction of safe drinking water, it was healthier to drink this than water, for the water used for the beer was boiled as part of the brewing process, and the alcohol killed off any subsequent bacteria. The term came to be used early on for something that is insignificant. Shakespeare used it several times in his plays – in *Othello* (1602–4), for instance, Iago dismisses a virtuous woman as fit only 'to suckle fools and chronicle small beer' (II.1). **Small potatoes**, which is used in the same way, dates from nineteenth-century America and is still more common in American English, although the poet Samuel Taylor Coleridge had written in a letter of 1797, 'The London literati appear to me to be very much like little potatoes, that is no great things.' And Byron had written, 'Who knew this life was not worth a potato' in his 1823 poem *Don Juan*, which pre-dates the first American use of the expression proper, in Davy Crockett's *Exploits & Adventures in Texas* (1836): 'This is what I call small potatoes and few of a hill.' However, weak drink may not **hit the spot**. This comes from target practice, where if you hit the central spot on the target, you are *spot on*. It was transferred to being right *on target* for what was wanted to satisfy thirst or hunger in the middle of the nineteenth century in the USA. While to the British 'hit the spot' conjures up images of the world of P. G. Wodehouse or a genial pub, in the USA it is closely associated with an advertising jingle of the Prohibition-blighted 1930s and 1940s: 'Pepsi-Cola hits the spot, twelve full ounces, that's a lot'. You may choose to **wet your whistle** on something stronger. Chaucer, describing the Miller's wife getting tipsy in *The Reeve's Tale*, says, 'So was her jolly whistle well y-wet', showing that the idea of using whistle, for the source of the sound, the throat, is by no means new; nor wetting it for having a drink. The alliterative phrase was so popular that by the mid eighteenth century there was even a slang expression 'whistle-drunk' to mean exceedingly drunk. If in convivial company, you may want to join in a toast by saying, **I'll drink to that**. The idea of drinking to someone or something in this sense has been around since at least the sixteenth century. By the early twentieth century 'I'll drink to that' had become a stock expression for agreeing to have a drink, and by the middle of the century it had taken the small step to being used as a catchphrase for general assent or agreement. This development took place in the USA and spread gradually to the UK. A big boost to the currency of the expression was given, on both sides of the Atlantic, by its use as a catchphrase in the highly successful television comedy *Rowan and Martin's Laugh-In* (1968–71). If in poor spirits you may feel that you are **drinking in the last chance saloon**. This became a cliché of media and politics in the 1980s, used as a more emphatic version of 'last chance'. It may, however, be quite a bit older. The Last Chance Saloon was the place Frenchie (Marlene Dietrich) ran in the 1939 western film *Destry Rides Again*. Whether the saying gave the saloon its name or vice versa is not clear, but a similar expression was in use soon after, when Eugene O'Neill used 'It's the No Chance Saloon' in his 1946 play *The Iceman Cometh*.

All our remaining clichés are euphemistic terms for being

drunk to some degree or other, although the degree may range from no worse than being **in your cups** to a **drunken stupor**. 'In your cups' has been a cliché in English since the early seventeenth century, although the same image was used by the Romans well before this. The expression has survived, even though 'cup' has been replaced by 'glass' where alcoholic drink is concerned. The first example of 'drunken stupor' I have been able to find is in a report in *The Times* from 1831 describing 'Recent riots in Bristol': 'Men stretched in drunken stupor beside puncheons of rum: women in loathsome shapes, bearing the outward marks of the sex, in the same state of beastly degradation'. 'Stupor' technically means a state of unconsciousness or near unconsciousness, so it is interesting to note that many modern uses of the expression describe activity while in a drunken stupor. This reflects a growing trend to use it to mean a state of extreme drunkenness, rather than in its original sense of passed out from drink – such unthinking misuse being a good indication that something is a cliché. You may choose to use drink to **drown your sorrows** – an alternative for expressions such as 'drown yourself in drink' or 'drown yourself in wine', which have been around since the Middle Ages. *The Times* again provides an early example of its use. In 1863 it printed an excerpt from a letter in an American paper describing, in highly patriotic terms, the captured Mexican general Santa Ana:

Santa Ana is a very ordinary-looking man, and the greatest coward the world ever produced. As proof of this I will give you an instance that came under my own observation. He and his officers were sent on board our vessel at Velasco, for safe keeping. He had not been with us over a few days when the people became dissatisfied, and sent for him. As soon as he was informed of this, he judged our people by his own, and thought they were going to butcher him. The wretch exclaimed in Spanish – 'Mercy, mercy! Oh God! If they wish to kill me, let them come and shoot me here – don't let them take me ashore.' We could not persuade him that his life was safe. He rushed below, and, like a Turk, took opium to drown his sorrows. As soon as the effects of the drug were over, we hurried him over the side of the vessel into the longboat; and as he went the tears trickled down his pusillanimous cheeks.

If Santa Ana was drowning his sorrows in opium, which even if in liquid form would not have constituted *copious draughts*, then it is likely that the expression had already travelled far from the idea of a sufficient quantity of liquid for drowning, and so was well established.

If you **drink like a fish** you can also be **full to the gills**. Fish do not, of course, drink very much. However, they do appear to be gulping liquid down as they open and close their mouths to pass water over their gills, and this, combined with their liquid environment, means that they have been associated with excessive drinking since the sixteenth century. The gills have been used jokingly of human throats since the same century. The *OED* lists a polychrome collection of phrases describing people's gills: rosy if in good health; white, blue or yellow about the gills for illness (but strangely not the now common green for feeling sick, which dates from at least the nineteenth century); and red for anger. However, to be full or up to the gills for having eaten a large amount, or drunk too much, is missing from this list, which suggests it is a comparative innovation. Finally, the ultimate euphemism for drunk is **tired and emotional**. This term for drunk was memorably used in 1967 to describe the then Foreign Secretary George Brown in the satirical magazine *Private Eye* and subsequently became its standard term for the state.

3. Manners, Moods and Mores

This section covers social structures, social conventions, attitudes to life and individual ways of behaviour – what the *News of the World* would call **all human life**. The slogan 'All human life is there' has been used since the late 1950s by the newspaper, but researchers have found it in a Henry James work, *The Madonna of the Future* (1879): 'Cats and monkeys – monkeys and cats – all human life is there!' Quite how much influence Henry James has had on the notorious 'News of the Screws' is debatable.

If we start with social life in the loosest, most popular use of the term, we find the **gala occasion**, usually indicating a do arranged for money. Originally 'gala' by itself was enough, having been used to mean 'a festive occasion' since about 1700. However, nowadays it is used to mean 'special, elaborate, memorable', or just to indicate some vague air of distinction. Someone enjoying themselves at such an event might be the **life and soul of the party**, which dates from the nineteenth century, and is quite often used ironically. If they get too lively, they may fail to **stand on ceremony** where required. 'Stand' here means to be scrupulous or attentive to something. The older form of the saying used 'upon' and is first recorded in a sermon of 1751: 'There is no occasion to stand upon Complaisance and ceremony with writers who have done so much mischief.' One social ceremony that is in flux at the moment is the act of opening doors for people, particularly a man holding open a door for a woman. Some women object to it as a sign of inequality; some object if it is not done on the ground of rudeness. For men it is a case of **damned if you do, damned if you don't**. This expression is only recorded in British English from the twentieth

century, but goes back to the American Evangelist Lorenzo
Dow, whose *Reflections of the Love of God*, published in 1836,
two years after his death, said that Calvinistic preachers 'make
the Bible clash and contradict itself, by preaching somewhat like
this: "You can and you can't – You shall and you shan't – You
will and you won't – And you will be damned if you do – And
you will be damned if you don't."' The whole business of
precedence – who goes first into a room or how you should
seat someone at a table – is a dying art, but nevertheless one
does still hear the dictum **age before beauty**, although only as
a feeble joke. This expression started life in the late nineteenth
century, probably as a graceful way for an older woman to
acknowledge the courtesy of a younger one who stands aside to
let her take precedence in entering a room. It soon came to be
a gallantry of an older man to a girl, and to be used jocularly or
maliciously between other pairs. Various ripostes developed –
schoolchildren would retort, 'Dust (or dirt) before the broom'
– but most famous is the exchange which has been attributed to
various couples but which is most often found in the form of an
anecdote that has Clare Booth Luce ushering Dorothy Parker
through a door with 'Age before beauty' only to have Dorothy
Parker sweep past with 'Pearls before swine'.

Ideas of correct social behaviour are closely linked with those
of class. Some think they are **a cut above** others. This rather
odd expression, notoriously popular as a name for hairdressers,
has been in use since the end of the eighteenth century. The
word 'cut' seems to have become an expression of superiority
via the use of 'cut' for the way clothes or hair are shaped. From
being something fashionably cut it came to mean 'fashion, style'
– as in the old-fashioned 'I don't like the cut of his jib', and
from there developed into an assessment of worth. Such people
could also be described as **high and mighty**. This was first
introduced as a literal expression in the fifteenth century, often
as a term of address to a ruler. By the seventeenth century it was
already beginning to move, via the sense of powerful, towards

its modern sense of arrogant and conceited. Some might consider these people **too big for their boots**. This expression suggests someone whose own idea of their importance has outgrown their real size. It dates from the late nineteenth century, the similar **too big for his britches** being half a century older. A similar image is found in being **big-** or **swollen-headed**. If behaving very formally, a person could be described as a **stuffed shirt**. This is generally linked to the idea of a shirt on display in a shop window, stuffed to make it look occupied, the idea being of an underlying emptiness. However, the term 'stuffed shirt' is usually linked not just with pomposity, but with stiffness, and it may be that the image also involves the highly starched formal dress shirts worn at the turn of the century, when this was coined in America (of the kind that gave rise to OFF THE CUFF; see Chapter 15). These were so stiff down the front that an occupant might well have about as much movement as he would were he stuffed, as well as being occupied by those with well-stuffed bellies. In addition, illustrations of the time show that the fashionable cut of such shirts made the wearer look rather pigeon-breasted, adding a further stuffed effect. Another word to describe such people is **toff**, which has had a strange revival in recent years. Until recently it was a very old-fashioned term, redolent of Victorian England, and rarely used except in parody of the sort of condescending writing that indicated a character was working class by means of a dated and distorted accent. Its resurgence is in part linked to the debate over fox-hunting, which led to the revival of a number of terms from the class war. Toff has a curious history. Its origin is not established, but it is thought to be a corruption of 'tuft'. In the Oxford and Cambridge of the past an undergraduate who had an aristocratic title wore not the plain black tassel on his mortarboard, but a gold one. These gentlemen become known as 'tufts', and those social climbers who cultivated them, 'tuft-hunters'. The childish term 'toffee-nosed' comes from the adjective 'toffy' derived from 'toff', combined with the image of the nose in the air, and not 'toff' from 'toffee-nosed' as some have supposed. Another obsolescent term that has been revived within much the same context is to **doff your cap**. However, as so often with revived terms, some of the usages can be a bit odd, as with the hunt supporter (usually considered to be the toff) who wrote a letter to the *Independent* newspaper saying, 'We won't doff our caps to the townies' (18 September 2004). 'Doff' is one of those words that have been kept alive only in a set phrase. It is a medieval contraction of 'do off', a way of saying 'take off'.

There are fewer clichéd terms for those who consider themselves superior to describe the lower sort. **Hoi polloi** is from the Greek, meaning literally 'the many'. The hypercorrect will tell you that it should never be used in the form 'the hoi polloi' since 'hoi' already means 'the', and to use both shows your ignorance. In fact, this is a twentieth-century worry, 'the hoi polloi' being standard in earlier uses. John Dryden is the first recorded user of the term in English, and he set the pattern and the tone for its use when he wrote, 'If by the people you understand the multitude, the hoi polloi, 'tis no matter what they think; they are sometimes in the right, sometimes in the wrong: their judgement is a mere lottery' (*Essay of Dramatic Poesy*, 1668), and Byron also writes of 'the hoi polloi' in his letters. Even lower than that are the **scum of the earth**, but this is not a term used by the well-mannered. 'Scum' has been used to describe the **lowest of the low** since Christopher Marlowe wrote of the 'Scum of Africa' in his play *Tamburlaine* (written about 1586), and scum of the earth is first recorded in 1712, presumably modelled on the biblical 'salt of the earth'. However, it probably gained cliché status thanks to the Duke of Wellington's description of the British army fighting Napoleon as 'composed of the scum of the earth – the mere scum of the earth'. A person so described may think of themselves not as inferior, but as just a **regular guy**. 'Regular' is a word that has expanded its range enormously in recent years and is now used for all sorts of things, including the ubiquitous 'regular coffee', which confusingly describes coffee that is not overly fancy or over-priced, as well as being a euphemism for 'small'.

If we turn now to general modes of behaviour, bravery is found in **to have the courage of your convictions**. This expression seems to have come into English from the French expression (recorded in the mid nineteenth century) '*le courage de son opinion*'. For a while it could appear as either 'the courage of your convictions' or 'of your opinions' but, as so often in English, the alliterative version won in the end. Nowadays it is often used in the negative, to point to someone lacking the necessary courage, rather than having it. On the same theme, when Dorothy Parker interviewed Ernest Hemingway for the *New Yorker* in 1929 she asked him what he meant by 'guts' and got the answer **grace under pressure**. This phrase has become increasingly popular, although it will be interesting to see what long-term effect its use as the title of a television series will have. A related expression is a **stiff upper lip**. The image here is of a lip that would be trembling with emotion being kept stiff by rigid self-control. Surprisingly, for an attitude that is felt to be so typically British, belonging to the sort of person who would use the consciously Edwardian expression **young feller me lad**, 'stiff upper lip' is first recorded in the USA in 1815. Another phrase indicating toughness is **take it like a man**. It is an attitudinal cliché, like A MAN'S GOTTA DO WHAT A MAN'S GOTTA DO (see Chapter 5), and associated with the same sort of film. Toughness is also found in **tough love**, a recent coinage of the counselling industry, a more positive way of saying CRUEL TO BE KIND (see Chapter 7).

A very different attitude to life is found in **laid back**, an expression as redolent of the hippy era (it is first recorded in 1969) as to **do your own thing**. The latter is particularly popular with writers of travel brochures in an attempt to evoke total relaxation and a lack of stress and worry. The sentiment it expresses goes back at least to Rabelais's *Fay çe que vouldras* ('do what you like') written above the entrance to the Abbey of

Thélême in his *Gargantua* (1534). Another expression of the 1960s is **let it all hang out**, the opposite of *uptight*. It developed in Black American slang and spread rapidly to the rest of the English-speaking world. There has been much speculation as to what 'it' might be. **Go with the flow** is yet another cliché of the era, which was well established by the mid 1970s. The image of letting the tide or stream of water take you where it will links this expression with terms like 'mainstream' and Shakespeare's 'There is a tide in the affairs of men' (*Julius Caesar* (1599), IV.3). **Life goes on** is a more resigned version of the same idea. More recently to be **absolutely fine with** something has begun to be used instead. Other leftovers from the hippy generation are **get your act together, get it together** and **get your head** (i.e. what's going on in your mind) **together**. Also originally from the 1960s, but not widely known in the UK until the 1980s, is **touchy-feely**, usually used derogatorily. The now ubiquitous **have a nice day** (to which the younger grouch might respond **get real**) belongs with this attitude. It has actually been a common phrase since the 1920s, but became widespread in the 1970s, and for some reason irritates a lot of people, probably because they feel it is intrusive or insincere – although few people have the same reaction to 'How do you do?', equally impertinent if taken literally. 'Have a nice day' in its modern use first became popular in the USA, once again in the 1960s, from the language of CB radio as used by long-distance lorry drivers, who had been using it for a decade. It came to the UK a little later, and for many is still felt to be something of an Americanism. Some alternatives – **take care** or even worse **take care, now** or, worse still, **don't be a stranger** – are even more intrusive.

Chattering classes has only been recorded in print in 1984, but thanks to BBC Radio 7's regular repeats of old comedy programmes can be heard in an edition of *Round the Horn* from 1965. People who object to their **dulcet tones** (dulcet, meaning 'sweet', is another of those words rarely found outside a set phrase) may suffer from **innate conservatism**. While this now has negative connotations, earlier uses, from at least the 1880s, use it to express a pride in fine British traditions. A final type, and one who may have few **redeeming features** (well established by the middle of the twentieth century) is one prepared to **fiddle while Rome burns**. According to legend, the music-mad Emperor Nero fiddled while a devastating fire swept through Rome, a fire he is also supposed to have started himself in order to be able to rebuild the city on the scale he wanted. He blamed the arson on the Christians and they were persecuted. In fact, this could not have happened, since the violin had not been invented at the time. Nero's instrument OF CHOICE (see Chapter 24) was the lyre. However, he really did do nothing much to stop the fire, and Roman historians do claim that he sang while the fire was burning. Whatever the truth, since the nineteenth century to 'fiddle while Rome burns' has been a cliché for doing nothing at a time that demands action. Presumably the choice of 'fiddle' was to pun on its other meaning.

If we turn now to moods and emotions, we find there a number of clichés for feelings of anger and bad temper. In the days when the ordinary man had but two shirts, if that, anyone with any sense at all would strip off their precious shirt as well as their jacket before getting into a fight. Thus stripping off would be a sign of being ready to fight, and to **keep your shirt on** meant staying calm and avoiding a fight. It is first recorded in the USA in George W. Harris's 1854 book *Spirit of the Times*: 'I say, you durned ash cats, just keep yer shirts on, will ye?' If you lose your temper you can be said to **blow your top**. There is quite a complex history behind this and other expressions involving 'blow' and temper. To 'blow up' is related to **storm at** someone (a cliché now usually restricted to romantic novels and related forms). In *Oliver Twist*, published in 1838, Dickens wrote, ' "That's it!" observed Mr Sikes, approvingly; "women can always put things in fewest words. – Except when it's blowing up; and then they lengthens it out." ' This idea of blowing a storm has got mixed up with steam pressure (blow a gasket) and electricity (blow a fuse) and it has even been suggested that 'blow your top' itself, the history of which is not fully known, comes from oil wells, although there is no need to reject steam or water power. Certainly cartoonists use this image when they show steam coming out of the ears or top of the head of angry people. A recent term for aggressive or angry behaviour is **in your face** (or **in yer face**), which only appeared in the 1970s. There is also the strange aggressive use of **excuse me**, sometimes combined with **I don't think so**, no doubt used **with attitude**. This sort of forthright behaviour makes an old term like to **take umbrage** seem positively genteel. Umbrage appears in the fifteen century and originally meant 'shade, shadow'; from there it came both to mean to be in the shadow of someone's displeasure and, by way of a shadowy outline, to mean a suspicion. By the 1680s 'take umbrage' was in use to mean to take offence, the suspicion having turned into something *without a shadow of a doubt*. **High dudgeon** or **high horse** is now also comparatively mild, although it was not in the past. High dudgeon is so much a set phrase that no other type of dudgeon exists any longer, and even the origin of the word is lost. It first appeared in the sixteenth century, when you could simply be 'in dudgeon' when angry or resentful, and even in 1816 Scott could write about 'deep dudgeon', but it has been fixed at high since about the middle of the nineteenth century. If you get in high dudgeon, you might also be tempted to get on your high horse. This apparently metaphorical expression reflects physical reality. The original sense of high horse was the sort of massive charger that was ridden by knights in battle or tournament. These were bred for size and power, not only to carry the weight of an armed knight, but also because the size and weight could give you an advantage in battle. They were also exceedingly expensive. One authority has said that their cost in the Middle Ages was the equivalent of buying a Ferrari today. Thus the idea of being mounted on your high horse (a form of the expression found in the past) manages to convey a combination of rank, wealth and aggression.

Milder disapproval has thrown up a number of other clichés. The comment that someone **can't hold a candle to** another, or is **not fit to hold a candle to** them goes back to the days before electric or gas light when servants might assist someone by holding a candle to help them see. Thus Jessica, running away from her father Shylock in *The Merchant of Venice* (1596– 8), says that she is glad that it is night, so that her lover Lorenzo cannot see her disguised as a boy. Lorenzo replies that she must act as his torch-bearer, and Jessica replies with, 'What! Must I hold a candle to my shames?' (II.6). From this sense the term came to be used to mean a lowly status, so that someone who is not fit to hold a candle to someone else is, to use the more extreme expression found in *The Garden of Kama* (1901) by 'Laurence Hope', 'Less than the dust, beneath thy Chariot wheel'. You can also say you **can't be doing with** someone or something. This is a dialect term that has recently become more and more common in standard prose. Interestingly, the *OED* marks the construction 'to be doing with' as obsolete, recording it only between the years 1601 and 1724. The concept of 'faint praise' has been around since at least 1633, when Phineas Fletcher wrote in *The Purple Island*, 'When needs he must, yet faintly then he praises', but the expression **damn with faint praise** comes from 1733, when Alexander Pope published a poem called 'An Epistle to Dr Arbuthnot', in which he advised a literary critic to 'Damn with faint praise, assent with civil leer, / And, without sneering, teach the rest to sneer.' In these lines he used 'damn' in a special sense, which had been around for about a century, of 'publicly condemn a work of art as a failure'. The expression 'damn with faint praise' summed up so well the ability of critics to condemn by condescending or hesitant praise that it soon passed into the general language.

More upbeat moods are found in **game for a laugh**, where 'game' is used to mean 'eager, willing', but obviously also con-

tains the idea of something entertaining. You may consider such
people a **shot in the arm** or a pain somewhere else. This
expression for a much needed stimulant or encouragement
comes from 1920s America. Whether we should see it as an
injection given by a doctor to put you back on your feet, or as
the effect of narcotics, is in doubt: a shot in the arm was certainly
part of drug slang in the 1930s. Comments meant to amuse may
be greeted with a **wry smile**, literally a twisted smile, which
meant an expression of disgust when it was introduced in the
late nineteenth century, but which is now usually used to indicate that you are the butt of the joke or some other form of
qualified amusement; while those hoping to charm may go for
an **impish grin**, which dates from the mid nineteenth century.
Someone who is a **wet blanket** might describe the situation as
no joke or **no joking** or **laughing matter**. Things have been
described as 'no laughing matter' since the sixteenth century,
but 'It's no joke' dates only from the early nineteenth century,
although **joking apart** is found from a century earlier. **You've
got to be joking** is probably only from the second half of the
twentieth century. Wet blankets were a standard means of putting out fires in the nineteenth century, when the phrase was
introduced, their effect on laughter being similar. They may
speak in self-pitying **hollow tones**. 'Hollow' has been used to
describe sounds that are insubstantial or sepulchral since the
sixteenth century, but the set phrase 'hollow tones' seems only
to have been used since the mid nineteenth century in this sense
– although in a more literal sense, describing the echoing effect
of sound in a cavernous place, it is earlier. Nowadays, someone
who does not want to **join in the fun** or **join the club** (in
common use on both sides of the Atlantic since the 1940s) is as
likely to be called an **anorak** as a wet blanket. 'Anorak', one of
the few words in English to come from a native Greenland
language, has only been used for the garment since the 1920s,
and is only recorded in this derogatory sense since the 1980s.

A handful of remaining clichés that belong here but do not fit into any particular grouping includes **girl talk**, a condescending cliché that covers both what might be more staidly described as 'women's interests' in the media, and the sort of communication more often found among exclusively female groups – what gets said when women are being **all girls together**. Use of the expression was no doubt boosted by the success of a song called 'Girl Talk' in 1966. Optimists might have **high hopes**. The idea of high hopes has been about since at least the seventeenth century. The playwright John Fletcher wrote that 'His jollity is down, valed to the ground Sir, And his high hopes ... Are turned tormentors to him' (*Wife for a Month*, 1624) and Milton wrote in 1644 of people with 'High hopes of living to be brave men, and worthy Patriots'. Modern uses of the expression are sometimes influenced by the tone of the 1959 song 'High Hopes' from the film *Hole in the Head*, a hit for Frank Sinatra, which has ants and suchlike attempting the impossible because of their 'high, apple-pie-in-the-sky hopes' (see also PIE IN THE SKY, in Chapter 16).

4. Sports and Games

Britain has long been a nation obsessed with sports, games and competitions of all sorts, and these passions seem to have been taken with the language to other English-speaking countries. I have included here few of the overwhelming number of specialist clichés used by sports journalists. Not only are these almost too easy a target, but they have been adequately dealt with by other writers elsewhere; for example, in Fritz Spiegl's *'A Game of Two Halves, Brian'* (1996). One of the oldest organized sports, horse racing, has been dealt with in Chapter 22, under 'Horses'.

   We start with general sporting clichés before looking at those attached to particular sports. The whole point is (or at least was originally) to have **fun and games**. This expression for exciting goings-on dates from the early twentieth century, and is an elaboration of the simple 'fun' used in the previous century. It is often used in an ironic or disparaging sense, and also functions as a sexual euphemism. Early uses tend to be military, and the origins of the expression may lie in typical forces braggadocio or understatement. Other clichéd uses of 'game' include **the name of the game** and **play the game**. The first of these is an Americanism while the second is quintessentially English. 'The name of the game', meaning something that is important or central, what really matters, probably developed in sporting circles in the USA and is recorded from the beginning of the twentieth century. It did not spread to the UK until the 1960s. 'Play the game' has a much longer and more complex history. Although this expression for playing fair or honourably is recorded from the early nineteenth century – it is one of the many turns of phrase first recorded in Sir Walter Scott's novels – it really came into its own in later years. Two enormously popular poems used it in a way that established its associations. In the UK Sir Henry Newbolt wrote 'Vitaï Lampada' (1897) with 'Play up, play up and play the game' as a chorus. The poem opens:

> There's a breathless hush in the Close to-night –
> Ten to make and the match to win –
> A bumping pitch and a blinding light,
> An hour to play and the last man in.
> And it's not for the sake of a ribboned coat,
> Or the selfish hope of a season's fame,
> But his Captain's hand on his shoulder smote –
> 'Play up! Play up! And play the game!'

The rest of the poem explains how the sort of experience you get from a public school cricket match trains you to die for the Empire. To act otherwise would be **not cricket**, which dates from the mid nineteenth century. In the USA in 1941 the sports writer Grantland Rice wrote *Alumnus Football*, echoing Newbolt's sentiments:

> For when the One Great Scorer comes to mark against your
>   name,
> He writes – not that you won or lost – but how you played the
>   Game.

When playing one would hope, both literally and metaphorically, for a **level playing field**. Surprisingly for an expression that is so well established (and, one has to say, when used appropriately is such a neat way of expressing the idea) it is not recorded before 1979. It is one of the many such expressions that come from American English. For half of the players that playing field is likely to be their **home ground**. 'Home ground' was being used to describe the pitch on which a team regularly played by the beginning of the nineteenth

century. It does not seem to have been transferred to familiar
territory or the place someone or something comes from until
the middle of the twentieth century. Those allowed out on the
hallowed turf need to be **team players**. Interestingly, the
OED has no record at all of hallowed being used other than in
a literal sense of 'blessed'. *The Times* has a linking of the words
'hallowed' and 'turf' from 1928 in a rather dire poem, showing
the original use of the phrase to mean a sacred place for the
dead, but first comes up with the sporting cliché in 1969. Team
player is found in the *OED* from 1886 in its original sense of
someone who plays the game to support the team rather than
for individual gain. It has now become an almost inevitable
cliché of longer job advertisements, although many will admit
that they are baffled about exactly what is meant. However, the
OED comes up with the perfect definition in their only other
illustration of the term. Quoting from the American magazine
Newsweek from November 1980, it says, 'Reagan wants "team
players" for his Administration – men and women loyal to him
personally and to his philosophy generally, willing to argue over
policy, but not fundamental ideology.' Those who fail to **hang
(on) in there** (another Americanism from the mid twentieth
century) will **fail to impress** – a sporting cliché, used by journalists to DAMN WITH FAINT PRAISE (see Chapter 3). This may be
because they lack the **killer instinct**. This has been in use since
the 1930s, and at first seems to have been primarily associated
with boxing, but is now used very generally. When it is **all over
bar the shouting** (in use as early as 1842, often in the form
'. . . but the shouting', still the standard form in the USA) it will
be time for the **long walk** or **to take an early bath**. The latter
is primarily used of footballers sent off; the former used both of
footballers and in cricket for batsmen who are out. **Blow the
whistle** is associated with these terms. In the world of sport,
when the referee blows his whistle everything stops. From this,
two senses of 'blow the whistle' have developed. Firstly it is used
simply to mean bring to a halt. Secondly, from the stopping of

play after a foul, it is used to mean to report crime or misconduct to the authorities or to make it public, particularly unacceptable behaviour on the part of one's employers. **Off the wall** also appears to be sports-derived. In use since the mid 1960s, but now less common than in its heyday, it is thought to come from the image of a squash ball or ice-hockey puck bouncing off the court wall unpredictably, but it may also have been influenced by the idea of someone mad or angry after being *driven up the wall*, coming down to give their views from another perspective. To **rest on your laurels** was originally a sporting cliché. In the ancient world both victorious athletes and generals were crowned with laurel wreaths to mark their success. The expression 'to rest on your laurels' grew up in the nineteenth century to indicate being satisfied with the laurels you already had achieved, but quite what is behind the phrasing of this uncomfortable-sounding image is not clear.

Individual sports

Since so many sporting expressions come from the USA it seems appropriate to start our look at individual sports with that most American of sports, baseball. **Ballpark figure** comes from 'ballpark', the place baseball is played. Surprisingly, its clichéd use for 'roughly, approximately' comes from the space programme. In the early days of space travel, when landing a spacecraft was perhaps a rather more hit-and-miss affair than it is now, and space capsules would be landed by parachute in the sea to cushion the impact, the term was used to indicate the general target area. Thus the first quote the *OED* has for the term, from 1960, reads, 'The Discoverer XIV capsule . . . came down 200 miles from the center of its predicted impact area, but still within the designated "ballpark" area.' **On the ball**, an expression for being efficient and alert, dates from the beginning of the twentieth century. The image was originally of a baseball pitcher putting spin on the ball, but for most British users the image is more likely to be associated with to **keep an eye on the ball**, which has the same meaning and dates. The expression to **take a rain check** comes from the custom, in use by 1884, of issuing rain checks (or cheques) entitling you to a free ticket to another game, if rain stopped play at a baseball match. From this the expression came to mean simply to postpone something until another time. However, in UK business circles it has been widely mis-analysed as coming from the verb 'to check', and understood to mean 'to check if it is raining' and used in a similar manner as *to see which way the wind is blowing*. Although this mistaken use is less common than it used to be, it means that this expression is in the unusual position of being both a cliché and a solecism at the same time. To **touch base** can have two meanings – to cover all possibilities (not frequent in British English, but used in American) and to make contact. Although some have argued for a military origin, it is more generally thought that the term comes from baseball, where a runner has to touch the bases that mark the diamond he runs around in order not to be out, and where all bases have to be touched to make a run. This is supported by the existence of 'off your base', all but unknown in British English for 'crazy', the opposite of touching base. American English also uses the related 'cover your bases' or 'cover all bases' for 'cover yourself against something', and 'caught off base' for 'caught unawares', and has a whole slew of other baseball expressions, such as 'to play hardball with' and 'get to first base' (or second, or third) for steps towards your objective (often with a sexual connotation).

Cricket is probably the British equivalent of baseball, but it has not produced quite as many clichés. **Off your own bat** is one of them. This originally referred to the runs a batsman makes after hitting the ball with his own bat (as opposed to the running he does when the ball has been hit by the man at the other end of the wicket), and is found in this sense from 1742. Hence, it came to mean 'by your own effort' and from that 'on your own initiative'. As 'A Wykhamist' wrote in 1843 in his *Practical Hints on Cricket*, 'The secret of all good Batting . . . is the playing with a straight or upright Bat', and someone who can **play with a straight bat** is someone who knows how to PLAY THE GAME (see above). If he plays in this way he might **have a good innings**. 'Innings' has been used to mean 'a period of activity' since at least the 1830s, about a hundred years after it was first recorded of cricket. The callous 'She's had a remarkably good innings, and persons can't expect to live for ever' is found as early as 1870. On the fielding side you want someone who is a **safe pair of hands**, a term found from the mid nineteenth century for someone who can be relied on to hold a catch in cricket. At an unknown date it was transferred to other sports, including football, and in recent years has spread to more general use, to mean someone who can be relied on to handle things well. It has become particularly popular in the last few years, and is often found in the context of politics and business.

Boxing has been a rich source of expressions, reflecting its importance as a sport in the nineteenth and first half of the twentieth century, when it was taught in many schools, particularly the linguistically influential public schools. To succeed as a boxer you have to be **fighting fit**. To get into training you may make use of a **sparring partner**, to HONE YOUR SKILLS (see Chapter 8). The term is found from the beginning of the twentieth century in the literal sense of someone with whom you practise, and by about mid-century had been transferred to mean someone with whom you constantly argue or skirmish, but not in a FIGHT TO THE FINISH (see Chapter 11). A commentator on a boxing match may give you a **blow by blow** account of events and will tell you if someone has a **fighting chance**. For this the man will have to be good at **ducking and diving** or else risk being **hit where it hurts**. While this is often used literally as an alternative for to *hit below the belt*, it is also used in a metaphorical sense, either of emotional violence, or of *making an impact* in some other way. A recent addition to this list of metaphors is **that's got to hurt**. A losing boxer may be **saved by the bell** at the end of the round, a term that was transferred in the middle of the twentieth century to any last-minute reprieve. If not, he will be **out for the count**, stunned or unable to get to his feet for the full count of ten that constitutes a knockout. It is used figuratively in much the same way as that other sporting image, KICK INTO TOUCH (see below).

Personality has always been important in boxing. Focus on individuals has led to quotations and nicknames being attached to individuals, and some of these have moved across into general use. **The bigger they come** or **are, the harder they fall** is a nineteenth-century catchphrase from the world of boxing, a useful sentiment for the underdog. It is often attributed to the boxer 'Ruby' Robert Fitzsimmons (1862–1917), but what he actually said, when faced with a match against James J. Jeffries in 1900, was 'You know the old saying, "The bigger they are, the further they have to fall" ', so he was not claiming to have invented the expression. The saying was particularly appropriate in this context, for Fitzsimmons, who had already lost his world heavyweight championship to Jeffries the previous year and was to lose to him again, was light enough to have boxed and won the world championship at both middleweight and light-heavyweight, and weighed only 170 pounds. Jeffries, nicknamed 'The Boilermaker' and later known as the **great white hope**, was 6 foot 2½ inches tall and weighed 220 pounds. It was a real DAVID AND GOLIATH match (see Chapter 16), but this time Goliath won. Fitzsimmons was British-born, but spent much of his fighting life in the USA, and the saying still has strong American associations. As a catchphrase, the expression was particularly popular among troops in the First World War. Jeffries got his nickname the Great White Hope when he was to meet the first black heavyweight boxing champion, Jack Johnson, in 1910. Johnson won. Users are now often unaware of the racist connotations, using 'white' as if it were the equivalent of 'shining' (as in *shining example*) or without any idea of its meaning.

The origin of **the real McCoy** as an expression for the genuine article is muddled, but has boxing links. Some say the expression comes from a brand of whisky, for the Mackay whisky distillery were promoting their whisky as 'the real Mackay' by 1870, and this expression seems to have had some currency, at least in Scotland, for Robert Louis Stevenson used it in 1883. In the 1890s there was an American boxer who boxed under the name of Kid McCoy. The expression is strongly linked to him, but this may be in echo of the earlier one. There are various stories about his being 'the real McCoy' rather than an imitation – either other boxers trying to cash in on his fame, or his having to prove his identity in a bar by knocking out a challenger, but certainly in 1899, after he won a particularly spectacular fight, the *San Francisco Examiner* used as its headline 'Now you've seen the real McCoy', phrasing that suggests the expression was already current. **He can run, but he can't hide** was said by the boxer Joe Louis of his opponent, the swift-footed Billy Conn, who it was thought could **run rings round** him, before a match in 1946, showing that pre-match hype is no new thing. Nor was the sentiment new, being found in the Bible and elsewhere. However, Louis's form stuck, and was reinforced by US President Ronald Reagan, who used it as a warning to international terrorists in 1985.

The game of soccer has come to dominate international sport. One cliché that is often said to come from football, but does not, is **back to square one**. It is true that in the early days of broadcasting (late 1920s to mid 1930s) the *Radio Times* used to print a numbered grid for readers to use when following commentary on football matches, so that commentators could tell them which grid the ball was in; but there is no evidence that this is the source of 'back to square one'. It seems to be from snakes and ladders rather than football, with the player sliding down the unfortunate ladder to end up where they started. Certainly, after much searching, including the use of television audiences, the *OED* has managed to push its first quote back from 1960 to one from 1952 that has an explicit reference to snakes and ladders. Football is famously **a game of two halves**. This is a notorious cliché of sports writers and managers, used to mean that a losing team may well make a comeback in the second half of the match. Often it is no more than a filler of the 'you never can tell' type. A similar cliché is **everything to play for**, which is used most often when a football team has scored against the leading side, and now has a chance to avoid defeat. It has now been extended to non-sporting use. To **get a result** means **giving it your best shot** if you are to get **back in the game**. Of course, if someone has **moved the goalposts** you are in trouble. You may even score an **own goal**. This expression reached a wider public in the 1970s when it was the sardonic term used by the British Army in Northern Ireland to describe terrorists who were blown up by their own bombs before they could use them to kill others. A player driven to distraction by all these clichés may have **suffered enough**. This modern cliché is often heard excusing the behaviour of some figure of popular culture, particularly a footballer, suggesting that he should no longer be condemned because 'he's suffered enough' already. In the past a successful team might be described as **over the moon**. Although this expression of joy, a cliché since the 1970s, is chiefly associated with footballers and their managers, its origins are very different. It was a part of the special slang used by a group of aristocratic, art-and-philosophy-loving Victorians and Edwardians known as The Souls, who used to communicate with each other in a highly precious, specialized language that effectively excluded outsiders. They used the term in much the same way as the footballers, to express great pleasure, a desire to **jump for joy**, and took it from the nursery rhyme in which 'The cow jumped over the moon'. The earliest recorded use is from as far back as 1857. That other great cliché of footballers, SICK AS A PARROT (discussed in Chapter 22 under 'Birds'), has now died. But these clichés leave out that essential element of matches, the spectator.

Football followers have a bad reputation, the most common words associated with them being 'hooligan' or 'thug'. Few people note the remarkable ability of football crowds to work together to sing and create football chants, although there have been a few academic studies of the latter. The most mindless of the chants is **Here we go**, once a simple comment of resignation, now known to inspire fear. Also known as 'The Earwig Song', this consists of endless repetition of the words ' 'ere we go, 'ere we go, 'ere we go' to the tune of the central section of Sousa's 'Stars and Stripes'. As Fritz Spiegl says in *'A Game of Two Halves, Brian'*, 'Even the thickest fan can memorise them after a little practice.' A more recent chant that has moved into the realm of cliché, even being used for the title of a radio series, is **Who ate all the pies?** Sung to the tune of 'Knees up Mother Brown', it has spread throughout the UK and is used to jeer at anyone on the pitch who looks overweight. The full words of the chant are simple, being, with variations: 'Who ate all the pies? Who ate all the pies? You fat bastard, You fat bastard, You ate all the pies.' It has been traced back to Sheffield United at the turn of the nineteenth to the twentieth century. Their team's goalie was William Foulke, 6 foot 2 inches tall and weighing in at 24 stone. Modern use was associated with the Aston Villa player Micky Quinn, who is said to have picked up and eaten a pie thown on to the pitch by a fan. Quinn, who later used 'Who ate all the pies?' as the title of his autobiography, already had a reputation for chunkiness, one of the more complimentary chants associated with him being, 'He's fat, he's round, he scores at every ground, Micky Quinn!' **There's only one . . .** is another football chant that has passed into clichéhood. Sung to the tune of 'Guantanamera', it is used to support a particular player. Typically in the past it might have been 'One David Beckham, there's only one David Beckham', but the chant is adaptable to anyone whose name will fit the scansion, and when an England international squad included two players both called Gary Stevens the chant became 'Two Gary Stevens, there's only two Gary Stevens'.

Tennis gives us **the ball is in your court** and **game, set and match**. These come from lawn tennis, but the earlier form of the game, now called real tennis to distinguish it from lawn tennis, seems to be the source of the expression **from pillar to post**. There have been claims that this comes from the pillory and whipping post of the past, but there is no evidence to support this. Real tennis is played on an indoor court and its complex rules involve the ball bouncing off walls, roofs and buttresses. Early uses of 'from pillar to post', which was pretty much a cliché by the sixteenth century, involve someone being 'tossed' (partly because at the time it rhymed with 'post') from pillar to post like the ball in tennis.

The jargon of American football gives us **game plan**, originally used to describe a strategy worked out in advance. It dates from at least the 1940s, and by chance is actually recorded slightly earlier in a figurative use – for a plan of campaign in a non-sporting context – than in a literal one. American football's close relative, rugby football, is the source of **kick into touch**. In rugger, when the ball is kicked into touch, it is out of play and the game is temporarily suspended, a useful tactic at times of pressure. Thus it has come in recent years to mean to postpone, shelve or get rid of a problem. **Kick into the long grass**, from golf, which also gives us **par for the course**, is a sneaky way of cheating by making the next stroke more difficult for your opponent. It should have a much darker meaning than 'kick into touch', but in practice the two seem to be used interchangeably. **When push comes to shove** has been linked to the rugby scrum by the great commentator on the American language William Safire, but the expression is undoubtedly American in origin, and this explanation does not convince. More likely is the view that it reflects the progress of a quarrel. Whatever the origin, this expression, which has largely replaced the older WHEN THE CHIPS ARE DOWN (see below), is recorded from the 1950s, but was not widely used until the 1970s. A more homely ball game is found in **beer and skittles**. Beer and skittles have stood for the pleasures of life since the nineteenth century. Thomas Hughes, in the novel *Tom Brown's Schooldays* (1857), famously wrote, 'Life isn't all beer and skittles', and the expression is often used in this form. In earlier times the pleasure of drink and company was expressed in the term 'cakes and ale', hence Shakespeare's 'Dost thou think, because thou art virtuous, there shall be no more cakes and ale?' (*Twelfth Night* (1601), II.3).

Pole position refers to the most advantageous position at the start of a motor race, given to the person with the best practice lap times. As well as meaning in the best position, it is sometimes used in the same way as PECKING ORDER (see Chapter 22). As a cliché it dates from the second half of the twentieth century. There are other clichés from more general types of racing. A RACE AGAINST TIME is discussed in Chapter 8, while someone who is **quick off the mark** will **leave you standing** and **see off the competition**. They are also likely to be **first past the tape. Toe the line,** meaning 'to stick to the rules', comes from running – from the starting line, marked in chalk, for a race. If you do not toe this line then you step OUT OF LINE (see Chapter 11). 'Toe the line' is a twentieth-century metaphor, to a large extent replacing the nineteenth-century **toe the mark** (as in 'on your marks, get set, go'), which came from exactly the same source. 'Toe the line' is often spelt as 'tow the line' as if it were a naval term, indicating that the expression is a dead metaphor.

Activities in the water, not necessarily sporting, give us **sink or swim**. This expression, used in various forms since Chaucer's time, is self-explanatory. There is no need to look for lurid antecedents in the trial by water of witches, as some have, but simply to the art of basic survival. Those who sink may find themselves **over a barrel**. This started life in the USA and comes from the former custom of putting someone rescued from drowning head-down over a barrel to help clear their lungs of water, hence its use to mean 'helpless', 'in someone's power'. It was not recorded until the 1930s, but is probably older. If you **go** or **swim against** or **with the tide** or **current** you are using an expression found as early as 1712 in the *Spectator*: 'There is no help for it, we must swim with the tide', but which is found in other cultures as well – for instance, in Confucius' *Analects* of about 500 BC. The other great water-based sport, fishing, gives us a **can of worms**, an American expression from the mid twentieth century showing the American preference for the word 'can' where the British might use 'tin'. It was originally used to mean something complicated, but is coming more and more to mean something unpleasant that someone does not want others to know about because it is going to cause problems. The expression is most commonly used with 'to open', and when you open a can of worms, certain people are always going to be worried about what might get out, hence the shift in meaning. **Hook, line and sinker** is another Americanism from the 1830s. Fish that take not just the bait and its hook but the hook, line and sinker swallow the whole of what the fisherman has put in the water. Traditionally, fishermen like to boast of the **one that got away**. Around the time of the Second World War the meaning of this cliché was transferred from the possibly imaginary giant fish they failed to land to anything that escapes.

If we turn now to less active entertainments, we come to the expression to **turn the tables on** someone. This is another example of an ancient term surviving fossilized in a cliché. 'Tables' goes back to the Middle Ages as a term for a gaming board, particularly a backgammon board, and to turn the tables was to reverse the gaming board in order to alter the advantages for the players. It has been in use metaphorically from at least the first part of the seventeenth century. Chess gives us **only a pawn in the game**, while another table-based entertainment gives us **piece together a jigsaw** or **pieces of the jigsaw**. The jigsaw puzzle came into popular use at the beginning of the twentieth century – *Punch* in 1910 wrote anxiously, 'What if the jig-saw epidemic spreads?' – and by the middle of the century the metaphorical use of the expression, for information that had to be assembled before something could be understood, was already well established.

Gambling is another sedentary pastime that has had an enormous influence on the language. The importance of dice in the past, before playing cards were widely available, is shown in the number of clichés from dicing and gambling in general. From Roman history we get the **die is cast**. This goes back to 49 BC, when Julius Caesar, according to Suetonius, said 'the die is cast' (*Iacta alea est*) as he took his troops south towards Rome across the Rubicon, a minor river just north of Rimini. The significance of this action was that the Rubicon marked the border between what the Romans regarded as Italy proper and the province of Gaul. Caesar was governor of Gaul, and had used his troops to conquer vast tracts of land there (see DIVIDED INTO THREE PARTS in Chapter 7), but no general was allowed to bring active troops into Italy. So when Caesar decided to **cross the Rubicon** his actions were a declaration of civil war, and if he failed he would die. He did succeed at this point, only to fall at his assassins' knives on **the Ides of March**. In this he could be said to have been **dicing with death**. The image of Death playing a game for the life of a living person is an ancient one, although perhaps most vividly realized in Ingmar Bergman's 1956 film *The Seventh Seal*, in which a knight plays chess with Death. Surprisingly, I have not been able to find the expression 'to dice with death' before 1925, when someone wrote to *The Times* using the expression in the form 'to rattle the dice with death'. Where, then, apart from the attraction of the alliteration, does it come from? There are other 'dice' images in the language, the idea of **staking everything on the fall** or **roll of a dice**, which goes back to the Middle Ages. Most significantly, the image of death combined with dice is found in that mainstay of school poetry classes, Samuel Taylor Coleridge's 'The Rime of the Ancient Mariner' (1798), where the Mariner witnesses Death and Life-in-Death playing dice for the lives of the crew of his ship, with the result that all of them die except him. The expression is mainly used by journalists, and is often associated with driving. Indeed the first recorded use in the *OED*, from 1941, writes of 'the journalists' former habit of writing about [drivers] being "speed demons dicing with death"'. If things are going well, your **winning streak** could be described as being **on a roll** (recorded from the 1970s).

Card games, particularly poker, have been a fertile source of clichés. To **show your hand** and **lay your cards on the table** are obvious examples. When you do this your opponents can see what you have in the way of strengths and weaknesses, and whether you have **played your cards right** or **wrong** (never, however pure a grammarian the speaker may be, 'rightly' or 'wrongly'). These are old expressions, for although the earliest recorded use of playing cards in the UK is not until about 1400, by 1581, the year of his martyrdom, Edmund Campion, the scholar, writer, Jesuit priest and secret missionary to England, is recorded saying, 'I would I might be suffered to show my cards.' Equally obvious in origin are the expressions to have an **ace up your sleeve** or **in the hole**, both coming from American poker. An ace up your sleeve is what the professional cardsharp would have to make sure he wins the vital hand. An ace in the hole, used for a good move or something kept in reserve for when it is really needed, is a term used in stud poker for an ace that is face down on the table, its value known only to the person in whose hand it is. Less obviously from cards is **open and above board**. This expression for 'patently honest and fair' preserves the old use of 'board' for table. In an honest game, players will keep their cards and dealings above board, where they can be seen, and thus avoid the suspicion of cheating. Both 'above board' and the now obsolete 'under board' (for 'secretly', 'deceivingly'), are found from the early seventeenth century, although the combination with 'open' is not recorded until the mid nineteenth century. If the game is not above board, the cards may be stacked, that is, arranged to give a player an advantage or disadvantage. This term was first recorded in 1825, but is probably older, as it was already being used figuratively, with someone commenting of an American election, 'It was impossible to win the game, gentlemen, the cards were stacked.' The cliché **the cards were stacked against him** was well established on both sides of the Atlantic by the second quarter of the twentieth century. **Come** or **turn up trumps** originates from the world of card games such as whist or bridge. In the nineteenth century the more logical 'turn up trumps', reflecting the fact that someone has to turn over a card in some games to decide which suit is trumps, was the expression; but as it has got more divorced from its origin and card playing has become less central to social life, 'come up trumps' has almost replaced it. Many card games involve gambling. The term 'chip' has been used for the token used by gamblers since at least the 1840s, and has been a slang term for money for almost as long. **When the chips are down** you find out if your **gamble has paid off** or not. If it is **your call** you may find you have to **put your money where your mouth is** or, more rudely, **put up or shut up**. A nineteenth-century expression, 'put up or shut up' has been connected either with gambling, demanding that a player produce his bet or keep quiet, the more probable source; or else with a simple challenge to put your fists up or keep silent. To a hardened gambler a particular game may be **the only game in town**. This expression comes from the USA and is still not fully naturalized in Britain. Used to mean the only important thing that is happening or the most important thing of its kind, although nowadays for sports fans it may be applied to whatever is their passion, early uses seem to refer to card games, possibly illicit. Certainly the first British instance I have been able to find, from *The Times* in 1960, is of a cartoon showing a card game. If you attend the game you had better not be **two cards short of a deck**, a formula phrase with innumerable variations used to describe the stupid. **Sit tight**, used either literally for 'to sit bunched up' or 'without moving', or figuratively meaning 'to take no action', has also been claimed to come from cards. It is indeed found as an expression in poker to describe someone who does not want either to bet or to throw his cards in. It has been suggested that this is the origin of the popular use; but since the first recorded instance is from 1738, used of women at their embroidery, this seems unlikely. It is more likely to come from hunting, as certain animals, such as hares, will sit tight until the hunter is almost on top of them. Less obviously from cards is **the buck stops here**. In nineteenth-century America poker players would keep some small object such as a pencil stub on the table. This was known as 'the buck' and would sit in front of the person dealing. When the deal passed to another player, the previous dealer would have to pass the buck to them. Why the word 'buck' was used is obscure, but perhaps a piece of buckshot was sometimes passed. From this custom the expression to **pass the buck**, meaning to pass responsibility or blame on to someone else, came into use, and became common from the early part of the twentieth century. The American president Harry S Truman (1884–1972) famously had on the presidential desk a sign that read 'the buck stops here', indicating that he took ultimate responsibility. From this sign the expression passed into popular use. Note that there is no full stop after the 'S' of the president's name, as it is not an abbreviation. He had no middle name, simply the letter. **The game is not worth the candle** is a cliché more obviously taken from pastimes. It was originally a French expression, '*Le jeu ne vaut pas la chandelle*', applied literally to card games where the money passing hands did not cover the cost of the candle used to illuminate them. It was well established in English by the later seventeenth century, and the advent of other forms of lighting does not seem to have dimmed its use.

More hidden in origin is **leave in the lurch**. This expression has nothing to do with 'lurch' in the sense of the sudden movement, but rather comes from an obscure gaming term. *Lourche* was a sixteenth-century game, said to resemble backgammon, although the exact nature of the game has been lost. In the form 'lurch' it was adopted as part of the scoring for games such as cribbage, when it meant a resounding defeat. From that developed the expression 'to give someone a lurch', meaning to get the better of them, put them in a bad position, and from this we get 'left in the lurch', meaning to be left in a difficult position, abandoned. All these terms are first recorded in the sixteenth century, and by 1600 'left in the lurch' was so well established that when Philemon Holland translated Livy's *Histories* he could write, 'The Volscians seeing themselves abandoned and left in the lurch by them . . . quit the campe and field.'

5. Popular Culture and the Arts

I very much suspect that many of the clichés and expressions from earlier popular culture have been lost – as the popularity wanes so the necessary knowledge to recognize the references is lost as well. Shakespeare's *King Lear* (1605–6) illustrates the way in which this can happen. There Edgar, disguised as a Tom of Bedlam, sings broken snatches of popular songs that must have been familiar to his audience but are lost to us. A briefest look at the headlines in any red-top newspaper will show the importance of lines from songs and television catchphrases in creating them. Although many are used with tedious monotony, they probably come under the heading of weak jokes rather than clichés and only the most pernicious are listed here. Similarly, in the clichés listed under quotations, we find a number from once influential but now little-read writers. This means that the majority of the clichés from popular culture listed in this chapter will be more recent than those from the more elevated arts.

Theatre and allied spectacles

Some of the clichés from the theatre and related arts are quite old. To **steal someone's thunder** is one such. This is an anecdote that grew into a cliché. The writer and critic John Dennis (1657–1734) had devised a new way of creating stage thunder for his play *Appius and Virginia*. The play, which was staged in 1709, was a flop, but the thunder effect was not, and was used soon after in a production of *Macbeth*. Dennis is recorded as saying, 'Damn them! They will not let my play run, but they steal my thunder', and from that the expression came to be used for stealing someone else's ideas or impressive gestures. The **greatest show on earth** started life as an advertising slogan for Barnum and Bailey's Circus, used from 1881 onwards, and is still in use by successor circuses. Use was given a boost when a film about circus life was made by Cecil B. DeMille in 1952 with the same title. The circus can also be described as **good clean fun,** a phrase that has been in use since the 1920s, usually to mean 'not obscene', although similar terms are found earlier – 'sane, clean and wholesome', for example, in 1867, and 'good, clean, wholesome' in 1911. Nowadays it is often used defensively, to protest that something others may not approve of is only good clean fun; or else ironically. The companion **all done in the best possible taste** is well-nigh impossible to use seriously, particularly since its use as a catchphrase by Kenny Everett in the character of Cupid Stunt, the buxom starlet in the television series *The Kenny Everett Video Show* (1978), who was constantly using this expression of the most dubious enterprises. While still on the vaudeville side of entertainment, the expression **gottle of geer**, meant to represent a ventriloquist's pronunciation of the phrase 'bottle of beer', is a catchphrase that is often used when ventriloquism is mentioned. It is also used to indicate that someone is being manipulated by someone else, like a ventriloquist's dummy, and is being extended to cover other fields, such as to indicate slurred or distorted speech through drink. Also from vaudeville is a **hard** or **tough act to follow**. It developed in the USA about the beginning of the twentieth century, but did not become a cliché in the UK until the middle of the twentieth century. A very successful or popular act would literally be a difficult one to follow, as the audience would inevitably compare you unfavourably. Those auditioning for a place on stage risk being told **don't call us, we'll call you**. This was originally a rejection formula from the performing arts, again originally from the USA where it is recorded from the middle of the twentieth century. It has spread first to cover a wider job market, and then into general colloquial use, where it has come to mean that the speaker is not impressed by something someone has just done or suggested. British in origin is the expression to put or get **bums on seats**, which has only been around since the 1980s and is even more recent as a cliché. Also very British is **cheeky chappie**, the epithet used by the music-hall comedian Max Miller (1894–1963). One of the bluest comics around in his day, he adopted the title in 1932 after it had been used in a review of his performance. It is now used in a wide variety of contexts, often as a put-down, as by the politician who referred to 'Labour's own cheeky chappie, Ken Livingstone' (*PM*, Radio 4, 13 May 2004). Another general theatrical cliché is **It's not for me, it's for my** (child, wife or whatever) – a standard excuse when asking for such things as an autograph. While this is still to be found used in all seriousness, it is most often nowadays a conscious cliché. There are two formula phrases that come from twentieth-century plays. The first of these is **look back in . . .** a formula phrase particularly found in headlines, based on the title of John Osborne's 1956 play *Look Back In Anger*. The second, **Who's afraid of . . . ?**, has a rather more complicated history. 'Who's Afraid of the Big Bad Wolf?' was the title of a popular song written by Frank E. Churchill and Ann Ronell in 1933, and used on the soundtrack of the Disney animation *The Three Little Pigs* of the same year. It was later recorded by Duke Ellington. In 1962 Edward Albee wrote a play called *Who's Afraid of Virginia Woolf?* which was made into a successful film starring Elizabeth Taylor and Richard Burton in 1966. The play title established the formula, much used in headlines, and adapted elsewhere, such as the title of Tom Holt's 1988 novel, *Who's Afraid of Beowulf?*

Television

Television has been another rich source of clichés. The enormously successful science fiction series *Star Trek* has been particularly fruitful. The original series, created by Gene Rodden-berry, ran from 1969 to 1971, and has given us **final frontier**. It was in use before this, used of places such as the Wild West, but nowadays it is associated in most people's minds with *Star Trek* and *The Next Generation*, every episode of which opens with the words 'Space, the final frontier . . . These are the voyages of the starship *Enterprise*'. The voiceover continues, 'Its five-year mission . . . **to boldly go where no man has gone before**', giving us 'to boldly go' as the language's best-known split infini-tive. **Beam me up, Scottie** was never used in the original *Star Trek* television series, but it became so popular in everyday speech, with many users convinced that they had heard it used in the series, that it was introduced in the *Star Trek* films. Unlike the other quotes, **it's life, Jim, but not as we know it** did not immediately become popular, but has gradually grown in use. Another television series with a fanatical following, *Monty Python's Flying Circus*, which ran from 1969 to 1974, with later films, has also engendered a number of catchphrases, although none of the expressions was an original coinage. Thus, for many people, **bereft of life** is not associated with Victorian mortuary pieties but with the 'Dead Parrot' sketch of 1969 ('It's not pining – it's passed on! The parrot is no more! It has ceased to be! It's expired and gone to meet its maker! This is a late parrot! It's a stiff! Bereft of life, it rests in peace – if you hadn't nailed it to the perch it would be pushing up the daisies! It's rung down the curtain and joined the choir invisible! **This is an ex-parrot!**'). **When I were a lad, we were so poor that . . .** is associated with other Python sketches and **look on the bright side**, in use since at least the 1830s, has been taken over by the final song (words by Eric Idle, music by Geoffrey Burgeon) from the 1979 film *Monty Python's Life of Brian*, 'Always Look on the Bright Side of Life', particularly since it became a popular choice with football crowds. Another comedy, *Blackadder*, is associated with **I have a cunning plan**. This was a long-established cliché of popular literature when it was deliberately used as such by the creators (Rowan Atkinson and Richard Curtis) of the *Blackadder* television series, which ran from 1983. The favourite phrase of the oafish servant Baldrick (Tony Robinson), it was used to introduce some fantastic idea that would either get a withering response from Edmund Blackadder (Rowan Atkinson) or else land him in the most excruciatingly embarrassing or dangerous situation. Among earlier uses of 'cunning plan' are those found in *The Book of Mormon*. Readers may decide for themselves when this was written, but it was introduced to the world as the work of an ancient prophet by Joseph Smith in 1827. 'O that cunning plan of the evil one! O the vainness, and the frailties, and the foolishness of men!' (2 Nephi 9.28). **I didn't get where I am today by** . . . was already a well-established cliché when it was given a new set of associations by its use by the pompous boss C.J. in the enormously popular television series *The Fall and Rise of Reginald Perrin* (1976–80), written by David Nobbs and based on his 1975 book, *The Death of Reginald Perrin*. The series also gave new resonance to **it made me what I am today**. Thanks to the success of the television series *One Foot in the Grave* (written by David Renwick, first shown in 1990), **I don't believe it** has also become a catchphrase cliché. It is the outraged cry of the lead character, Victor Meldrew, played by Richard Wilson as the archetypical **grumpy old man** as he finds yet something else to complain about. 'I don't believe it / this' had earlier been associated with the tennis player John McEnroe and his tantrums on court, and from this source we find a teen-speak cliché, **I *so* don't believe it**. Going back into what in television terms is the distant past, the formula phrase **never mind the . . ., feel the . . .** is based on **never mind the quality, feel the width**, a catchphrase meant to parody the patter of a market salesman, dating from the mid twentieth century. It was little known before it was used for the title of a successful television sitcom, which ran from 1967 to 1971. Another **blast from the past** (a catchphrase associated with the American disc jockey Murray the K in the 1960s and later taken up by British disc jockeys on the newly launched Radio 1) is **no hiding place**. An alternative to HE CAN RUN BUT HE CAN'T HIDE (see Chapter 4), 'no hiding place' was well used in the twentieth century, being adopted as the title of at least two books, in 1951 and 1962. To anyone middle-aged it has very strong associations with adventure and bringing criminals to justice, as it was the title of an enormously successful police drama that ran from 1959 to 1967, the theme tune of which entered the pop charts in 1960. More recent is the catchphrase **the truth is out there**, which has been enthusiastically adopted by journalists and caption writers from the series *The X Files*, first shown in America in 1993. Other catchphrases associated with the series are 'trust no one', 'deny everything', and 'I want to believe'. **Here's one** or **something I prepared** or **made earlier** is an expression chiefly associated with demonstrations of model-making on the children's television programme *Blue Peter*, but also used from the earliest days of television cookery demonstrations. It is now usually used ironically. The other *Blue Peter*-associated expression is **don't try this at home**, although again it has been used on other series. It is now nearly always a conscious cliché. Finally, when a television series starts showing episodes that do not seem to be going anywhere, that have no point, then you know that the scriptwriters have **lost the plot** – their sense of purpose, what the series is trying to say.

Film

The worlds of film and television are often closely linked, and some of their clichés overlap. Film writers can lose the plot, and

television may need to **rewrite the script**, although the habit
is more common in film. The cinema was the dominant entertainment from the 1920s until overtaken by television in the
post-war period, so it is not surprising that films have contributed
to the language. We have seen elsewhere how use of a cliché
can be boosted when it is taken up as a film title, and much of
this section on film could have gone in the section on quotations
instead. Right from the start of the introduction of the spoken
word on film the language has been influenced. **You ain't
heard nothing yet** dates from the original talkie. These words
were famously spoken by Al Jolson in the first ever talking film,
The Jazz Singer (1927), and **you ain't seen nothing yet** was
used the same year in a Broadway play called *The Barker* by
Kenyon Nicholson. However, 'You ain't heard nothing yet' was
already a Jolson catchphrase before the film. Jolson acquired it
in 1906 when he was singing in a San Francisco café and there
was a burst of noise from a nearby building site. Yelling 'You
ain't heard nothing yet', Jolson proceeded to sing at such a
volume that he drowned out the building noises. **All singing,
all dancing** goes back to 1929 and the first ever musical,
MGM's *Broadway Melody*, which was advertised as 'The New
Wonder of the Screen! All Talking, All Singing, All Dancing,
Dramatic Sensation'. The expression has become part of the
jargon of the financial and computing worlds as an alternative
to BELLS AND WHISTLES (see Chapter 15). **Blonde bombshell**
is an expression coined by Hollywood publicity people in the
1930s and used by them mainly of the blatantly sexual Jean
Harlow. *Blonde Bombshell* was the British title (in the USA it
was simply *Bombshell*) of a film she made in 1933, loosely based
on her life, and she made another one called *Platinum Blonde*. It
is now applied, as the *OED* rather coyly puts it, to 'a fair-haired
person, esp. a woman, of startling vitality or physique'. Harlow's
reputation was scandalous, summed up in the story that when
she met the wit Margot Asquith and persisted in mispronouncing
her name, she was corrected with the words, 'The *t* is silent, as

in Harlow.' (It has to be said that there is serious doubt that it was Margot Asquith who said this, and not another Margot.) The 1930s were also the great days of cartoon films. Warner Brothers' *Looney Tunes* series, the first of which was shown in 1930, used **That's all folks** to sign off at the end of each film, while **What's up, Doc?**, a catchphrase cliché from their Bugs Bunny cartoons, was first used in 1936. It was probably coined by Tex Avery, who was the chief writer of the cartoons, combining the already established catchphrase 'What's up?' and the slang use of 'Doc' as a term of address. The expression was given further currency when it was used as the title of a successful film in 1972. The year 1938 saw the release of *Angels with Dirty Faces*. This sentimental film showed the BATTLE FOR THE HEARTS AND MINDS (see Chapter 15) of a group of slum kids, between the gangster whom they admire and the priest determined to save them from going down the same path. In the end the tough gangster is persuaded to repel them by acting the coward when sent to the electric chair, and these innocents with the CARDS STACKED AGAINST them (see Chapter 4) are saved. The expression has retained the sentimentality of the original film. The next year saw one of the most successful films of all times – *Gone with the Wind*. Two lines stand out from the end of the film: Rhett Butler's weary **Frankly, my dear, I don't give a damn** and Scarlett O'Hara's 'After all, **tomorrow is another day**' as she resolves to fight on. Although the latter expression was by no means original to Margaret Mitchell's book, it is now firmly tied to it in most people's minds. The book *Gone with the Wind*, which was published in 1936, had been as much of a success as the film, but was the only book Mitchell published. 'Frankly, my dear, I don't give a damn' should strictly be attributed to the scriptwriter of the film, Sidney Howard, for what Mitchell wrote was 'I wish I could care what you do or where you go but I can't . . . My dear, I don't give a damn.'

Two important films dealing with events in the Second World War come next. **This could be the beginning of a beautiful**

friendship is the popular version of the final words of the film *Casablanca*, released in 1942. The script by J. J. Epstein, P. E. Epstein and Howard Koch was based on the play *Everybody Comes to Rick's* by Murray Burnett and Joan Alison. Rick (Humphrey Bogart) and Police Captain Louis Renaud (Claude Rains) have been in conflict throughout the film, united only in their apparent cynical self-interest, and in their indifference to the morality of the Nazis and to the plight of those trying to escape them. By the end, Louis has lost his position and Rick his bar and the girl he loves in order to help Ilsa and her Resistance hero husband escape to the USA. As they set out to join the Free French, Rick turns to Louis and says, 'Louis, I think this is the beginning of a beautiful friendship.' The film has been the source of a number of other popular quotations: **Play it again, Sam** (another misquotation); ROUND UP THE USUAL SUSPECTS (see Chapter 17); 'Of all the gin joints in all the towns in all the world, she walks into mine'; and 'Here's looking at you, Kid', as well as making the American expression 'It ain't worth a hill of beans' better known to English audiences. The other film was **Brief Encounter** (1945), an adaptation of Noël Coward's play *Still Life*. It starred Celia Johnson and Trevor Howard as the lovers who put duty before feelings, and, helped by the lush Rachmaninov music, became the ultimate weepy of its day. Ever since, 'encounter' rather than the more common 'meeting' has been the chosen pairing with 'brief'. It must be among the most parodied films of all time.

Film quotes from the 1950s show a radically different set of social attitudes from *Brief Encounter*. *The Wild One*, written by John Paxton, was released in 1953 in the USA, but was considered so controversial that it was not passed for public showing by the British Board of Film Censors until 1968, a full fourteen years later. This is the film that established a whole set of visual clichés, in particular the white T-shirt, the black leather jacket and the motorcycle as the paramount symbols of youthful rebellion. Nowadays the film seems pretty tame, certainly not justifying the advertising copy of 'Hot feelings hit terrifying heights in a story that really boils over!' or the portentous opening voiceover, 'This is a shocking story. It could never take place in most American towns – but it did in this one. It is a public challenge not to let it happen again.' As well as too many clichés of youth rebellion to list, the film is famous for the exchange between the motorcycle gang leader, Johnny (played by Marlon Brando at his most macho and sultry), and a girl at a dance: 'Hey, Johnny, **what are you rebelling against?**' '**What've you got?**' *Rebel Without a Cause* was a 1959 James Dean vehicle with a similar theme. The title has become a staple of headline writers, often as a formula phrase. Other 1950s film titles that appear in headlines with monotonous regularity, often with plays on the wording, are the *Sweet Smell of Success* (1957), *The Long Hot Summer* (1958) and *Never on Sunday* (1959).

The 1960s gave us **the great escape**, the title of a 1963 film and another journalistic cliché, and **if you've got it, flaunt it**, popularized by 'When you got it, flaunt it', one of the earliest recorded uses of this expression, in the 1968 Mel Brooks film *The Producers*. It is particularly, but not invariably, used of physical assets, and at least helps to resist the growing confusion between 'flout' and 'flaunt'. The year 1972 saw two significant films. The musical *Cabaret* has two songs that have influenced the language. **Money makes the world go around** from the song 'Money, Money' sounds like an old proverb, but is not. Less popular, but still used as a formula phrase, is **tomorrow belongs to . . . .** One of the most memorable scenes from the film, set in Germany during the rise of Nazism, was the perfect example of Aryan boyhood innocently singing the song 'Tomorrow Belongs to Me'. The song was written for *Cabaret*, but so convincing is this scene that in an interview a few years ago the writers said that people had come up to them to reminisce about having heard it in their childhood in Germany. The enormously influential film *The Godfather* of the same year gives us **I'll make him an offer he can't refuse**. The film was based on Mario Puzo's best-selling 1969 novel of the same name. In film and novel the line is said by a member of the Mafia and the 'offer' involves coercion, but although it was often used in this way at first, it has now largely lost its violent overtones. Puzo's line was not entirely original: the John Wayne film *Riders of Destiny* (1933) contains the line 'I've made him an offer he can't refuse.'

The 1980s brings in the tough-man movie, giving us **make my day**. To make someone's day, in the sense to give them pleasure, has been in use since the early part of the twentieth century. However, the expression was given new resonance by the 1983 film *Sudden Impact*, written by Joseph C. Stinson and starring Clint Eastwood as Dirty Harry. In a famous scene in this film, Harry invites a robber to 'make my day' by giving him a chance to shoot him. Because of this, the expression is now aggressive if used alone, although not in forms such as 'he made my day'. The *Dirty Harry* line is often misquoted in forms such as 'Make my day, punk', which is a blend of the *Sudden Impact* line and one from the earlier film in the series, *Dirty Harry* (1971), where Harry says to a villain, as he urges him to take the risk that there are no bullets left in his gun after a shoot-out, 'What you need to ask yourself, punk, is **are you feeling lucky?**' Another 1980s catchphrase cliché and quotation is **I'll be back**, used as a threat by the Terminator (played by Arnold Schwarzenegger) in the 1984 film *The Terminator* and its 1991 sequel, *Terminator 2*. The latter is also the source of other catchphrase clichés: **hasta la vista, baby** and 'He's back – and **this time it's personal**.'

The 1990s brings us the film **The Full Monty** (1997). This expression, for something thorough or complete or the full amount, has been around as a colloquialism for a while, but only became a cliché with the success of the film. It is said that there are at least sixteen explanations of the origin of the phrase in existence, but there are only two realistic contenders. One is that it refers to the former chain of Montague Burton tailor shops, so that the full monty would be a smart three-piece suit and tie outfit, suitable for SUNDAY BEST (see Chapter 16). The alternative links the expression to the nickname of Field Marshal Montgomery, who, it is said, insisted on a full English cooked breakfast, even in the heat of Egypt. However, evidence for the expression's existence only dates from the 1980s, rather late for both these sources, and one has to admit that the origin is obscure. From 1997 comes the film ***Men in Black***. Again, the term for people believed to visit those who have had encounters with aliens was not new – it has been traced back to 1963 – but the film gave the term currency. Nor is the type of formation new. Terms such as the **boys in blue** for either policemen or sailors date back to the mid nineteenth century. It is interesting, though, to observe the clash of ideas that has been involved in the popularizing of the term 'men in black'. The idea of 'baddies', particularly in Westerns, being dressed in black or as 'black hats' is so strong that the term is pulled in several directions and 'men in black' has acquired an even more sinister overtone than the original warranted.

Westerns have been deliberately left out of the list above, as they form a genre all of their own. In fact, many clichés that are associated with Westerns are not directly from films, but were adopted by the genre. Thus, to **bite the dust**, so strongly associated with old cowboy and Indian films, goes back to some of the earliest literature we have. The expression is used by Homer in the *Iliad* – 'May his fellow warriors . . . fall round him to the earth and bite the dust' – and was copied by Virgil. The origins of the expression in English can be seen in translations of these two. Dryden, translating the *Aeneid* in 1697, has 'So many Valiant Heros bite the Ground' and Pope, translating the *Iliad* in 1718, has 'First Odius falls, and bites the bloody sand'; but the first recorded use of 'dust' comes from another translation, that by Smollett of Lesage's *Gil Blas* of 1749. The formula phrase **the only good . . . is a dead . . .** was originally 'the only good Indian is a dead Indian', a cliché of old Westerns no longer acceptable because of its racism. The history of the original is obscured by folklore. Traditionally General Phil Sheridan is supposed to have said this when he met the Comanche Chief Toch-a-way at Fort Cobb in 1869. In fact Toch-a-way introduced himself as 'Me Toch-a-way, me good Indian', and Sheridan is said to have responded, 'The only good Indians I ever saw were dead.' If Sheridan did say this, he was merely repeating the sentiments expressed earlier by Montana Congressman James Cavanaugh, who said, 'I have never in my life seen a good Indian . . . except when I have seen a dead Indian.' The expression **wild and woolly**, associated with the sort of mayhem that happens when the **boys ride into town**, comes from *Tales of the Wild and Woolly West*, the title of a book by Adair Welcker published in 1891. Welcker's publisher provided a note saying 'Woolly . . . seems to refer to the uncivilized – untamed-hair-outside, wool-still-in-the-sheepskin-coat – condition of the Western Pioneers.' The origin of **a man's gotta do what a man's gotta do** has yet to be traced. It sounds like something from a Western film, but claims that it comes from the 1939 John Wayne film *Stagecoach* have not been substantiated. The nearest quote that has been found is in John Steinbeck's 1939 novel *The Grapes of Wrath*, which contains the line, 'A man got to do what he got to do', but this may well only reflect an expression that was already current. It has been in popular use since about 1945 and is now usually used as a conscious cliché. To **ride off into the sunset** is a visual cliché of Westerns, bringing to an end a film in which the hero has done those things that a man's gotta do, and righted the wrongs of the townsfolk. Not quite a HAPPY EVER AFTER ending (see Chapter 1), because this sort of hero is one who WALKS A LONELY ROAD (see Chapter 13), but still suggesting a job well done.

There remains a handful of general film clichés that are not attached to a particular film, but associated with genres or Hollywood. **The show must go on** is very much a cliché of the 1930s–50s Hollywood film, but appears to have originated in the nineteenth-century circus. **Let's do** or **put on the show right here** is a companion cliché, supposedly a line from a 1930s American musical film, although no such line has yet been traced. It is used to indicate naive enthusiasm for a project, usually with an implication of success. Some kind of location, particularly 'in the old barn', is often added. **The rest is history** is a clichéd sign-off of old films, which has been recorded in print from 1877. The clichéd tough-guy threat of **you're history**, on the other hand, has only been recorded from 1981. It is usually the hero rather than the villain who gets to **bang heads together**. Too much violence and you get a **video nasty**, a coinage of the 1980s. Horror or science fiction films have spawned the formula phrase **the . . . that ate . . .**, which is meant to be based on format titles of old horror films, although it is hard to find a source. It is a development of the later twentieth century, and has given rise to headlines such as 'The Movie That Ate Hollywood' or 'The Zombie Movie That Ate Toronto'. There was a 1974 film called *The Cars That Ate Paris*, but this was probably itself derived from the format. There are certainly earlier films with titles starting *The Monster that . . .*, such as *The Monster That Challenged the World* (1957).

Music and song

Music and especially songs are another rich source of clichés. As with film, clichés from songs are often phrases that were already established in the language, but which were turned into hackneyed expressions, sometimes with a new twist, by their use in song. We will start with a number of general music-related clichés. To **make a song and dance about** something, used to mean to make an unnecessary fuss about something, dates from the mid nineteenth century. By the end of the century this idea of elaborating something simple into a show had spread, so that a song and dance could also, in the USA, be used to mean

a long, usually evasive, explanation. Also involving dancing is to
strut your stuff. It is tempting to try to link this to Shakespeare's
'Life's but a walking shadow, a poor player / That struts and frets
his hour upon the stage' (see further under SOUND AND FURY,
Chapter 7) but this is not possible. The expression is in fact
Black American slang, derived from the use of 'strut' as the name
of a type of dance, 'strut your stuff' starting life as a general term
to encourage someone to show off. Early uses are found from
the 1920s, and tend to be found in Blues lyrics. Only in recent
years has it become an English cliché, and it still keeps some of
its original sense, in that it is mainly used of popular music and
the media. Several stages up from those who strut their stuff are
the **wild men of** rock or whatever. Just as football has its **hard
men**, so music has its wild men, people who exemplify all the
SEX AND DRUGS AND ROCK AND ROLL lifestyle (see Chapter
15) that goes with the job. Those that have different tastes could
be said to be **singing a different tune** or **song**. Sorting out
the set of clichés that cluster round 'different tune' or 'different
song' is no easy matter. To **sing another song** or **sing a
different tune**, meaning to speak or act in a different way, is
very old, going back to at least the fourteenth century. In the
twentieth century one can also **dance** or **march to a different
tune** or a **different beat** or even a **different drummer**. This
last has its source in H. D. Thoreau's *Walden* (1854), where he
writes, 'If a man does not keep pace with his companions,
perhaps it is because he hears a different drummer.' On the
other hand, those who follow the latest fashion **jump on the
bandwagon**. A literal bandwagon is the sort of large wagon
that would carry a band in a parade. Those caught up in the
excitement of such a parade might be tempted to join the
performers by jumping or climbing on to the bandwagon. Hence
the expression, in use since the end of the nineteenth century.

The first songs that have contributed clichés date from the
end of the nineteenth century, although as I have said elsewhere,
I suspect that intensive research into popular culture would

reveal earlier ones. The exact origin of **the life of Riley** is confused. In the 1880s in America a performer called Pat Rooney was a popular success with a song called 'Are You the O'Reilly?' which described all the things O'Reilly would do if he were rich. Then, around 1900, another popular song, by Lawlor and Blake, was called 'The Best in the House is None too Good for Reilly'. By this time Reilly or Riley must have been proverbial for someone who is living a comfortable or carefree life, so it is hardly surprising that the actual wording of the expression is first found in yet another popular song, 'My Name is Kelly', which has the words 'Faith and my name is Kelly Michael Kelly, / But I'm living the life of Reilly just the same.' 'Motley' is a medieval word, originally meaning 'variegated', 'mixed in colour', which also came to be used for the term for the many-coloured costume worn by a court jester. 'Motley' then developed the sense of 'various things', 'a mixed bag', and **motley crew** became a set phrase by the start of the nineteenth century, and had already been used literally by 1748 in 'With this motley crew . . . Pizarro set sail' (*Anson's Voyage Round the World*). **On with the motley**, the older version of **the tears of a clown** (the title of a 1970 hit written by William Robinson, Henry Cosby and Stevie Wonder) comes not from this, but from the words of the tragic jester in Leoncavallo's opera *I Pagliacci* (1892) as he struggles, despite his broken heart, to carry on. It is used to indicate both a SHOW MUST GO ON mentality (see Chapter 5), and the idea of struggling to carry on as normal in the most difficult circumstances, putting **a brave face** on something. **Merrie England** is also from opera. As a literal description, using 'merry' in an obsolete sense meaning 'delightful', 'merry England' dates back to at least the fourteenth century. The form 'Merrie England', used to indicate all that is **olde worlde**, is found by 1839 in a book entitled *Merrie England in the Olden Time*, but received a great boost with the enormous success of a comic opera with the name *Merrie England* (libretto by Basil Hood, music by Edward German) in 1902. It is now rarely used without irony, at least outside the tourist industry. **Merry men**, based on Robin Hood and his Merry Men (although Robin was by no means the only one to have his gang described as 'merry men'), is found in the original sense from the fourteenth century. It is first recorded in 1873 in the modern sense of 'followers' or 'supporters': 'Moderate Liberals had been glad to give Mr Daubeny and his merry men a chance' (Anthony Trollope, *Phineas Redux*).

The source of **all dressed up and nowhere** (or **no place**) **to go** is a song written by the Americans Silvio Hein and Benjamin Burt in 1913, 'When You're All Dressed Up and No Place to Go', although a song with a nearly identical title, 'When You're All Dressed Up and Have No Place to Go', was published in 1912 (which makes one suspect we should be looking for another source, such as a cartoon, that made the expression current). The Hein and Burt song was in a show called *The Beauty Shop* produced on Broadway in 1913 and in London in 1916. The expression is often found as a political insult thanks to its use by the polemical journalist William Allen White (1869–1944), who described the Progressive Party, after Theodore Roosevelt had retired from the presidential contest in 1916, as 'all dressed up with nowhere to go'.

The American experience of the First World War is reflected not in clichés of suffering as one might expect, but in **down on the farm**, for the source of this peculiar construction is the 1919 American hit song 'How 'Ya Gonna Keep 'em Down on the Farm (After They've Seen Paree)' (words by Sam M. Lewis and Joe Young). The song refers to the US soldiers who had been to Europe in the war. For journalists, particularly headline writers, events hardly ever take place 'on a farm', but nearly always 'down on the farm'.

The **best things in life are free** started out as the title of a song written by Buddy de Sylva, Lew Brown and Ray Henderson for the 1927 Broadway musical (later filmed) *Good News*. The title of this song was then used in 1956 as the title of a musical film biography of the song's writers, following their life from Broadway to Hollywood. However, the strongest modern musical associations for most people are probably from the very different lyrics of the 1963 Janie Bradford and Berry Gordy Jnr song 'Money (That's What I Want)' made famous by the Beatles, with its opening claim that although the best things in life may be free, what the singer wants is money. The Beatles were later to popularize the sentiment that 'Money Can't Buy Me Love'. Spike Milligan played on a similar idea when he said, 'Money couldn't buy friends but you got a better class of enemy' in his novel *Puckoon*, also from 1963.

Although **anything goes** is best known as the title of a song written by Cole Porter in 1934, Porter himself was picking up an expression of disapproval that was already well established. For instance, in 1921 the *Ladies' Home Journal* could write, 'One of the few real "movie" fortunes has been made by a man who . . . has constantly exploited the vicious theory that "anything goes in fun".' Porter was thus mocking the strait-laced supporters of VICTORIAN VALUES (see Chapter 14) when he wrote that even a glimpse of stocking may have shocked in the past, but the modern world has a very different attitude.

While 'anything goes' is still used in a disapproving way, it can also be used in a positive sense, and this use probably owes much to Porter's jaunty, upbeat song. Another jaunty song appeared in 1936, again using an established expression, when Jerome Kern and Dorothy Fields wrote a song with the instructions '**Pick yourself up**, / Dust yourself down, / And start all over again'. Yet more upbeat American positivism is to be found in **accentuate the positive**, from a 1944 song by Johnny Mercer, properly written 'Ac-cent-tchu-ate the Positive', the opening lines of which run (ignoring the phonetic spellings):

> You've got to accentuate the positive
> Eliminate the negative
> Latch on to the affirmative
> Don't be Mister In-between.

Going back briefly to the 1930s, the song 'Winter Wonderland' by Felix Bernard and Richard B. Smith, published in 1935 (although some say 1934) and recorded by everyone from Perry Como and the Andrews Sisters to Cyndi Lauper and Radiohead, has become a cliché of anything you want to promote concerning Christmas or cold weather. Even worse, it is now often categorized as a Christmas carol. Much more downbeat is **you always hurt the one you love**. This comes from the title of a song written by Allan Roberts and Doris Fisher in 1944. Oscar Wilde's earlier 'Yet each man kills the thing he loves' (*Ballad of Reading Gaol*, 1898) probably lies behind it.

The 1950s was a quiet time for song clichés, and it is not until 1961 that we find Ray Charles's 'Hit the Road, Jack'. Yet again this appropriates an old expression, for **hit the road** (or 'hit the trail') had been used in the USA since the mid nineteenth century, but it entered popular consciousness and the vocabulary of headline writers via the song. **They'll be dancing in the streets tonight** is another favourite of journalists, particularly sports journalists, to indicate celebration. It is often found in conjunction with, or as an alternative to, **(champagne) corks will be popping**. Both clichés date from the middle of the twentieth century. 'Dancing in the streets' had its position in the language reinforced by the success of the 1964 song, written by William Stevenson and Marvin Gay, with that title. The Beatles reappear in 1966 with **with a little help from my friends**. Although this was already a cliché when they used it as a song title, the song's popularity not only boosted use of the expression, but added a whole new dimension to its meaning, derived from the lyrics.

We skip another decade, the 1970s, and find a final two cliché songs in the 1980s. The first is the 1984 Tina Turner hit song 'What's Love Got to Do with It?' (written by Terry Britten and Graham Lyle), which has led to the formula phrase **What's . . . got to do with it?** The other is **material girl**, the title of a song written by Peter Brown and Robert Rans, which was a great hit for Madonna in 1985. Although firmly associated with Madonna – often found described in the press as the Material Girl – it is also used to reflect a hedonistic lifestyle.

Two final general music-derived clichés. On an organ the stops control which pipe the air can pass through to make the sound. If you want to use a particular set of pipes you **pull out the stops** that govern them. If you **pull out all the stops** then the organ is played at maximum volume. Thus, in the nineteenth century, 'pull out all the stops' came to be used for 'doing your utmost', 'to work as hard as possible', although it is now more usually used for 'at maximum capacity' or, an image which could be from the same source, 'full blast'. A keynote is the note that determines the key of a musical piece. It has been used in the sense of 'the main idea of something', 'something that sets the tone', since the later eighteenth century, but expressions such as **keynote speech** or **statement** date from the USA in the early twentieth century. They have become very common in recent years.

Cartoons

One might expect cartoons to be too minor an art form to influence the language, but they have contributed at least five clichés. **Collapse of stout party** was the standard punchline in a considerable number of mid nineteenth-century cartoons of the type that used to appear in *Punch* magazine. These were usually drawn in great detail, with lots of heavily etched lines, showing two people and with a long dialogue underneath. One of the characters would usually be blustering or pompous, and something deflating said by the other would lead to the collapse of this stout party. **What a** (or **hell of a**) **way to run a railroad / railway** is a catchphrase from North America, expressing general disgust at mismanagement, which probably originated in the late nineteenth or early twentieth century. It must have been well enough known to be instantly recognized when it was used in a famous cartoon in the 1920s that showed a signalman looking out of his box at two trains about to collide and saying, 'Tch-tch – what a way to run a railroad!' The year 1934 saw the start of the American cartoon strip *Li'l Abner*, created by Al Capp (1909–79). There a character called Evil-Eye Fleegle claims to be able to put a hex or, as he calls it, 'shoot a whammy' on people by pointing a finger towards them with one eye open. If necessary he can put in a **double whammy**, with both eyes open. The expression was not introduced to the general British public until the Conservatives' General Election campaign of 1992. In 1941 a cartoon drawn by Peter Arno appeared in the *New Yorker*. It showed a crashed plane surrounded by frantic rescue workers, while in the foreground a little man, obviously the designer, is rolling up his blueprints, and with apparent unconcern is saying, 'Well, back to the old drawing board.' Arno was probably using an expression that was already in use, but this much-reproduced cartoon certainly spread it. **Back to the drawing board** reached an even wider audience when it was taken up by the makers of the Warner Brothers' *Looney Tunes* animated cartoons, and used by characters such as Bugs Bunny, and Wile E. Coyote (when he was allowed to talk). It has now become a standard way of indicating, usually with resignation, that something must be rethought because it does not work. Finally, **take me to your leader** is a cartoon cliché that became a catchphrase. From about 1950 a series of cartoons of little green men showed this expression being used in various comic circumstances – for example, the alien making this demand of a petrol pump. The expression itself was probably used because it echoed earlier tales of explorers and heroes in the wild dealing with 'primitive' tribes, and the expression may well go back to the 1860s.

Painting and the visual arts

Painting has contributed its own batch of clichés. You can be **pretty as a picture**, which has been used as a term of praise since the nineteenth century, although it now has a rather dated ring, or **not a pretty picture**, a more recent development and now more common. You can ask to be **put in the picture**, an image which is probably one of belonging, of knowing what is going on because you are a part of a group, and in a photograph of a team or of friends. The expression dates from the early years of the twentieth century. You can ask for your picture to be **warts and all**. This is the popular version of words supposed to have been used by Oliver Cromwell when the fashionable, and generally flattering, portraitist Peter Lely (1618–80) was painting him. He is quoted as saying, 'Mr Lely, I desire you would use all your skill to paint my picture truly like me, and not flatter me at all; but remark all these roughnesses, pimples, warts, and everything as you see me; otherwise I will never pay a farthing for it.' Hence, the expression is used to mean 'as things really are' or 'despite its faults'. The artist needs to add the **finishing touches**, an expression that dates from the eighteenth century, and which still has artistic connotations, even if it is now more often used of the applied or domestic arts. The finished product may be **large as life (and twice as natural)**. 'Large as life' was originally used as an alternative to 'life size'. 'And twice as natural' therefore becomes a fairly obvious extension of 'and (looking) as natural' or similar expressions. Although 'It's as large as life and twice as natural' is best known from Lewis Carroll's *Through the Looking-Glass* (1872), it was already well established by the time Carroll used it, being found at least forty years earlier. It is now used as a formula phrase. **Larger than life** for 'imposing', 'impressive', 'on a grand scale', is easily transferred from a gigantic statue like Michaelangelo's 'David' to a large-scale personality. **Come up and see my etchings** is a conscious cliché, used as a humorous invitation to join one in the bedroom. The origin is that of the caddish seducer of the innocent maiden using an apparently innocent stratagem to get her into his clutches. The expression may well have been used seriously in an early talking film (it has that sort of a ring about it), but, if so, no one has yet spotted which one. The great Eric Partridge, in his *Catch Phrases* (1977), suggests that it is American in origin, and quotes a correspondent who says he knew it by the 1920s, and suspected it was earlier. Partridge also points out the line in Susannah Centlivre's 1710 play *The Man's Bewitched*, 'There is a very pretty Collection of Prints in the next Room, Madam, will you give me leave to explain them to you?' used in the same way as 'come up and see my etchings'. In fact the motif goes back even further, to William Wycherley's 1675 play *The Country Wife*, where both pictures and a collection of porcelain are used as an excuse for a couple to be alone together; and is no doubt even older if one knew where to look. The earliest example using the word 'etchings' is by Dorothy Parker, writing in the *New Yorker* of 25 July 1931: 'Come down to my apartment – I want to show you some remarkably fine etchings I just bought'; but this is not thought to be the original.

Literature

The world of criticism is almost too easy to attack for its clichés. The jargon and buzzwords grate not just because they are overused, but because they are so often unthinkingly or inaccurately used. While these buzzwords are also employed by art critics and those in other fields, the literary critics seem to use the widest range. **Postmodern** means almost whatever they want it to; **relevant** is used without any indication of what something is relevant to; **contemporary** is thrown in unthinkingly, often with no indication of whether the critic is referring to the present day, or to the same time as the historical events they may be writing about; **homage** often fails to be distinguished from something that is **derivative** or plagiarized; **knowing** equals 'I'm too lazy to want something new either'; and **paradigm** has been attacked for years without much effect. Other horrors include **name-check**, **deconstruction**, **structuralist** and **post-structuralist**, **existential** (currently enjoying a revival), **concept** and **conceptual**, **self-referential**, **pastiche**, **ephemeral** and **seminal** – all perfectly good words when used with care, but so often abused. In everyday speech, clichés derived from criticism include **critical acclaim**, meaning little more than 'praise', while 'acclaim' itself is rarely seen outside publicity for a performance.

If we turn now to writers rather than critics, the classic description of **deathless prose** in English literature is to be found in Shakespeare's Sonnet 18, when he says of his 'eternal lines': 'So long as men can breathe, or eyes can see, so long lives this, and this gives life to thee.' Nowadays, however, you would be hard put to it to find anyone using 'deathless prose' in any way but ironically. From popular fiction we find heroes with **steely eyes** from the second half of the nineteenth century, although they did not become **steely-eyed** for another hundred years. An alternative is **piercing eyes**, which do not sound any more comfortable. **Wax lyrical** is another literary cliché. It is a curious expression, and almost the only use of wax in the sense of 'to grow' other than for the phases of the moon. People were being described as 'growing lyrical' in the nineteenth century. Why then the change to 'wax'? It would appear to be a consciously over-literary use, for it normally has a slightly mocking sense, suggesting the enthusiasm of the person it describes seems slightly odd to the listener. It certainly has this feel already in the first example I have been able to find, in an obituary in *The Times* from 1936, which is nearly thirty years earlier than the 1965 quotation in the *OED*.

★

Finally, a handful of oddments from popular culture. **Go directly to jail, do not pass go, do not collect £200** or **$200** are the instructions on a Community Chest chance card in the game of Monopoly. The game was created by Charles Darrow in 1931. Any part of the expression can be used as an alternative to 'bad luck!' or when someone has lost out. As the great wit Tom Lehrer put it in his song on the effects of all-out nuclear warfare, 'We Will All Go Together When We Go':

> You will all go directly to your respective Valhallas.
> – Go directly, do not pass go, do not collect two hundred dolla's.

The nursery rhyme 'Old Mother Hubbard' gives us the expression **the cupboard was bare**. However, the formula phrase **alive and well (and living in . . .)** has a more complex history. The expression 'alive and well' was established by the middle of the nineteenth century, but was used mainly in a literal sense until the middle of the twentieth century. At about this time it took on a more ironic tone, and the addition 'and living in . . .' really took off. There was, in particular, a well-known 1960s graffito, 'God is alive and well and living in Argentina' (and variants), created in response to Nietzsche's statement, much debated at the time, that 'God is dead', and to various newspaper stories of Nazis still being alive and well and living in South America – in particular Adolf Eichmann, the Nazi SS officer responsible for running the death camps, who had been living under an assumed identity in Argentina, was kidnapped by the Israelis in 1960, taken to Israel, and tried and executed in 1961. A further boost was given to the expression by the musical *Jacques Brel is Alive and Well and Living in Paris*, which ran in London from 1968 to 1972.

6. Proverbs and Fables

Proverbs

Proverbs make up one of the most fruitful sources of clichés. These proverbs are often not a particularly English phenomenon, being found in various versions throughout Europe. The folk wisdom they represent crosses boundaries both national and temporal. When clichés, they are usually not quoted in full, but used in shortened forms or merely alluded to. Their variety of subject makes them a sort of short version of the whole book.

The natural world appears in the expression **let sleeping dogs lie**. This is found from the early fourteenth century in French, and reaches England by about 1385 when Chaucer uses the saying in his *Troilus and Criseyde*: 'It is nought good a sleeping hound to wake'. 'Hound' was the usual general term for dog throughout the Middle Ages. Where the word 'dog' comes from is a bit of a mystery. It appears to have been used first of a particular much-admired breed of dog developed in Anglo-Saxon England, and the word was exported, presumably with the animal itself, to various Continental languages, usually with the word for English in front of it as the name of this breed. 'Dog' had become the normal term by the time John Heywood wrote in 1546, 'It is evill wakyng of a slepyng dog', but the form of the proverb usual today is not recorded before the nineteenth century. More exotic animals are found in **the final** (or **last**) **straw that broke the camel's back**, frequently shortened to **the final straw**. The shortened 'the last straw' came into use by the nineteenth century, while the variant 'final straw' seems to be a twentieth-century innovation. The earliest examples, from the mid seventeenth century, refer not to the exotic camel but to the homely horse, in the form 'It is the last feather may be said to break an Horses back', and even in the eighteenth century it could be feathers breaking the camel's back. Quite why the expression changed from horse to camel I have no idea, although it has been suggested that it was an invention of Charles Dickens in *Dombey and Son* (1848): 'As the last straw breaks the laden camel's back, this piece of information crushed the sinking spirits of Mr Dombey.' However, it cannot be Dickens's invention for *The Times* for 10 April 1841 has:

A case may arise in which *one vote* may be wanted to save the MELBOURNE Administration – not from disgrace, for to that Ministers have become accustomed, but – from another minority, which, like the 'last straw that breaks the camel's back,' may oblige the noble leader in the Commons, the author of a Treatise on the British Constitution, by surrendering his office, 'to act,' as he said Sir ROBERT PEEL did in 1835, 'in the spirit of that Constitution'.

(I often worry that my sentences are too long and convoluted; I take comfort from this sentence.) When we speak of the **worm that turns** we are using a shortened version of the proverb found variously as 'tread on a worm and it will turn' or 'even a worm will turn'. It has been used in English since at least the sixteenth century. Another animal-related cliché that has lost touch with its original proverb is **every little helps**. It is usually a feebly encouraging expression. Those irritated by it might like to take comfort in the fact that the user is most probably unaware that it is a development of a proverb found from the sixteenth century, 'Every little helps as the ant said as it pissed in the sea at midday.' This seems to be a very ancient sort of joke. Even the ancient Sumerians had a story about a fox that urinates in the sea and then brags that the whole sea is his urine. The ant proverb is first found in French in 1590. However, when the proverb appears in English a few years later the ant has become a wren. Why the change? Perhaps because there are so many stories about the wren in British folklore, and the saying reflects the chutzpah associated with it. The wren is the smallest of our birds, but is also said to be the king of them, thanks to trickery. The birds, it is said, agreed that they would elect as king the bird who could fly the highest. Not surprisingly this was the eagle. But what the eagle did not realize was that the little wren had stowed away on the eagle's back, and when the exhausted eagle could fly no higher, the fresh and unstressed wren took off and managed to fly higher still.

Wealth figures in a number of proverbs. **Money**, we are told, **can't buy you love** or **happiness**. This seems to be a fairly recent proverb, not being recorded before the middle of the nineteenth century. It is a proverb that many find irritating, feeling that it is one that has definitely been formulated by those who have money rather than those who do not, and has inspired a number of cynical alternative versions, including 'money can't buy you happiness, but it can rent you some for a while' and 'whoever said money can't buy you happiness didn't know where to shop'. The role of the Beatles in popularizing similar sentiments is discussed in Chapter 5. **Money talks** is a much older, international proverb. It can be found in Italian in the seventeenth century, and even earlier in a negative form, 'The tongue has no power when gold speaks' (Stefano Guazzo, *La Civil Conversatione*, 1586). It appears in English in 1681 in Aphra Behn's play *The Rover*, as 'Money speaks in a Language all Nations understand' (II.3). The modern form 'money talks' has not been found before 1880, but has been much played with in the twentieth century. Perhaps the best-known of these versions is Bob Dylan's 'Money doesn't talk, it swears' ('It's Alright, Ma (I'm only bleeding)', 1965). **Ill-gotten gains** is all that is left in general use of a proverb that ran 'Ill-gotten gains never prosper'. A form of this is found in Latin in Cicero's '*male parta, male dilabuntur*', 'things ill gotten slip away in evil ways', which first appeared in English in 1519 in the form 'Evil gotten riches will never prove long'. Shakespeare has it in the form 'Didst thou never hear/

That things ill got had ever bad success' (*Henry VI, Part 3* (1592),
II.2). 'Ill-gotten gains' had become separated from its proverb by
the late seventeenth century, and was a cliché by at least the
nineteenth century. **Beggars can't be choosers** is a proverb-
cliché that was in use by 1546 when it appeared in a book of
proverbs compiled by John Heywood, in the form 'Folk say
alway, beggers should be no choosers'. Once mainly used to
indicate resignation about one's situation, nowadays it is often
used more aggressively, of other people's situations, implying
'like it or lump it'. Another proverb, 'If wishes were horses,
then beggars would ride' (early seventeenth century) approaches
the situation from a different angle; but this is more rarely used.

If you want to make money you have to take risks, or, as
the proverb says, **nothing ventured, nothing gained**. The
sentiment is found in French in the fourteenth century as 'he
who never undertook anything never achieved anything', and
is first found in English in Caxton's 1481 publication *Reynard
the Fox*, his delightful translation of the international folk tales,
ultimately inspired by and derived from Aesop, about the wily
fox who tricks and exploits all the other animals. The proverb
here takes the form 'He that will wynne he muste laboure and
auenture.' The proverb appears as 'I see hee that nought venters,
nothinge gaynes' by 1624. The use of nothing ventur*ed*, nothing
gain*ed*, rather than using the present tense, seems to be modern,
as the earliest I have been able to find dates from 1921. You must
also **grasp** your opportunity **with both hands** if you are to
succeed. The image of grasping, or holding on hard, is a powerful
one. As well as grasping with both hands – taking hold of
something as fully as possible – which is probably a development
of 'to grasp at', meaning 'to accept with alacrity', it has given us
to **grasp the nettle** for 'to tackle a difficult problem head on',
from the fact that a nettle touched tentatively will sting, but if
taken hold of firmly will not. And it has given us to **grasp at
straws**, a development of 'A drowning man will clutch at a
straw', a proverb found from the sixteenth century in a wide

variety of forms. The verb used is variable, 'clutch' and 'catch' being particularly common. That cliché for the interplay of profit and loss, 'What you lose on the swings you win on the roundabouts', is from the twentieth century as one might expect, the earliest example being from 1912 in the form 'losses on the roundabouts means profits on the swings' (swings themselves are not recorded in English before 1687). It is most often found as a cliché in the shortened, allusive form **swings and roundabouts**. **Talk is cheap** is another proverb the sentiment of which has been around for a long time but which was slow to settle in a fixed form. It appears as 'Woords are but wordes, and payes not what men owe' about 1600, but has not been found in its modern form until the 1840s. It echoes an earlier proverb, current from the seventeenth century, 'talking pays no tolls'.

When things go wrong we can comfort ourselves with the idea that **lightning never strikes twice**. This piece of spurious science – in full, 'lightning never strikes the same place twice' – is not found before the middle of the nineteenth century. The problem may have come about because you chose to **play with fire**. The proverb 'if you play with fire you get burnt', meaning if you involve yourself in dangerous things you must expect to be hurt, is first recorded in 1655 in the allusive form we use today – 'I played with fire, did counsel spurn . . . But never thought that fire would burn' (Henry Vaughan, *Silex Scintillans*) – which strongly suggests that it was well established by this date. Stronger still than 'play with fire' is **live fast, die young**. This companion cliché to I WORK HARD AND I PLAY HARD (see Chapter 9) and to **live dangerously** (a saying of Nietzsche's), has a rather obscure history. It will not be found in dictionaries of proverbs or indeed in most dictionaries of quotations, although it qualifies as a modern proverb and is also a quotation. 'Live fast' by itself has been used to mean 'live dangerously' since the late seventeenth century, but the second element seems to be modern, certainly as a cliché. It is often associated with James Dean, who died in a car crash in 1955, and has been attributed to him. However, its association with Dean is from the way in which it fits his public and acting persona; its actual source is a 1948 novel by the American writer Willard Motley called *Knock on Any Door*, although, as will be seen, the expression is presented in a way that suggests it may have been current by the time Motley was writing. The novel tells the story of Nick Romano, a good Catholic Italian-American boy who at one time has aspirations to join the priesthood. However, poverty, resentment and the casual cruelty of the adults with power over him turn him into a ruthless, nihilistic killer. In chapter 34 Nick is with a group of young toughs:

When the beer came Nick lifted and tilted the brown liquid in past the yellow foam. 'Live fast, die young and have a good-looking corpse,' he said with a toss of his head. That was something he had picked up somewhere and he'd say it all the time now. Always with a cocky toss of his head.

The novel is a powerful one, although Motley is now a largely neglected author. The use of the expression, often in the variant form '. . . make a good-looking corpse', took off not directly from the novel, but from the film of it starring John Derek and Humphrey Bogart that was made in 1949.

Another source of accidents is that, where danger is concerned, **familiarity breeds contempt**. This is found in the writings of St Augustine (354–430) as *familiaritas parit contemptum*, which is translated by Chaucer as 'Men seyn that "over-greet hoomlynesse [familiarity] engendreth dispreisynge".' The proverb reverts to the literal translation of 'familiarity breeds contempt' by the sixteenth century. Others may justify their actions on the basis that **all's fair in love and war**. This proverb has been used in various forms since the sixteenth century. In the earliest examples the emphasis is on love, as in the first recorded use, from John Lyly's interminable *Euphues* of 1578: 'Anye impietie may lawfully be committed in loue, which is lawlesse.' It had settled into the modern form by the middle of the nineteenth century. It is well known that in this sort of situation **he who hesitates is lost**. Although this is now the standard form of the saying, the proverb was once usually applied to women. The earliest known version is 'When love once pleads admission to our hearts ... The woman that deliberates is lost', in Joseph Addison's *Cato* (1713). Even though you may feel you have reached your **darkest hour** (from 'the darkest hour is just before the dawn', in use since the seventeenth century), you may find that you have a **friend in need**. This is from the proverb 'A friend in need is a friend indeed', a sentiment that goes back to at least the third century BC, when Ennius wrote that 'a sure friend is known in unsure times'; an even earlier expression of the same idea is found in the fifth century BC, in Euripides' *Hecuba*: 'for in adversity good friends are most clearly seen'. Another form of the proverb, 'a friend shall be known in time of need', was used by the Anglo-Saxons. The use of 'a friend in need' for 'a dependable friend' goes back to the nineteenth century. Finding a good friend may make you feel that 'It's an ill wind that blows no one any good', which has been a proverb in English since at least 1546, when it appeared in John Heywood's collection of proverbs. The image is originally from sailing, but it has long lost any connection with that, and as a cliché occurs in the shortened form **it's an ill wind ....**. You may even feel that this gives you **the last laugh**. This is based on the saying 'He who laughs last laughs longest', itself based on an earlier proverb, 'He laughs best who laughs last', first recorded from about 1607. The modern version is not recorded before 1912, but by 1925 'the last laugh' was well-enough established to be used as a film title. We may conclude from our experiences that we **live and learn**, a proverb found in the sixteenth century in English, but inherited from the ancient world, an extended version of which ran: 'One may live and learn, and be hanged and forget all.' It is used almost as a catchphrase, to indicate that one can learn from experience, or as an exclamation of surprise when discovering something new. There is an obvious link between this and **live and let live**, a proverbial saying encouraging tolerance which has been in use since the seventeenth century. This was given a new twist by the 1973 Bond movie *Live and Let Die*. There are a number of proverbs related to this saying, such as **it takes all sorts (to make a world)**, current since the seventeenth century, expressing in a different way the earlier Roman proverb '*de gustibus non est disputandum*' – there's **no accounting for taste**. A more homely version is **there's nowt so queer as folk**. 'Nowt' is a northern dialect form of the word 'nought' or 'nothing'. 'There's nowt so queer as folk' is only recorded from the beginning of the twentieth century, and although it is still used proverbially, it is now often used as a conscious cliché, to indicate rusticity. A more PROACTIVE (see Chapter 24) version of 'live and let live' is **do as you would be done by**. This warning against selfishness has been endured by generations of children, ever since Charles Kingsley used the proverb in *The Water Babies* (1863). There Tom, the ignorant and abused chimney sweep, is taught how to behave with consideration to others by Mrs Doasyouwouldbedoneby, and taught the consequences of not doing so by Mrs Bedonebyasyoudid. George Bernard Shaw, in his *Maxims for Revolutionists* (1907), cast a new light on the maxim: 'Do not do unto others as you would they should do unto you. Their tastes may not be the same.' 'Do as you would be done by' is a snappier version (dating from the late sixteenth century) of the earlier 'Do unto others as you would they should do unto you', which, in the form 'What you do not wish others to do to you, do not to other men', goes back to Anglo-Saxon times. These sayings may make you want to try to **mend fences** with opponents. The proverb 'good fences make good neighbours' has been recorded in various forms since the seventeenth century. In 1879 the American Senator John Sherman made a speech in Mansfield, Ohio, saying, 'I have come home to look after my fences.' Whatever Sherman may have meant by this it was interpreted, no doubt under the influence of the proverb, to mean that he had come to campaign. Within ten years 'mend fences' had become an Americanism for 'to look after your interests', and since then has mutated to mean 'to rebuild good relationships'. Perhaps some of this change, and certainly a greater awareness of the proverb, comes from Robert Frost's poem 'Mending Wall' (1914), which includes the lines, 'My apple trees will never get across / And eat the cones under his pines, I tell him. / He only says, "Good fences make good neighbours."' Of course, all of this effort may be of no use, and you may find it is easier to **save your breath**. Although this cliché is to be heard all the time, the original proverb 'save your breath to cool your porridge' is more rarely heard, although it will be familiar to readers of R. L. Stevenson. It dates from the sixteenth century.

Proverbs based on domestic life have also become clichés. The most obvious is **home is where the heart is**. This proverb was well established by the 1870s, and has been popular ever since. A much-quoted variant of this is from Robert Frost again: 'Home is the place where, when you have to go there, / They have to take you in' ('The Death of the Hired Man', 1914). Homes mean housework, which brings us to the **new broom**. This expression for a newly appointed person who arrives at a job full of ideas and enthusiasm for change comes from the saying 'a new broom sweeps clean'. The earliest example, from 1564, is: 'Som therto said, the grene new brome swepith cleene', which reminds us that brooms were once made from the plant broom. Homes need a family, ideally one based on a **marriage made in heaven**. Used literally, this is an old expression, represented in two sixteenth-century proverbs: 'Marriages be done in heaven and performed in earth' and 'The first marriages are made in Heaven, and the second in Hell.' Figurative use is mainly a twentieth-century development. Children figure surprisingly little here, the only example being **boys will be boys**. The modern form is surprisingly sexist when compared with the past. The Latin proverb was *pueri sunt pueri, pueri puerilia tractant*, which at first glance seems to mean 'boys are boys and do boyish things', but this ignores the fact that *pueri* in Latin can mean either 'boys' or 'children' (in the same way that until quite recently the word 'man' could quite happily be used for a man or mankind), so the Latin should probably be translated as 'children will be children . . .'. This is certainly the sense used by Thomas Deloney in *A Gentle Craft* (1597): 'Youth will be youth.' The form 'boys will be boys' is not recorded until the nineteenth century. A section dealing with domestic affairs is probably a good place to slip in a proverb on dress – 'if the cap fits, wear it', usually shortened to **if the cap fits**. This has been around since at least the early eighteenth century, and is probably older. A work of 1600 called *Pasquil's Fools-Cap* has the passage: 'Where you finde a head fit for this Cappe, either bestowe it upon him in charity, or send him where he may have them for his money', which suggests that the expression was known then, and also reminds us that the cap to be worn is a dunce's cap. In America this saying is more likely to be found in the form **If the shoe fits** or even, perhaps under the influence of the Cinderella story, **If the slipper fits**. Appearance is also commented on in **beauty is only skin deep**. This proverb, reminding us not to be taken in by appearances, has been in use since the sixteenth century. Nowadays, developments such as 'more than skin-deep' are quite common. To say that someone **looks as if butter wouldn't melt in his/her mouth** is also a warning against being taken in by appearances. It has been an English proverb since at least the sixteenth century. Thackeray sums up the type in *Pendennis* (1849) when he writes, 'When a visitor comes in, she smiles and languishes, you'd think that butter wouldn't melt in her mouth', while Swift produces a more elaborate version of the saying with 'She looks as if butter would not melt in her mouth, but I'll warrant cheese won't choke her' (*Polite Conversation*, 1738). The idea behind the expression is probably that reserved innocence is cool, as opposed to the fiery passion of the forward or experienced. The idea of coldness was certainly picked up on by the English actress Elsa Lanchester, who is reputed to have said of the Irish actress Maureen O'Hara, 'She looked as though butter wouldn't melt in her mouth. Or anywhere else.'

Moving out from the home to the farmyard, we come to the problem of finding a **needle in a haystack**. This expression for trying to do or find the impossible is only found in the form we use at present from the mid nineteenth century, but the idea is much older. In the past the image was a little less ambitious, as people looked for the needle not in a whole haystack, but in a 'bottle of hay', the old equivalent of a bale – still an all-but-impossible task. The origin of this expression may be LOST IN THE MISTS OF TIME (see Chapter 20), for it exists in a number of other languages, and may have reached English from one of them. Also on the farm we find apples. The importance of apples as a source of food and cider to English speakers in the past is illustrated by the number of proverbs they appear in. These include 'the apple never falls far from the tree' and 'an apple a day keeps the doctor away'. The only one that concerns us here, though, is the **rotten** or **bad apple** you find in every barrel. Surprisingly, this expression, seemingly so well established, has yet to be found in print before 1971, and features on the *OED*'s current list of terms that it hopes the general public can find earlier examples of, for it seems much older. The sentiment is certainly old. There is a Latin proverb that says 'a rotten apple quickly infects its neighbours', and similar sayings have been found in English from the fourteenth century. Only the modern, allusive use is new.

Before leaving proverbs, there are a handful that do not fit comfortably into any category. **Better late than never** goes back to the ancient world. It is found in Greek in the writings of Dionysius of Halicarnassus (first century BC) in the form, 'It is better to start doing what one has to late than not at all' and in the Latin of his near-contemporary Livy. It is in English by about 1330. Also from Latin is a **word to the wise**. This is the

English translation of the Latin proverb *Verbum sapienti sat est*, 'a word is enough for a sensible man', itself a cliché in the shortened form **verb sap**. It has been used in English in various forms since the thirteenth century. In the 1590s Ben Jonson showed it was already well understood as a warning or even threat, in his play *The Case is Altered*: 'Go to, a word to the wise; away, fly, vanish.' **It's now or never** has been in use since the time of the ancient Greeks, and is recorded in English from Chaucer onwards. For many, the words are irrevocably associated with the adaptation by Aaron Schroeder and Wally Gold of the Italian song 'O Sole Meo', which was a hit for Elvis Presley in 1960 under the title 'It's Now or Never'. **Great minds think alike** has been around since the early seventeenth century, in the form 'great minds (or wits) jump', 'jump' being used in an old sense meaning 'coincide'. The modern form of the proverb is not recorded before the very end of the nineteenth century, and is usually used ironically. **Third time lucky** is more recent, not having been recorded before the nineteenth century.

Fables

Greek historians said that Aesop was a slave in Thrace who lived in the middle of the sixth century BC. Whoever he may have really been, if he ever existed, the collection of animal fables attributed to him were translated into Latin and from Latin spread throughout Europe, changing and acquiring further stories and details as they went. Their influence is still widely felt, even though not many people read them in their original forms, and modern tellings nearly always leave out the moral, once a vital part of the story. However, the moral part is often still implicit in the clichéd references to them. One of the best-known of the fables is that of the **dog in the manger**, in which a dog, lying comfortably in a manger full of hay, refuses to let an ox come and eat the hay, even though the ox (or in some versions, horse) is hungry and, as the ox mildly points out, the dog cannot eat the hay itself. It was firmly fixed in the language by the sixteenth century as a term for a selfish person, although the story was widely known before that. **Sour grapes** comes from Aesop's fable of *The Fox and the Grapes*, which tells of a fox's struggles to get at some grapes hanging out of reach. When at last it has to give up, it walks off muttering to itself that it knows they are nasty sour things anyway. A carnivorous fox's desire for grapes may seem rather odd to us, and at first I thought this was another example of the ancient Greeks' ineptitude at natural history. They thought, for instance, that kingfishers built their nests floating on the sea. According to legend, the original kingfishers were the metamorphosed forms of King Ceyx and his wife Alcyone, daughter of the wind god Aeolus. When Ceyx was drowned, Alcyone tried to commit suicide by drowning herself, but the gods, out of pity, turned them into kingfishers. Because Alcyone was Aeolus' daughter, he made sure that there was a two-week period of calm around the winter solstice while she was brooding her eggs on her floating nest so that it did not get swamped. This period became known as the **halcyon days**, 'Halcyon' being a form of Alcyone's name. (The Latin name for the kingfisher family is still *Halcyonidae*.) Well into the twentieth century this was a clichéd term for a happy, ideal time, but the expression has now fallen out of favour and I find many young people have never heard of it. To be fair to the Greeks, as kingfishers nest in tunnels in banks their nests are difficult to spot, and you can search as many trees as you like and never find one. However, to return to *The Fox and the Grapes*, I am assured by my local winegrowers, the excellent Bothy Vineyard at Frilford Heath near Oxford, that foxes really do have a passion for grapes. Being carnivores, they get an upset stomach from the fruit, but, nevertheless, they are so persistent in their liking for ripe grapes that the plants have to be fenced off to protect them from both foxes and badgers.

A fable that is little known today, although once well known in the days when Horace's *Odes* were widely studied in schools, is the source of the **naked truth**. It tells the story of Truth and Falsehood's going bathing together. Falsehood got out first and stole Truth's clothes, but Truth preferred to go naked rather than be seen dressed in Falsehood's clothes. The expression has been familiar in English since the Middle Ages. An alternative cliché is the UNVARNISHED TRUTH (see Chapter 17). The expressions **cat's paw** and to **pull chestnuts out of the fire** both come from the same fable, often associated with Aesop, although there is another version that links the story to a monkey owned by Pope Julius II (pope from 1503 to 1513). In the story a persuasive monkey wants to get some roasting chestnuts out of a fire and persuades the cat to do it for him. In another version the cat is actually sleeping by the fire and the monkey grabs the cat's paw to use as a rake. While neither expression really counts as a cliché, the story is too good to miss out.

Not all such fables are linked to Aesop. To **add insult to injury** goes back to the Latin fables of Phaedrus, written in the first century AD, which include the story of a bald man bothered by a fly, which bites him on the head. The man swats at the fly and hits himself on the head, at which the fly comments, 'You wished to kill me for a touch. What will you do to yourself since you have added insult to injury?' The actual wording first appears in the mid eighteenth century in English. The story behind the phrase to have an **axe to grind** is usually attributed to Benjamin Franklin, but it seems in fact to come from a column written by the American Charles Miner for the *Wilkes-Barre Gleaner* in 1811. In this he told the story of how, in his childhood, a stranger asked to use the grindstone in his family backyard, and through a mixture of charm and flattery he got the young Miner to do the hard work of turning the grindstone, while the stranger simply held the axe. Miner concludes, 'When I see a merchant over-polite to his customers, begging them to taste a little brandy and throwing half his goods on the counter – thinks I, that man has an axe to grind.' The confusion with

Franklin may come from a passage in his autobiography, when he tells of his attempts to improve himself:

I made so little progress in amendment, and had such frequent relapses, that I was almost ready to give up the attempt, and content myself with a faulty character in that respect, like the man who, in buying an ax of a smith, my neighbour, desired to have the whole of its surface as bright as the edge. The smith consented to grind it bright for him if he would turn the wheel; he turn'd, while the smith press'd the broad face of the ax hard and heavily on the stone, which made the turning of it very fatiguing. The man came every now and then from the wheel to see how the work went on, and at length would take his ax as it was, without farther grinding. 'No,' said the smith, 'turn on, turn on; we shall have it bright by-and-by; as yet, it is only speckled.' 'Yes,' said the man, 'but I think I like a speckled ax best.'

E. Cobham Brewer, the author of *Brewer's Dictionary of Phrase and Fable* written in 1870, tells a story, to account for the expression a **skeleton in the cupboard**, of a wide-ranging search for someone who had perfect contentment. The searchers thought they had found someone so blessed, but the woman selected took the searchers to her bedroom, showed them a skeleton in the cupboard, and told them it was that of a rival killed by her husband in a duel years before, and that he forced her to kiss it every night. Alas, Brewer does not say where he got this fantastic rigmarole from, and it sounds suspiciously like something made up to account for the saying. The expression came into use in the early nineteenth century, at a time when the Gothic horror novels so well parodied by Jane Austen in *Northanger Abbey* (written 1798) were popular, so it may be inspired by these, or perhaps Brewer's story may come from one of them. In the USA the saying takes the form of **skeleton in the closet**, and since for many years homosexuality was considered such a skeleton, this has given rise to **come out of the closet** for to be open about one's homosexuality.

7. Quotations

An examination of the quotations that have become clichés offers us an interesting insight into the reading of the past, and the impact their authors had on their readers. It also reveals what were felt in the past to be gaps in the language. The following section is by no means the only place that quotations appear in this book. Many of the quotations that have entered the language have been included in other chapters, as they fit more neatly under those subject headings. Quotations from popular songs and films in particular are listed in Chapter 5. However, enough are collected here to give material for thought. Shakespeare, left until the last section of this chapter, and the Bible, covered in Chapter 16, are, of course, the commonest sources of quotation clichés in the language. Other sources have been grouped below according to the periods in which their authors wrote. I have tried to indicate when they crossed over from quotation to cliché, although this is not always easy to ascertain. As will be seen, sources cover most of the periods from which we have records of written language, and they also show the influence of some authors little read today.

The Classics

Some of the clichés translated from Latin are easily recognized. Almost everyone using the expression **bread and circuses** knows it comes from Latin, if only because it is hard to imagine a **baying mob** (unrecorded in the *OED*, and the two words are not found joined in *The Times* until 1974) demanding a modern circus. The Roman poet Juvenal (AD 60–130) complained in his tenth *Satire*: '[The Roman people] long for two things only: bread and circuses.' Both of these were provided for Roman citizens for free or at subsidized prices, so Juvenal was saying that as long as the people had their cheap food and entertainment, they didn't much care what happened. At a later date a similar idea was expressed as the OPIUM OF THE MASSES (see below). There is no mistaking the fact that **O tempora! O mores!** is Latin. The great Roman orator and master of spin Cicero, who also coined the phrase **men of good will**, used this expression in one of his most telling political speeches. In the year 63 BC Cicero was one of the two Consuls – the most senior officials – of Rome, and a poor but capable rival called Catiline was trying to foment revolution. What was really going on is not clear, since the main evidence we have against Catiline is Cicero's speech attacking him, and Cicero was quite capable of twisting facts. In his speech he gives an account of the depravity and general worthlessness of Catiline and his followers, lamenting that such things should be possible, exclaiming, 'O tempora! O mores!' The reason that this expression is usually kept in Latin is that while the first part is easily translated as 'O what times!', the word *mores* presents problems. It is used in modern English to mean the customs and conventions embodying the fundamental values of a society. In Latin it literally means 'customs' and is used by Cicero in a sense that falls about halfway between the modern English 'morals' and 'lifestyle'. The expression has been a cliché since at least 1770. **Divided into three parts (like Caesar's Gaul)** is also self-evidently Roman. When Julius Caesar became governor of Gaul he made up his mind to make a political name for himself, and started a campaign of conquest that turned what had been a small province into one of the largest then under Roman rule. The legality of this was dubious, so, being a master of propaganda, he sent home a brilliantly written series of dispatches justifying his actions. These were then collected into a book, *The Gallic Wars* (*De Bello Gallico*), studied by generations of later schoolchildren, the opening words of which are: 'All Gaul is divided into three parts' (*Gallia est omnis divisa in partes tres*). By 1892 it was a well-enough established cliché for a writer to be able to play on it, saying, 'All golf . . . is divided into three parts – driving, iron play, and putting.' The decline in Latin in schools does not seem to have stopped its use, although it now has a decidedly old-fashioned ring to it. The DIE IS CAST and to CROSS THE RUBICON also come from Caesar (see Chapter 4 for both).

The coiners of the phrases above were skilled at creating weaselly, but memorable, phrases because in Greece and Rome, rhetoric – the art of choosing your words carefully and persuasively – was highly admired, not just for its own sake, but because much of the law was run by people standing up in the open market-place and persuading others to think their way. The study of rhetoric sometimes encouraged people to use over-elaborate language, and both Greek and Roman writers describe as preferable the simple language of **calling a spade a spade**. Yet again we quote that paragon of public speakers, Cicero, who said, 'A wise man will call a spade a spade.' This idea was picked up by English writers of the sixteenth century, and it is easy to see how the idea of choosing plain words could drift into the idea of plain speaking, or not mincing matters. The expression was very common in the nineteenth century, and Oscar Wilde uses a variant of it when, in *The Importance of Being Earnest* (1895), he has Cecily say, 'When I see a spade I call it a spade', to which the refined Gwendolen replies, 'I am glad to say that I have never seen a spade.' By the early nineteenth century, someone who spoke with unnecessary bluntness could be described as one who **calls a spade a shovel**, now usually elaborated into 'calls a spade a bloody shovel'.

Not all of the clichés borrowed from Latin, though, are highly rhetorical or obviously from classical literature. 'Custom is **second nature**,' wrote Plutarch in the first century AD. This had been translated into English by the fourteenth century. The concept of a period of life when you are at your peak is even older, going back to Plato's *Republic*, but the expression **prime of life** only attained cliché status in English in the nineteenth century. The alternative version, **in your prime**, is particularly associated with Muriel Spark's 1963 novel *The Prime of Miss Jean Brodie*, whose protagonist considered herself to be in hers, and told her pupils, 'One's prime is elusive. You little girls, when you grow up, must be on the alert to recognise your prime at whatever time of life it may occur. You must live it to the full.' **So near and yet so far** seems to appear first in English in a 1755 translation of the Latin poet Martial's *Epigrams*, but probably owes its clichéd status to a line in Tennyson's poem on his dead friend, *In Memoriam* (1850): 'He seems so near and yet so far.'

From the Renaissance to the Augustans and the Enlightenment

Once we get to clichés pulled out of the body of English literature, it becomes difficult to distinguish between these and overused quotations, as there is no true dividing line between the two. The clichés I have included here are mostly those where the speaker might be pushed to identify the source. They are, in other words, unconscious quotations, or at least unthinking ones. There is also a problem dividing the clichés into groups by period. Some quotations may actually be expressions that had been used over a long period of time, but that only became clichés thanks to a particular use by a particular person, and are thus difficult to place in time. And ways of thought do not sit comfortably within discrete centuries. The quotations in this section are more or less those from the sixteenth to the eighteenth centuries, but some from the end of the eighteenth belong in the next section (and indeed, some people may feel that some of those in the later section should arguably be with the earlier quotations).

If we take the selected clichés in chronological order, we find first of all the formula phrase **a . . . for all seasons**. This is an example of an expression that became a cliché long after it was coined. It started being used widely after becoming the title of Robert Bolt's 1960 play about Sir Thomas More, *A Man for All Seasons,* which was made into a highly successful film in 1966. But Bolt took the title from a sixteenth-century description of More. More, who was born in 1478 and executed in 1535, was described while still at the height of his power as 'As time requireth, a man of marvellous mirth and pastimes, and sometime of as sad gravity, as who say: a man for all seasons' in Robert Whittington's 1520 book *Vulgaria*, a series of toadying verses with which the schoolmaster hoped to win favour at court. Even then Whittington was not being original, as indicated by his words 'as who say', but was echoing the great humanist scholar Erasmus's description of More, in the preface to Erasmus's satire *In Praise of Folly* (1509), as *omnium horarum hominem,* 'a man for all hours'. Thomas More was canonized in 1935, and our next quotation comes from another saint, and was also popularized by a twentieth-century writer. The Spanish Christian mystic St John of the Cross (1542–91) used the expression **the dark night of the soul**, *la noche oscura del alma* in the original Spanish, as the title of one of his books. He used it in a technical sense, to describe a period of spiritual aridity suffered by a mystic. It does not seem to have become a cliché until the twentieth century, and its popularity was probably helped by F. Scott Fitzgerald's comment, 'In a real dark night of the soul it is always three o'clock in the morning, day after day' ('Handle with Care', *Esquire,* March 1936). The shorter form, *the dark night of . . .,* is being used increasingly just to mean 'difficult time', rather than a period of mental or spiritual depression.

Despite his canonical status, John Milton (1608–74) has not been a major source of clichés, having provided only two in this list, and both of those are misquotes. **Fresh fields and pastures**

new is the usual misquotation of the line 'Tomorrow to fresh Woods and Pastures new' from his poem 'Lycidas' (1638). It is often shortened to just **fresh fields** or **pastures new** and is occasionally found in its correct form. To **skip the light fantastic** (often just 'the light fantastic') is an adaptation of Milton's lines from 'L'Allegro' (1632): 'Come and trip it as you go, / On the light fantastic toe'. 'Trip' was probably changed to 'skip' to avoid ambiguity, although again the correct form, 'trip', is still sometimes found. The political philosopher Thomas Hobbes (1588–1679), Milton's longer-lived contemporary, wrote in his *Leviathan* (1651) of the state of uncivilized man: 'No arts; no letters; no society; and which is worst of all, continual fear and danger of violent death; and the life of man, solitary, poor, nasty, brutish and short.' Nowadays **nasty, brutish and short** can often be found as a jibe aimed at the personal behaviour and appearance of an individual, but it is still the standard summing up of life without the benefits of modern society – even though we would probably apply it to the civilization in which Hobbes himself lived.

Moving on to the Restoration period, we come to the Poet Laureate John Dryden (1631–1700). He was once considered one of the greats of English literature, and no one who considered himself educated could admit to not having read his works. Today, while the dictionaries of quotations are still full of his lines, he is little read. And to be fair, the smooth heroic couplets he wrote can seem monotonous today, only jarred by the fact that many of his rhymes, thanks to changes in pronunciation in the last three hundred years, no longer actually rhyme. Added to this, much of his best work was political satire and can no longer be appreciated without reading up on the history of the time. Among the quotes you will find in the dictionaries is a couplet from one such satire, *Absolon and Achitophel* (1681), which just about sums up why clichés are so common in our language: 'But far more numerous was the herd of such / Who think too little and who talk too much' (pt 1, l. 533). Despite his former pre-eminence, I have only been able to track down one cliché that comes from his work, although there may be more. He wrote so much, and he is so neglected, that it is quite possible there are more undetected. The cliché is **a blaze of glory**, which appears in Dryden's poem *The Hind and the Panther* (1686), where he writes, 'Thy throne is darkness in the abyss of light,/A blaze of glory that forbids the sight.' 'Blaze of glory' quickly became used to mean the way in which a fire can burn brighter just before going out, and nowadays is usually found in the form 'to go out in a blaze of glory'. The other quotation cliché from this period is from an author, politician and courtier who is attacked in Dryden's *Absolon and Achitophel*. George Villiers, second Duke of Buckingham (1628–87), was a prominent figure in the court of Charles II, and among his many activities was writing. He wrote verses, now even less well known than Dryden's, but he is still remembered as a dramatist. His work affects the cynical wit of dramatists of that time; his comment 'The world is made up for the most part of fools and knaves, both irreconcilable foes to truth' is typical of the period. His best-known play is the burlesque *The Rehearsal* of 1715. In Act III, scene 1 he comments, 'What the devil is the plot food for, but to bring in fine things?' This leads, in the next scene, to the line, 'Ay, now the plot thickens very much upon us.' **The plot thickens** became a cliché of Victorian melodramas, or at least parodies thereof, and is now unlikely to be found used except as a joke or as a conscious cliché.

Villiers serves as a link to our next period, the Augustan Age, for Alexander Pope (1688–1744) describes his deathbed:

> In the worst inn's worst room, with mat half hung,
> The floors of plaster, and the walls of dung,
> On once a flock-bed, but repair'd with straw,
> With tape-tied curtains, never meant to draw;
> The George and Garter dangling from that bed,
> Where tawdry yellow strove with dirty red,

Great Villiers lies: – alas! how chang'd from him,
That life of pleasure, and that soul of whim!
Gallant and gay, in Cliveden's proud alcove,
The bower of wanton Shrewsbury and love;
Or, just as gay, at council, in a ring
Of mimic'd statesmen, and their merry king.
No wit, to flatter, left of all his store!
No fool to laugh at, which he valued more.
There, victor of his health, of fortune, friends,
And fame, this lord of useless thousand ends.

(*Moral Essays, Epistle III*)

Pope, too, is not as much read as he once was, although he is less neglected than Dryden. Nevertheless, he is still much quoted. Many of these quotations are outside our scope, as they are not quite clichés: an example would be 'Do good by stealth, and blush to find it shame' (often just 'do good by stealth'), which comes from his *Imitations of Horace* (1738). Two of his lines have, however, pretty well reached the status of proverbs (and indeed the first is an adaptation of a Latin proverb). Both come from his *Essay on Criticism* of 1711. The first is **to err is human**. The line in full, which is quoted less often, is: 'To err is human; to forgive, divine.' Exactly one hundred lines further on in the work comes **fools rush in where angels fear to tread**. It, too, is often found in a shortened form, 'fools rush in'; while 'where angels fear to tread' is well known as the title of an E. M. Forster novel published in 1905. Pope is also the source of **hope springs eternal**. This comes from *An Essay on Man, Epistle I* (1733), and is rather more ironic in full quotation than in its general use: 'Hope springs eternal in the human breast:/Man never Is, but always To be blest.'

Thomas Gray (1716–71), Pope's younger contemporary, supplies three clichés from a single poem, his 'Elegy Written in a Country Churchyard' of 1751, which is, perhaps, the most quoted poem in the language. One of these clichés is **kindred**

spirit: after he has mused over the dead poor buried in the churchyard, Gray imagines Nature speaking to him of what may happen when he dies, and what may be said, 'If chance, by lonely contemplation led, / Some kindred spirit shall inquire thy fate'. The expression was picked up over half a century later by John Keats, who wrote in 1817 in his 'O Solitude! If I must with thee dwell': 'and it sure must be / Almost the highest bliss of human-kind, / When to thy haunts two kindred spirits flee.' **Mute inglorious Milton** might at first seem a borderline candidate as a cliché, but research shows it is still used surprisingly often. In the poem Gray writes of the apparently ordinary people who are buried in the churchyard, who might in their own ways have been as heroic as those who are famous for withstanding oppression:

> Full many a flower is born to blush unseen . . .

> Some village-Hampden, that with dauntless breast
> The little tyrant of his fields withstood;
> Some mute inglorious Milton here may rest,
> Some Cromwell guiltless of his country's blood.

('Hampden' refers to John Hampden, whose refusal to pay what he felt was an unlawful tax was a key element in the lead-up to the English Civil War.) More familiar is **far from the madding crowd**. Gray wrote of the villagers buried in the churchyard, 'Far from the madding crowd's ignoble strife, / Their sober wishes never learned to stray'. Thomas Hardy used the phrase as the title of his 1874 novel *Far from the Madding Crowd*, which made it even more widely known, and it was given a further boost when the novel was made into a highly successful film in 1967. Since 'madding' is such a rare word, it is sometimes misquoted as 'maddening' – indeed, this is the original meaning of 'madding' – but since 'maddening' subsequently developed the sense 'irritating', 'madding' conserves the sense of 'making insane'. Gray's 'Ode on a Distant Prospect of Eton College' (1742) is the source of **ignorance is bliss**: 'Where ignorance is bliss / 'Tis folly to be wise'. In the poem the blissful ignorance is of the future that lies in store for the schoolboys, of whom he has already said:

> Alas, regardless of their doom, the little victims play!
> No sense they have of ills to come,
> Nor care beyond today.

'Ignorance is bliss' had developed into the expressions **blissfully ignorant** and **blissful ignorance** by the late nineteenth century.

The final three clichés in this group come from abroad. **To encourage the others** comes from Voltaire's satirical novel *Candide* (1759), in which he wrote, 'In [England] it is considered good to kill an admiral from time to time to encourage the others', and this ironic use caught on. It is often used in the original French, '*pour encourager les autres*'. The sentiment that in unity is strength goes back to the ancient world, but the way we usually express this idea, **united we stand, divided we fall**, is adapted from John Dickinson's 'Liberty Song' (1768): 'Then join hand in hand, brave Americans all, / By uniting we stand, by dividing we fall.' Finally, **from the sublime to the ridiculous** has a similar story behind it. The contrast between the sublime and the ridiculous was made in Latin literary criticism, but the expression we use today comes from a saying attributed to Napoleon, who is supposed to have said, after the retreat from Moscow in 1812, 'From the sublime to the ridiculous is but one step.' This was not, however, original to Napoleon. Tom Paine had already written in *The Age of Reason* (1795): 'The sublime and the ridiculous are often so nearly related, that it is difficult to class them separately. One step above the sublime, makes the ridiculous; and one step above the ridiculous, makes the sublime again.' Napoleon might have read Paine, but the saying may well have been proverbial before either used it.

The Romantics and Victorians

Some people might want to argue that the last few quotations belong in this section, for there is no clear dividing line between the two, and the dates overlap. However, there can be no doubt that Samuel Taylor Coleridge (1772–1834) belongs with the Romantics. His 'Rime of the Ancient Mariner' (1789) is the source of the following cliché, contained in the lines:

> He went like one that hath been stunned,
> And is of sense forlorn:
> **A sadder and a wiser man**,
> He rose the morrow morn.

One of his younger contemporaries, the Scottish poet Robert Burns (1759–96), is the source of two more clichés. **Fast and furious**, which has been a popular cliché with journalists since the nineteenth century, comes from his 1793 poem 'Tam O'Shanter': 'As Tammie glow'red, amazed, and curious, / The mirth and fun grew fast and furious.' His 1786 poem 'Man Was Made to Mourn' furnishes us with **man's inhumanity to man**, in the lines 'Man's inhumanity to man / Makes countless thousands mourn.' Another Scottish poet, Thomas Campbell (1777–1844), provides two more clichés. Campbell is another of those poets once popular but now neglected. His 1809 'Battle of the Baltic' was once a standard school text, and his 'Lord Ullin's Daughter' of the same year a mainstay of the public reciter. It is, however, a phrase from the poem with which he made his name, 'The Pleasures of Hope' of 1799, that has entered the language: '' 'Tis **distance lends enchantment** to the view, / And robes the mountain in its azure hue.' When the Queen made her famous *annus horribilis* speech in 1992, she picked up on the full quote when she said, 'Distance is well-known to lend enchantment, even to the less attractive views.' The expression

few and far between also probably owes its elevation to cliché status to the poetry of Campbell, although it has been in the language since the mid seventeenth century. In the same poem he wrote, 'What though my wingèd hours of bliss have been,/ Like angel-visits, few and far between'. We continue the Scottish theme with the poet Lord Byron, for although his father, 'Mad Jack' Byron, was English, his mother (whose surname, Gordon, his father adopted to get his hands on her money) was very Scottish and Byron was brought up in Scotland. His *Childe Harold's Pilgrimage* of 1812–18 gives us **let joy be unconfined**, found in the lines:

> On with the dance! Let joy be unconfined:
> No sleep till morn, when Youth and Pleasure meet
> To chase the glowing Hours with flying feet.
>
> (canto 3, stanza 12)

Since it has a ring of artificial enthusiasm, modern uses are often ironic. The final Scot in this group is the man who, in the nineteenth century, largely created the Scottish tourist industry, giving rise to a craze for the Highlands and all things associated with them, which included Queen Victoria's regrettable decision to decorate Balmoral throughout in mixed tartans, down to the carpets. Sir Walter Scott (1771–1832) made his mark first as a poet on Scottish themes, and then as a novelist. It is to one of the poems, 'The Lay of the Last Minstrel' (1805), that we owe the idea of someone who is not honoured being 'unsung', found in the cliché **unsung hero** – although the sentiment in Scott's poem is very different and the exact wording of the cliché is not recorded for another fifty-five years. Song and heroism have long been associated, for one of the most important of the poet's original tasks was to **sing the praises** of soldiers. Back in Roman times, Virgil, for instance, opens the *Aeneid* with 'of arms and the man I sing'. 'Unsung' has been used in this way since Milton, but the most famous line containing it is Scott's. I quote part of his poem here at length, as the second stanza has been so influential in literature promoting Scotland, and thus qualifies as the original of a whole set of visual and advertising clichés:

> Despite those titles, power, and pelf,
> The Wretch, concentred all in self,
> Living, shall forfeit fair renown,
> And, doubly dying, shall go down
> To the vile dust, from whence he sprung,
> Unwept, unhonoured and unsung.
>
> O Caledonia! stern and wild,
> Meet nurse for a poetic child!
> Land of brown heath and shaggy wood,
> Land of the mountain and the flood,
> Land of my sires! What mortal hand
> Can e'er untie the filial band
> That knits me to thy rugged strand!
>
> (canto 6)

The first recorded use of the term 'unsung hero' is also in verse, and seems to have been heavily influenced by Scott's style. It is found in the marvellously named *Merry's Museum & Parley's Magazine* of January 1860:

> And many an unsung hero
> Now as in days of yore,
> Enacts his part in silence
> Upon some desert shore.

Again, he may not have originated it, but Scott is probably also responsible for popularizing the expression **a far cry**. The expression 'within cry of', meaning 'near enough for a shout to be heard between two points', is found in English from the mid seventeenth century, but 'a far cry', meaning 'a long way', is not found until 1819, when Scott, a great reviver of rustic phrases as well as an inventor of new ones, wrote in his *Legend of Montrose*, 'One of the Campbells replied, "It is a far cry to Lochow", a proverbial expression of the tribe, meaning that their ancient hereditary domains lay beyond the reach of an invading army.' There is further evidence to link early uses of the expression in its literal sense to Scotland, but by the later nineteenth century its figurative use had become a cliché in general English. Scott is also responsible for **pride and joy**, which comes from a line in his poem 'Rokeby' (1813), in which he describes children as 'a mother's pride, a father's joy', and for COLD SHOULDER (see Chapter 19).

Pride forms a link with the next quotation cliché in chronological order, the opening of Jane Austen's 1813 novel *Pride and Prejudice*: 'It is **a truth universally acknowledged**, that a single man in possession of a good fortune, must be in want of a wife.' These words were once judged the most well-known opening of any English novel. As the phrase is so well recognized, the criteria we are using to define a quotation cliché would seem to exclude it from our list. But it has become such a formula for journalists wanting to imbue their work with Austen's mildly cynical wit – appearing in guises such as 'It is a truth universally acknowledged that a single woman in possession of an interesting past must be in want of a chat show' – that it qualifies on other grounds. Our next cliché, **wild surmise**, has, however, become so much a part of the language that very few think of it as a quotation. It comes from John Keats' sonnet 'On First Looking into Chapman's Homer' (1817). In this he writes of the tremendous sense of revelation he felt when he first read the translation of Homer from Greek into English made by the seventeenth-century poet and dramatist George Chapman. He compares the experience of new worlds unfolding to that of Europeans seeing the Pacific for the first time, after the Spanish invaders under Hernán Cortés crossed the Darien Peninsula in Central America:

Stout Cortez . . . and all his men
Look'd at each other with a wild surmise –
Silent, upon a peak in Darien.

The year 1817 also saw the publication of Thomas Moore's collection of poems and prose *Lallah Rookh*. Moore is mainly remembered today for his Irish songs, such as 'The Harp that Once Through Tara's Halls' and 'The Minstrel Boy', but he was popular in his day for many other exotic and wildly romantic works, as well as later being notorious for having agreed to the burning of Byron's memoirs, which Byron had entrusted to him before he died. One of the poems in *Lallah Rookh* was called 'The Fire Worshippers' and seems to have popularized the expression **('twas) ever thus**. The poem contains the lines:

Oh! Ever thus from childhood's hour,
I've seen my fondest hopes decay;
I never loved a tree or flower,
But was the first to fade away.
I never nursed a dear gazelle,
To glad me with its soft black eye,
But when it came to know me well,
And love me, it was sure to die!

These melodramatic, self-pitying lines were widely parodied – often giving the opening in the form ' 'twas ever thus', although **it was ever thus** is now rather more common. The latter, for instance, is the title of a parody by H. S. Leigh (1837–83), which runs:

I never rear'd a young gazelle,
(Because, you see, I never tried);
But had it known and loved me well,
No doubt the creature would have died.

> My rich and aged Uncle John
> Has known me long and loves me well,
> But still persists in living on –
> I would he were a young gazelle.

While Charles Dickens has:

'It has always been the same with me,' said Mr Swiveller, 'always. 'Twas ever thus – from childhood's hour I've seen my fondest hopes decay, I never loved a tree or flower but 'twas the first to fade away; I never nursed a dear Gazelle, to glad me with its soft black eye, but when it came to know me well, and love me, it was sure to marry a market-gardener.'

(The Old Curiosity Shop, ch. 56)

Lewis Carroll (1832–98) wrote a version, a theme with variations, which begins:

> *I never loved a dear Gazelle* –
> Nor anything that cost so much:
> High prices profit those who sell,
> But why should *I* be fond of such?

> *To glad me with his soft black eye*
> My son comes trotting home from school;
> He's had a fight but can't tell why –
> He always was a little fool! . . .

James Payn (1830–98) wrote what is probably the best-known parody:

> I've never had a piece of toast
> Particularly long and wide,
> But fell upon the sanded floor,
> And always on the buttered side.

All these parodies attest to the enormous popularity and recognizability of the text, for you do not publish a parody that no one will recognize.

It was a dark and stormy night is a conscious cliché that is also much parodied. It is best known from children's jokes, such as the one that runs, 'It was a dark and stormy night, and the Bo'sun said, "Captain, tell us a story" and this is the story he told: "It was a dark and stormy night . . ."' and so on, ad infinitum. Its origin lies in *Paul Clifford*, a novel from 1839 by Edward Bulwer Lytton, which opens:

It was a dark and stormy night; the rain fell in torrents – except at occasional intervals, when it was checked by a violent gust of wind which swept up the streets (for it is in London that our scene lies), rattling along the housetops, and fiercely agitating the scanty flame of the lamps that struggled against the darkness.

This has inspired the annual Bulwer-Lytton Fiction Contest (the name is correctly spelled without a hyphen, but often appears with one), in which contestants must write a single opening sentence to an imaginary novel. The winner for 2006, Jim Guili Carmichael, produced:

Detective Bart Lasiter was in his office studying the light from his one small window falling on his super burrito when the door swung open to reveal a woman whose body said you've had your last burrito for a while, whose face said angels did exist, and whose eyes said she could make you dig your own grave and lick the shovel clean.

Bulwer Lytton is also responsible for **the pen is mightier than the sword**, which appears in his historical verse drama *Richelieu* (1839). The idea is by no means original and can be traced back to at least Cicero's Latin *cedant arma togae* ('arms give way to persuasion'), but no one had previously expressed the idea so neatly. Unfortunately, the proverb is rarely quoted with the proviso that Lytton included: 'Beneath the rule of men entirely great / The pen is mightier than the sword.' Bulwer Lytton is another of those literary figures famous in their own time but now almost entirely neglected. He was a best-selling author in the mid nineteenth century, with editions of his works known to sell out on the day of publication, as well as being a radical politician and campaigner for social reform. *Paul Clifford* had as its hero a highwayman, and was a campaigning novel attacking the cruelty of the penal code of the day. In its own way the final sentence, 'The very worst use to which you can put a man is to hang him', is as memorable as the first. Alas, Bulwer Lytton's orotund style grates on the modern ear, and he is now unread. Perhaps his most lasting influence has been on dress codes. Lytton was over six foot tall, wore his hair in auburn ringlets and was a great dandy. His second novel, *Pelham, or, The Adventures of a Gentleman* (1828), a huge best-seller with which he made his name, had a hero who took dandyism to extremes. One of his affectations was to wear black for evening dress, and so successful was the book that people began to imitate Pelham's style, which is why we still wear black evening clothes today.

Scarcely less ignored today is the once-revered Thomas Babington Macaulay (1800–1859), politician, historian and essayist. 'Every schoolboy knows who imprisoned Montezuma, and who strangled Atahualpa' appears in his 1840 essay 'On Lord Clive', a statement that may make us react as Lord Melbourne did, with 'I wish I was as cocksure of anything as Tom Macaulay is of everything.' Macaulay uses **as every schoolboy knows** elsewhere, and the expression has become particularly associated with him, although it was already beginning to be something of a cliché at the time he was writing. In the later twentieth century the statement became mixed up with the language (and spelling) of Nigel Molesworth, Geoffrey Willans's great creation, found in a series of books telling of school life from a horrid boy's point of view (*Down with Skool!*, *How to be Topp* and *Whizz for Atomms*) that appeared in the 1950s with

illustrations by Ronald Searle. It was an immense success in its
day, although not widely known today by those under fifty.
One of Molesworth's favourite expressions is 'as any fule kno',
and this has, with wonderful inappropriateness, become blended
with Macaulay's pronouncements. Another savant of the period,
Thomas Carlyle (1795–1881), once as famous for his book *The
French Revolution: A History* as Macaulay was for his *History of
England*, attributes the expression **the iron hand in a velvet
glove** to Napoleon, although it has also been attributed to earlier
rulers. The iron hand as a symbol of powerful control is found
in English from the early 1700s (**the iron fist** appears in 1740).
As a cliché the expression is highly variable, 'iron fist' being
as common as 'iron hand' and other variants including 'steel
fist', 'MAILED FIST' (see Chapter 11) or 'silk glove'. Like Bulwer
Lyttons' literary style, Carlyle's has not aged well, and he is best
known today for the story that he lent the unique manuscript
of *The French Revolution* to John Stuart Mill, whose housemaid,
thinking it was scrap paper, used it to light a fire. Carlyle, with
commendable control, did not allow this to interfere with his
friendship with Stuart Mill, and diligently set about rewriting
the whole work. He is also known for his tumultuous relationship with his wife, Jane. Jane Carlyle was a sharp-tongued wit
with a brain to match her husband's, and has been described as
the greatest female letter-writer in English. Her letters are now
more read than her husband's work, and she is also remembered
for the charming rondeau written about her by Leigh Hunt:

> Jenny kissed me when we met,
> Jumping from the chair she sat in;
> Time, you thief, who love to get
> Sweets into your list, put that in!
> Say I'm weary, say I'm sad,
> Say that health and wealth have missed me,
> Say I'm growing old, but add,
> Jenny kissed me.

In contrast with the preceding writers, the name of Karl Marx is not forgotten, even if his theories are out of fashion. **The opium of the people** (or **masses**) comes from his comment that 'Religion . . . is the opium of the people' (*A Contribution to the Critique of Hegel's Philosophy of Right*, 1843–4). This was not a particularly original idea. About the same time (1848) the Revd Charles Kingsley was writing in his *Letter to the Chartists, no. 2*, 'We have used the Bible as if it was a constable's handbook – an opium-dose for keeping beasts of burden patient while they are being overloaded', but Marx's version is much snappier and caught on, the word 'masses', so common in Communist writing, often replacing the original 'people'. It is now a formula phrase, with whatever the speaker thinks is being used to keep the populace quiet and content being substituted for 'religion'. In Roman times the poet Juvenal expressed much the same idea in BREAD AND CIRCUSES (see above).

At the same time that Marx was writing, in France the very different Alexandre Dumas was publishing *The Three Musketeers* (1844), the source of the slogan **all for one and one for all**. Ten years later, Alfred, Lord Tennyson published his description of the mess that was being made of the Crimean War in 'The Charge of the Light Brigade'. A few lines – 'Theirs not to make reply, / Theirs not to reason why, / Theirs but to do and die' – both give us the cliché **theirs not to reason why** and play with another. The alternatives DO OR DIE (see Chapter 18) have been recorded since the sixteenth century; but Tennyson's soldiers do not have the alternatives. Nothing they do, however heroic, is going to save the majority from death. Tennyson is also the creator of **it's better to have loved and lost**. This appears in his 1850 poem *In Memoriam*: ' 'Tis better to have loved and lost / Than never to have loved at all.' However, although Tennyson's words give us the form in which we use it, the sentiment was not original to him. In 1700 William Congreve wrote, 'Say what you will, 'tis better to be left, than never to have lov'd' (*Way of* *the World*, II.1), and in 1812 George Crabbe wrote, 'Better to love amiss than nothing to have lov'd' (*Tales in Verse*, 14).

We now move on to Charles Dickens. When he used **great expectations** as the title of his 1861 novel he was not coining a new phrase, but turning it into a cliché. 'Expectations' in the sense of 'what someone is expected to inherit' has been in use since the seventeenth century, and 'great expectations' was already well established by 1777 when Sheridan wrote in *School for Scandal*, 'I have a rich old uncle . . . from whom I have the greatest expectation.' **It was the best of times, it was the worst of times** are the opening words of Dickens's 1859 novel of the French Revolution, *A Tale of Two Cities* (which has plot episodes very close to some in a novel written twenty years earlier by Bulwer Lytton). Often used to describe a love-hate relationship, the phrase can also be used to express the idea of something that was GOOD IN PARTS (see below), but terrible in others. Sydney Carton's words in the book as he goes to the guillotine in place of the husband of the woman he loves, 'It is **a far, far better thing** that I do, than I have ever done; it is a far, far better rest that I go to, than I have ever known', although much quoted and parodied, probably still count as a quotation rather than a cliché.

We come back to John Stuart Mill again with a **conspiracy of silence**. So overused has this expression been, that simply to use it risks making you sound as if you have a persecution complex or at the very least a BEE IN YOUR BONNET (see Chapter 22), however true the accusation may be. It probably entered the language from French, as the earliest known use of it is in Mill's 1865 book on the French philosopher Auguste Comte (1798–1857): 'M. Comte used to reproach his early English admirers with maintaining the "conspiracy of silence" concerning his later performance.' By the late nineteenth century it was so well established that when Sir Lewis Morris asked Oscar Wilde what he should do about the conspiracy of silence among reviewers who were ignoring his publications, Wilde could curtly respond, 'Join it.' Still in the 1860s, we find **sweetness and light** gaining cliché status. This is an expression coined in the eighteenth century by Jonathan Swift, but it was popularized by Matthew Arnold, who used it a number of times, saying for instance, 'Hellenism, and human life in the hands of Hellenism . . . are full of what we call sweetness and light' (*Culture and Anarchy*, 1869). Arnold's use turned it into such a cliché that it is now rarely used without irony.

As we move on to the 1870s, the tone of the clichés and their authors gets lighter. In *Through the Looking-Glass* (1872), Lewis Carroll writes, 'The rule is jam tomorrow and jam yesterday – but never jam today.' This quotation is rarely used in full, but in shortened form, as **jam tomorrow**, means a reward or pleasure that never comes. (The other Alice book, *Alice in Wonderland*, actually belongs in the 1860s, for it was published in 1865, and is the source of **curiouser and curiouser**.) In 1874 the American poet and academic Henry Wadsworth Longfellow's *Tales of a Wayside Inn, part 2* introduced **ships that pass in the night**. He writes of:

> Ships that pass in the night, and speak each other in passing,
> Only a signal shown and a distant voice in the darkness;
> So on the ocean of life we pass and speak one another,
> Only a look and a voice; then darkness again and a silence.

This cliché has to some extent been superseded by **strangers in the night**, the title of a song by Charles Singleton, Eddie Snyder and Bert Kaempfert, which was a hit for Frank Sinatra in 1966, and which seems to owe something to Longfellow's words. Longfellow is another of those poets whose work was once immensely popular but is now little read. Some of his poems, particularly *Hiawatha*, are still known, and at least the stories of some of his most popular poems have entered the folklore of the USA, but although his influence lingers on, his name does not. Few, for example, would be able to name him as the author of the lines 'I shot an arrow in the air, / It fell to earth I know not where.' A few more might link his name to:

> The **shades of night** were falling fast,
> As through an Alpine village passed
> A youth, who bore, 'mid snow and ice,
> A banner with a strange device,
> Excelsior!

If only because they know the parody by A. E. Housman:

> The shades of night were falling fast
> The rain was falling faster
> When through an alpine village passed
> An alpine village pastor.

Longfellow's poem 'Excelsior', published in 1841, is also responsible for the use of Excelsior as a brand name. Although he never published them in his lifetime, Longfellow is also said to have made up, to sing to his second daughter, when a **babe in arms**, what are probably his most famous, though not his best, verses:

> There was a little girl
> Who had a little curl
> Right in the middle of her forehead.
> When she was good
> She was very, very good,
> But when she was bad she was horrid.

These lines were capped by Mae West, with: 'When I am good I am very, very good, but when I am bad I am better' in the 1933 film *I'm no Angel*. Longfellow also introduced **the patter of little** (often now **tiny**) **feet** in the first volume of *Tales of the Wayside Inn* (1862):

> I hear in the chamber above me
> The patter of little feet,
> The sound of a door that is opened,
> And voices soft and sweet.

It became a general term for small children, either actual or expected, but since at least 1920 has rarely been used straight, but instead ironically, or twisted into something like 'the thunder of little feet'. **Into each** (or **every**) **life a little rain must fall** also owes something to Longfellow. This is a modern proverb with a complex history. In 1842 Longfellow published a poem called 'The Rainy Day', which contained the lines:

> Thy fate is the common fate of all,
> Into each life some rain must fall,
> Some days must be dark and dreary.

This was picked up in 1944 by Allan Roberts and Doris Fisher, who used Longfellow's line in a song: 'Into each life some rain must fall, / But too much is falling in mine.' Despite the fact that the song uses the poem's words, it is usually known by the title 'Into Each Life a Little Rain Must Fall', and from this comes the proverb. Despite its modern sound, **movers and shakers** is also a product of a now obscure poem. Although the expression had been used before, its use as a cliché comes from Arthur O'Shaughnessy's 1874 'Ode', which reads:

> We are the music-makers,
> We are the dreamers of dreams,
> Wandering by lone sea-breakers,
> And sitting by desolate streams.
> World-losers and world-forsakers,
> Upon whom the pale moon gleams;
> Yet we are the movers and shakers,
> Of the world forever, it seems.

> With wonderful deathless ditties
> We build up the world's great cities,
> And out of a fabulous story
> We fashion an empire's glory:
> One man with a dream, at pleasure,
> Shall go forth and conquer a crown;
> And three with a new song's measure
> Can trample an empire down.
>
> We, in the ages lying
> In the buried past of the earth,
> Built Nineveh with our sighing,
> And Babel itself with our mirth;
> And o'erthrew them with prophesying
> To the old of the new world's worth;
> For each age is a dream that is dying,
> Or one that is coming to birth.

This poem, in praise of the creative powers of art, is far removed from the modern business world, in which the term 'movers and shakers' is now most commonly used. The poem may also have reinforced use of **dreamer of dreams**, a term that goes back to the Bible.

In the original novel *The Strange Case of Dr Jekyll and Mr Hyde* (1886) by Robert Louis Stevenson, Dr Jekyll was a benign doctor and researcher who discovered a potion that could change him physically and mentally into someone he called Mr Hyde who expressed all the evil impulses Jekyll had suppressed. With time the change became irreversible. It took only a year or two for **Jekyll and Hyde** to be taken up to describe someone with conflicting characteristics. Modern use is becoming detached from the details of the story, and the expression is now being used more and more loosely to describe any kind of conflicting trend. Two years later W. E. Henley, yet again a very popular poet in his day as well as a successful playwright, but who is now looked down on for his facile sentimentality, published his poem 'Invictus' ('Undefeated'). This has contributed two clichés to the language. **Bloody but unbowed** comes from the verse:

> In the fell clutch of circumstance,
> I have not winced or cried aloud:
> Under the bludgeonings of chance
> My head is bloody but unbowed.

While to be **master of your fate** comes from a later stanza:

> It matters not how strait the gate,
> How charged with punishments the scroll,
> I am the master of my fate:
> I am the captain of my soul.

The 1890s was when Rudyard Kipling started publishing, beginning a career that went on until his death in 1936. He gave us, in 'The Ballad of East and West' (1892), 'Oh, East is East, and West is West, and **never the twain shall meet**', while 'The Colonel's lady an' Judy O'Grady are sisters under their skins' (usually found as **sisters under the skin**) is the chorus of the poem 'The Ladies', published in 1896.

That monument to Victorian humour, *Punch* magazine, was, I very much suspect, a major influence on the language, but until someone can find the time to go through *Punch* carefully, this cannot be proved. For our purposes it is simply the source of COLLAPSE OF STOUT PARTY (see Chapter 5) and the **Curate's egg**. The latter comes from the title of a cartoon which appeared in volume 109 of Punch in 1895, showing a formidable bishop and a timid curate over breakfast. The caption read, ' "I'm afraid you've got a bad egg, Mr Jones." "Oh no, my Lord, I assure you! Parts of it are excellent!" ' Hence 'like the Curate's egg – **good in parts**'. The final cliché for this decade is from Thorstein Veblen's statement that 'Conspicuous consumption of valuable goods is a means of reputability in the gentleman of leisure' (*The Theory of the Leisure Class*, 1899). Veblen was an American economist and sociologist who lived from 1857 to 1929. **Conspicuous consumption** has such a modern ring, and seems to be such a modern problem, that it is salutary to find that it was coined well over a hundred years ago.

We end this section with an undatable quotation cliché. There has been much debate as to who actually coined the saying about a **better mousetrap** and the world beating a path to his door. It has long been attributed to Ralph Waldo Emerson (1803–82), but Elbert Hubbard (1859–1915), coiner of 'Life is just one damn thing after another', claimed it for his own. It does not, in fact, appear in Emerson's published writings, but a Mrs Sarah Yule published a book called *Borrowings* in 1889, containing the following words, which she later claimed to have written down from a lecture given by Emerson: 'If a man write a better book, preach a better sermon, or make a better mouse-trap than his neighbour, tho' he build his house in the woods, the world will make a beaten path to his door.' Hubbard was never the most reliable of witnesses, but then the evidence for Emerson is not all that sound either. Readers will have to make up their own minds.

The Twentieth Century

As we ended the last section with a difficult quotation, we shall start this with another complex one. In the popular imagination Sherlock Holmes belongs firmly in the Victorian period, and indeed some of the stories that Sir Arthur Conan Doyle wrote about him were published in the 1890s, although others did not appear until the twentieth century. However, the quote for which Holmes is best known, **elementary, my dear Watson**, does not appear in Doyle's writing, although it was used in some sequels written by his son Adrian with John Dickson, and, most importantly, in the 1930s Basil Rathbone films based on the Sherlock Holmes books. It was from these films that the saying rapidly caught on. (For DOG IN THE NIGHT-TIME, see Chapter 22.)

Speak softly – sometimes found as 'talk softly' – **and carry a big stick** is a saying associated with President Theodore Roosevelt (1858–1919), who used it several times. In a letter of 1900 he wrote, 'I have always been fond of the West African proverb: "Speak softly and carry a big stick; you will go far."' By 1917 Kipling could write, 'The secret of power . . . is not the big stick. It's the liftable stick' (*A Diversity of Creatures*). At first the expression was used mainly of international power (hence the expression **big stick diplomacy**), but nowadays it is used more generally.

From 1912 onwards H. M. Bateman (1887–1970) produced a series of cartoons that showed some poor person shrinking in embarrassment at having committed some minor social gaffe, while pompous types around him swelled with indignation. The caption of these would typically be 'The Man Who . . .', followed by a description such as 'Passed the Port the Wrong Way', although the formula could be varied: for instance, one cartoon entitled *The Spoilsport* has a court scene and the caption 'The Culprit Who Admitted Everything'. Although the expression is found less commonly than in the past, **the man who . . .** has entered the language. Bateman was also responsible for the illustrations to the Second World War Ministry of Health slogan (from 1942) **coughs and sneezes spread diseases**, another expression that has entered the language. The name of the copywriter is not known. Another cartoonist who made his name at the beginning of the twentieth century was Bruce Bairnsfather. His cartoon Tommy from the First World War, Old Bill, was immensely popular. One cartoon showed two soldiers in a shell hole under intensive barrage, with one saying to the other, 'Well, if you know a better 'ole, go to it.' 'If you know a better hole' became for many years a catchphrase, if not

a cliché, but is now comparatively rare. Still surviving from the
First World War is the phrase **foreign field**. These words come
from Rupert Brooke's rousingly patriotic poem 'The Soldier'
(1915):

> If I should die, think only this of me:
> There is some corner of a foreign Field
> That is forever England.

At the end of the First World War Lytton Strachey wrote his
attack on the mores of the previous century, *Eminent Victorians*
(1918). He wrote of Florence Nightingale, 'She was a **legend
in her own lifetime**, and she knew it', which is the first
recorded use of the expression. The jocular variant **legend in
his own lunchtime** was in use by the mid 1970s, usually said
of journalists, media types and other exponents of the three-hour
lunch. A **living legend** is a further form of the cliché. **Legend-
ary** and **the stuff of legend** are equally clichéd.

The year 1925 saw the publication of the downbeat, deeply
serious poem 'The Hollow Men' by T. S. Eliot, with its lines
'This is the way the world ends/**Not with a bang but a
whimper**.' While it is still associated with the end of the world
or other cataclysmic event, this cliché is often used today with
a sexual innuendo, as a formula phrase or with some facile play
on noise – a fate that would make Eliot despair. In complete
contrast, the same year saw the publication of Anita Loos' bright
and witty book GENTLEMEN PREFER BLONDES (see Chapter
15). This tells the story of the not-as-dumb-as-she-seems Lorelei
Lee and her search for a rich husband. The book was turned
into a musical in 1953 by Leo Robin and Jule Styne, who wrote
the song '**Diamonds are a Girl's Best Friend**'. The song in
turn was based on words from Loos's book: 'So I really think
American gentlemen are the best after all, because kissing your
hand may make you feel very very good but a diamond and
safire [*sic*] bracelet lasts forever', words which may also have

inspired the slogan **A Diamond is For Ever**, used to advertise diamonds since 1939.

The 1930s brings another new style to literature in the tough prose of Ernest Hemingway. **The moment of truth** first appears in English in Hemingway's work in praise of the bull-fight, *Death in the Afternoon* (1932), where he writes, 'The whole end of the bullfight was the final sword thrust, the actual encounter between the man and the animal, what the Spanish call the moment of truth.' The non-technical sense of the expression, a turning point or test, was in use by the 1950s, undoubtedly thanks to Hemingway's influential book. Equally macho is the comment made by Leon Trotsky (1879–1940) of the rival Mensheviks in his *History of the Russian Revolution* (1933), vol. 3, ch. 10: 'You are pitiful isolated individuals; you are bankrupts; your role is played out. Go where you belong from now on – into **the dustbin of history**!' A very different writer gave a new twist to **a good time was had by all**. This is a cliché of society reports and works outings, which became a literary cliché after Stevie Smith published a volume of verse using it as a title in 1937. She said she got the expression from parish magazines. The crack that 'she was the original good time who had been had by all' has been attributed to various people, most frequently to Bette Davis. Twenty years later Smith published the poem '**Not Waving but Drowning**', which is passing from quotation to cliché, if it has not already done so. A brilliant evocation of what it feels like to be lost in life, it ends:

> Oh, no no no, it was too cold always
> (Still the dead one lay moaning)
> I was much too far out all my life
> And not waving but drowning.

Although **my lips are sealed** was known before the 1930s, this expression really took off only after the then Prime Minister, Stanley Baldwin, made a speech on the Abyssinia crisis on

10 December 1939, saying, 'I shall be but a short time tonight. I have seldom spoken with greater regret, for my lips are not yet unsealed. Were these troubles over I would make a case, and I guarantee that not a man would go into the lobby against us.' After this speech the cartoonist David Low took to drawing Baldwin with a piece of sticking plaster over his mouth, and 'my lips are sealed' became something of a catchphrase.

While one might expect the 1940s to have produced many war-related clichés, it is actually literature that dominates. 'Down these **mean streets** a man must go who is not himself mean,' wrote Raymond Chandler in his essay 'The Simple Art of Murder' (1944). Chandler himself is probably echoing 'I am . . . a citizen of no mean city' (St Paul, in Acts 21:39), once a popular quotation. St Paul's 'mean' means 'insignificant' and Chandler was probably deliberately ambiguous in his use of the word. George Orwell was also playing with language when he wrote his 1945 political satire *Animal Farm*. In this novel the pigs justify their power and privilege in a society where everything is supposed to be shared, with the slogan: 'All animals are equal but some are **more equal than others**.' This cynical manipulation of the truth has become a popular description of privilege, particularly when power has been used to obtain unfair perks. Orwell's words are themselves an echo of the American Declaration of Independence: 'We hold these truths to be self-evident, that all men are created equal . . .' In the same vein, politicians of all types like to use **equal but different** to justify inequalities. In the bleak future society described by George Orwell in the 1948 novel *1984*, England is run by a sinister dictator known as Big Brother whose image is everywhere, often accompanied by the slogan '**Big Brother is watching you**'. From this, 'Big Brother' has come to mean an overly restrictive or intrusive aspect of the POWERS THAT BE (see Chapter 16). Orwell chose to call his tyrant Big Brother because one of the themes of his book is the power of propaganda to twist things, and, at the time he was writing, 'big brother' was used as an image of care and protection. However, such was the power of his book that the term soon came to be used in his sinister way, and had become a cliché by the 1960s.

Nice guys finish last is the result of a misunderstanding. In 1946 the American baseball player and manager Leo 'The Lip' Durocher was watching his players practise. His listed his players' names, and then commented, 'Take a look at them. All nice guys. They'll finish last. Nice guys. Finish last.' This comment was really one of resigned despair, but by the 1970s 'Nice guys finish last' meant something rather different, having become the excuse for who knows what mayhem on the sports field. This expression probably also lies behind such formula phrases as 'X, soccer's Mr Nice Guy' and **No more Mr Nice Guy**. The latter came to prominence in the early 1970s, when it was announced that Senator Ed Muskie had decided that it was going to be 'No More Mr Nice Guy' in his 1972 campaign to stand for the presidency. Then, in 1973, Alice Cooper had a hit record with a song of the same name. However, the expression was around before this, for an old joke about Hitler agreeing to come back from the dead – 'But this time – no more Mr Nice Guy' – has been dated to the mid 1950s.

The American politician and twice-failed presidential candidate Adlai Stevenson (1900–1965) was one of the few of his kind to have the flair to use wit in his campaigns in the dour 1950s. To him has been attributed the expression **dragged kicking and screaming into the twentieth century**. I have been unable to track this down, but Nigel Rees quotes Kenneth Tynan, who wrote in 1959, 'A change, slight but unmistakable, has taken place; the English theatre has been dragged, as Adlai Stevenson once said of the Republican Party, kicking and screaming into the twentieth century.' With the new millennium the expression has had to be updated. The expression **no pain, no gain** – brought to wider public attention by Stevenson in a noted speech he made in 1952 when he accepted nomination at the Democratic National Convention: 'Let's talk sense to the

American people. Let's tell them the truth, that there are no gains without pains' – is said to date back to at least the sixteenth century. In the 1980s 'no pain, no gain' was a slogan associated with Jane Fonda's immensely popular fitness videos. John Major tried out a substitute when he said of his economic policy in 1989, **If it isn't hurting, it isn't working**. The only other person who created a cliché that belongs in this list was another American, the flamboyant pianist Liberace (1919–87). He was enormously successful with audiences, but viciously attacked by critics. His frequent response to this, from about 1954 onwards, was to say that he had **cried all the way to the bank**, and there was no doubt that, despite the critics, he became very rich. In the UK the more obvious **laughed all the way to the bank** is now far more common than the original. Search UK websites using Google, and one gets fewer than 500 pages for 'cried' and well over 17,500 for 'laughed'. Although the expression is very much associated with Liberace, it should be noted that Walter Winchell had used the expression in a newspaper column first, and it may have been doing the rounds at the time.

Although the scholar Marshall McLuhan (1911–80) is often thought of as an American, he was, in fact, Canadian. He first used the term **global village** in 1960: 'Postliterate man's electronic media contract the world to a village or tribe where everything happens to everyone at the same time: everyone knows about, and therefore participates in, everything that is happening the minute it happens. Television gives this quality of simultaneity to events in the global village' (Carpenter and McLuhan, *Explorations in Communication*); although it is better known from his 1962 book *The Gutenberg Galaxy* in the form: 'The new electronic interdependence recreates the world in the image of a global village.' This handy term, coined with great prescience long before the arrival of satellite television and mobile phones, let alone the Internet, would not qualify as a cliché were it not used both too often and too loosely, frequently as nothing more than an alternative for **it's a small world** (an expression in use since the late nineteenth century). McLuhan is also known for **the medium is the message**, used in his 1964 book, *Understanding Media*.

More means worse is the popular adaptation of a comment made by Kingsley Amis, also in 1960, in *Encounter* magazine. He vehemently opposed the expansion of universities that was then taking place, even though it was small compared to what has happened since:

The delusion that there are thousands of young people about who are capable of benefiting from university training, but have somehow failed to find their way there, is a necessary component of the expansionist case. I wish I could have a little tape-and-loudspeaker arrangement sewn into the binding of this magazine, to be triggered off by the light reflected from the reader's eyes on to this part of the page, and set to bawl out at several bels: More will mean worse.

The expression was quickly seized upon as a pithy way of expressing the balance between quality and quantity, but Amis objected to the popular version of his saying, and when in 1983 *The Times* misquoted him, using 'more means less', he sent them a furious letter that included the comment, 'Laziness and incuriosity about sources are familiar symptoms of academic decline.' Amis himself was probably using the expression allusively, for one year earlier the architect Mies van der Rohe had written in the *New York Herald Tribune*, 'Less means more.' Between them these two statements have spawned a whole family of variants.

One unchangeable cliché is **Catch-22**. 'There was only one catch and that was Catch-22, which specified that a concern for one's own safety in the face of dangers that were real and immediate was the process of a rational mind.' This definition comes from the 1961 novel by Joseph Heller, *Catch-22*, which created the expression. In the novel, Yossarian, flying combat missions in the chaos of the Second World War, tries to feign madness to avoid getting himself shot down and killed; he finds that he can only be reassigned to other duties if he applies for a medical certificate, but that the very act of applying for such a certificate is taken as evidence that he is in his right mind, for no sane person would want to fly combat missions. It did not take long for this handy term for a NO-WIN SITUATION (see Chapter 17) to catch on as a useful term for something we meet so often in modern life.

Let's see how it plays in Peoria, and its variants, is a cliché from an undefined date in the 1970s. The *Independent*'s obituary of one of President Nixon's more notorious aides, John Ehrlichman (1925–99), stated that he coined it. Others simply say that **It will play in Peoria** was a catchphrase associated with the Nixon administration, and that it comes from an old music-hall joke current in the 1930s. Ehrlichman was caught by the notorious Watergate tapes saying of Patrick Gray, director of the FBI, whom Nixon had decided to throw to the wolves without warning, 'I think we ought to let him hang there. Let him twist slowly, slowly, in the wind', which has also been much quoted. Another saying that became a cliché in the 1970s, but which is not directly attributable, is **when the going gets tough, the tough get going**. Some maintain this was a favourite saying of Joseph P. Kennedy (1888–1969), father of President J. F. Kennedy, but it has also been attributed to Knute Rockne (1888–1931), the American footballer and coach, although the *Yale Book of Quotations* has found it used by the football coach Frank Leahy in 1954. Rockne is also associated with the expression 'win one for the Gipper', a catchphrase of President Reagan's. Reagan, in his acting career, had played a character called George 'The Gipper' Gipp, a real-life football star who had died young, in a film with the magnificent title of *Knute Rockne, All American Hero* (1940). Gipp's dying words, delivered to Rockne, were 'Win just one for the Gipper.'

It (or **the opera**) **ain't over till the fat lady sings** is usually said to have been created by the American sports commentator

Dan Cook in 1979, while commenting on a basketball game, to mean that the result could change at any time right up to the end of the game, an elaboration on **it ain't over till it's over** (quoted in different forms, and said by the American baseball player Yogi Berra, when commenting on the National League pennant race in 1973). However, the *Yale Book of Quotations*, published as the last few pages of this book were being written, has come up with an earlier instance of the 'fat lady' saying, this time by the sports commentator Ralph Carpenter, in 1976. It became popular in sporting circles, and gained wider currency in 1982 when it was used in an advertising campaign by the Baltimore Orioles baseball team, which showed a large, aggressive looking Valkyrie, over the caption 'She ain't sung yet'. Although individuals may be credited with the expression, similar sayings were already current, including 'Church ain't out till the fat lady sings', and there is anecdotal evidence of similar uses going back to at least the 1950s, which would explain why it caught on so quickly.

The key quote of the 1980s must be **There is no alternative**. It was used by Margaret Thatcher on several occasions in the 1980s about her economic policies. As a result, when used in a way that marks it as a quotation, it has come to be used, both seriously and jokingly, to show firm conviction that is not open to argument.

Finally, only one cliché from the 1990s fits neatly into this list, the format phrase '**I wouldn't get out of bed for . . .**', derived from the comment by the Canadian-born supermodel Linda Evangelista in 1990, 'I don't get out of bed for less than $10,000 a day.'

Shakespeare

I have left the dominant figure of Shakespeare to the end so that
he did not overshadow the other writers who have added so
much to the language. Not all the quotations from Shakespeare
in this book are listed here, as a few fit more comfortably
elsewhere. Many of these expressions are not peculiar to him,
but are simply part of the language of his day; however, Shakespeare is probably instrumental in keeping them alive. An
example of this is **thereby hangs a tale**. This not very impressive pun on tail/tale, used to indicate that more information
could be forthcoming, was revived in the nineteenth century.
Shakespeare used it in four of his plays, and, judging from the
characters he gives it to, it was already a cliché in his day. Indeed,
it was also used by contemporaries of his.

Taking the plays in alphabetical order, the first cliché we
come to is **all's well that ends well**. Versions of this proverb
have been around since the fourteenth century, but it is nowadays identified as the title of the Shakespeare play rather than
as a proverb. *All's Well that Ends Well* (1603–4), often classed as
a tragi-comedy, is a story of bad behaviour and deceit which is
finally resolved in harmony, the title implying that whatever
may have gone before, the future will be calmer for those
involved.

From *Antony and Cleopatra* (1606–7) we get two clichés. The
first is **salad days**, meaning a time of innocence or ignorance.
In Act I, scene 5 Cleopatra talks of her 'salad days, / When I was
green in judgement', 'green' here meaning 'ignorant' (as in the
modern 'greenhorn'), a very common use in Shakespeare's day.
Twentieth-century cliché status was reinforced by the success
of the 1956 musical by Julian Slade, showing the *Salad Days* of
newly qualified students just launching themselves into the adult
world. It is a monotonously frequent caption for magazine
articles dealing with salads. **It beggars description** appears in

Act II, scene 2, in Enobarbus' wonderful speech describing Mark Antony's first view of Cleopatra:

> The barge she sat in, like a burnished throne,
> Burned on the water; the poop was beaten gold,
> Purple the sails, and so perfumed, that
> The winds were love-sick with them; the oars were silver,
> Which to the tune of flutes kept stroke, and made
> The water which they beat to follow faster,
> As amorous of their strokes. For her own person,
> It beggared all description; she did lie
> In her pavilion – cloth-of-gold of tissue –
> O'er-picturing that Venus where we see
> The fancy outwork nature.

'Beggars description' had passed into general use by the end of the eighteenth century, and was also found in other set phrases such as 'beggars compare', but it is now quite unusual to find 'beggar' used as a verb outside 'beggars description' and the emphatic **beggars belief**.

Hamlet (1601) is famous for the number of quotations that it contains, so many that it is difficult to separate the play itself from the bits we all know. **To be or not to be** is the best known of these quotations, and our first from the play, being the opening of Hamlet's great soliloquy in Act I, scene 2. **Slings and arrows** also comes from this speech, as Hamlet wonders:

> Whether 'tis nobler in the mind to suffer
> The slings and arrows of outrageous fortune,
> Or to take arms against a sea of troubles,
> And by opposing end them.

Later on in that scene Hamlet's friend Horatio describes the appearance of the ghost of Hamlet's father. Hamlet asks him about the ghost's expression, and Horatio describes it as **more**

in sorrow than in anger. Shortly before this, he had explained
that the ghost was silent throughout its appearance; Horatio had
challenged him, **But answer made he none**. In the next scene
Laertes warns his sister against paying too much attention to
Hamlet's attentions to her. She is not impressed by his presump-
tion and comments:

> Do not, as some ungracious pastors do,
> Show me the steep and thorny way to heaven,
> Whiles, like a puffed and reckless libertine,
> Himself the **primrose path** of dalliance treads,
> And recks not his own rede.

Shakespeare repeats the idea in *Macbeth* with 'the primrose way
to the everlasting bonfire' (II.3). In *Hamlet* the following scene
returns to Hamlet and Horatio. Their conversation is disturbed
by the noise of guns and trumpets used to mark the court's
drinking session. Hamlet finds this objectionable and provides
two clichés in short succession when he comments:

> But to my mind – though I am native here,
> And **to the manner born** – it is a custom
> **More honour'd in the breach than the observance**.

Thus the original sense of 'to the manner born' is that he grew
up with the custom. However, since it has been used so often
of people at ease with wealth or position, it has come to be
written sometimes in the form 'manor' as if of someone born
into a privileged background, a form which has no doubt
become more common after the success of the television series
To the Manor Born (1979–81, with multiple repeats since). 'More
honoured in the breach than the observance' is also often misused, some people failing to realize that Hamlet is saying it is
better to drop the custom than follow it. In scene 5 Hamlet is
again talking to Horatio when his father's ghost appears. Hamlet

runs after him, and the ghost breaks his silence to tell of his murder. He describes how his own brother poured poison into his ear while he was asleep, and describes it as '**Murder most foul**, as in the best it is;/But this most foul, strange and unnatural.' 'Murder most . . .' has become a formula phrase for headline writers. Returning to Horatio, Hamlet tells him, 'There are **more things in heaven and earth**, Horatio,/Than are dreamt of in your philosophy'. We then skip forward to Act II, scene 2 when Hamlet is winding up Polonius with his comments which seem to be mad, but which at the same time are both pointed and shrewd. Polonius comments, 'Though this be madness, yet there is method in it', usually summed up as **method in his madness**. The **witching hour** is not, as the unsuspecting might suspect, from *Macbeth* (1606), but from Act III, scene 2 of *Hamlet*, being an adaptation of: 'Now is the very witching time of night,/When churchyards yawn', an allusion to the belief that witches and ghosts were thought most likely to be active and powerful at midnight. It was an established cliché in the form 'witching hour' by the middle of the nineteenth century. In the 1980s the expression took on a special sense in stock-market jargon as a time when accounts had to be settled. When you say that someone **protests too much**, you are quoting from the same scene: 'The lady doth protest too much, methinks', comments Hamlet's mother, Gertrude, about the Player Queen's protestation of fidelity in Hamlet's 'Mousetrap' play, never realizing that she is meant to see herself in the Player Queen. The whole line is rarely quoted in full now, but is frequently alluded to. In Act III, scene 4 Hamlet upbraids his mother for her incest in marrying her deceased husband's brother (banned by the Church; see further at FLESH AND BLOOD, Chapter 15) and makes her realize the difference in quality between his father and his murderous brother. He leaves Gertrude with the words, 'I must be cruel only to be kind', containing an equivocal pun on the many meanings of 'kind' then current, which included our modern meaning; 'relating to proper behaviour'; 'natural'; and 'relating to family, kin'. However, in modern use **cruel to be kind** simply means to act in a way that seems harsh, but is for that person's ultimate good, and it is used as an alternative to the more recent TOUGH LOVE (see Chapter 3). **Hoist with your own petard** is a similarly slight adaptation of 'For 'tis the sport to have the engineer / Hoist with his own petar' (III.4), said by Hamlet as he prepares to turn the tables on Rosencrantz and Guildenstern. An engineer in this context is the equivalent of a sapper in the modern Army, and a petard – which gets its name from the French word for to fart – is a primitive type of bomb or grenade, used to blow open city gates. Explosives were, in those days, even more unreliable than today, and fuses likely to ignite a device as soon as touched, so it would be no rare thing to have an engineer blown up ('hoist') by his own petard as he tried to use it. Finally, **the rest is history**, found from the nineteenth century, but with no known origin, may perhaps be modelled on Hamlet's dying words, 'The rest is silence.'

Three plays on three kings named Henry give us three clichés. **Once more into the breach** is an adaptation of the speech made by Shakespeare's Henry V at the siege of Harfleur, where he encourages his faltering troops back into the attack on the city walls with 'Once more unto the breach, dear friends, once more; / Or close the wall up with our English dead' (*Henry V* (1599), III.1). It is used today as a wry or resigned comment when getting back to the task in hand. One of Shakespeare's earliest plays, *Henry VI, Part III* (1592), contains the lines:

> Why, love forswore me in my mother's womb;
> And, for I should not deal in her soft laws,
> She did corrupt frail nature with some bribe,
> To shrink mine arm up like a wither'd shrub;
> To make an envious mountain on my back,
> Where sits deformity to mock my body;
> To shape my legs of an unequal size;

To disproportion me in every part,
Like to a chaos, or an unlick'd bear-whelp
That carries no impression like the dam.

(III.2)

With these words, Gloucester (later Richard III) describes his deformities, referring to a legend, inherited from the ancient world, that bear cubs are born a shapeless mass, and have to be licked into shape by their mothers. This is the origin of to **lick into shape**, first found in the late seventeenth century, although the idea had been expressed in similar words since the early fifteenth century. Although Shakespeare does not use the exact words of the expression, it is probable that they kept the idea before the public and helped with the term's survival. Similarly, to **dance attendance**, used to mean 'to pay obsequious attention to someone', 'to be ready to carry out their least whim', has been in use since the middle of the sixteenth century, was well-used in the later sixteenth and seventeenth centuries, and has always carried a suggestion of sarcasm or contempt, an image of the overeager courtier. Since we have little or no use for 'attendance' to mean 'paying attention' nowadays outside this expression, we probably owe its survival as a set phrase in English to Shakespeare, who used 'To dance attendance on their lordship's pleasures' in Act V, scene 2 of *Henry VIII* (1613).

Julius Caesar (1599) gives us **all Greek to me**. In Act I, scene 2 Cicero (for whom see the beginning of this chapter), off-stage, makes a speech in Greek, and Casca, who is giving an account of events, claims not to have understood what he said because 'for mine own part, it was Greek to me.' From this, 'all Greek to me' has become a way of saying something is incomprehensible, usually with the implication that it is above your head. In Act III, scene 2 Mark Antony shows the Roman crowd the cloak Caesar was wearing when assassinated, and points to where Brutus struck, saying how much Caesar loved him, and adding, 'This was the most **unkindest cut** of all.' 'Unkindest' here originally meant 'unnatural', but is now always used in the sense 'most unkind'. Even in the middle of the nineteenth century the expression was being used jokingly, and nowadays is most often found with reference to neutering animals.

We get yet another misquote in **gild the lily**. The original form of this expression was 'to gild refined gold, to paint the lily', which comes from Act IV, scene 2 of *King John* (1591–8). It is included in a list of things that it would be superfluous to do, which includes 'To smooth the ice, or to add another hue / Unto the rainbow', all of which 'Is wasteful and ridiculous excess'. The spoiling of the point by compressing the quote to 'gild the lily' seems to be comparatively recent. Byron in *Don Juan* (1819–24) wrote, 'But Shakespeare also says, 'tis very silly "To gild refined gold, or paint the lily," ' (canto 3, stanza 76), and 'paint the lily' can still be found in the early years of the twentieth century. However, nowadays the correct quotation is only used by pedants.

More sinned against than sinning is from Act III, scene 2 of *King Lear* (1605–6), when the outcast king says, 'I am a man / More sinned against than sinning.' The expression still tends to be used in self–justification.

Macbeth (1606) is a fertile source of clichés. When, in Act I, scene 3, Lady Macbeth is trying to nerve her husband to murder his way to the throne, she expresses her fears that he is not ruthless enough: 'Yet do I fear thy nature; / It is too full o' the **milk of human kindness**.' The image behind this is probably a combination of the idea of the baby at the mother's breast (Lady Macbeth later says, 'Come to my woman's breasts, / And take my milk for gall, ye murthering ministers' (I.5) and 'I have given suck, and know / How tender 'tis to love the babe that milks me: / I would, while it was smiling in my face, / Have pluck'd my nipple from his boneless gums, / And dash'd the brains out, had I so sworn as you / Have done to this' (I.7)); and derived from this, the idea of milk being childish and weak, found in words such as *milksop*. Interestingly, despite all these references to motherhood, no mention is ever made in the play

to any children that she has had, which has led to much speculation about what has happened to them. The **be all and end
all** of something is a cliché that is not often recognized nowadays
as a quotation. Shakespeare uses it in *Macbeth* (I.7) in a rather
different way from its current sense. Macbeth is trying to steel
himself to murder Duncan, and worries that the act will not be
without knock-on effects. In a famous soliloquy he says:

> If it were done when 'tis done, then 'twere well
> It were done quickly. If th'assassination
> Could trammel up the consequence, and catch,
> With his surcease, success; that but this blow
> Might be the be-all and the end-all here,
> But here, upon this bank and shoal of time,
> We'd jump the life to come.

Shortly afterwards he compares Duncan's saintliness with his
motives for murder:

> I have no spur
> To prick the sides of my intent, but only
> **Vaulting ambition**, which o'erleaps itself,
> And falls on the other.

Macbeth is, of course, famous for its witches, and Act IV, scene 1,
the scene when the witches are gathered round their cauldron,
chanting, gives us **eye of newt**, the mixture they are using
containing:

> Eye of newt, and toe of frog,
> Wool of bat, and tongue of dog,
> Adder's fork, and blind-worm's sting,
> Lizard's leg, and owlet's wing,
> For a charm of powerful trouble,
> Like a hell-broth boil and bubble.

While this is a borderline cliché, it has become a standard short-hand for indicating the contents of a witch's brew, either directly or as a formula phrase. Thus in a cartoon of witches you are likely to get eye of newt in the recipe, or a quote from earlier in the scene, 'Double, double, toil and trouble' (often misquoted as 'Bubble, bubble . . .'), or else you find parodies of the whole scene, as in Terry Pratchett's vegetarian recipe in *Wyrd Sisters* (1988):

> Wholegrain wheat and lentils too,
> In the cauldron seethe and stew.

Cheer to the echo has moved some way from 'I would applaud thee to the very echo / That should applaud again' (V.3). This obscure quotation is explained by the *OED* as 'so vociferously as to produce echoes'. It has been a cliché from at least the nineteenth century, surviving in its original form into the works of Dickens. **Sound and fury** is from Act V scene 5. After he hears of the death of his wife, a despairing Macbeth says:

> Life's but a walking shadow, a poor player
> That struts and frets his hour upon the stage
> And then is heard no more. It is a tale
> Told by an idiot, full of sound and fury,
> Signifying nothing.

More despair is to come two scenes later. Macbeth, deluded as in so many things by the witches, believes himself invulnerable in battle, for, as he tells Macduff, 'I bear a **charmed life**, which must not yield / to one of woman born.' However, Macduff answers him, 'Despair thy charm . . . Macduff was from his mother's womb / Untimely ripp'd', thereby winning a psychological victory which is soon followed by a physical one. By the nineteenth century 'charmed life' had become a cliché to describe anyone who had DICED WITH DEATH (see Chapter 4) and survived, and in the twentieth century expanded even to cover the inanimate.

Gone to a better place is a cliché for death, in contrast with going to that worst of places, 'the other place', hell. The expression is first recorded in this sense in Act IV, scene 2 of Shakespeare's *Measure for Measure* (1604), but there the speech puns on the sense of 'promotion' that 'better place' could have in his day. By the eighteenth century it was being used in sentimental poetry for heaven, and 'gone to a better place' has remained a stalwart of sentimental grief ever since.

'A **Daniel come to judgement**! Yea, a Daniel!/O wise young judge, how I do honour thee!' are the words spoken by Shylock the moneylender in praise of Portia's legal wisdom in agreeing with his case, in Act IV, scene 1 of *The Merchant of Venice* (1596–8). He is referring to the biblical prophet Daniel's status as a judge in the Bible, an Old Testament reference that Shakespeare uses to emphasize Shylock's Jewishness (see further on Daniel in Chapter 16, Bible and Religion). The expression is used, usually in rather literary contexts, to hail an opinion that one agrees with. However, there is often an ironic twist to its use, for while Portia agrees with Shylock's plea that he is entitled to his **pound of flesh** if the loan he made to Antonio has not been redeemed, Shylock soon finds that he ceases to admire Portia's judgement when she tells him he can only have it if he takes no blood with it. 'Pound of flesh' has been used to signify an unjust or excessive payment, or something exacted in revenge, since at least the nineteenth century. **Life blood** is also in *The Merchant of Venice*, although not in this scene, as one might suppose. Instead, it is used in Act III, scene 2 to foreshadow Antonio's possible fate, when Bassanio, for whom Antonio has taken out the loan that puts his life in danger, gets a letter telling him that Antonio is financially ruined and so will not be able to repay the money to Shylock: 'Every word in it a gaping wound/Issuing life blood' is his response.

Foregone conclusion is a common cliché, which comes

from *Othello* (1602–4): Othello responds to the comment 'This was but his dream' with the deeply obscure 'But this denoted a foregone conclusion' (III.3). The extraordinary thing about it is that no one is really sure what Shakespeare meant by it. As the *OED* says, it is 'a Shakespearian phrase, variously interpreted by commentators . . . Now used for: A decision or opinion already formed before the case is argued or the full evidence known (hence *foregone intention, opinion*, etc.); also, a result or upshot that might have been foreseen as inevitable.' There is no such problem with **not wisely but too well**. This is a quotation from Act V, scene 2, where Othello describes himself as 'One that loved not wisely, but too well' as an excuse for murdering his wife. It has been a cliché since the early nineteenth century, and is often used today to describe overindulgence in food and/ or drink. We do, however, find another slightly unusual use of language in Act IV, scene 2, in the expression **seamy side**. While the outside of a garment may be smooth and neat, a look inside the lining will reveal the rough edges of the seams and the hidden signs of how the outer appearance is achieved. This is the image that lies behind the term, first recorded in Shakespeare's 'He turned your wit the seamy side without.' It seems to have made the transition to the modern sense in the nineteenth century.

The best-known source of to **kill with kindness** is from Shakespeare's *Taming of the Shrew* (1592) when Petruchio says in Act IV, scene 1, 'This is the way to kill a wife with kindness.' However, Shakespeare was using an already well-established saying, in its full form 'to kill with kindness as fond apes do their young', a reference to the belief that apes could literally hug their young to death. Although this sounds like a companion proverb to the biblical **spare the rod and spoil the child**, it is, in fact, usually used in kinder, domestic situations, and of adults, rather than of the more abstract principles of upbringing.

If I had to come up with just one cliché that I hate most of all, it would be **sea change**. It comes from Act I, scene 2

of *The Tempest* (1611), where Ariel sings to the shipwrecked
Ferdinand:

> Full fathom five thy father lies;
>> Of his bones are coral made:
> Those are pearls that were his eyes:
>> Nothing of him that doth fade,
> But doth suffer a sea-change
> Into something rich and strange.

'Sea change' began to be used in the nineteenth century for a
profound change, and it is today a very popular journalistic
cliché, often used where a mere 'change' is perfectly adequate.
I think I find it so particularly objectionable in part because it is
used for redundant and unnecessary emphasis; but most of all it
is for the unthinking way in which it abuses the original. There
is never any sense of the wondrous change 'Into something rich
and strange', and people who use it also miss the point that in
the play the whole scene involves a deception. Not only has no
'sea change' taken place, but Ferdinand's father is not dead at
all, but safe and well on another part of the island and on course
for redemption. **Strange bedfellows** I have no such problems
with. It is derived from the comment in Act II, scene 1 that
'Misery acquaints a man with strange bedfellows.' Since sharing
a bed with other people was normal, even in inns, at the time,
there is no sexual element in the saying. We find another
common misquote in **the stuff that dreams are made of**.
What Prospero actually says in Act IV, scene 1 is 'We are such
stuff as dreams are made on', but popular use has changed it to
the more conventional grammar. **Brave new world** is a double
quotation: in *The Tempest* (V.1) Shakespeare has the naive
Miranda, brought up on an island with only her father for human
company, respond to seeing a group of shipwrecked men, who
mostly turn out to be corrupt, with the words, 'O brave new
world, / That has such people in it' ('brave' here meaning 'fine,

handsome'). When Aldous Huxley wrote his novel of a future world where babies were reared in bottles, and sex was encouraged, but love and affection, and especially individuality, were taboo, he called it *Brave New World* (1932), and it is from this that we take the phrase for a nightmare society. The irony of both Shakespeare's and Huxley's use is now often missing.

Our last Shakespearean cliché is **some are born great** ... In Shakespeare's *Twelfth Night* (1601), when the roistering Sir Toby Belch, Sir Andrew Aguecheek and the maid Maria want to get their own back on the puritan Malvolio, who has tried to put a stop to their enjoyment of the good things of life, they decide to trick him into thinking his employer, Olivia, is in love with him. As a part of this they leave a letter for him to find, in which she appears to tell him, 'Be not afraid of greatness: some men are born great, some achieve greatness, and some have greatness thrust upon them.' (II.5). This quotation has now become a formula phrase. It is still used ironically, as in this quote from the *Evening Standard* on 28 August 1998: 'On her tombstone should be written this: Some are born great. Some achieve greatness. And some hire great PR companies.'

8. The Working World

This chapter will look at clichés that arise from the world of work. These fall into four groups. There are the general clichés that cover work in general; there are those that belong to particular jobs and trades; and then there are two special sections, one on school, which is the work of children and teachers, and one on journalism, which has what almost amounts at times to its own language. The worlds of business and money, and of advertising, have been dealt with separately (see Chapters 9 and 10), and other aspects of work appear in subsequent chapters.

Work in general

There are many general clichés belonging to the world of work, where you **earn** or **win your daily bread** (or **crust**). This expression for earning your living or food is from the Lord's Prayer: 'Give us this day our daily bread.' It was already in general use by the seventeenth century, but really took off as a cliché in the nineteenth century, with 'crust' not appearing until the early twentieth. The more pompous may call work **gainful employment**, an expression used in legal documents to avoid arguments about what a job is – gainful employment meaning that it must be something you are paid to do and recognized as such. For those who enjoy their work it may be **just the job**, an expression that became forces slang for 'just what is needed' in the 1930s, and spread to the general population by the 1950s. For those struggling with their work, being helpful may be **more than my job's worth**, which was well enough established by 1925 to be used in advertising copy, and which had developed into that marvellous term, a 'jobsworth', for someone who acts in this way, by the 1970s. In a similar way, **just doing my job** is used to justify your actions, or stonewall objections to a lack of co-operation.

Jobs for the boys, meaning giving appointments to your friends or contacts – 'cronyism' is the current vogue word for it – is at best cynical and at worst corrupt. The phrase was well established by the middle of the twentieth century. The first instance in this sense in *The Times* archive is from a parliamentary report from 1946: one speaker comments that 'many changes had occurred in the House since the General Election, but perhaps the strangest was the Socialists [i.e. the Labour Party] should be defending privilege and members of the Opposition seeking to restrict it', which is greeted with a cry of 'Jobs for the boys.' It has a strangely modern ring. **Nice work if you can get it** is also usually used cynically. It was popularized by a 1937 George and Ira Gershwin song. Ira Gershwin later said that he had got the expression from a *Punch* cartoon by George Blecher, but this has yet to be traced. For some it may be **all in a day's work** to do **dirty work**. While 'all in a day's work' is regularly used as a cheerful response to having been thanked, this twentieth-century cliché is also used to indicate resigned acceptance of circumstances. Two expressions have fallen together to produce 'dirty work'. Firstly, there is the simple idea of work that involves getting dirty being unpleasant, so that 'dirty work' comes to mean anything that is unpleasant to do, as in the catchphrase 'It's dirty work but somebody has to do it.' Secondly, there is a shortening of the nineteenth-century expression 'dirty work at the crossroads', meaning foul play. The source of this expression is rather obscure, but probably comes from the idea of a crossroads being an ideal place for highwaymen and robbers to hang out, as well as a place where suicides were traditionally buried. Its history is further complicated by the fact that around the First World War 'dirty work at the crossroads' was also used as an expression for sexual activity. The full form of the expression is rarely heard in any sense today.

To succeed in a job you may feel (if you are rather old-fashioned) that you have to **take pains**, an expression that dates from the sixteenth century and is a development of the medieval 'to pain yourself', meaning to make an effort. This obsolete use of 'pain' also survives in the expression 'painstaking'. A more modern **up and coming** worker may prefer to be **hands on**. 'Up and coming' originally developed in the USA in the late nineteenth century with the sense 'energetic, active', the wording reflecting the behaviour of the person. However, that sense of energy had been transferred to mean someone promising, beginning to show success, presumably through their efforts, by the 1920s. 'Hands on' also implies active, practical involvement. It appeared in the 1960s, and was particularly associated with computers, but has now spread to other fields. If you do not work hard you may find yourself **taken to task**. As might be expected, the original meaning of this, in the sixteenth century, was to take on something as a task. From there it came to mean to take a person or thing in hand, and it was but a small step to meaning tell someone off for what they had done, which had happened by the eighteenth century. **A harsh** or **hard task-master** may even **let you go** as **surplus to requirements**, both unpleasant twentieth-century euphemisms for giving someone the sack.

Particular jobs and trades

Carpentry is the occupation that has the most clichés associated with it in this section. When working wood or any material with a natural grain, it is much easier to work with the grain than across or against it, hence the development of **against the grain**, in use since at least the seventeenth century, to mean much the same as to RUB THE WRONG WAY (see Chapter 22). The 'fair' part of **fair and square** is self-evident, and 'square' can still be used to mean honest and straightforward. The expression comes from the idea that something that is truly square, each corner a right angle, each side lined up with a carpenter's square, is the opposite of crooked or twisted. 'Square' is first recorded in this sense at the end of the sixteenth century, and only a few years later, in 1604, we find the first use of the rhyming doublet 'fair and square'. **Square deal** comes from the same idea. It has been around since the seventeenth century, but really took off as a cliché much later, when US President Theodore Roosevelt used it to sum up his policies, particularly his statement that 'If elected, I shall see to it that every man has a square deal, no less and no more' (1904). The opposite is a **raw deal**, which dates from the same period as square deal, and uses 'raw' to mean crude, unrefined, rough (as in 'raw silk'). The history of **to a T**, meaning 'exactly', 'to perfection', is not entirely clear. It is first recorded in the late seventeenth century, and it has been suggested that it is a shortening of the early seventeenth-century 'to a tittle', referring to doing something well down to the smallest mark (see NOT A JOT OR TITTLE, Chapter 16). This would convince, were it not for the fact that many early uses involve something 'fitting to a T', which suggests the carpenter's T-square, linking the expression to 'fair and square'. The old technique for splitting wood into usable pieces, still used to make logs for fires, is to insert the **thin end of the wedge**. This will go easily into the wood, and you can then hammer it in down to its full thickness, which causes the wood to split. The figurative use of this term dates from the nineteenth century. To work wood successfully you need to keep your tools sharp. The technical word for 'to sharpen' tools is to 'hone' them. This gives us to **hone your skills**. Although the image of using a honing stone to sharpen something is an ancient one, and 'hone' as a noun goes back to Old English, the *OED* does not record it as a verb until the nineteenth century, when the literal and figurative uses appear almost simultaneously. Continuing with the idea of sharpness, we are brought to **razor's edge** and **razor sharp**. The image of the razor's edge for an acute dilemma, where things could *cut either way*, is adopted directly from a line in Homer's *Iliad*. It first appears in English in George Chapman's translation of the *Iliad* (1611): 'Now on the eager razors edge, for life or death we stand.' 'Razor's edge' is also used, as is 'razor sharp', for *incisive, cutting* intellectual ability, and these uses, along with 'razor' by itself used as an adjective (**razor wit**, most typically) are all clichés of the twentieth century.

Building work has also made its contributions to the stock of clichés. 'Build' itself goes very deep into the language, producing **build your life around something**, 'building arguments' and all sorts of other metaphors. Bricklaying gives us **lay it on thick** or **with a trowel**. The image here is of someone piling on flattery or similar things, like a bricklayer spreading a thick layer of mortar. The expression comes from Shakespeare's *As You Like It* (1599), Act I, scene 2: 'Well said, that was laid on with a trowel.' As a cliché it dates from the nineteenth century, although that century offers interesting alternatives such as the comment from *Law Times* in 1893: 'It is nauseous to hear the adulation of Mr Neville, who laid butter on with a spade.' 'To lay it on' is simply a shortened version, which has largely ousted the full version in the USA. A variation is attributed to Disraeli, who did not get on particularly well with Queen Victoria, and as something of a dandy probably did not understand bricklaying very well: 'Everyone likes flattery, and when it comes to Royalty, you should lay it on with a thick trowel.' Bricklaying is also found in **one brick** (or **two bricks**) **short of a load** or **wall**. To describe someone using this expression is to imply that their ideas are wrong, not because they are **as thick as two short planks**, but because they are *not all there*. The expression **one card** (or **two cards**) **short of a deck** is equally well used. The formula has been a popular one, seized on as a chance to show off one's wit, and giving rise to similar expressions such as the not-uncommon *one sandwich* (or *several sandwiches*) *short of a picnic*, or one-off coinages such as a political party in an election being *several policies short of a manifesto*. General building involves

some digging: **dig a hole for yourself** (probably from DIG
YOUR OWN GRAVE, see Chapter 18), is also found as **dig yourself
into** or **out of a hole** and leads to the advice **when in a hole,
stop digging** (all twentieth century). Digging also gives the
expression to **delve into** something. 'Delve' is another of those
words pretty well obsolete except in this set phrase, being an
old alternative for 'dig' and an unnecessary archaism. **Hard as
nails** is another building image. Anyone who has been clumsy
while hammering in a nail will know that nails are not, in fact,
particularly hard, but bend quite easily; however, what they are
good at is being hit, at *taking a hammering*. 'Hard as nails' replaced
earlier expressions such as 'hard as a stone' or 'as flint' in the
second half of the nineteenth century. As anyone who has
reglazed a window will know, putty, when fresh out of the tin,
is both stiff and sticky. To make it into a substance that is soft
and malleable and able to hold the shape you want it to, you
have to knead it in your hands, working the oil back into it and
warming it. Thus someone who is **like putty in someone's
hands** has been *worked on* until they will do what that person
wants. The expression dates from the first quarter of the twentieth century. The duller side of building is found in **as interesting as** or **like watching paint dry**, and its variants, which are
only recorded from the 1970s. Unfortunately, builders have a
reputation for not doing the job properly, which means we can
put **rough and ready** and **quick fix** here. 'Rough and ready'
for 'crude but effective', or simply an extension of 'rough',
became a cliché in the early nineteenth century. As one writer
has pointed out, we might expect the wording to be 'rough *but*
ready', and it is tempting to counter this with a vision of a surly
workman muttering about having something rough and ready,
or properly finished next year. A 'quick fix' is a set phrase that
has only been around since the middle of the twentieth century.

Metal and mechanics come next in this section. If you have
several **irons in the fire** you have several courses of action open
to you; if you have too many, you have taken on more than

you can manage; and if you put all your irons in the fire you are trying every possible course of action. All these come from the blacksmith and the pieces of work he has heating in his forge. As each one cools too much to be workable he can put it back in the fire to soften and work on another ready waiting for him. The image has been in use since the mid sixteenth century. It has been suggested that it is actually taken from heating the pre-electric irons for ironing, which had indeed to be put on a stove to heat, and which were used in at least pairs, so that one heated while the other was in use; however, I doubt this is the case. To start with, you would not put that sort of iron *in* the fire, or your nice clean linen would get covered in soot marks when you used your iron. Secondly, the smoothing iron is not recorded until some fifty years after the first record of our expression. Thirdly, all the early uses of this expression are just too masculine for this origin – they refer to people like the great Roman general Pompey or to the Pope putting all their irons in the fire, and it seems unlikely that the image here is of preparing a nice smooth shirt. Finally, there is a related term that definitely comes from the blacksmith – **to strike while the iron is hot** (and therefore still malleable). This has been in use since Chaucer's day. Once the metal has been worked and made into machinery, it can be wrecked if someone chooses to **throw a spanner in the works**, when things will literally **grind to a halt**. The first of these expressions is only recorded from 1934, but as the preferred American version, 'to throw a monkey wrench', is recorded from 1907, it may well go back to the nineteenth century. Before you can do all this metalwork, you need to dig the ore for it out of the ground, which gives us the term a **mine of information**. Current from at least the beginning of the twentieth century, this is not entirely a dead metaphor, for it has been extended to cover the art of extracting relevant information out of the vast databases computers have now made possible, which is now known as *data-mining*.

Trades associated with fabric give us **dyed-in-the-wool**.

Often used of political parties or beliefs, this cliché is first found in America in 1830. Wool can be dyed at four different stages of manufacture: in the wool, before it is spun; in the yarn, before it is woven; in the piece, when it is a length of cloth; and garment dyed, once it has been made up. The earlier in the process it is dyed, the more thoroughly the colour is incorporated into the final garment and, in the past, the more likely it was to be permanent. **To have your work cut out for you** comes from tailoring. This expression looks at first sight self-contradictory – how can you have a job still to do if it has already been cut out for you? However, 'to cut out work' for someone has been used to mean 'to plan or prepare work' for them since the early seventeenth century. In the days before sewing machines, once the work was cut out there remained the long hard grind of stitching it all together. Because we often associate the word 'mill' with cotton spinning (as in that cliché of drama, 'trouble down at t'mill') it might look at first as if **run of the mill** is also associated with cloth. However, while it can refer to the products of a yarn mill, the expression is much more general. The *OED*'s first example of this sort of expression is from a dictionary of 1909, which gives the examples: '*Run of the kiln*, bricks of all kinds and qualities just as they happen to come from the kiln . . . *Run of the mine*, coal just as it comes from the mine, large and small sizes and all qualities together.' Other examples of 'run of the mill' suggest the production of a sawmill. The expression means 'ordinary', because it refers to products that have not been graded for quality. A different type of mill is found in the **daily grind**, meaning work. Here the image is of being ground between the stones of a corn mill. 'Grind' for 'hard work' appears as slang in the middle of the nineteenth century, with 'daily grind' appearing by the end of that century.

A rather rarer occupation gives us the final cliché in this section. **Shooting the messenger** comes from stories of tyrants in the past who punished the bearer of bad news with death, giving rise to the saying 'Don't shoot the messenger who brings bad news.' Shakespeare used 'beate the Messenger, who bids beware / Of what is to be dreaded' in Act IV, scene 6 of *Coriolanus* (1608), and there are examples of 'kill the messenger' over subsequent centuries. However, the form with 'shoot' seems to be twentieth century. The *Revue of Economic Studies* has 'shoot the messenger boy' in 1963, and *The Times* of 1973 has 'The American public, like most others, tends to shoot the messenger of bad news.' I did think I had found a nineteenth-century example in *The Times* of 1839, but it turned out to be a literal instance of shooting the messenger: 'Mr Morris Myers, said to be a man of large property, was charged with threatening to shoot a messenger of the Bankruptcy Court', which creates a vivid enough picture and raises enough questions to be the start of a novel.

School

Clichés from schools and education tend to concentrate on the basics of schooling, or its rewards. In February 2001 Alastair Campbell, then the spokesman for the Prime Minister, commented that 'the day of the bog-standard comprehensive is over', linking the term **bog standard** – which had not previously emerged from the linguistic substratum of slang and was unknown to many – in the popular mind with schooling, and turning it into an instant cliché. The term 'bog-standard' is not recorded in print before the 1980s, although anecdotal evidence suggests it was around in the 1960s. There have been many stories suggesting where it comes from, the most convincing of which is that it is an alteration (probably under the influence of 'bog' for lavatory) of the factory term 'box-standard'; that is to say, a standard factory product that comes boxed off the production line, rather than an upgraded or customized product (compare RUN OF THE MILL above). Even a bog-standard comprehensive will try to teach the basic skills. They should teach

you how to **put pen to paper**. As an elaborate way of saying
'to write', this was obviously considered objectionable even by
the 1650s, when a certain Mr Osborne wrote in a letter, 'The
fellow thought that putting "pen to paper" was much better
than plain "writing".' The skill should enable you to **make
your mark** – originally the way in which the illiterate signed
their name, with a cross or some other symbol. Someone not
very good at reading who comes to a difficult word may·need
to **spell it out**. The modern use of this phrase as a less aggressive
form of LAY IT ON THE LINE (see Chapter 9), meaning to make
things clear, has been around since the 1940s. The **dog ate my
homework** is a conscious cliché, the sort of desperate excuse
the class slacker might make, now used for comic effect. And
come the end of term report, the very best this sort of schoolchild
can expect is the clichéd **could do better**. All this work involves
a **learning curve**. Originally a graph plotting the rate at which
a skill was acquired (first found 1922), in recent years this has
become first a general term for the rate something is learned,
then a loose vogue term for 'experience'. The frequent 'steep
learning curve' shows a misunderstanding of the way the original
works. If the graph shows a curve that rises steeply, then progress
is being made, and the learner is learning quickly. Someone
struggling with a subject would, in fact, show a shallow learning
curve. The end result of all this work, critics would say, is that
all must have prizes (often quoted as **all shall have prizes**).
This expression is from Lewis Carroll's *Alice's Adventures in
Wonderland* (1865), where, in chapter 3, the Caucus race ends
with: 'At last the Dodo said, "EVERYBODY has won, and all
must have prizes."' This quotation is primarily associated with
liberal, non-competitive schooling, and *All Must Have Prizes* is
the title of a 1996 book by Melanie Phillips attacking such
education. If the child succeeds in their studies, they may end
up with **glittering prizes**. This expression, for highly attractive
rewards, dates from the late nineteenth century (and is found in
a literal sense from at least 1713), but has only become a cliché

more recently. It became better known after F. E. Smith delivered a much-quoted speech as Rector of Glasgow University in 1923 in which he said, 'The world continues to offer glittering prizes to those who have stout hearts and sharp swords', but its real leap to cliché status came in 1976, when BBC TV showed a series of six linked plays called *The Glittering Prizes* written by Frederick Raphael, which charted the lives of a group of Cambridge students from their undergraduate days in the 1950s, through to the 1970s. It was both a critical and a popular success. No doubt the title was chosen with Smith in mind. This fixed in people's minds a link between the expression and the results of a good university education. Those who do not go to university are stuck with the **university of life**. A similar concept to LIVE AND LEARN (see Chapter 6), and a cliché since the early twentieth century, this implies that the knowledge gained in the REAL WORLD (Chapter 15) is of equal (or superior) value to mere book learning, and generally carries a sense of pomposity or self-satisfaction with it.

Journalism

Journalism has a special need of clichés. Notoriously, the job of a journalist is to write words for today, only to have them end up as tomorrow's wrapping paper. This means that journalists often have to write quickly and efficiently, and because many readers read their newspapers with only limited attention, clichés can be an effective way of getting the point across. However, this is no excuse for some of the journalistic horrors that are readily inflicted on the public, which in certain papers indicate a lack of thought and a lack of respect for the reader on the part of the writer. Individuals are frequently reduced to ciphers. Women over retirement age become **little old ladies**, unless they are **have-a-go grannies**, while attractive women are **stunners** (or 'stunnas'). 'Stunner' is a surprisingly old term, having been popular in the middle of the nineteenth century, and it is a curious sensation to read the letters of the Pre-Raphaelites and find the women painted in their pictures described as 'real stunners'. Any large man (or animal) who is not aggressive becomes a **gentle giant** (also in use since the nineteenth century). Any scientist risks being called a **mad genius**. As for children, they are either demonized as feral hoodies, or else referred to as **tiny tots**, possibly even **tug-of-love** tiny tots. 'Tot' in this sense is first recorded in the eighteenth century in Scotland, although it seems to be in other dialects too, and has the same origin as 'tot' for a small drink (found a hundred years later), but the inevitable pairing with tiny is twentieth century. 'Tug of love' is not recorded in the clichéd sense until 1973, although there was a 1907 comedy by I. Zangwill called *The Tug of Love*.

What pass for news stories in the red tops will claim to tell the **full story** (although **the full story may never be known**) of perhaps a **historic occasion** or **event**. They may **name and shame**. This is a recent journalistic development of the earlier journalistic cliché to **name names**, itself a development of the expression to **name no names**. The latter is first recorded in Fanny Burney's *Diary* from June 1792 where she writes, 'She desired he would name no names, but merely mention that some ladies had been frightened.' Un-named, however, will be their **reliable sources**. Those pestered by the press will have **no comment**, which has been used as a conscious cliché or catchphrase since the middle of the twentieth century. They will, however, receive **massive exposure** ('massive' is a favourite word, found in various combinations, including the frequent **massive investment**), although there may be a **question (mark) hanging over** them (a journalistic cliché that has flourished since the 1980s). A sex scandal often means behaviour that would make something less outrageous look like a **vicarage tea party**. Despite the fact that vicars spend so much of the time dealing with the problems of the REAL WORLD (see Chapter 15), in popular culture they still have a reputation for unworldliness and innocence. The tea party expression, and the associated catchphrase **More tea, vicar?**, have been in use as a comparative standard of innocence since at least the 1950s. An alternative format is 'makes X **look like a choirboy**' – behaviour that would not lead to receiving a **sumptuous repast** at the tea party. This latter cliché of the society report and local journalism has been in common use since the 1880s. It may owe something to Milton's 'Their sumptuous gluttonies, and gorgeous feasts' (*Paradise Regained*, 1671). I had thought 'sumptuous repast' was going out of fashion until I Googled it, and found a depressingly high number of hits.

Sorting things out could be a **race against time**, a useful expression spoilt by journalistic overuse. In the end there may be a **rude awakening**. This cliché, a set phrase since the 1890s, springs so readily to the journalistic mind that it was used as a headline after Ruud Gullit's first match as manager of Newcastle United by no less than five newspapers. The other set use of 'rude' is **rude health**. In both cases, 'rude' has retained otherwise rare senses. In the first case it means 'uncivilized' or 'rough' (also found in expressions such as 'a rude peasant hut') and in the second, which dates from the eighteenth century, it means 'vigorous'. Anything that involves two of something risks being headlined with the formula phrase **a tale of two . . .**, based on the title of Charles Dickens's 1859 novel *A Tale of Two Cities*. Any affection in the warmer part of the year risks being labelled a **summer of love**. The original Summer of Love refers to the heyday of hippydom in 1968 or more generally to the period around then (although **if you can remember it, you weren't there**). A dispute becomes a **war of words**. This is first recorded in Alexander Pope's 1725 translation of the *Odyssey*: 'O insolence of youth! Whose tongue affords / Such railing eloquence and war of words.' **Strange but true** has been used since the sixteenth century, and is connected with the proverb **truth is stranger than fiction**. The phrase is first recorded in a line from Byron's

Don Juan (1823), which combines the two: ' 'Tis strange – but true; for truth is always strange; stranger than fiction.' **X marks the spot** is a cliché from the earliest days of newspaper photography, where the scene of the crime would be shown with an X to mark where the deed was done, and it goes back even further in romantic accounts of such things as pirate treasure maps. The expression was being used jokingly by the 1920s, and now can be found as a formula phrase. **Watch this space**, a cliché of both advertising and journalism, is equally venerable, being recorded from as early as 1896.

Some clichés belong in definite sections of the paper. The women's pages will give you **beauty secrets** or **tips**. In the past these might have been described as **hints and wrinkles**, an expression no longer usable in the glamour industry now that all suggestions of wrinkles are taboo. **Luxury lifestyles** and the chance to **get away from it all** appear in the holiday section (even **action–packed** adventure holidays are 'away from it all', although what 'it' may be is never specified). **Eponymous** is a favourite of the music reviewer to describe a CD that is named after the performer or band. A **sideways look at** is a cliché of humorists, not recorded in the *OED* before the 1980s, but in *The Times* by 1959. Sportswriters are notorious for their clichés, but only a token few will be dealt with here (others appear in Chapter 4, Sports and Games). There is the **agony and the ecstasy** of **the sporting life**. *The Agony and the Ecstasy* is the title of an Irving Stone novel (1961), which was made into a film in 1965. The phrase describes the life and works of Michelangelo, the agony and the ecstasy being particularly associated with the triumph, physical labour and discomfort involved in painting the Sistine Chapel. **Walk tall** is an originally American expression, which received a boost in use when it was used as the title of a successful film in 1973. A less common alternative is to **stand proud. Pride and the passion** is a cliché of sports journalists trying to evoke the feelings of those playing in important matches, who are of course those who have **got what it takes**.

9. Wealth, Money and Business

Wealth

There are a number of different types of clichés linked with different aspects of wealth and wealth-making. We start with terms derived from precious objects. A miner or prospector who strikes gold or oil is going to get rich. By the end of the nineteenth century enough people had done this for the expression to **strike gold** or **oil** to be transferred, along with **strike it rich**, to a more general sense of wealth or luck. Gold also features in the phrase **good as gold**. But why should it be gold that people are as good as? The alliteration is obviously important, and gold is something generally considered good, or at least rare and precious, as is, perhaps, good behaviour. The expression dates from the nineteenth century, when money was still tied to the value of gold, so it also contains an element of 'as good as' in the sense found in the expression 'as good as money in the bank'. Gold also features in to **pan out**, which comes from panning for gold. The expression is found literally from the 1830s, and used figuratively from about thirty years later. Silver is linked to **sterling qualities** or **worth**, for 'sterling' is also found in the term 'sterling silver'. 'Sterling' comes from the name of the Norman English silver penny, the purity and reliability of which was once recognized throughout Europe. Because of this it came, from the seventeenth century, to be used as a term of excellence. The word was linked as a set phrase with both 'qualities' and 'worth' in the first part of the nineteenth century. Coinage also gives us the **ring of truth** and to **ring true**. When coins were made of precious metal it was worth forgers' while to make coins of base metal and cover them with gold or silver, or to make them out of an alloy that looked like a precious metal. As well as biting the coin to see if it was soft – a familiar scene from cinema – someone suspicious of the coin he was given could bounce it on a counter or similar surface and listen to the sound. A forged coin would give off a dull sound, but a genuine one would ring true or have the ring of truth about it. Precious metals again lie behind an **unalloyed delight**, **pleasure** or **joy**. The image here is of a precious metal in its purest form, unmixed with anything baser. 'Unalloyed' is actually recorded first in this figurative sense from around 1672, nearly a hundred years before the literal sense has been found. It is not clear if 'not to be able to **make head or tail** of' refers to the two sides of a coin or a literal head and tail. If the Latin phrase, which translates as 'neither head nor feet', used by Cicero to mean total confusion, is anything to go by, it does not belong with coinage in origin, although it is now closely associated with tossing a coin. 'Neither head nor tail' is found from the middle of the seventeenth century, although the construction with 'make' is not recorded until the eighteenth century.

Jewels are found in the phrase **rough diamond**, meaning someone who has intrinsic value but whose *lack of polish* initially obscures the fact. It is an old expression, the literal use for an uncut diamond going back to the early seventeenth century, the figurative first being recorded in 1700, when Dryden wrote, 'Chaucer, I confess, is a rough diamond.' **Diamond geezer** can be presumed to be influenced by 'rough diamond' as a turn of phrase, as well as by the simple equation that diamonds are valuable. It is a very recent term, at least as a cliché, owing its rise to the popularity of East End-based films and soap opera, and of Cockney (or at least Mockney). The **jewel in the crown** is an old phrase for the finest part of something, THE CROWNING GLORY (see Chapter 15). It has been used since at least the eighteenth century. It became a commonplace of Victorian Britain to describe the colonies, particularly India, as the jewel in the crown of the Empire, and it was this use that Paul Scott picked up when he called the first of his Raj Quartet novels *The Jewel in the Crown* (1966). Modern use of this cliché really took off after these novels were televised in 1984 under the title of the first one. While dealing with royal wealth we should look at the **king's ransom**. This expression appears to go back at least to the 1530s, when the proverb 'A peck of March dust is worth a king's ransom' is first recorded. It is one of many country proverbs dealing with the importance of a dry March, and is said still to be current. Such precious things also give us the term **precious few**. 'Precious' developed an emphatic sense in the early nineteenth century, being used to mean 'very' or 'extremely', and has been linked in a set phrase with 'few' from that date.

Two kings that were proverbial for their wealth were Midas and Croesus. Croesus was King of Lydia in Asia Minor in the sixth century BC, and reputed to be the richest man alive, until he lost everything to Cyrus, King of Persia. There is a story that Croesus was visited by the great Athenian lawgiver Solon, to whom he showed his wealth and asked who he thought was the most fortunate of men. Solon named various people, but not Croesus, to the latter's annoyance. Solon explained that you never know what the gods might bring to a man (he is sometimes said to have declared, 'Call no man happy until he is dead'). When the victorious Cyrus was about to burn Croesus alive, Croesus called on Solon's name. Intrigued, Cyrus enquired why. When he learned the reason, he spared Croesus' life, knowing that he too might suffer a reversal of fortune. Unfortunately, Solon and Croesus did not live at the same time, so this cannot have happened, but it makes a good story. Now rather old-fashioned, the expression **rich as Croesus** is an alternative to 'rich beyond the DREAMS OF AVARICE' (see below). Midas, son of Gordius, and King of Phrygia, was said to have looked after Silenus, drunken companion of the god Dionysus, when he wandered off and got lost, and as a reward Dionysus offered him whatever gift he might want. Midas chose the gift of changing anything he touched to gold, but when he found that this was taken more literally than he intended, and even the food he tried to eat turned to gold, he had to beg for the gift to be removed. The moral of this story – the dangers of greed – seems to be lost when people are praised nowadays for having **the Midas touch**. Midas' father, Gordius, was the man who tied the Gordian knot. According to legend, Gordius was a peasant who became king because an oracle had told the people of Phrygia to choose as a king the first man to approach the temple of Zeus in a wagon. Having become king in this strange manner, Gordius dedicated his wagon to Zeus. The wagon was attached to the yoke with a very complicated knot, and the legend developed that whoever could untie it would become ruler of all Asia. A further legend says that Alexander the Great, a master manipulator of propaganda, claimed Asia for his own, not by untying the knot, but by cutting through it with his sword. Thus a 'Gordian knot' came to mean something impossible to unravel, and to **cut the Gordian knot** to mean solving a problem not by finesse but by direct and often forceful means.

Money – whether you have it or not

The British are notoriously squeamish about talking about money, so have developed a rich vocabulary for avoiding the subject. The dream of acquiring wealth is reflected in **rags to riches** – a three-word summary of the Cinderella story. This cliché is much used by journalists, who often imply that it has happened **like a fairy tale**, even when the climb from poverty to wealth has involved extreme hard work. The reverse process, **riches to rags**, is not uncommon, but the language is well equipped with proverbs that do the same job. Americans use 'from shirtsleeves to shirtsleeves in three generations' (sometimes attributed to Andrew Carnegie (1835–1919), but never tracked down in his writings). This is a more up-to-date version of the old Lancashire proverb 'from clogs to clogs in three generations'. Sometimes things get blended together and we find 'from rags to riches in three generations'. The nineteenth century introduced **easy come, easy go** as a more general alternative. 'I am **rich beyond the dreams of avarice**' is a quotation from an obscure play called *The Gamester* written by Edward Moore in 1753, although the term 'dreams of avarice' in the sense of 'illusions' was already well established at this date. Moore's line, which has been used steadily since the eighteenth century, must have passed into the language quickly (unless Moore stole it from somewhere else) for it is used by Boswell in his *Life of Samuel Johnson* of 1781 in the somewhat unexpected context of: 'We are not here to sell a parcel of boilers and vats, but the potentiality of growing rich beyond the dreams of avarice.' It sometimes occurs in the form: 'Wealth beyond the dreams of avarice'. Avarice is, of course, one of the seven deadly sins. Religious condemnation of greed is also found in the expression **filthy lucre**. This comes from the Bible, 1 Timothy 3, where the personal qualities desirable in the leaders of the new religion are set out: 'A bishop then must be blameless, the husband of one wife, vigilant, sober, of good behaviour, given to hospitality, apt to teach. Not given to wine, no striker, not greedy of filthy lucre; but patient, not a brawler, not covetous.' It is found again at Titus 1:11. The original Greek of these passages uses words that would nowadays be translated as 'shameful gain', and the early translators of the Bible chose the word 'lucre' because it carried not only the meaning 'profit' from its Latin source, but also a secondary sense of 'avarice'.

Two examples of wealthy men have been discussed in the previous section, but there are two more clichés that deal with women's wealth. While the men are found in the ancient world, the women date from more modern times, reflecting the recent growth of the number of women joining the money economy (although, of course, women have always worked). ***Poor Little Rich Girl*** was the title of a 1917 film starring Mary Pickford, which, ironically, satirized the rich but made her the richest actress in the world. The expression was then picked up by Noël Coward and used as the title of a popular song in 1925, which is where most people know it from. **Poor but honest** is older, as is the problem that women face when their bodies are the only thing they have left to sell. It is a cliché of the Victorian age, which has rarely been used straight since the popularity in the First World War of the music-hall song 'She Was Poor But She Was Honest', with its chorus, 'It's the rich wot get the pleasure, but the poor wot get the blame.' The companion cliché, the **deserving poor**, from the same era, meaning those deemed to deserve help as opposed to those who have brought their troubles upon themselves, has suffered a similar fate.

If we turn to clichés of spending we find **shop till you drop**, a cliché of the yuppie, high-spending 1980s, reflecting the CONSPICUOUS CONSUMPTION (see Chapter 7) of the time. Your shopping list may also be a **wish list** (which came into use in the early 1970s), in that it contains things that can only be purchased **at vast expense**. The earliest example of the latter that I have found is in a *Times* article of 1811 with the very modern-seeming theme of the outrageous profits being made by the company running the lottery. It is a very common combination in the early nineteenth century, perhaps reflecting a fashionable popularity of both 'vast' and 'vastly' in the eighteenth and early nineteenth centuries that the word has now lost. **No expense spared** is a companion cliché to this from the same century, although it is frequently used ironically today. You may decide you are not prepared to **pay the price** of what you want. This expression can relate to something trivial, or something of inestimable value. Most cultures have stories that tell of heroes who have to sacrifice something of enormous importance to them to get what they want. In the Bible Jephthar finds out after the event that the price of victory is the sacrifice of his only child; Woden, in Germanic myth, sacrifices an eye to acquire wisdom. Criminals have been expected to pay the price in the sense of 'suffer a penalty' from the sixteenth century; but the older idea of sacrifice is also found, and is illustrated by Woodrow Wilson's 1916 speech: 'There is a price which is too great to pay for peace, and that price can be put in one word: One cannot pay the price of self-respect.' Paying for something expensive demands a **fat cheque** (although, with cheques being used more and more rarely today, it will be interesting to see if this is a cliché that dies out, or one of the ones that carries on being used long after the process it describes has died out). 'Fat' carries with it images of large size and abundance and has been used to refer to a good source of income such as a job or, most commonly in the past, a church benefice, since the fourteenth century. Milton, in 1642, uses it in his *Apology . . . against Smectymnuus*: 'I would wish him the biggest and the fattest Bishoprick.' The linking of this use of 'fat' with 'cheque' is probably twentieth century. A less obvious cliché from paying is **lay it on the line**. This term is found in the sense of 'pay' in the 1920s in the USA, and then, presumably via a similar idea to PUT YOUR MONEY WHERE YOUR MOUTH IS (see Chapter 4), came to be used to mean to be frank about something. This change came about around the 1950s. This is the dominant sense in the UK, but the paying sense was still strong enough in the USA for the sense 'put at risk, pay dearly' to develop in the 1960s. If you really want something you may be prepared to **give the shirt off your back** for it. The image of one's shirt being one's minimum possession goes back to the Middle Ages (Chaucer uses someone's lack of a shirt to indicate the ultimate in poverty), and the expression as we use it is found from the seventeenth century. Giving away your shirt as a symbol of generosity dates from at least 1771, when Smollett wrote in *Humphrey Clinker*, 'He would give away the shirt off his back', and the idea of giving away essential clothing as such a symbol is even older. St Martin of Tours, one of the most popular saints of the Middle Ages, was famous for cutting his cloak in half with his sword to share it with a naked beggar, after which he had a vision of

Christ wearing the cloak, and entered holy orders. Alternatives for this expression are **give your right arm** (or AN ARM AND A LEG, See chapter 15) or **give your back teeth** for something. For smaller purchases, particularly in a pub or similar places of entertainment, you could find out the cost by asking **what's the damage?** – often in the deliberately jocular, old-fashioned form, 'What's the damage, Squire?' This expression, although rather dated now, has a long history. 'Damage' by itself, as a slang word for 'cost', was in use by the mid eighteenth century, and, since slang is often slow to get into the written record, may well be earlier. The slang expression, in turn, probably developed from the legal use of the word (now always used in the plural, 'damages') for the estimated value of something lost or money to be paid in compensation. If this is an old-fashioned expression, more dated still is the idea that you can go out and **still have change from sixpence** or **a shilling**. Indeed, this comment on the effects of inflation, felt to be typical of old people reminiscing about the good old days, is now only found as a conscious cliché or joke, although you can hear remarkably similar comments couched in more up-to-date terms.

Getting this spending money demands a **nice little earner**, an expression popularized in the television series *Minder* (written by Leon Griffiths and running 1979–85, 1988–94), where it was a catchphrase of the **loveable rogue** Arthur Daley. Even better, you want to get on a **gravy train**. 'Gravy' was being used to mean money that had been easily acquired, or that was extra in some way, such as a bonus or tip, in the same way that gravy is an extra on top of the basics of a meal, by the beginning of the twentieth century. It could also be used for money obtained through bribery or other illicit means. A 'gravy train' was US railroad slang for an easy run where the pay was good. This was adopted into general speech in the 1920s. For some reason in the UK it has been particularly attached to those employed by the EEC. Best of all is **a licence to print money**. The Canadian-born industrialist Roy Thomson (later Lord Thomson of Fleet) is supposed to have commented, in 1957, on his commercial television company, 'You know it's just like having a licence to print your own money.' By the 1970s, this expression, in the form 'a licence to print money', had become a cliché. An alternative is to save up for what you want, but how old-fashioned this approach is considered can be seen by its only cliché – to have **money under the mattress**. This is a conscious cliché of the hoarding peasant who does not trust institutions with his wealth. It does, however, reflect the material progress of the peasant, in that it replaced an earlier image of money buried under a brick in the fireplace or in a hole dug in the earth floor. In the end it comes down to **the pound in your pocket**. The clichéd use of this expression comes from a radio broadcast made in 1967 by the Prime Minister Harold Wilson after the devaluation of the pound: 'It does not mean, of course, that the pound here in Britain, in your pocket or purse or in your bank, has been devalued.' This was immediately adopted in the form 'the pound in your pocket'.

Business

Keeping track of all the money made and lost in business has given us a number of clichés, not all of them obviously from this source. The most obvious term from accounting is probably the **bottom line**, the one that shows the profit or loss on the balance sheet. This became a cliché in the middle of the twentieth century, but by the 1970s it was beginning to spread its range to mean the ultimate criterion, the most important thing, or even the equivalent of THE FINAL STRAW. The **day of reckoning** is also an accounting term, for 'to reckon' originally meant 'to count', and very early on in its history 'reckoning' came to mean an account or bill. The day of reckoning is therefore the day you have to settle your account. 'Reckoning' took on a religious sense, to mean 'judgement day', early in the

Middle Ages. It is not clear when this was transformed into a
secular sense of the day when things have to be accounted for, or
'comeuppance'. Although the *OED* does not have an example
before 1839, *The Times* shows clearly that it was common from
the very beginning of the nineteenth century, so it is probably
much older.

To **keep (someone) posted** is an Americanism from the
first half of the nineteenth century, originally found in the form
'posted up'. It is accountancy jargon – you post (put) a figure
into the accounts and post up the books to bring them up to
date. If someone is kept posted they are therefore supplied with
the latest figures or information. Accounts themselves appear
in **creative accounting**, a term in use since the 1970s for
presenting financial information in a way that hides the real
situation, and now often used as a euphemism for outright fraud
or **cooking the books**, an expression for falsifying accounts
that has been used since the seventeenth century. The allied
study of economics gives us **trickle down**. A cliché of right-
wing economists, this theory that things that benefit the well-off
will eventually benefit the poor is a creation of 1930s America.
Tiger economy was originally a useful way to describe those
Asian economies that grew rapidly. Until the 1998 crashes it
seemed journalists were unable to discuss Far East economics
without using it. Since then it has been used to describe any
economy that is growing fast, so that Ireland, for example, gets
called the 'Celtic Tiger'. This complete disregard for the original
image – economies that were not only fierce and aggressive,
but were based in the same area as the few remaining tigers –
shows how far down the road to clichéhood this expression has
gone.

Getting a job

The clichés used in job applications could probably fill a whole
book on their own. One has only to look at the advertisements

in any paper to see just how prolific they are – so much so that only a representative sample can be covered here. Most of them are pretty recent, and few are more than about fifty years old – and even those took time to become clichés. Candidates are asked to be **self-starters** (as if they are some sort of old-fashioned car), TEAM PLAYERS (see Chapter 4) – or possibly **team leaders** (occasionally both at once), **results driven** (or **orientated** or **motivated**) with a good TRACK RECORD (see Chapter 22). They will be expected to subscribe to **best practice** (usually a vague phrase for something undefined, but which sounds suitably conscientious). Even if the job is **entry level** (also used of bottom-of-the-range products) they may need to be **of graduate calibre** (why not just 'graduates? No one is likely to turn up and claim that they could have got a degree if they wanted to, but just did not feel like it). And they must, of course, subscribe to the firm's **mission statement**. To get the job, the candidate must present the interviewer with their **USP** (unique selling point). The reader can, I am sure, supply many more.

Business jargon

There is much debate about where we should draw the line between jargon, slang and clichés. For our purposes, I have simply taken terms used both by business people and by the general public that are associated with business and that irritate from overuse. The sort of thing I mean is something like the use of **run something past someone** rather than the simpler and clearer 'ask them to have a look at it'. There are also much more extreme examples, such as **run something up the flagpole (and see if anyone salutes it)**. This is an expression coined in the USA in about 1950, and to be fair has now been so mocked that it is probably little used, or at least only as a conscious cliché, although it is too good an example to be left out. The source of the expression is self-explanatory, and it has obvious links to the imagery of expressions such as *to fly a kite* in the sense of to raise an idea and see how it is reacted to, or *to see which way the wind is blowing*. Since the UK has no tradition of saluting the flag, the full form of the expression always seemed an affectation when used by the British.

If we start at the top of the job ladder, we find the **captain of industry**. This expression was coined by Thomas Carlyle, who used 'Captains of Industry' as a chapter heading for his book *Past and Present* in 1843. It became a popular expression, particularly in newspapers, to describe the leaders of big business, but now has a slightly old-fashioned ring to it. Such people are nowadays more likely to be called the much less respectful FAT CATS (see Chapter 22). They may also be **self-made men**. A term from the first part of the nineteenth century, 'self-made man' is used to describe someone who has won wealth and position through his own efforts, rather than through the advantages of birth. It is rarely used without some element of snobbery or an indication that the person is at best a ROUGH DIAMOND (see above), and the quotation books abound in jokes made at his expense. One of the best known of these is Disraeli's comment on being told that he was perhaps being too hard on John Bright, as he was a self-made man, to which Disraeli replied, 'I know he is and he adores his maker' (often quoted in the form 'a self-made man who worships his maker'). If this boss heads a merger they can be said to **get into bed with** another company (well used since the 1970s). Someone they decide to **bring on board** to help the company may find themselves restricted by a **golden handshake** or **handcuff** or **hello**, 'golden', in these business clichés, referring to money or other reward. The earliest form of the expression, from about 1960, is the golden handshake, used when you say goodbye to someone. This is a payment to get someone to leave a job before their contract is up, so that they go quietly. Then, in the 1970s, came the golden handcuff, where you offer someone such an attractive package of long-term benefits that they cannot afford to disentangle themselves from the company. Then in the 1980s came the golden hello, where someone is paid a sum just for joining a company. A less common member of this group is the **golden parachute**, where company directors who think they may lose their jobs, for instance in a takeover, award themselves a big pay rise or bonus, to give themselves an easier descent from their position.

The new job may turn out to be a **poisoned chalice** – something that looks like a benefit, but that will actually be a disadvantage. The image is of nefarious goings-on in melodrama and films set in the Middle Ages, of the sort so admirably parodied in the 1955 Danny Kaye film *The Court Jester* (written by Norman Panama and Melvin Frank), with its famous tongue-twister 'The pellet with the poison's in the vessel with the pestle. The chalice from the palace has the brew that is true.' An alternative source would be the poisoning in *Hamlet* and other revenge dramas of the period. The person handed the poisoned chalice may feel that they have been **taken to the cleaners**. This expression, derived from being **cleaned out**, an early nineteenth-century gambling term for losing all your money, dates from the middle of the twentieth century. It carries a sense of being cheated that 'cleaned out' – a self-explanatory image – does not. At its worst, the deceit may be part of the **unaccept-able face of capitalism**. In 1973 the Prime Minister Edward Heath said of payments made to a politician by Lonrho, 'It is the unpleasant and unacceptable face of capitalism, but one should not suggest that the whole of British industry consists of practices of this kind.' The expression rapidly caught on, and is now also used as a formula phrase. But the new company may be a good buy – even a **cash cow**: a business or product you can *milk* for a steady income. Although the expression is recent, the idea is old. 'Milk' has been used in this sense since the early sixteenth century. The purchase may have been **cheap at the price**. This was originally a huckster's cry of good value, and the expression still carries with it a certain feeling of suspicion

that all is not as it should be. The objects for sale may not be
cheap and nasty (a cliché from the early nineteenth century)
nor **cheap and cheerful** (a modern cliché), but are, the seller
would argue, good value for money. Ironically, this was the
original meaning of the word 'cheap'. Originally 'cheap' meant
the act of buying or bartering, and from that the price of something. We only got our adjective 'cheap' in the sixteenth century,
when the expression 'good cheap', meaning 'a good price', 'a
bargain', was shortened to just 'cheap'. The ambiguous elaboration **cheap at half the price** probably goes back to the nineteenth century.

If we move down the command structure to the managers
we meet the **grey suits**. A cliché of the 1990s, this expression
reflects the fact that senior management has to wear sober, grey
suits in dull conformity, which is also felt to reflect the lack of
imaginative thinking in such people. The expression is now
often shortened to 'suit'. The opposite stereotype is represented
by the comment **I work hard and I play hard**. Managers at
this level are the people who have to deal with the regular crises
in business. If there is a crisis they will find themselves **fire
fighting**, a term which is spreading from management to other
areas. Alternatively they could **focus on addressing the challenge**. If they do not respond to the **wake-up call**, they may
find themselves **consigned to the history books**, **scrap heap**
or **scrapyard**, all clichés of the mid twentieth century, with
'scrapyard' being particularly popular among journalists describing redundancies. They may decide they need to take a **basket**
or **raft** of actions (a recent empty filler that is steadily spreading).
They may want to grab themselves a **piece of the action**. An
Americanism that still has a slightly transatlantic feel for British
users, this developed from the concept of buying a piece of
some business or activity (recorded from the 1920s), which was
blended with the slang use of 'the action' for an important or
significant activity (recorded from the 1930s). The two together
are not recorded before the 1960s, but the phrase is probably

older. Nearly every article on pizza that you see in the news-papers or magazines puns on this. Under the influence of the stock market they may talk of **playing the market**, hoping to **hit a (new) high** (not **low**). Shares were hitting new highs in the USA in the 1920s, and by 1937 this was being used metaphorically in the headline 'Nazi epithets at U.S. set a new high.' Arrangements they make may be a **done deal**, but if they feel that it involves information they do not need to know about, then it may be **above my pay grade** or **beyond my job description**.

A final group of miscellaneous business-based clichés are **stake-holder** – a particular favourite of the government, often mean-ing little more than people with a vague interest in something working; **we deeply regret**, an apology that both keeps an emotional distance and avoids any commitment to do anything about the problem, used by both business and politicians; and **unavoidable delays**, occurrences that are often being regretted. **Give and take** comes originally from trade. It has been an expression for reciprocal concessions or a fair exchange since the eighteenth century, and is found even earlier in the literal sense. Edmund Burke, for instance, speaking of America, said in 1775, 'Every prudent act is founded on compromise and barter . . . we give and take; we remit some rights, that we may enjoy others.' Finally there is the slogan **the customer is always right**, adopted by H. Gordon Selfridge for his stores in about 1909, which rapidly spread through the business world.

10. Advertising

Advertising copywriters devote their lives to trying to get their slogans into our brains and into the language. Given how often we may hear a slogan, it is not surprising that many succeed. Most of them do not survive very long after the campaign is over. One has only to look at the selection included in a dictionary of quotations that is a few years old to prove this. Some, however, do work their way into long-term use, and some of these even achieve the status of clichés. Yet, if I were a copywriter, I would be depressed by the frequency with which the memory of the slogan outlives the memory of what it was advertising. For example, many people will remember that **we won't make a drama out of a crisis** was a heavily advertised slogan for an insurance company in the 1980s, and 'to make a drama out of a crisis' is fixed in the language, but how many remember that it was the slogan of Commercial Union? The other financial services cliché, **that'll do nicely**, which was already an established expression when it was used in the 1970s, is remembered as the slogan of American Express, probably because the name was said just before the slogan. Similarly, **it's good to talk** is still identified with telephones after its use by British Telecom from 1994, even though it was already a general cliché before it was used. A fairly recent addition to the stock of clichés contributed by advertising is **Because I'm worth it**, currently used by L'Oreal. However, among the ones I have selected to include here, recent advertising has not been very influential, perhaps a result of the narrower targeting of audiences by advertisers (although it is always a possibility that this is merely a reflection of the television I watch).

The 1980s were, however, a productive period. **Naughty**

but nice has been a cliché since it was used to promote cream cakes in the 1980s in an advertisement campaign said to have been written by the novelist Salman Rushdie, who once worked in advertising – although it was in use before then, for example as the title of a film released in 1939. Zanussi's the **appliance of science** dates from the same period. **Vorsprung durch Technik** (progress through technology) is the MISSION STATEMENT (see Chapter 9) of the German car manufacturers Audi, written up over the factory gates. It was used heavily in advertising campaigns from 1986 and came to be used to symbolize the modern Germany.

Other slogans are older, and may no longer be recognized as advertising. **Never knowingly undersold,** used sarcastically of the self-promoting, has been the slogan of the John Lewis Partnership shops since the 1920s. **Sinking feeling** has been a way of describing hunger since the late nineteenth century, although it has since been transferred to other things. The expression became well known in the 1920s, when there was a vigorous advertising campaign which used the slogan 'Bovril prevents that sinking feeling.' **Say it with flowers** is one of the oldest advertising slogans still in use, having been adopted by the Society of American Florists in 1917. But some slogans can be deceptive. While familiar as a cliché of advertising for washing powder, **whiter than white** is not a modern expression in itself: Shakespeare has the lines 'Who sees his true-love in her naked bed / Teaching the sheets a whiter hue than white' in his *Venus and Adonis* (1593). The expression is not recorded again until it appears in one of the *OED*'s own definitions, where *exceeding-white* is defined, in 1924, as 'exceeding or surpassing white, "whiter than white"', which suggests the expression was already current by then.

We turn now to expressions that are associated with general advertising copy. Some of these are single words that we have all learned to distrust, such as 'genuine', always a sign to doubt the provenance of anything that feels it needs to claim it. If you are offered a 'free exclusive T-shirt' you know very well that it is not 'exclusive' for thousands will have been produced, and it is unlikely to be genuinely free (there being NO SUCH THING AS A FREE LUNCH; see Chapter 2). Longer phrases often seem designed to lull you into turning off your critical faculties. **In the comfort of your own home** means no more than 'at home', but manages both to flatter and imply that you are in control. Flattery is also present, although more crudely, in **for the man who has everything**. It became widely used in the USA in the 1920s or 1930s, and is still used both seriously and as a conscious cliché. The persistent search of modern society for eternal youth is flattered in **children of all ages**. A cliché of advertisers since the middle of the twentieth century, this represents an unconvincing attempt to imply that something will be fun for everyone. Even worse are variants such as **children from seven to seventy**. Other such expressions are **sun-drenched** (popular since the 1920s and used to describe anything from holidays to citrus fruit); 'treasured', found used variously in **treasured memories, treasured possessions** and **a . . . you will want to treasure**; **has to be seen to be believed**; a DREAM COME TRUE (see Chapter 18); and **that special moment** – all fine examples of **style over substance**.

11. Fighting and the Forces

It is a cliché of social commentators to say that the importance of fighting is a sad reflection on our society. However, there is no getting round the fact that conflict and the forces have supplied us with many of our clichés, and that the language is, to use another cliché, **soaked in blood**.

General fighting

This section covers general fighting, rather than that associated with armed forces, although some phrases mentioned are also applicable to war – what might be categorized as **blood on the streets** (by the early nineteenth century). Those looking for trouble might be **armed to the teeth**, which may conjure up images of Caribbean pirates, but which has been around since the fourteenth century. The hero may succeed **armed with nothing but** something insignificant, looking for a **fight to the finish** (late nineteenth century). If you get your **backs to the wall** you may be able to **hold your own** (sixteenth century) or **fight to a standstill**. 'Fighting with your backs to the wall' is both a cliché of the adventure film and an expression which, although in use since at least the sixteenth century, gained a whole new resonance when General Haig sent out the following order on 12 April 1918, couched in resounding terms, but of small comfort to the cannon-fodder actually facing the enemy:

Every position must be held to the last man: there must be no retirement. With our backs to the wall, and believing in the justice of our cause, each one of us must fight on to the end. The safety of our

Homes and the Freedom of mankind alike depend upon the conduct of each one of us at this critical moment.

The result of this string of high-sounding and sentimental clichés was **mass slaughter** – a fine example of what can be done when you know how to manipulate the language. Those who expect others to **risk life and limb** (seventeenth century, with the typical doubling-up of that period) may be said to have **blood on their hands**, once used to mean that someone was a murderer, but now often meaning nothing more than that a person did something or was the guilty party. A crude way to say that people have been killed violently is to say they have been **blown away**. It has been suggested that the expression 'blown away' for 'dead' comes from a New Orleans tradition of marching a coffin through the streets to the accompaniment of a jazz band, and that this was known locally as 'blowing a friend away'. However, this theory both has little evidence to support it, and is unnecessarily complicated. A much simpler explanation comes from soldier's slang, perhaps from the Second World War, describing the effects of heavy gunfire. The expression comes from America, and by the 1950s had expanded, at least in Black dialect, to include the sense 'impressed very much', a transition from killing to an expression of appreciation also made by the word 'slay'. An earlier use of 'blown away' for 'killed' is even grimmer. In the eighteenth century rebellious troops in India were punished by some of their number being strapped to the mouth of a cannon. This was fired, and they were literally blown away. It is first recorded in 1776, with the simple statement: 'I ordered . . . the artillery officers to blow them away', and *The Times* for 4 January 1785 seems quite comfortable with the whole idea, a correspondent writing:

The trial and condemnation of Capt. M'Kenzie being now very much the subject of public conversation, we think it will not be deemed incurious to give the origin of blowing human beings away from the cannon's mouth. On the investigation of India affairs, before the House of Commons, at the time that Lord Clive's conduct was much arraigned, General — confessed in evidence, that a black or sepoy regiment having deserted, he had sent a sufficient force to bring them back, and had fifty of the ringleaders tried by black officers, who condemned twenty-five out of the fifty to be blown away from the mouth of the cannon. 'I ordered the sentence to be executed,' said the General, 'when, of the number, twelve grenadiers of the black regiment cried out, that as they were always first upon service, they now claimed the honour of being the first blown away, and I accordingly gratified them.'

After this gruesome account the correspondent blandly continues in the next paragraph, 'The rigour of the present season has turned out very fortunate for the States of Holland . . .' The Lord Clive referred to is Robert Clive (1725–74), 'Clive of India', whose running of the East India Company had been much investigated in the 1770s, while *The Times* of 8 January 1785 tells us, 'We have heard from good authority that Lieutenant (not Captain) M'Kenzie, now under sentence of death in Newgate, for shooting a soldier from the mouth of a cannon, at Fort Miree on the coast of Africa, has received the Royal promise of a free pardon.' Returning to 'blow away', it is unlikely that the barbaric behaviour of the British Army is the direct ancestor of the current use for 'to kill'; however, combined with a sporting slang use of the same term for 'to shoot a bird' (also the simple 'to blow' and the source of the familiar 'blow to pieces'), it could have supplied a background memory for the more obvious effects of modern munitions.

All this **mindless violence** depends on **brute force**. 'Brute' here means action like that of an animal ('brute' as an adjective is rare outside this set phrase; 'brutal' is used elsewhere). As might be expected, this cliché is the product of the Enlightenment, setting reason against the animal side of nature. A sermon of 1726 laments that 'Some kind of brute Force within, prevails over the Principle of Rationality.' Those **spoiling for a fight** (a mid nineteenth-century Americanism, with a change in the sense of the verb 'to spoil' that has not really been explained) may have a **chip on their shoulder**. This expression grew up in the early nineteenth century in the USA as a way of proving your machismo. As the *Long Island Telegraph* of 1830 put it, 'When two churlish boys were *determined* to fight. A *chip* would be placed on the shoulder of one, and the other demanded to knock it off at his peril.'

We can round off the list of clichés dealing generally with violence with an opposed pair. The likes of General Haig would no doubt urge his troops to **fight the good fight**. This is a quotation cliché, best known from the hymn, sung in countless schools and Sunday gatherings, 'Fight the good fight with all thy might', written by the Irish cleric John Monsell in 1863. Monsell was himself quoting the Bible: 'Fight the good fight of faith, lay hold on eternal life' (1 Timothy 6:12), followed in the Second Epistle (4:2) by 'I have fought a good fight, I have finished my course, I have kept the faith.' That this had reached clichéhood by the nineteenth century can be seen from Oscar Wilde's waspish description of W. E. Henley: 'He has fought a good fight and has had to face every difficulty except popularity.' The opposite view is found in **wreak havoc**. 'Wreak' is an extremely old word, meaning 'to express' or 'give vent to', going back to earliest records of English, but which is now obsolete outside this sense, and is rarely found without being coupled to 'havoc' or sometimes 'vengeance'. (Just hours after writing this I came across 'wreak damage' in a newspaper, forcing me to change 'never found' to 'rarely'. However, it reads oddly.) Curiously, the *OED* does not record a past tense in the form 'wrought', giving instead forms such as 'wreaked', although the earliest example of the phrase I have been able to find is 'wrought havoc' from *The Times* in 1832. Those who like to **fight dirty** may get a **stranglehold** (1901 in a metaphorical sense) or **put the boot in** (early twentieth century).

Fighting in the past

Before we turn to clichés more obviously connected with the modern armed forces, let us look at those from the armies of the past. From the classical world we get the term **Pyrrhic victory**. The Greek general Pyrrhus was a skilful general and had ambitions to emulate his second cousin, Alexander the Great. He agreed to lead the Greeks of southern Italy against the encroaching Romans, and the two forces met at the Battle of Asculum in 279 BC. Pyrrhus and his forces were victorious, but lost so many men that they were never able to follow up their success, and Rome was the real winner in the long run. After the battle Pyrrhus is said to have exclaimed, 'One more such victory and we are lost.' 'Pyrrhic victory' began to be used to describe this sort of situation by the middle of the nineteenth century, but, with the decline of knowledge of the classics, is now being replaced by **won the battle but lost the war**. Also from the ancient past, perhaps surprisingly, is **parting shot**, which refers to arrows and not, as might be expected, to guns. All the might of the Roman Empire could never manage to subdue the Mesopotamia-based Empire of the Parthians, their only serious rivals as a world power. The reason for this was that the Romans fought as massed infantry, while the Parthian army was of lightly armed skirmishing cavalry that the Roman army could never get to grips with. If the Romans tried to engage them they would scatter, turning round over their horses' rumps to fire devastating arrows at the Romans. This ability to attack while running away became known as the Parthian shot, found in the form 'Parthian blow' as early as the sixteenth century.

Swords and other bladed weapons now obsolete have had a considerable influence on the imagery of the English language. Arguments have long been described by terms such as *sharp* or *cutting*. Some designs of edged weapons were designed to **cut both ways**, that is, have two cutting edges, which would give an obvious advantage in some fights to those trained to use them effectively, but could inflict unintentional harm with a thoughtless backswing. The development to the modern sense can be traced from the literal use in the description of some sabres by Viscount Valentia in 1809: 'They were all Persian, but had been lengthened in Egypt at both ends, so as to give the Mameluke point, which cuts both ways' via the transition to figurative use in J. Martineau's *Essays* (1866): 'The charge . . . is double edged, and cuts both ways.' The violence of Elizabethan London is reflected in **at daggers drawn**. It is first found in the sixteenth century, in the form 'at daggers drawing', which explains the rather odd 'at', used originally to signify 'at the point of'. It appears in its modern form by 1668. A similar idea is found in the expression **at each other's throats**, but because the action is not obsolete this has not lost its sense of physical violence in the same way that 'daggers drawn' has. Older still is the origin of the term to **fall on your sword** for those who accept the consequences of their mistakes. This expression comes from the Old Testament, 1 Samuel 31:4–5 (the story is repeated in very similar words at 1 Chronicles 10). King Saul had been defeated by the Philistines and wounded:

Then said Saul unto his armour bearer, Draw thy sword, and thrust me through therewith; lest these uncircumcised come and thrust me through, and abuse me. But his armour bearer would not; for he was sore afraid. Therefore Saul took a sword and fell upon it. And when his armour bearer saw that Saul was dead, he fell likewise upon his sword, and died with him.

The same action occurs in Homer, and defeated Roman generals would also commit suicide in the same way. Shakespeare clearly used the biblical passage as a source for the conspirators' suicides at the end of *Julius Caesar* (1599), and this, given the enormous influence Shakespeare has had on the language, may have helped spread the expression. Swords are also implied in the imagery of a **crushing blow**, a set phrase since at least the middle of the nineteenth century. This expression usually, but not invariably, starts with the old-fashioned 'deal' instead of 'give', which suggests the language of knighthood and links it to the original image of a hand-to-hand fighter bringing a weapon down in a blow that would literally crush.

With the archaic business of swords goes armour. Clichés seem to have concentrated on the armoured covering of hands. The most recent is the **mailed fist**. This term for armed force or superior might is a direct translation from German. In 1897 Kaiser Wilhelm II made a speech in which he said, 'But should any one essay to detract from our just rights or to injure us, then up and at him with your mailed fist.' At first 'mailed fist' was used to describe Germany's aggressive foreign policy, then of similar behaviour by other countries, and from there it spread to general use. It is sometimes used to replace the 'iron fist' in THE IRON FIST IN THE VELVET GLOVE (see Chapter 7). **Pick up** or **take up the gauntlet** together with **throw down the gauntlet** are genuine hangovers from the Middle Ages and were in use metaphorically by the seventeenth century. They reflect the medieval custom of throwing down a glove or gauntlet as a means of challenging someone to a fight, and of picking it up as a sign of acceptance. **Run the gauntlet** has, however, a completely different origin. It comes from a Swedish word, *gatlopp*, formed from words meaning 'lane' and 'course', and refers to a traditional military punishment for crimes like theft from your fellows, where the guilty party had to run, stripped to the waist, down a lane formed by two ranks of men who would strike at him as he passed. The word entered English in the form 'gantlope', and because of a perceived similarity of sound this was changed to the more familiar 'gauntlet', although 'gantlope' can be found into the nineteenth century. The figurative use, for something difficult or dangerous that has to be passed through, has been used for as long as the literal sense.

Early firearms also left their mark on English. Their poor

reliability is reflected in **flash in the pan**. This cliché, in the sense 'a brief spurt of success', came into use in the 1920s, although it was used in the previous century to mean an abortive effort. The literal use of the expression goes back much further. Early firearms would have a pan of priming gunpowder designed to ignite the charge in the barrel. Sometimes, however, the gunpowder in the pan would ignite with a flash, but the combustion would not be carried through to the charge. Then you were left waiting to see what was going to happen, knowing, as with a faulty firework, that if you interfered you risked finding it was working after all. **Bite the bullet** supposedly reflects the primitive treatment for those wounded in the wars in the days before anaesthetics. A man wounded in battle might be given a bullet to bite on to help prevent himself screaming while being operated on. It would also help him not to swallow his own tongue. Early uses of 'bite the bullet', such as Rudyard Kipling's use in *The Light That Failed* (1891) – 'Bite on the bullet, old man, and don't let them think you're afraid' – retain an idea of using the bullet to control evidence of fear, but nowadays it is used simply to indicate doing something unpleasant or difficult. However, there is something not quite right in this explanation of the origin of the phrase. The bullet used would have to be a cylindrical rifle bullet. The earlier, spherical musket bullets would just have choked a man. Although the principle of rifling guns had been established by the end of the eighteenth century, rifles did not replace the musket until the middle of the nineteenth century, and the modern-shaped bullet, rather than cartridge, that you could bite came even later; they seem not to have been general British Army issue until the 1880s. Anaesthesia was already beginning to be introduced, although no doubt not for the common soldier, by the middle of the nineteenth century. And then there is the consideration of the bullet itself. If you used an unfired bullet there was always the danger of it going off, and you would be reprimanded for wasting ammunition; but would a fired one be in any condition to bite? Finally, it has been said that this custom came from surgery on the battlefield. But surgeons had long used a leather strap to put in the mouths of patients. This served the triple function of giving them something to bite on, stopping them swallowing their tongues and being usable to restrain them. Straps would surely have been taken on to the battlefield by surgeons, so a bullet would not have been needed. It may be significant that the expression does not start appearing in *The Times* database until the 1920s, well after the custom would have disappeared. There is a distinct suggestion of folk myth about the whole thing.

Earlier forms of large-scale warfare have also made their impact. To **hold the fort** has been used figuratively for centuries – a writer in 1592, for instance, described women as 'Having but . . . weak feeble Hands To hold their Honour's Fort unvanquished.' In the nineteenth century, however, two things happened to boost the use of the phrase. First, in 1864 during the American Civil War General Sherman signalled another general to 'Hold the fort!' which became something of a catchphrase in the USA. Then, a few years later, the great American hymnwriters and evangelists Moody and Sankey picked up the expression, and produced a popular hymn with the immortal lines:

> 'Hold the fort, for I am coming,'
> Jesus signals still;
> Wave the answer back to heaven,
> 'By thy grace we will.'

Failure to hold the fort might result in a **last-ditch effort**. The last ditch of your defences would be the final rallying point, your last chance to avoid defeat. William III of England (1689–1702) is supposed to have claimed, 'I will die in the last ditch', and during the American War of Independence the Citizens of Westmoreland issued a grandiloquent proclamation in 1798 saying, 'In War We know but one additional Obligation, To die in the Last Ditch or uphold our Nation.' The expression was being used figuratively by the 1820s. Once the walls of the fort start to go, you need people to **step into the breach**. This seems to be a development of the earlier 'stand in the breach', which is found from the seventeenth century. No doubt use of this expression has been reinforced by Shakespeare's ONCE MORE INTO THE BREACH (see Chapter 7). An attempt to break out of a besieged fort might involve **a forlorn hope**. When this expression was first introduced into English in the late sixteenth century it was as a translation of the Dutch *verloren hoop*, 'lost troop', used of the soldiers who led an attack and were most likely to be killed, or of a skirmishing party. However, instead of choosing 'heap', the nearest English equivalent to the Dutch *hoop*, it was anglicized by the reliably linguistically inept English as 'hope', which introduced almost the opposite idea. This soon started to affect the meaning, and it developed the modern sense of a faint or desperate hope. Any survivors of the forlorn hope would be unlikely to **pass muster**. This comes from military jargon, where a 'muster' meant an inspection, and 'to pass muster' meant to pass the inspection. It is found used figuratively from 1574, and by the eighteenth century was being used frequently enough to count as a cliché. A victorious army would be able to come off the field **with flying colours** – that is, with its flags flying. In the first recorded instance found so far, in *The Play of Dicke of Devonshire* of about 1626, attributed to John Heywood, the expression is used to describe an army that had been defeated, but whose troops were allowed to leave the field in good order, still with their pennons flying, rather than being routed and disgraced. That it has become a cliché and that the metaphor has been lost to many users is shown by the frequency with which the term appears as 'with flying collars'. The same use of colours for a military standard is found in the once popular 'stick to your colours', but **nail your colours to the mast** is self-evidently naval rather than army.

We do not need to look only at the distant past for war clichés.

The Second World War has left a surprising legacy of clichés, and more recent wars have also contributed. Articles on slimming are headlined with tedious frequency the **Battle of the Bulge**. The original Battle of the Bulge was fought in 1944, when the German forces broke through Allied lines and at one point advanced sixty miles into Belgium. The Allies were forced into a desperate action to contain this German breakthrough that formed a bulge in the lines of troops encircling German forces. The expression became popular after a successful film of the same name appeared in 1965. The same campaign to invade Germany brought us a **bridge too far**. This developed after the publication of Cornelius Ryan's 1974 book *A Bridge Too Far*, which was made into a highly successful film in 1977. The book was an account of the part of the Allied operation of 1944 that parachuted troops into Holland to capture eleven bridges needed to secure the approaches to Germany. Lieutenant-General Sir Frederick Browning is supposed to have protested to Field-Marshal Montgomery at the time that eleven might be 'a bridge too far', but this is probably spurious. 'A bridge too far' rapidly degenerated into a formula phrase, much used in headlines. These events were preceded by **D-Day**. In Army jargon, in use since the First World War, D-Day and H-Hour mean the designated day and hour that an operation is due to begin. For most people, however, the historical D-Day means 6 June 1944, when Allied forces landed in Normandy and started an operation that was to lead to the end of the Second World War. Nowadays its meaning has been diluted, and it is often interchangeable with DAY OF RECKONING (see Chapter 9). **Loud and clear**, in the sense 'understandable, emphatically', comes from the use of the expression in military circles to confirm that a message is getting through on communications systems. 'Receiving you, loud and clear' became a well-known expression during the Second World War. The Home Front supplied **make do and mend**. It comes from a Second World War propaganda slogan, used to encourage people either to conserve materials in a time of shortage by mending things rather than replacing, or to make do with what they have (or do without). However, it was based on a combination of 'make' and 'mend' that had been in the language since the fourteenth century. More directly it was a variant of the nineteenth-century naval term 'make and mend', a weekly half-day introduced to provide sailors with time to make and mend their clothes and equipment.

Even more recent events have provided further clichés. **I counted them all out and I counted them all in** is probably now a lapsed cliché, but was much used in the aftermath of the 1982 Falklands War. At the time there were strong feelings among some of the public and journalists that there was too much heavy-handed censorship by the military of what information was allowed to be made public. In one radio report the journalist Brian Hanrahan told listeners, 'I'm not allowed to say how many planes joined the raid, but I counted them all out and I counted them all back.' The neat way in which Hanrahan both revealed the extent of the restrictions and sidestepped them was much appreciated, and the phrase was widely used for some time afterwards. At the start of the First Gulf War, in January 1991, Saddam Hussein declared, 'The great, the jewel and the mother of battles has begun.' During the war the 'mother of all battles' was much cited, often, given the emptiness of Hussein's rhetoric, ironically, and **the mother of all . . .** caught on as a formula phrase. Previously, from the beginning of the century, the **daddy of all . . .** had been used, but usually only in a light-hearted or highly colloquial way. Currently, conflict gives us two clichés: **war on terror**, coined for George Bush after the 9/11 attack on the World Trade Center in New York, and, from the initial invasion of Iraq in 2003, **shock and awe**.

Modern Forces

If we look at clichés from life in the modern Army, we find that they come from both daily life in the forces and the events of armed combat. From the parade ground we find the **rank and file**, troops lined up in ranks (side by side) and files (one behind another), forming a platoon, while the officers stand apart. The term has been used literally since the sixteenth century, and figuratively since the eighteenth, and is particularly a cliché applied to political party members. Any who **get** (or **step**) **out of line** will be in trouble. Although this has been used in the modern sense since at least the 1930s, it has been particularly overused in the last ten years, perhaps as a reflection of the growing conformity of our society. If the troops PASS MUSTER (see above) then their sergeant-major can report to the officer in charge, **all present and correct**. To reach this state the troops will no doubt have expended a fair bit of **spit and polish**. While we think of spit and polish in a literal sense as being strictly a forces process, this technique so beloved by the Army, of raising the high shine on boots by repeated rubbing with a polish-soaked rag lubricated with spit, was also obligatory at the author's school in the so-called swinging sixties. All school shoes were regularly inspected, and those that were not mirror bright were sent back, repeatedly if necessary, for further work. By the late nineteenth century it came to mean all that goes into keeping things excessively neat and clean in barracks, and by the 1920s to mean exaggerated cleaning in general. To do this they would have had to **rise and shine** early. This was originally an example of forces humour, demanding that the sleeping troops should be like the sun and rise and shine at dawn. First recorded in the early twentieth century, it has now become a general term for 'wake up'. The cruder alternative, 'hands off cocks and on with socks', while classable as traditional, is not widely enough used to count as a cliché. **Catch napping** contains the opposite idea.

It is an old expression – in use by Shakespeare's day – and is self-explanatory. Someone who is asleep can be approached without being seen, a particularly dangerous position for a soldier to be found in.

There are a good number of clichés from active service. Expressions like 'an **army of** ants **invading** a house' (or, in a more extreme form, as one journalist wrote recently, 'the **vanguard** of an unimaginable army of insects') are pretty clichéd uses of the whole idea of an 'army'. Overuse of such terms can be dangerous. To quote from another newspaper:

There was a slightly uncomfortable collision between figurative and literal speech in this paper earlier this week. On Tuesday, the caption to a photograph of British troops in Iraq explained that the soldiers it depicted had '**come under fire**', near Basra, while the opening sentence of the adjacent article reported that Tony Blair 'came under fire in the Commons . . . yesterday'. By accident, I guess, a familiar cliché of parliamentary journalism had been reconnected to its origins and the result was a galvanic jolt. (Thomas Sutcliffe, *Independent*, 23 May 2006)

Images from war in general are much used to describe any conflict, but have a special role in the area of class conflict. How far this can go is demonstrated in another quote from the *Independent*, from a letter on banning fox hunting: 'Too much **ground** had been **given** to the **class-warriors** and inverted snobs within the party who love a bit of **toff-bashing** even if it means RIDING ROUGHSHOD OVER [see Chapter 22] civil liberties.' Since the invasion of Iraq we have been exposed to all the old clichés for describing fighting. We are told the **battle raged around** the soldiers (also popular metaphorically), that **crack troops** have been involved, and that **chaos and carnage** reign. The war has also led to an increase in the sort of double vision that Thomas Sutcliffe describes above. The fact that we are meeting military expressions in their literal senses is altering the way we respond to them. If you read that someone has come under **heavy flak**, is this severe criticism (alternative cliché, to come under a **barrage of criticism**) or literal? Until the recent **outbreak of hostilities** such clichés were dying metaphors. Suddenly they seem real again. In addition, a number of new clichés have developed, or older ones become more common. The American **not on my watch** (a favourite of politicians trying to identify with the military) has recently passed into British English, and to **watch someone's back** now occurs in the military buddy sense of 'to look out for someone' much more frequently than the older clichéd sense of a warning that you might be STABBED IN THE BACK (see Chapter 14). To **save the day** does not seem to have been affected, but a **shot in the dark**, in the sense of a wild guess, may be a little too close to reality not to have declined. A **smoking gun**, for a clue or evidence that will **give the game away**, and that comes from the world of the detective rather than the military, is, however, increasing.

If we move to the world of officers and of the strategy they make, we find a further clutch of clichés. The officers themselves can be classed as **top brass**, which was originally an American expression. It comes from a disrespectful allusion to the gold braid worn on officers' hats (known as 'scrambled eggs' in the UK). Such people became known as 'brass hats' and then, from the late nineteenth century, they became 'big brass'. 'Top brass' was in turn a development of 'big brass', which then spread rapidly to bosses in general. Alternatively, you could call people in charge **big guns** or **big shots**. 'Big guns' in this sense dates from the early nineteenth century; but the alternative sense – bringing up the heavy artillery to bully someone into doing what you want – is more recent. When **zero hour**, which dates from the First World War, comes the officers may decide to **steal a march** on their enemy. This expression was being used literally for 'manoeuvre by stealth into a position the enemy does not know about' in the Middle Ages, and was being used in the modern way by the eighteenth century. Alternatively they could **stand their ground**, an expression used from about 1700 to mean 'to hold a position'. It began to be used figuratively in the nineteenth century. Similarly they could **make a stand** or **stand and fight**. The subtle difference here is that to 'stand your ground' is simply not to retreat when attacked, while the other two phrases contain a suggestion of possible defeat, and so may be the action of those who **fight a losing battle**. Metaphorically, someone who makes a stand can be said to **take up arms** in defence of their cause. 'Make a stand' has been used in a military sense since the seventeenth century, and figuratively since the late eighteenth. If the troops do lose their battle, it is to be hoped that the enemy do not decide to **take no prisoners** (a fairly recent business cliché indicating a ruthless **fight to the death** in pursuit of the company's aims) but will look after the **walking wounded**, originally a military term to distinguish those who can get themselves off the battlefield from those who are stretcher cases, first recorded in the First World War. Unlike their troops, defeated generals can still claim the **moral high ground**, currently a very popular term. While in the past generals would seek the high ground either as a **vantage point** from which to direct a battle, or else as a desirable position because it was difficult to attack, those who take the *moral* high ground simply use it as a place from which to look down on those that who other views.

The Army is not the only service that has given us clichés. The Air Force has yet to make a **significant impact**, although it has been a rich source of slang, dealt with elsewhere in this book. The Navy, on the other hand, has provided us with many clichés. For convenience all those relating to the sea and shipping have been included in this section, even if civilian. Not strictly a cliché, but still a source of discomfort for purists, is the current use of the term **careen** to mean something like the verb 'career', as in the radio announcement that 'The Genesis capsule came careening into the atmosphere today' (Radio 4, 6 September 2006). 'Career' is a technical term used when you put a ship on its side to clean or repair the underneath, a state of static helplessness very different from the violent motion suggested by the changed use. This new use seems to have developed in the early twentieth century, and is first recorded in the USA. There are two other terms used of a ship out of water. 'Hard', in nautical terms, is used to mean 'secure, securely', so that a ship that is hard aground is not easily going to be refloated. **Hard and fast** was used to describe a ship in dry dock or similarly out of the water, with 'fast' meaning firm. **High and dry** has much the same sense, being used either for a ship in dry dock or for one stranded out of water. Both were being used figuratively by the mid nineteenth century. You have a ship in dry dock to build or repair it. When you launch a new ship you crack a bottle on it and probably have a bit of a party afterwards. This ceremony was the origin of the term **push the boat out**, originally (from the 1930s) used to mean 'to buy a round of drinks', but now used to mean 'spend lavishly' in general. A new ship will be **spick and span**. This expression, which keeps alive two otherwise obsolete words, was originally applied to ships, when it meant 'brand new'. 'Spick' is a form of 'spike' and referred to nails; 'span' is a chip of wood, and a spick-and-span new ship would have everything new, down to these little bits. The expression is found used literally from the sixteenth century, and began to be used of something so neat and tidy it looked new in the nineteenth. Once the ship is on the water, passengers will have to **get on board**. The overuse of this term, used as an alternative to the sporting **join the team**, is comparatively recent. Those left behind will have **missed the boat**, which, in its clichéd use, seems to date from the 1930s. If the passengers are lucky, it will all be **plain sailing**. This was originally 'plane sailing', the art of navigating by plotting your position as if the world were a flat plane rather than a sphere, which works for short, simple journeys. By the mid eighteenth century this had become 'plain sailing' used in the sense 'easy sailing', avoiding **troubled waters**. The ship may travel **at a rate of knots** (a knot in this sense having originally been one of a series of knots on a rope used to judge the speed of a ship by measuring the rate of knots running out behind the ship in a given time) providing no one **rocks the boat** (a cliché of the 1920s) until it can finally **drop anchor** in a **safe haven**. 'Haven' is another word that is kept current by its clichéd use. It was much used in the 1990s during the wars in former Yugoslavia, and is also popular jargon in the financial world for a safe investment. The idea of somewhere providing shelter for a ship also being used to mean 'spiritual refuge' is an old one. John Wesley used the word 'haven' to mean 'heaven' in one of his popular hymns, 'In Temptation' (1740): 'Jesu, lover of my soul, / Let me to thy bosom fly . . . Safe into the haven guide, / O receive my soul at last', an idea that Gerald Manley Hopkins picks up in his 1864 poem 'Heaven-Haven'. In worldly terms, a year after Hopkins's poem, someone was writing in *The Times* about 'One safe haven where no nicotine perfume intrudes', which has a remarkably modern ring.

To be guided to a safe haven a ship may need a **leading light**. This is an alternative to GUIDING LIGHT (see Chapter 16), a light that a ship can follow safely into a harbour. *Luminary* is a more grandiose term with the same idea. The popularity of 'leading light' may have been influenced by an association with Cardinal Newman's immensely popular 1834 hymn 'Lead, kindly light'. When leaving the haven the ship may have to **stem the tide**. According to the normal rules, this expression should not exist. There are two possible meanings of 'to stem', with opposite senses, and usually in such cases one of the words drops out of use, thereby avoiding confusion. (The classic example of this is when, in the sixteenth century, changes in pronunciation meant that the words 'Queen' and 'quean', the latter an insulting term for a woman, came to be pronounced in the same way. You find the occasional 'quean' in Shakespeare and his contemporaries, but it disappears soon after.) The usual meaning of 'to stem' is 'to stop', but a ship that stems the tide is one that is making headway against it, travelling in the direction the tide is coming from – yet another example of words kept alive by clichés. The ship will then have to **steer clear of** the shoals, a phrase which was being used in the modern way by the early eighteenth century.

The above are all general shipping terms, but the following come from the Navy proper. Before going into battle a ship needs to **clear the decks** of anything that might get in the way. Anyone who has visited one of the old ships of the line that have survived will know under what cramped conditions sailors worked, and how easily the everyday things they were surrounded with could become lethal in a battle. The expression is used in two senses – to tidy up or make everything shipshape, and to get ready for action. The literal sense is found from the middle of the eighteenth century, but the figurative is a cliché of the nineteenth century. One of the things that could have got in the way was a **loose cannon**. Weighing several tons, guns on sailing ships were only secured by ropes, for a degree of movement was needed to take up the recoil. If one came loose in a storm or battle it could do incalculable damage to both people and the ship. **Son of a gun** is said to be a term for someone born in the shadow of the guns to one of the women who often travelled illicitly with sailors. Used as a jocular or disparaging term for a person, or, in the USA, as a largely meaningless exclamation, it is recorded from 1708, used much as we do today. In Admiral W. H. Smyth's *Sailor's Word-Book* (1867) there is a statement that it is 'an epithet conveying contempt in a slight degree, and originally applied to boys born afloat, when women were permitted to accompany their husbands to sea; one admiral declared he literally was thus cradled, under the breast of a gun-carriage.' Some commentators, however, have doubted that it comes from being born on a gun-deck, and think that it is simply a rhyming euphemism for 'son of a bitch'. The term is also found in other languages, the name of the Russian author Pushkin translating literally as 'son of a gun'.

Women and children first is also from the Navy, although for once we can link a cliché to a particular event: the wreck of the *Birkenhead* in 1852. One of the first iron ships commissioned by the Navy, the *Birkenhead* was a troop-ship sailing to South Africa. She struck a rock off the Cape of Good Hope (now known as the Birkenhead Rock) and went down with 487 officers and men in shark-infested waters. The wreck became famous, the subject of many paintings and poems, because of the unusual discipline shown by the troops in evacuating the ship, ensuring that the women and children really were put in the lifeboats first and saved.

12. The Law and Logic

Historically, the study of logic has always been linked to preparation for a legal career, the training in the former being seen as the best way to win your argument in the latter, so I have kept the link here. Some of the clichés from the law are still very obviously connected with the courts; some are so generally used that we tend to forget their legal connections; and others have been so well absorbed into the language that their legal connections are only recognized by specialists.

The law

Perhaps the only law to have become a cliché is the Riot Act of 1716. The provisions of this were that if twelve or more were gathered together and someone in authority read a certain portion of the act out loud, those people automatically became criminals if they did not disperse within the hour. The act was not repealed until 1973. By the early nineteenth century **to read the riot act** had become another way of saying 'to issue a severe warning or telling off' about someone's behaviour. The use of **charter**, on the other hand, to mean a licence to do something that the speaker objects to, is a recent but popular cliché, particularly in the red-top newspapers, which love to write in outrage at something being, for example, 'a scrounger's charter'. 'Out of court' is a legal expression used of someone who has lost their right to be heard in court. Thus **laughed out of court** originally meant something so ridiculous or comic that it would have no right to be considered. As a concept it goes back to ancient Rome where Horace wrote, 'The case will be dismissed with a laugh. You will get off scot-free' (*Satires*, Book 2, No. 3). As an expression of general ridicule it dates from the early twentieth century. The transfer of the term **the jury's out on** from the law courts to a general judgement seems to have happened in the twentieth century. The first example I have found is from 1971, but it has been used metaphorically in earlier examples, although not in this sense, and the change in meaning is probably earlier than 1971. If you have been arrested by the **strong arm of (the law)**, you may hope to escape through a **legal loophole**. In the days when might and right went hand in hand, a strong arm represented power, and has been used to mean this since the early seventeenth century. However, the form 'the strong arm of . . .' did not become common until the nineteenth century, then and now most commonly used of the law – perhaps because it is combined in people's minds with the **long arm of the law** (from its ability to reach everywhere) to mean something that can both reach far and impose its will. The use of 'loophole' to mean something that allows you to get round the spirit of a law while sticking to the letter of it has a surprisingly long history. Why a narrow opening designed to shoot an arrow through or to let in light should become a means of escape is not quite clear. Perhaps the idea is of something you can just squeeze through; perhaps it is influenced by the old Dutch word *loopgat*, of much the same meaning, where *loop-* comes from 'to run' and *-gat* means 'hole'. Whatever the reason for the change in its meaning, it had occurred by the middle of the seventeenth century, and is usually used of the law. The alliterative 'legal loophole' is first found in 1768, in the form: 'A legal loop-hole . . . for a rogue now and then to creep through.' Witnesses under oath have to swear to tell **the truth, the whole truth and nothing but the truth**, which has in turn become a formula phrase. The *OED* first records it outside a legal sense in 1931 in the extraordinary line 'The truth, the whole truth, and no cray-fishing, so help me God' (V. Palmer, *Separate Lives*). Clichés that contain the word 'law' include that favourite of politicians, **law and order**. Aristotle wrote that 'Law means good order' in his *Politics* in the fourth century BC, and the two concepts are a natural coupling. As a cliché, however, 'law and order' has been used as a political rallying cry since at least the mid nineteenth century. In recent British political history the call for more law and order often seems to have carried a jinx, and to have been the precursor of some scandal. Politicians also like to **lay down the law**. 'To lay down', here, is used in an old sense of 'to establish, formulate' and 'to lay down the law' originally meant, and in some cases still does, 'to interpret the meaning of the law', 'to legislate'. In the sense 'to be dogmatic or pontificate' it dates from the nineteenth century. Some people may seem to be a **law unto themselves**. 'These [Gentiles] . . . are a law unto themselves' is a quotation from the Bible (Romans 2:14). Although the *OED* does not record its use as an expression meaning 'to set your own rules', 'to be unconventional, unpredictable', until the late nineteenth century, it can be found in *The Times* by 1824. In modern use it is often used with resignation, if not outright disapproval, but in the original biblical epistle it was used approvingly, for Paul says that those outside the law of the Jews, by following it, become part of the law. Even those who like to go their own way will find there are **unwritten laws**. In a literal sense there is a distinction between the written parliamentary laws of Britain, and the traditional unwritten law that is the basis of common law. In this sense the expression was in use in the Middle Ages. It was transferred to mean 'generally accepted conventions and concepts' in the seventeenth century. Sometimes it gets confused by writers with the LAW OF THE JUNGLE (see Chapter 22), and we find uses such as 'She had always accepted the unwritten law of the pop jungle – all publicity is good' (Sasha Stone, *Kylie Monogue*, 1989).

Among those expressions that we use without considering their legal implications is **to give someone the benefit of the doubt**. In law you are innocent until proved guilty, and if there is any doubt about your guilt, you must be given the benefit of the doubt and considered innocent. 'Benefit of the doubt' began to be used figuratively in the nineteenth century, and had become a cliché by the end of that century. **Hue and cry**, which has existed as a legal phrase since the thirteenth century, used for an outcry raised while hunting a criminal, literally means 'noise and cry'. By the nineteenth century it was being used metaphorically, and nowadays is sometimes diluted to mean little more than 'fuss'. The frequent misspelling 'hew' shows that knowledge of the origin is being lost. In the cliché **throw the book at someone**, the book referred to is the one containing the laws, or more generally the rule book, and 'throw' reflects the element of indiscriminate accusation suggested by the expression. It has been in use since the 1930s. If you do something **by the book**, which dates from the mid nineteenth century, you are again following the rules or law.

To **come of age**, meaning 'to reach the age of majority and legal responsibility', is a sign of maturity, and in recent years 'come of age' has come more and more to be used figuratively to mean 'matured'. To **come into your own** is derived from the same idea, that of taking control of one's own affairs when one has reached the necessary legal age. One thing you can do at eighteen is to put your name to a contract, but if you enter into a contract to supply something, you must **deliver the goods**. The term has been in use from the eighteenth century. Its modern use, 'to perform as expected', does not seem to have developed until the middle of the twentieth century. When you get a **new lease of life** you are using the image of a lease on something abstract, which goes back to the sixteenth century when the Countess of Pembroke wrote of 'A lease of bliss with endless date'; there is also Shakespeare's famous 'Summer's lease hath all too short a date' (Sonnet 18). The idea of someone who has recovered from illness taking on a new lease of (or on) life is recorded from the beginning of the nineteenth century, and had been transferred to mean a more general renewal before the end of that century.

Less obviously legal is **after due consideration**. 'Due consideration' has a quasi-legal meaning, in that if you can be shown to have acted without the consideration due to something, then you can be in trouble. In this sense, the wording has been around since the sixteenth century. From this has come the cliché, popular in business letters and formal pronouncements, meant to imply serious thought, but in fact adding little or nothing to a statement. To **call in(to) question** goes back to the days when lawyers all had fluent Latin, so they would be familiar with the Latin legal term *in dubium vocare*, meaning 'to call in question, or doubt'. This literal translation appeared in English by the late sixteenth century, and from the start, although it was also used in the legal sense of 'to summon for trial', was used in contexts where a simple 'question' would do just as well. 'Call into . . .' was an alternative form of the expression from the first, and this is now the commoner form, although 'call in' was the norm until the twentieth century, and is still much used in the States. If you do something with **malice aforethought** you are using a legal term for premeditated harm, what in law distinguishes murder from manslaughter. The date at which this was transferred to more general speech is not known, but is probably relatively recent. Many English expressions that repeat the same idea in two ways within one phrase come from legal language, where lawyers have tried to cover themselves against misinterpretation of their words or people weaselling out of the spirit of the law while obeying the letter of the law. One example of this is **part and parcel**. 'Parcel' here is used in the original sense of the word – a small part, a particle – rather than in its modern sense of something you get through the post. Thus 'part and parcel', in use in a legal sense from the sixteenth century, means 'part and sub-division of that part'. It has been used more generally to mean 'all', 'every bit', since at least the beginning of the nineteenth century. Another of these doublets is **all and sundry**. This has been in use since the fourteenth century. **Flotsam and jetsam** comes from ancient maritime law, where flotsam, from the French *floter*, 'to float', is salvage found floating on the waves, and jetsam, a shortening of 'jettison', that which has been deliberately thrown overboard. By the nineteenth century this had become a cliché for odds and ends, while terms such as 'human flotsam' have been much used to describe the outcasts of society in modern times. The **man on the Clapham omnibus** also has a legal origin. **The man in the street** is a nineteenth-century expression for the ordinary man, and should perhaps escape the stigma of being a cliché on the grounds that substitutes usually have a political or social implication. The elaboration or elevation of this expression comes from Judge Lord Bowen, who, during a trial in 1903, asked the jury to interpret a point in the case from the point of view of the average man, saying, 'We must ask ourselves what the man on the Clapham omnibus would think.' For some reason the expression struck the public imagination, and has stuck in the language. **Vested interest** is a cliché with a complicated history. 'Vested' originally meant 'dressed', particularly of priests in their vestments. Special clothing or uniforms are worn to show that you have a right to be what you claim to be, that you have been invested in a certain rank, and by the eighteenth century 'vested' had come to mean 'established', 'definitely assigned to something or someone'. By the early nineteenth century 'vested interest' had become a legal term meaning 'a right to property', and from there it was transferred to mean 'a personal involvement or stake in something'.

Logic

If we turn to the area of logic and debate used to train lawyers in the past we find first of all the **moot point**. 'Moot' started life as an Anglo-Saxon term for a meeting, and by the early Middle Ages had acquired the sense of a discussion. From the sixteenth century it was also used for a special gathering of law students, where interesting points of law were examined via hypothetical cases (a practice and term that live on in university law departments). Thus a moot point was originally something worthy of debate in a moot. By the eighteenth century the term had spread to cover any debatable question. A moot point can also be a **vexed question**. This is a literal translation of a Latin term, *vexata quaestio*, where the 'vexed' part has the meaning 'troublesome, difficult', a vexed question being something that needs debate. It has been in use in this sense since the seventeenth century, but modern use tends to be influenced by the more usual sense of vexed, 'irritated, angry'. **Beg the question** is another term from logical debate, and although perhaps not a cliché is certainly an abused phrase. It is a bad translation of the Latin *petitio principii*, and in origin did not have any sense of 'lead one to ask'. Rather 'beg' here means 'take for granted' and the expression originally meant that a speaker had taken as already proved something he was asserting, but which may be a circular argument or a logical fallacy. Another such term that has had its meaning reversed is **the exception that proves the rule**. The original meaning of this expression (in use in English by 1640, but based on a Latin saying) was that the fact that there *can* be an exception proves that there is a rule, for otherwise it could not be broken, 'prove' here having the sense 'test'. Nowadays it is often used simply as a comment on something that does not fit an expected pattern, or which has gone wrong.

We end with two historical expressions. **Draconian measures**, **powers** or **punishment** goes back to events of the seventh century BC, when the city of Athens appointed a man called Draco to reform its laws. He took punishment for crimes out of the private sphere and handed it over to the state. Traditionally – although modern scholars doubt this – Draco's laws were very severe. When he was asked why most crimes were punished with death he is said to have replied that small offences deserved death and he knew of no severer penalty for great ones. It was said that he wrote his laws in blood not ink. Most of these laws were repealed a century later, but their reputation lived on. However, the word 'Draconian' only appeared in English in the nineteenth century (although 'draconical' was used from the seventeenth), and set phrases such as 'Draconian powers' only became clichés of journalism in the middle of the twentieth century. The fact that the word is now often written with a small 'd' shows how thoroughly it has been absorbed into the language. The history of something being written in **letters of fire** is rather obscure. It sounds biblical, but is not. In ancient Scottish law there was a process known as 'letters of fire and sword', a licence for the authorities to use force against a wrong-doer. Such warrants, for instance, were drawn up in the expectation of trouble from the Highlanders when James II was deposed, and provided some legal basis for the massacre of Glencoe in 1692. This would appear to lie behind the expression, with, again, a popular misunderstanding of the word 'letters' – originally meaning 'documents' but now understood to be letters of the alphabet. However, there may be an alternative origin, for in 1797 *The Times* printed a report from Paris of the Revolutionary French celebrations of the anniversary of the abolition of the monarchy, containing the remarkable information that 'At nine at night a splendid fire-work was played off in front of the Camp, when the words "*Liberty or Death!*" appeared written in letters of fire.' Whatever its history, it was in use figuratively by the 1830s.

13. Transport and Travel

Wandering through the world

Travellers **go out into the world** or **a world away** in search of **new horizons** (this last in use by the early nineteenth century) or to feel **worlds apart** (twentieth century). They often travel to the **ends of the earth**, a cliché from at least the nineteenth century, which comes from Psalm 65: 'O God of our salvation: who art the confidence of all the ends of the earth.' The similar **four corners of the earth** or **world** is also found in the Bible (Isaiah 11:12 and Revelation 7:1). The persistence of an expression once it has become fixed is evident in the way that no one is uncomfortable with these phrases, despite the fact that flat-earthers are now FEW AND FAR BETWEEN (see Chapter 7). Travellers are often looking for both novelty and comfort – **the best of both worlds**. This has been linked to Voltaire's 'all is for the best in the best of all possible worlds' ('*tout est pour le mieux dans le meilleur des mondes possibles*', *Candide*, 1759), but although the common linking of 'best' and 'world' may have reinforced use, the connection does not seem essential. More work needs to be done on the history of the expression. It was certainly well-enough established by 1853 for Thomas Binney to have published a book called *Is it Possible to Make the Best of Both Worlds?*, which was reissued in 1895 as simply *The Best of Both Worlds*. It **goes with the territory** (twentieth century – perhaps a use of territory in the sense used by travelling salesmen) that the traveller **scours the area** for things of interest. 'Scour' is a confusing verb, with two meanings. You can scour pans to get them clean in one sense, but the other sense, to search restlessly, is rarely found other than in 'scour the area' and the occasional 'scour the shops for something'. Of course, the traveller may not have gone willingly. They may have been **sent packing** by people who want to **put a distance** between themselves and the traveller. 'To pack' has been used to mean 'to send someone away' since the beginning of the sixteenth century, and is still found in the expression 'to pack someone off somewhere'. It is from this sense that the term 'to send someone packing' comes. It may be because they have *gone too far*. The opposite to this is the recent horror – **don't go there**.

Roads

Roads themselves have provided many images that have in turn become clichés. You can make life easier for people if you **pave the way** for them (used since the sixteenth century) until they reach the **end of the road,** which rarely means more than 'the end'. The use of 'end of the road' as a cliché may owe something to the 1924 song '(Keep Right on to) The End of the Road', by Harry Lauder and William Dillon, for the expression is not recorded before then. The variant, **end of the line**, from railroads, is not found until nearly twenty-five years later. If you come to **a parting of the ways** you are at a junction or **at the crossroads**. 'A parting of the ways' has been used in the literal sense since the Bible: 'The king of Babylon stood at the parting of the way, at the head of the two ways' (Ezekiel 21:21). It took until the nineteenth century before it was transferred to mean people *going down different paths* in their lives, a separation of some sort. 'At the crossroads' has been used since the same century as a cliché for a point in life where decisions have to be made about which path in life to choose. The expression is also used semi-literally of larger geographical features, such as 'the crossroads of Europe'. Alternatively you may **turn the corner**. A rather puzzling expression, if you think about it literally, usually used of financial recovery, but also of things like illness.

This use dates from the nineteenth century. Since it can also mean to pass round the corner of a racecourse, perhaps it comes from the idea of approaching the HOME STRETCH (see Chapter 22), with the *end in sight*. In the eighteenth century it was a rather charming term for those who were out of sight because they had *passed on*. **Ins and outs** is found from the late seventeenth century, although it did not really become established until the nineteenth. The image is of the intricacies of the situation being like the twists and turns of a winding path. You can also **explore every avenue**. 'Avenue' comes ultimately from the Latin for 'to come towards, approach', and its original meaning in English (from about 1600) was an approach. This became a standard military term for a way of access, a passage, the sort of thing a wise commander would make sure was thoroughly explored before he took his troops through it. However, 'to explore every avenue' did not become a cliché until the twentieth century. According to an article in the *London Morning Post* in 1936, quoted in James Rogers' *Dictionary of Clichés*, it was 'invented by the Marquis of Landsdowne when he was Foreign Secretary at the turn of the century' and has 'exercised a mortal fascination over politicians . . . The exploring of avenues has become one of the main preoccupations of political life.' An alternative cliché with the same meaning is **leave no stone unturned**. The source of this expression goes back to the fifth century BC and the Greek playwright Euripides, who tells the story of how the Persians were defeated at the Battle of Plataea in 477 BC. Their general, Mardonius, was said to have left behind a great treasure, and when Polycrates of Thebes could not find this, he asked the Delphic Oracle for help. He was given the advice 'Move every stone', which, in the form we now use, had entered the language by the middle of the sixteenth century. The reversed form, **leave no turn unstoned**, has all but become an independent theatrical cliché. Finally, there is **the middle of the road**. This expression has acquired a variety of connotations, which can range from approving moderation to outright scorn. In politics it can still be used to indicate lack of extremism; in general application it indicates average, for good or bad; but in music, while it can just mean music with mass appeal, it is often a term of condemnation, particularly when shortened to MOR.

Transport

Transport also supplies a number of clichés, whether it be going in **fits and starts** or travel in **the fast lane**. 'Fits and starts' – both words rarely used in these senses outside this set phrase – has been in regular use since the early seventeenth century. The term 'fast lane', in its literal sense, is only recorded in English from 1966, yet by 1978 an American magazine was writing of 'the image usually associated with the superjet, "fast lane" set', showing how quickly a descriptive phrase can move from creation to figurative use to cliché. Those who LIVE LIFE IN THE FAST LANE (see Chapter 18) must, of course, accept the risk that they will LIVE FAST, DIE YOUNG (see Chapter 6). You may show **get up and go** (an expression originating in the USA in the form 'get up and get' or 'get up and git', which is found as early as 1864; the joke 'my get up and go got up and went' almost qualifies as a cliché in its own right) or not know if you are **coming or going**. This term for being confused or in a whirl is not well attested before the twentieth century, but that it was well established by the late nineteenth century is suggested by the characters of Mr Cummings and Mr Gowing, friends of the immortal Charles Pooter in George and Weedon Grossmith's *Diary of a Nobody* (1892). If you are **going places** (a twentieth-century expression from the USA, first used in a literal sense meaning 'to go out and about', but by the 1930s being used to mean 'to get ahead or be successful') you may **continue apace**. This set phrase is the only time most people will ever use the word 'apace'. It comes from the Old French *a pas*, literally 'at pace', understood as 'at a considerable pace, quickly'. The expression has been ignored by philologists, and little is known of its history, but it does not seem to have become a cliché until the beginning of the twentieth century. The earliest quotation I have been able to find in *The Times* is a report from Japan of 1903 which says, 'War preparations continue apace, and naval transports are ready to sail.' You may be **in for a bumpy ride** – in popular speech sometimes a misquote of Bette Davis's remark in the 1950 film *All About Eve*, written by Joseph L. Mankiewicz, 'Fasten your seat-belts, it's going to be a bumpy night', meaning 'look out, here comes trouble.' In which case you have to hope you do not have to **go the extra mile, down a long, hard road**. 'The extra mile' is based on a passage from the Bible (Matthew 5:43): 'Whosoever shall compel thee to go a mile, go with him twain', one of the precepts for Christian conduct that goes with 'turn the other cheek'. This instruction derives from the power of officials in the Roman Empire to make inhabitants of occupied territories do forced labour, such as acting as porters, at little or no notice. Although 'road' has been used metaphorically since the days of Shakespeare, as have versions of the proverb 'it's a long road that has no turning', both 'a long road' and 'to go down a long, hard road' seem to be modern. **Royal road** for 'an easy path' has been used since the eighteenth century, but cannot really be taken back beyond that, for the saying attributed to Euclid (who lived about 300 BC) in which he told Ptolemy I 'there is no royal road to geometry' should strictly be translated 'no royal short cut'. **Going forward**, a comparatively recent import from America, sees an unnecessary addition to 'go ahead' (another, older American import) and 'progress', both of which use the same image. If you are out of reserves, near to grinding to a halt, then you are **running on empty**. Another development from the USA, this expression spread after the success of Jackson Browne's 1978 song 'Runnin' on Empty'. Our final car-based cliché is the **U-turn**. This image of a car turning round and going back the way it came has been a popular cliché since the 1980s. It is nowadays almost invariably used of any change in government policy. It is something to be avoided in **two-way traffic** or **street** (only used to mean 'reciprocal' since the 1950s). Other driving-based clichés, all obviously relatively modern and needing no explanation, are **road map**, **move up a gear**, **take a back seat**, **go down the same road**, **streets ahead**, and **a one-way street**.

Foot-based travel is found in a **step in the right direction**. A cliché from the later nineteenth century, this is one of a number of expressions, like *putting your best foot forward*, that equates life with a journey. Surprise can **stop you in your tracks**. This is one of a number of related terms expressing human movement in terms of tracks – *make tracks, lose track of, cover your tracks* and so on. **Fleet of foot**, thankfully a dying cliché, was much used in the nineteenth century. It has the feel of a quotation cliché, but if so it has yet to be traced. To **walk a lonely road** is a cliché from the MAN'S GOTTA DO WHAT A MAN'S GOTTA DO (see Chapter 7) school of literature and film. It is a member of a group of related phrases that have spread through the language, from clichés like A LONG, HARD ROAD, above, to Bob Dylan's Zen-like 'How many roads must a man walk down/Before you can call him a man?' ('Blowin' in the Wind', 1962). **Plough a lonely furrow** has been used in the same sense since the nineteenth century. Another archaism, this time more common, is to **wend your way**, much used in the nineteenth century to replace the simple 'go'. 'Wend' was the standard Anglo-Saxon word for 'to go' in the sense of 'travel', and all but died out at the end of the Middle Ages except in dialect and a few technical senses, although Shakespeare does use it three times. It was revived in about 1800 by Sir Walter Scott and similar writers of medieval romances at the beginning of the nineteenth century, and this particular phrase stuck in the language thereafter. The verb 'wend' does, however, still survive in one form in everyday speech, for its past tense was 'went', adopted as the past of the irregular verb 'to go'.

Other forms of transport also have their clichés. Trains give us **hit the buffers**. The buffers are there on the railway line to make sure a train comes to a full stop at the END OF THE LINE (see above), hence 'to hit the buffers' means either to grind to a halt or to run out of control. Its history has been surprisingly neglected, but it seems to be a twentieth-century term. A search of *The Times* archive (which runs up to 1985) does not record even a literal use until 1928. Anything approaching a figurative use does not appear before the 1980s, and even then the examples are all still linked to trains, whereas a search of the Internet will show ample current use with no train connection. The first example of figurative use dates from 1981, although the context shows that it was in use earlier:

Many . . . echo the view once expressed by the late Iain Macleod of Mr Enoch Powell on economic policy. 'He's a marvellous companion on a train journey, but you need to jump off before you hit the buffers.'

A headline the following year looks promising, reading, 'Sir Peter Hit the Buffers', but while this suggests that the expression was being used in the alternative modern sense by then, it is clear from the article that 'Sir Peter' is Sir Peter Parker, Chairman of British Rail, and that the piece is about his problems negotiating with rail unions. Miles Kington uses 'his train of thought hit the buffers' the same year. In 1984 we find the line 'after two days, that line of conversation had already hit the buffers', which looks like the modern use – but even then it appears in an article about the sponsorship of a sporting event by Intercity Trains! A train that is **off the track** will need work before being **back on track** (twentieth-century clichés). Shipping has mainly been dealt with elsewhere, but also gives us to **enter calmer water** and to have **hidden depths. Across the pond** (or **over**, or **on this side of the pond**) can apply to shipping or aeroplanes. 'Pond' has been used humorously for the sea since the seventeenth century, and has been found for the Atlantic since the later eighteenth. **Touch and go**, first found in the seventeenth century, has been used as a cliché since the nineteenth century, originally to refer to something a bit closer than a near miss, where vehicles touch each other in a glancing blow but do not actually crash. The phrase is also used in aviation, where 'touch and go' is used to describe a manoeuvre where a plane touches down and then immediately takes off. Transport in general is covered by the punning use of **transports of delight**. 'Transports', for keen emotional feelings, has been in use since the middle of the seventeenth century, but the *OED* has no record of 'transports of delight', although it does have a 'transports of joy' from 1715. This suggests that the expression may not have become a cliché until the twentieth century. It was certainly well-enough established by 1960 for Flanders and Swann to use it as the title of a song about London buses, and the expression now lives a double life as a straightforward cliché and a punning one used by travel writers.

14. Politics, Politicians and Weasels

The language of politics is one of the most cliché-ridden areas of English. This is not surprising, as clichés are both efficient and effective for political purposes. They are instantly recognizable, do not encourage critical thinking, and one of the things they do best is to communicate vague and often emotive sentiment. Thus they are obviously perfect tools for political speeches. This chapter will deal not only with those clichés coined by or associated with particular politicians, but also with specifically political clichés, finishing with a collection of weasel words and expressions which, while often used by politicians, are not exclusive to them.

Quotations

Thanks to the radio and other media, political speeches still have a wide audience, and the language used in them can be very influential. What is perhaps more surprising is the way in which some of these sayings have lasted – in a number of cases for hundreds of years. The oldest such phrase is **let well alone**. This was the motto of the eighteenth-century Prime Minister Sir Robert Walpole (1676–1745), although as a proverb it goes back to the sixteenth century. In the UK today, 'leave' is often substituted for 'let' as the latter is now rather archaic, but in the States 'let' is still current. **The tyranny of the masses**, an expression mainly used in political circles to sum up the dangers of democracy, comes from Alexis de Tocqueville's 1835 book *Democracy in America*. **Snare and delusion** is a simplification of a judgement given by Lord Denman, the Lord Chief Justice, in the House of Lords in 1844, when he said that without reforms 'trial by jury itself, instead of being a security to persons who are accused, will be a delusion, a mockery and a snare.' This expression was immediately picked up, particularly by other political figures, and much used. By 1851 it was being simplified to 'delusion and snare', and appears in its modern form by 1856. You might not associate the expression to be **on the side of the angels** with politics, but it comes from a speech given by Benjamin Disraeli in 1864, on the then hotly debated subject of evolution: 'Is man an ape or an angel? Now I am on the side of the angels.' Still in the nineteenth century we come to **drop the pilot**. This rather dated cliché comes from a *Punch* cartoon drawn by Sir John Tenniel (illustrator of Lewis Carroll's *Alice* books) in 1890. It was inspired by events in Germany, when the Kaiser forced Bismarck to resign as Chancellor, after he had piloted his country through political difficulties for many years. The cartoon showed Bismarck leaving a ship, dressed in the sort of uniform a pilot who guided big ships through difficult waters would have worn, and had the caption 'Dropping the Pilot' (an expression used for the point when the pilot disembarked and the ship was left to make its own way). Although not met with regularly, this expression is still used when some prominent leader is sacked, and was very much in evidence when Mrs Thatcher was ousted from power in 1990 and again when Helmut Kohl lost his post as Chancellor of Germany in 1998. In 1896 the Canadian politician Sir George Foster delivered his *Official Report of the Debates of the House of Commons of the Dominion of Canada*, which contained the words: 'In these some-what troublesome days when the great Mother Empire stands splendidly isolated in Europe'. *The Times* reported this the next day under the headline '**Splendid isolation**' and thus was a new cliché born. We return to Germany, via France, for **place in the sun**. The French philosopher, theologian and mathematician Blaise Pascale (1623–62) wrote in his *Pensées*: 'This dog is mine, the poor children would say; this is my place in the sun;

in this is the beginning and picture of the usurpation of the World.' Modern use of the expression comes from the period of expanding rival empires and the build-up to the First World War. Germany wanted to expand its empire in both the East and Africa, much of which was already occupied by the British and others. Picking up on Pascale, in 1897 the then German Chancellor, Bernard von Bülow, made a speech saying, 'We desire to throw no one into the shade, but we also demand our own place in the sun', and the demand for a place in the sun was used on several occasions afterwards by the Kaiser, Wilhelm II.

The twentieth century starts with **wait and see**. Although the expression had already been in use for many years, it became a catchphrase in 1910 when the Liberal Prime Minister used it repeatedly in the House of Commons when asked when he was going to reintroduce a rejected budget. This won him the nickname 'Old Wait and See', and explains the provocative or coy associations it still has as a tag. The **lunatic fringe** appears surprisingly early in the century. It was coined by American President Theodore Roosevelt, who used it a number of times. In his *Autobiography* (1913) he wrote, 'There are the foolish fanatics always to be found in such a movement and always discrediting it – the men who form the lunatic fringe in all reform movements.' **Power without responsibility**, originally said by Rudyard Kipling in a conversation with Lord Beaverbrook in about 1917, was borrowed by his cousin Stanley Baldwin for a speech made in 1931 attacking the popular press for being propaganda machines: 'What the proprietorship of these papers is aiming at is power, and power without responsibility – the prerogative of the harlot throughout the ages.' The then Duke of Devonshire is supposed to have exclaimed when he heard this, 'Good God, that's done it, he's lost us the tarts' vote.' A much higher tone is found in **rendezvous with destiny**, which comes from a speech given by Franklin D. Roosevelt in 1936, when he claimed, 'This generation of Americans has a rendezvous with destiny.' There may, perhaps, be an echo here of the poem written by the American poet Alan Seeger in 1916, the year he died fighting in the First World War, which begins, 'I have a rendezvous with death / At some disputed barricade.' Roosevelt's successor, Harry S Truman (President from 1945 to 1953), famous for THE BUCK STOPS HERE (see Chapter 4), also used **if you can't stand the heat, get out of the kitchen**, probably coined by General Harry Vaughan, long-standing friend and aide to Truman. The original version is rumoured to have been much less polite. **We name the guilty party** or **men** was boosted by a pamphlet written by 'Cato' (Michael Foot) in 1940 called *The Guilty Men*, which accused Chamberlain and his followers of appeasement. The idea of someone who does more harm to himself than others can do to him goes back to Greek and Roman times, but the form we have it in, **his own worst enemy**, is twentieth century. A famous comment by Ernest Bevin (1881–1951) involving the phrase is recorded by Sir Roderick Barclay in his book *Ernest Bevin and the Foreign Office* (1975):

A Ministerial colleague with whom Ernie [Bevin] was almost always on bad terms was Nye Bevan. There was a well-known occasion when the latter had incurred Ernie's displeasure, and one of those present, seeking to excuse Nye, observed that he was sometimes his own worst enemy. 'Not while I'm alive 'e aint!' retorted Ernie.

Similar exchanges have been attributed to others, and Bevin is also reported to have said it of Herbert Morrison. We owe the much-used **corridors of power**, meaning the senior levels of government, where influence is more important than the rule book, to C. P. Snow, novelist and scientist, Labour politician and, after he became Baron Snow, member of the House of Lords. He first used it in his 1956 novel *Homecomings*, then as the title of a novel published in 1964. Snow also coined *The Two Cultures*, the title of a lecture series on the conflicting cultures of the arts and sciences he gave in 1959. Also from the 1950s is a **little local difficulty**. In 1958, shortly before the

Prime Minister Harold Macmillan (Lord Stockton) was due to go on a Commonwealth tour, his Chancellor of the Exchequer Peter Thorneycroft, and two other Treasury ministers, Enoch Powell and Nigel Birch, sensationally resigned over government spending targets. At the airport Macmillan, a master of what would later be called the **sound bite**, nonchalantly dismissed the uproar this caused with: 'I thought the best thing to do was to settle up these little local difficulties, and then turn to the wider visions of the Commonwealth.' In political circles this saying still carries overtones of the original circumstances, but elsewhere it can be used without irony. Two years later, in a speech made in Cape Town, Macmillan said, 'The **wind of change** is blowing through this continent, and, whether we like it or not, this growth of national consciousness is a political fact.' Much later in life, Macmillan, who lived 1894–1986, created another cliché. In a speech made to the Tory Reform Group in 1985, in which he attacked the Thatcherite privatization of national assets, he described the process in these terms: 'First of all the Georgian silver goes, then all that nice furniture that used to be in the saloon. Then the Canalettos go.' This was summarized in the press as **selling off the family silver**.

The 1960s, that time of changing mores, brings us the formula phrase **a . . . is a long time in . . .**, based on the saying attributed to Harold Wilson *c.*1960 that 'a week is a long time in politics'. It is still used of circumstances where events can change radically in a short time, but as a formula phrase it is also used facetiously. **Ask not what . . . can do for you; ask what you can do for . . .** – based on the 1961 inaugural address of American President John F. Kennedy, with its famous 'And so my fellow Americans: ask not what your country can do for you – ask what you can do for your country' – has also become a formula phrase, sometimes in very convoluted form, such as the article title 'Ask Not What Post-Secondary Education Can Do for Psychology; Ask What Psychology Can Do for Post-Secondary Education' (*Canadian Psychology*, February 2006). The collapse of the old guard in England is linked by many to the Profumo affair, which introduced a new meaning to **he would, wouldn't he?** Although the expression was well established at the time, these words became full of innuendo, in 1963, during the scandalous trial of Stephen Ward, charged with living off immoral earnings. Mandy Rice-Davies had supplied a list of men she had had relationships with, which included the name of Lord Astor. When asked in court, 'Do you know Lord Astor has made a statement to the police saying that these allegations of yours are absolutely untrue?' she replied, 'He would, wouldn't he?' This was greeted with shocked delight at a time when such informal language in court came as a surprise, as did her offhand assumption that a lord would lie. The expression has been used in similar contexts ever since.

President Richard Nixon forms a link between the 1960s and 1970s. In 1969, the year he was elected, Nixon made a speech in which he said that he was sure that 'the great **silent majority** of my fellow Americans' would not want to get out of the Vietnam War except on honourable terms. Since then, many politicians have claimed to speak for the silent majority, but without explaining how they know what the silent majority wants. MIDDLE ENGLAND (see below) or 'Middle America' are alternative terms. On 17 June 1972 burglars broke into the national headquarters of the Democratic Party in the Watergate building in Washington DC, looking for material that could be used by the Committee for the Re-election of the President (CREEP) to smear the Democratic Party and their candidate. This bungled break-in and attempt to tap the telephones led to the **Watergate** hearings and the resignation of President Nixon in 1974. By August 1973 **-gate** was already established as a journalistic suffix, used to indicate a scandal or a secret that needs to be revealed, and the use has not died down with time, as is shown by such recent coinages as Whitewatergate, Nannygate, Camillagate, Cronygate and Zippergate. Another 'contribution' to the English language from the affair was the extraordinary use of the word 'inoperative' when White House press secretary Ronald L. Ziegler said on April 17 1973 that all previous statements issued by the White House about events surrounding Watergate were 'inoperative', i.e. lies. The expression **expletive deleted** also comes from the Watergate scandal. When transcripts of the Watergate tapes, the secret recordings made of conversations between Nixon and his colleagues, were published in 1973, the exceedingly salty language used by the President and his associates was bowdlerized, '[expletive deleted]' replacing the words it was felt would shock the general public. The expression immediately caught on as an alternative for an asterisk, or euphemism.

Meanwhile, in England **at a stroke** was becoming a cliché. It has been used to mean 'with a single blow' since Chaucer's day, and had come to mean 'at once', 'immediately', by the eighteenth century. It is particularly associated with a statement issued by the Conservative leader Edward Heath two days before he became Prime Minister in 1970, in which he proposed tax cuts and a price freeze, claiming, 'This would, at a stroke, reduce the rise in prices, increase productivity and reduce unemployment.' Of course it did no such thing. In the election contest the losing Labour Party had used on their posters the slogan **yesterday's men** below grotesque caricatures of the leaders of the Conservatives, causing such an outcry that the posters had to be withdrawn, but the phrase lived on, used of anyone whose career was over. A possible inspiration for the slogan was a 1965 song written and performed by Chris Andrews called 'Yesterday Man'. In 1977 Bert Lance, US President Jimmy Carter's Director of the Office of Management, was reported as saying, **If it ain't broke, don't fix it** when asked about government reorganization. Whether or not the saying originated with him, his use of it caught the public imagination at the time, and it rapidly became a catchphrase cliché, although the grammar is sometimes tidied up. Back in England again, the Conservative minister William Whitelaw was reviving an expression from

The Cat's Pyjamas

a comic opera. In *The Mikado* (1885) one of Gilbert and Sullivan's famous patter songs, on the subject of execution, describes the condemned: 'Awaiting the sensation of a **short, sharp shock**, / From a cheap and chippy chopper on a big black block.' The political use, recommending a short, sharp shock as a treatment for young offenders, dates from a speech made in October 1979 by Whitelaw, when he introduced a particularly harsh new regime for young offenders.

Originally, **on your bike!** (or 'on yer bike!') was a British expression that grew up in the 1960s meaning 'push off', 'go away', the sort of thing a policeman might say to a youth he suspects is up to no good (the Americans, meanwhile, could use 'on your horse' in the same way). From this it had also developed a more general sense of 'get a move on'. However, in 1981, shortly after a series of violent poll-tax riots, the then Conservative Minister of Employment, Norman Tebbit, said in a speech at his party's political conference: 'I grew up in the thirties with our unemployed father. He did not riot, he got on his bike and looked for work.' Once again, newspapers changed the wording in their summing-up of the text and it was interpreted by the tabloid newspapers as an unsympathetic minister saying 'On yer bikes' to the unemployed. Ever since then the expression has both kept its original sense and adopted the sense of 'go and look for work'. **Read my lips** is an expression used for emphasis dating from the 1970s, which became a cliché after American President George Bush Snr said, 'Read my lips: no new taxes' in a speech (written for him by Peggy Noonan) given in 1988 when accepting the Republican nomination. The latest political cliché, **not fit for purpose**, is discussed in the Introduction (p. xiii).

The language of politics

Other political clichés can be divided roughly into two groups – those that are used *of* politics, and those that are particularly used *by* politicians, although there is considerable overlap between the two. There are two clichés that sum up what it is to be American, for some people. The first is the **American Dream**. In use since at least 1835, this expression is used for the traditional values that the USA is held to stand for. However, what exactly is meant is often rather vague, and it is often used emotively, rather than with any precise meaning. **Apple pie**, particularly **Mom's apple pie**, has come to represent all that is comforting and homely, and the domestic bliss that is part of the American Dream. As Joseph Heller wrote in his novel of American troops in the Second World War, *Catch-22* (1962), 'The hot dog, the Brooklyn Dodgers. Mom's apple pie. That's what everyone's fighting for.' It is often found in the form **American as apple pie**. We have seen that America has a RENDEZVOUS WITH DESTINY, above, but the more pompous of politicians may use the cliché **day of destiny**, although it is more likely to be found now used by sports journalists when describing an important match. The term **uncrowned king** or **queen** now has political connections only from its wording, although originally it was used, from the beginning of the twentieth century, for someone who had the sort of power a ruler used to have. By the 1930s it had come to indicate anyone who was pre-eminent in their field. It is particularly commonly used of people in the fields of sport and entertainment. The **great and the good**, however, can be political. Defined by one wit as a group of people too eminent to need to be competent, the expression has been in use since at least the second half of the nineteenth century, frequently ironically. By 1904 it was enough of a cliché for the English classicist and humorous poet A. D. Godley to play on it, writing:

> Great and good is the typical Don, and of evil and wrong the foe,
> Good, and great, I'm a Don myself, and therefore I ought to
>   know.

> *(Megalopsychiad)*

Middle England is another grouping of people, but exactly who these people are is sufficiently complex a question to have supported a whole radio series in search of an answer. The term, rarely used to flatter, is often defined in terms of newspaper readership and more or less covers the middle classes outside London, particularly those with conservative or old-fashioned views, although this definition seems to be shifting. It is often felt to constitute a not-so-SILENT MAJORITY (see above). Although 'Middle England' has been in use since the middle of the nineteenth century, it has only recently passed from a geographical location to a state of mind, when it really took off as a cliché. Another disparaging group term is **rent-a-mob** or -**crowd**, used to indicate that the supporters of a cause – usually left-wing – are unthinking clones. It dates from the 1970s, and is based on hire services using 'rent-a- . . .' in their title, such as 'rent-a-van' services. There are other formations of the 'rent-a- . . .' formula, but this has to some extent been replaced by **dial-a-. . .** – reflecting the growth of businesses that provide services that can be ordered over the telephone, and often, in cases such as dial-a-pizza services, delivered to your door.

To return to politicians rather than the people who may or may not vote for them (or who may **vote with their feet**, a truly democratic term that dates from the 1960s): first of all they must be **politically correct**. Originally coined in the early 1980s to describe words or behaviour that was sensitive to the feelings or needs of minorities or the disadvantaged, this rapidly became a cliché also used to attack and condemn those trying to reform usage. If the politicians succeed, there will be complaints of **political correctness gone mad**. They must also be careful not to be **off message** ('on message' exists, but is much rarer). An ugly way of saying 'toeing the party line', this expression has been associated with the Labour Party since its election campaign of 1997, and has spread from there to more general use. It is particularly associated with following the advice of spin doctors and has to some extent replaced the similar 'sending the right signals'. **Spin doctor** itself was coined in the 1980s in America, and in Britain was again initially particularly connected with New Labour, although it has now spread to other parties and fields. An older cliché for 'being on message' is **speak with a single voice** or **with one voice**. The idea of a group speaking unanimously (which literally means 'with one mind') has been expressed by 'with one voice' since the Middle Ages, and became so much a part of the language that in the seventeenth to eighteenth centuries the term 'univocal' was used as an alternative to 'unanimous'. 'With a single voice' seems to be a recent variant, no doubt used because it alliterates with 'speak'. Ambitious politicians may seek a **high profile**. This is a badly under-researched expression. The *OED* deals with it only in passing, without any definition, so the dates of the citations – almost all from the 1990s – are no help. *The Times* used the term literally a number of times in the nineteenth century, when describing buildings or ships. Then in 1939 it printed an advertisement for Dunlop tyres, which contains the text: 'The Teeth on Dunlop Tyres constitute the greatest development in tyre construction since the introduction by Dunlop of the flat tread and high profile tyre in 1931.' (You would typically expect to see high profile tyres on a model T Ford – the distance from the edge of the metal hubs to the ground is greater than the width of the tyre that touches the ground; these are now deeply unfashionable, and the low-profile tyre dominant.) I mention this simply because it may have made the use of 'high profile' more widespread, and therefore made it easier to adopt as a cliché in a new sense. The opposite is **low profile**, which has the same range of senses, with the figurative use appearing by 1970. But prominence brings with it the risk of being **stabbed in the back** – a cliché based on the idea of an assassin or mugger creeping up behind, with strong overtones of the death of Caesar – particularly if the person involved is losing a HOTLY CONTESTED (see Chapter 19) election which may lead to **regime change**. In this case they might need to

deliver an ultimatum, an expression, adopted from the world of diplomacy, that has become a much-used substitute for 'threaten'. Ultimatums (*ultimata* would be overly pedantic, even for a book on clichés) can also be **issued**, as can **dire** or **stark warnings**. 'Stark' is another of those words that is rarely used outside set combinations, often paired with 'choices', 'staring mad' and 'naked'. In the end a politician **stands or falls by** his ideas. But to **gain currency** these ideas must, in a particularly ugly image, **have legs**, or, in the rising cliché, **gain traction**.

What they say

If we turn now to expressions used by politicians either to persuade or to obfuscate, one of the most dangerous has been **Victorian values**. It was an expression much used by politicians in the 1980s, those on the right using it to mean order, free enterprise, self-restraint and other old-fashioned values; those on the left pointing out that the Victorian age was one of gross inequality, poverty, squalor and widespread child prostitution. The expression got mixed up with various political scandals of the time, becoming associated with that Victorian vice, hypocrisy, and is now usually used mockingly. Its equally dangerous companion cliché is **back to basics**, which also suggests that there was once some nebulous, innocent golden age, before things were spoilt by theorists or by over-complication. The expression had been used as a slogan by educational reformers in the USA in the mid 1970s, but became famous in 1993 when the British Prime Minister, John Major, made a speech at the Conservative Party Conference saying, 'The message from this Conference is clear and simple. We must go back to basics . . . The Conservative Party will lead the country back to these basics, right across the board: sound money, free trade, traditional teaching, respect for the family and the law.' Although Major was prepared to go into apparent detail, his speech was, in fact, little more than a string of clichés, leaving the listener no clearer as to what exactly 'basics' were. The slogan soon became discredited, in much the same way as 'Victorian values' did, when the government was beset with a series of sexual scandals. (More recently New Labour's **joined-up government** has been as much of a millstone round the neck of the party as any of the Conservatives' slogans.) The opposite of these backward-looking approaches is the **ground-breaking initiative**, which seems to COME TO GRIEF (see Chapter 18) equally often. 'Ground-breaking' is found as early as 1907 when William James, philosopher brother of the now more famous Henry, wrote in a letter, 'I am going to settle down to the composition of another small book, more original and ground-breaking than anything I have yet put forth.' However, further research will probably turn up earlier uses, for 'breaking ground' was used throughout the nineteenth century in a wide range of often idiomatic ways, and can be found much earlier in a literal sense. 'Breaking new ground' was used from quite early in the nineteenth century in the way we use it, and is presumably the source of 'ground-breaking'. But 'breaking ground' could also be used, for instance, for 'starting to speak', sometimes in the way we would use 'breaking the ice' today, and was also widely used metaphorically for 'starting a new project'.

When politicians feel attacked over the way things are run, they will defend themselves by saying that the Health Service (or television, or theatre, or whatever) is the **best in the world** (often prefaced by 'We in Britain' and without feeling any need to provide evidence to support this) or, even worse, that it is **world class** or **world-beating**. On the same theme, it may be the **envy of the world**, a cliché that is a more blatant attempt to stir up national pride. They will **categorically reject** or **deny** or else **condemn without reservation** any attacks on them, using expressions that sound grand but are in truth vague and insubstantial. 'Categorically', in particular, is a wonderfully legal-sounding word that is rarely used by the majority of people, and in practice means almost nothing in this context. The denying may even be done **once and for all**. In the form 'once for all', this expression dates from the fifteenth century. The politician might then go on to claim that the **way forward**, a modern cliché used to create an atmosphere of upbeat positiveness without being too specific, is to **stand up and be counted** and to **think the unthinkable**. 'Stand up and be counted' is a twentieth-century cliché that grew up in America, from public meetings where votes are cast by literally standing up to be counted. Although 'think the unthinkable' has been particularly associated with the Labour government *c.*2000, the idea had been around for some time before. In 1962 Herman Kahn published a book called *Thinking the Unthinkable*, and two years later the American politician J. William Fulbright made a speech about the USA having better relations with the USSR containing the words, 'We must dare to think "unthinkable" thoughts.' Politicians may even claim that there are **no two ways about it**, an expression recorded as early as 1818. They may further justify themselves by appealing to the people. Although expressions such as **people power** are quite recent, 'the people' have, of course, been invoked since the foundation of Socialism in the modern sense, with the will of the *demos* (as in 'democracy') invoked since at least the time of ancient Athens. **Power to the people** is particularly associated with the Black Power movement in America, which used it from about 1968, although it has been used by others, most memorably as the title of a John Lennon song of 1971. Many other emotive uses of 'the people' can be found from about this time. More recent, but fortunately on the wane thanks to the mockery it has received, is the clichéd formula **the people's . . .** This does have a back history. The Chartists in the 1840s, for instance, campaigned for the People's Charter, and **the People's Choice** is an old political campaign slogan. But with the election of the Labour Party in 1997 and the death of Diana, Princess of Wales, in the same year, the formula took on a new lease of life. **The People's**

Princess was coined by the Prime Minister's press secretary, Alastair Campbell, in the aftermath of Diana's death, and subsequent uses of 'the people's . . .' have been so prolific that it is now used ironically.

Radio interviews seem to bring out the worst in politicians. You could sit and listen to some of them and fill pages noting down their clichés – indeed, I have done so. Many of them are euphemisms. Perhaps the most famous is the claim that someone has resigned to **spend more time with their family**, generally taken to be a polite way of saying 'I've been sacked', a sad end for so laudable a sentiment. *Private Eye* has been known to use the variant 'to spend more time with his money' of those politicians who have extensive business interests or inherited wealth. Just before resigning they could be **considering their position**. When pressed for answers by interviewers about what they plan to do about something, politicians have a wide range of ways of trying to hide the fact they have no idea what to do. They can be **monitoring the situation, keeping all their options open** or **keeping the situation under review**. In so doing they will not **relax their vigilance**, will show **zero tolerance** and will not **take their eye off the ball**; nor will they **lose momentum**. When they have done nothing, they will say that we must **move on**, make **a fresh start**, and will **draw a line under** events. In this way they will **keep the faith**.

The power of clichés to change the whole way people look at things, as long as they chime with current feelings, is shown by the rise of the term **nanny state**. It is found from 1965, but took off in the 1980s when opponents of the idea of the CRADLE TO GRAVE (see Chapter 1) welfare state started attacking it by talking in terms of a dependency culture and describing a state that looked after its citizens in this way as a nanny state. Since the Labour victory of 1997 the term has been expanded to cover any interference in private life by the state. Although it is so new, the terms 'nannyist' and 'nannyism' have already developed from it. The negative force of 'nanny' has been used effectively to make it very difficult to present any government-based caring or nurturing work in a positive light. Instead of being supported by the state when in need, every member of a **hard-working family** is supposed to be a STAKEHOLDER (see Chapter 9) in the country. Other political slogans that have become clichés since the WAR ON TERROR (see Chapter 11) began are **free society** and **flying the flag** (a particular favourite of George Bush Jnr).

Weasels

Weasel words are those that evade the issue or equivocate in some way. We all use them at some time and they are much used by advertisers; but they are most easily spotted and most frequently heard in the speech of politicians, which is why they are listed at this point. The one weasel that is not associated with politicians and that has been a joke since it was first used, but that illustrates the type well, is the **wrong kind of snow**. This was an excuse offered by British Rail spokesman Terry Worrall in February 1991 when the company's snow-clearing equipment could not clear the tracks. It has stuck in the national consciousness as the ultimate unconvincing or outrageous excuse. The train services have learned nothing from it, for they have not dropped their 'the wrong kind of . . .' formula (rapidly turning into a formula phrase); Virgin Trains have been known to excuse opaque train windows as 'due to the wrong kind of dirt'.

Some weasels are single words such as **arguably**, which means little or nothing but gives the appearance that the speaker is being reasonable. Others, like **industrial action**, are classic statements of the opposite of their apparent meaning. Weasel words are not a new phenomenon. **Men of goodwill** is a literal translation of the Latin used by that brilliant propagandist Cicero in the first century AD. In Latin it is the elegantly simple *boni*, 'the good', in its masculine plural form. When told by one so eloquent as Cicero that certain behaviour patterns are those of the *boni*, it takes a man of great courage to mark himself as a member of the opposite side. But although weasels are as ancient as the art of rhetoric, the frequency with which they are used, and the way in which politicians and their spin doctors are trained in their use, has made them particularly prominent at the moment. Some ring immediate alarm bells. If you hear someone say **to be honest** you start looking for the evasion, although you might be surprised and hear them come out with the cliché that they will **put their hand up** and admit something, thus reducing the confession to the schoolchild level of crime. They might claim that they would like to take action, but with the **best will in the world** and **despite their best efforts**, **to all intents and purposes** their **hands are tied** (a clutch of clichés from the mid nineteenth century). An alternative to 'hands are tied' is the more emphatic **tied hand and foot**. This might be because of **circumstances** or **forces beyond their control** (from the nineteenth century). They might even claim to be a **victim of circumstances**. This was obviously well established when Kenneth Grahame used it in *The Wind in the Willows* (1908) of Toad's escape from jail in disguise:

Toad was delighted with the suggestion. It would enable him to leave the prison in some style, and with his reputation for being a desperate and dangerous fellow untarnished; and he readily helped the gaoler's daughter to make her aunt appear as much as possible the victim of circumstances over which she had no control.

This view might be offered **with respect** (a pretty sure sign that respect is lacking) along with the claim that they have **implicit confidence** in the people involved, and that it is their **considered opinion** that **in due course** (that is, when they get round to it) things will be sorted out.

15. Sex, Science and Technology

As it is a cliché of advertising that working the word 'sex' into anything increases its attraction, it seems appropriate to include it in this chapter title. As so often with advertising, the reality is more prosaic than the come-on. This chapter will deal with all the sciences, including human biology, and that minor aspect of it, sex. The exception is geology, which is found in Chapter 21.

Technology

Technology, used here very loosely for anything mechanical, is largely created by researchers in the **back room**. The use of the term 'back room' to mean a place where support work, or sometimes secret work, is carried out dates from a speech made in March 1941 by Lord Beaverbrook, who said, 'Now who is responsible for this work of development on which so much depends? To whom must the praise be given? To the boys in the back rooms. They do not sit in the limelight. But they are the men who do the work.' A few years earlier, using a catchphrase invented by the cartoonist Tad Dorgan (1877–1929), Marlene Dietrich famously sang, 'See what the boys in the back room will have' in the film *Destry Rides Again* (1939). In this song she is using 'back room' in its literal sense. However, the film is known to have been a favourite of Beaverbrook's, and one he had watched not long before he made his speech, and it has been suggested that it had an influence on his choice of words. Of course, much that is done in the back room is theoretical, and has to be tested in the **real world**. Telling someone that what they suggest will not work in the real world, to accuse them of being impractical or of living in an IVORY TOWER (see Chapter 16), was common by the 1960s. Such criticism may **push** or **press** researchers' **buttons**. This idea has probably been around for as long as machines have had buttons – a writer in the 1930s showed an early stage in its development when he said, 'These terms . . . have become push buttons which touch off emotional reflexes' – but it has not become a cliché until recently. A related term, although with a rather different meaning, is **to pull (someone's) strings**, where the imagery comes not from machinery but from puppets. Redundant research can be said to be an attempt to **reinvent the wheel**, an expression from the second half of the twentieth century which may owe something to the prevalence of cartoons showing the invention of the wheel. But research cannot be expected to go **like clockwork** every time. Things were being compared to clockwork from the early seventeenth century, and by 1679 John Goodman, in *The Penitent Pardoned*, was approaching our modern use with 'Their Religion was a kind of clock-work . . . moving in a certain order, but without life or sense', although the actual wording 'like clockwork' is not recorded until the end of the next century. Engines have given us the **nuts and bolts of** for basic elements that hold something together, and **firing on all cylinders** dates from the early days of motoring when vehicles were much less reliable that they are today. **Fine tuning** looks as if it should owe its origins to car engines, but the record (the *OED* has it only from 1969 in both literal and figurative senses) suggests that scientific instruments are more likely to be the source. The technical aspects of rocket engines give us **all systems go**, adopted in the 1960s and 1970s when the launching of manned flights, particularly the flights to the moon, was prominently featured on radio and television, and the expression became something of a catchphrase. More recently **it's not rocket science** has become a common space-related cliché, reflecting the complexity of space exploration.

The world of computing, although new, has been surprisingly

productive of clichés, although many of them are connected
with advertising and sales. Thus aficionados of the latest developments are keen to acquire the latest **cutting–edge technology**.
This term began to be used in the scientific community to mean
'research that is out in the forefront of things, breaking new
ground' in the middle of the twentieth century. By the 1970s it
was passing into general use, and had become a cliché by the
1980s. An alternative expression is **leading edge**, used in much
the same way. The expression originally came into use in the
1870s to mean the foremost edge of a propeller or aeroplane
wing. The figurative use developed some hundred years later.
Cynics battered by too many unfortunate encounters with 'the
leading edge of technology' have developed a new term, christ-
ening it the **bleeding edge**. Also from aeronautics is to **push
the envelope**, originally meaning to go to the limit of performance. It became a cliché after it was popularized in the USA in
Tom Wolfe's 1979 book about the space programme, *The Right
Stuff*. Yet another term for the latest thing is **state of the art**.
This is first recorded in 1889 in the form 'the present status of
the art'. From being a description of where things had got to, it
had, by the 1950s, become an adjective used to describe something that was the most up to date. The latest product may come
with all the newest **bells and whistles**. This term comes from
the multitude of bells, whistles and other noise-making devices
found on old-fashioned fairground organs, and is used in much
the same way as ALL SINGING, ALL DANCING (see Chapter 5).
A similar expression, also based on lavish embellishment, is **with
knobs** or **bells on**. Although the *OED* does not record 'with
knobs on' until 1930, Eric Partridge dates it and 'with bells on'
to the late nineteenth century, which the *OED* ignores. 'With
knobs on' is particularly associated with the insults traded by
schoolchildren, and is used to mean 'and the same to you', in
which case it is often used in the form 'with brass knobs on', as
if referring to some ornate Victorian bedstead. While the history
of 'with bells on' is untraced, it is worth noting that horse

harnesses could be decorated with bells, and such harnesses are often evidence of wealth in folk and fairy stories. **User-friendly** is another term used to promote computer sales. It dates from the 1970s, when computer users were often greeted by a blank screen that needed programming before the computer could be used, and spread rapidly to other areas. It has spawned a new combining form, with '-friendly' tacked on to all sorts of other words. Terms more closely associated with the actual functioning of the computer include **real time**, originally an expression used in computing to distinguish data that was processed at the time of gathering rather than at a later date. For instance, accounts could be processed as the transactions were made, rather than all the information being gathered and processed at the end of the month. The expression was coined in the 1950s, but it took until the 1980s before the general public was exposed to the exciting developments in the computing world that made this term a buzzword and started its transference into a clichéd way of saying 'as it happens, now'. Another is **in** or **out of the loop**. A loop is an element of programming that repeats itself, and this has been transferred to the idea of an information loop, a continuous pattern of passing information between a group of people. If you are in this loop, you get the information; if you are out of it, you do not.

Physics is responsible for one of the silliest misunderstandings ever to become a cliché, in **quantum leap**. The use of the phrase as an alternative to Mao's **great leap forward** is the exact opposite of its true meaning, which is a sudden change that happens at a subatomic level, about the smallest scale you could be working on. The term came into use among physicists in the 1950s and was being used figuratively only about five years later. Astrophysics gives us a **black hole**, from the collapsed star with gravity so strong that everything, even light, is sucked into it. The term was only coined in 1968, yet was being used metaphorically by 1980 to replace other terms that conjured up images of limitless capacity and no hope of return, such as the biblical **bottomless pit** or **abyss**. Astronomy also gives us 'galaxy' as in a **galaxy of stars**, surely the coinage of some Hollywood publicity genius, just as the whole concept of 'stars' was. This cliché is now used as much of the football world as it is of film actors. Radio gives us **on the same** or **a different wavelength**. To pick up a radio broadcast, you have to tune into the same wavelength. 'To be on the same wavelength' as someone therefore means being able to understand them, to pick up the signals they are sending you. The figurative use dates from the early days of radio in the 1920s. A change in electrical voltage in a very short time is called by physicists a **step change**, which in recent years has passed into management speech and that of politicians.

There are a number of other clichés that come more loosely from physics, in that they refer to phenomena that are the realm of physics, rather than being directly associated with science and scientists. Light waves give us **the light at the end of the tunnel**. This expression probably entered the language in the later nineteenth century – the earliest instance of it in *The Times* is from a political speech in 1900. The image has been a productive one, giving rise to graffiti such as: 'Will the last person to leave the tunnel please turn the light off', and the pessimistic joke: 'The light at the end of the tunnel is the light of the oncoming train' (later used by Robert Lowell in his poem 'Day by Day' (1977)). Gravity is involved in **hang in the balance**, which dates from at least the fifteenth century, while the image of the two pans of a scale being turned by the least weight added to either pan goes back to biblical times. It would have been a familiar visual image in the Middle Ages from the many paintings in churches of the souls of the dead being weighed in judgement against the weight of a feather. Anyone who has ever used such an old-fashioned pair of scales will know that two almost equal weights can oscillate for some time before they **come down on one side or the other**. The related **hang by a thread** goes back to the world of the ancient Greeks, to the story of the Sword of Damocles. Damocles, who lived in the fourth century BC, was an inveterate flatterer at the court of Dionysius, Tyrant of Syracuse. Dionysius grew tired of constantly hearing that he was the most fortunate man alive and decided to teach Damocles a lesson. He held a magnificent banquet with Damocles in the seat of honour, but as he enjoyed the feast Damocles realized that suspended over his head was a sword, hanging by a single thread, by which Dionysius meant to teach him the dangers and discomforts of supreme power.

The science of surface tension necessary to form bubbles lies between physics and chemistry. If someone is elated or uplifted, we tend to describe them as bubbling over with happiness or with similar images. If you destroy their happiness or shatter their illusions, you **burst their bubble**, and they become deflated.

Maths is closely associated with physics, so I will conclude this section with two mathematical clichés. Firstly, a perversion of maths gives us **110 per cent**, a modern expression used to indicate maximum or extra effort, users of which seem to have no problem with the fact that per cent means 'out of every hundred', so that anything over 100 per cent is a mathematical impossibility. And secondly, the diameter of a circle gives us **diametrically opposed to**, already in use in the literal sense by the seventeenth century.

Chemistry

Chemistry itself gives us the expressions **good** or **bad** or **the right chemistry**. The use of the word 'chemistry' to describe the reaction between people or their personal characteristics actually goes back to the sixteenth century, Queen Elizabeth I being the first recorded user. However, as a cliché, paired with terms such as 'good' or 'bad', it belongs to the twentieth century. This use probably developed with the spread of knowledge of human physiology, particularly the biochemical processes involved in attraction between people, as shown in the expression **sexual chemistry** for physical attraction. An early example of this is found in George Bernard Shaw's *You Never Can Tell* (1898): 'No, no, no. Not love: we know better than that. Let's call it chemistry . . . Well. You're attracting me irresistibly – chemically.' From the idea of sexual attraction, 'chemistry' spread to cover other areas of getting on together.

The phrase **the acid test** comes from the use of nitric acid as a diagnostic test to find out the proportion of gold present in a piece, particularly to find out if gold coins were genuine. It has been used since the early twentieth century to mean a test of the success or value of something.

The explosives produced by chemists have also provided clichés. **Explosive mixture** has been used as a cliché since the 1970s. The word 'dynamite' is first recorded in English in 1867, and took about fifty years to be used metaphorically. **Political dynamite** is a particularly common coupling. Gunpowder is another explosive that crops up in clichés. If the type of firework known as a squib gets wet, then all you get is a splutter or nothing at all. Hence **damp squib**, in use since the middle of the nineteenth century, for something that does not meet expectations, that fails to develop. The successful use of fireworks is found in **light the blue touchpaper and retire**, an instruction frequently found on fireworks. Guns are the source of the cliché **lock, stock and barrel**. This is an expression from the late eighteenth century, and refers to the three main parts that form a gun: the firing mechanism (lock), the stock that holds it, and the barrel.

Biology

Biology and related sciences give us **survival of the fittest**, an expression of the process of evolution that comes from Herbert Spencer's book *Principles of Biology* (1865), and not from Charles

Darwin as is often assumed, although Spencer is describing Darwin's ideas. 'Fittest' means here 'most suited, best adapted', but is now often used as if it meant 'fit' as in 'in good physical condition'. Evolution also gives us the **missing link**. The original image here is of a chain of events, which will not be complete without all of its links. Also related to evolution is the **lowest form of life**, which has itself evolved from its original use to describe single-cell creatures to being an insulting term for the humblest, least significant person in a team or group, to being a general insult. Attempts to impose human design on evolution give us **Frankenstein** as a term of disparagement. Baron Frankenstein was the scientist who created the monster in Mary Shelley's 1818 novel, but 'Frankenstein' has long been used as a shortening of the more correct 'Frankenstein's monster'. It has now progressed to being used as an adjective to describe the creations of modern science, with particular reference to genetically modified foods, which are sometimes described as 'Frankenfoods' or other such compounds. Finally the biologists and psychologists investigating rat behaviour give us the **rat race**, a term derived from experiments that put rats through mazes to discover, for example, how good their memories are. Its development as an expression used of a highly competitive working life was probably helped by the fondness of cartoonists for showing such experiments. It first developed in the USA in the 1930s.

Human biology

If we travel down the body from top to bottom, we can start with **head held high**, a cliché since the nineteenth century, although the idea behind holding one's head up, rather than bowed in shame, goes back much further. In fact, two expressions seem to have become blended here. Originally, 'to hold one's head up' meant to behave arrogantly or proudly, while 'to hold up one's head' referred to keeping one's dignity or self-respect. Both these date from the sixteenth century. Related is **head and shoulders above**, a cliché for something that stands out from or towers above the rest of its class, first recorded in the 1840s. It has echoes of Newton's famous comment, very nearly a cliché if not fully one: 'If I have seen further it is by standing on the shoulders of giants' (in a letter to Robert Hooke, written 5 February 1676). Newton, however, was not being original. In 1159 John of Salisbury wrote that Bernard of Chartres (who had died some thirty years earlier) 'used to say that we are like dwarfs on the shoulders of giants, so that we can see more than they, and things at a greater distance, not by virtue of any sharpness of sight on our part, or any physical distinction, but because we are carried high and raised up by their giant size'. **Heads will roll** is another quotation, surprisingly from a speech by Adolf Hitler from 1930 when he said, 'If our movement is victorious there will be a revolutionary tribunal which will punish the crimes of November 1918. The decapitated heads will roll in the sand.' Further violence is found in **I need that like a hole in the head** and its variants. This started as slang in the USA in the 1940s, and had reached the UK by the 1950s, although it did not become really popular until rather later. It may be Jewish-American in origin, as an identical Yiddish expression is used in the States: *ich darf es vi a loch in kop*. Marshall McLuhan was an early user of it, writing in *The Mechanical Bride* in 1951: 'A smart operator needs a dame like he needs a hole in the head', and in 1959 'hole in the head' was used as a film title, no doubt spreading its use. Such a hole may damage the interior of the head, the main **nerve centre**. Originally a term for a group of nerves, by the 1870s it had come to mean the administrative centre from which an organization was controlled.

If we turn to the individual parts of the head, starting at the top we find a **bad hair day**. A fairly recent cliché from the United States (first recorded in 1988), it is used to mean a day when everything goes wrong, starting with getting up in the morning and finding you can't do a thing with your **crowning glory**. 'Crowning', in the sense 'completing, most perfect', is recorded from the mid seventeenth century, when Oliver Cromwell wrote of 'crowning mercy'. 'Crowning glory' in the sense of 'high spot, best bit, greatest achievement' is a journalistic cliché of the nineteenth century. The *OED*'s first citation of it as a description of a woman's hair is from 1922, from James Joyce's *Ulysses*. The earliest that I have been able to find is from *The Times* of 17 April 1917, which has a classified advertisement that runs: 'A Woman's Crowning Glory is her Hair. Rowland's Macassar Oil Makes it More Glorious Still.' Unless further research proves otherwise, it is quite reasonable to assume that this is the source of the expression for hair. It would be typical of Joyce to quote from an advertisement, and we have seen in the chapter on the influence of advertisements on clichés how easily they unconsciously slip into the language.

Moving on down the head, people can be **all ears**. This is found as early as 1634, in John Milton's masque *Comus*: 'I am all ear and took in strains that might create a soul under the ribs of death.' It is easy to see how the rather uncomfortable image of a person being nothing but a single listening ear changed to the less meaningful, but more comfortable, 'all ears'. The opposite cliché is **deaf as a post**, the origin of which is not entirely clear. Presumably a post was chosen because it is an inanimate object; however, it is common in English for such comparisons to alliterate, and in the past people were described as being deaf as a door or deaf (rather than dead) as a doornail. Yet in the nineteenth century the comparison with the unalliterating 'post' became the norm. A post is more humanoid than a door in shape, which may have had some influence. Another influence may have been the unfortunate tendency to regard the hard of hearing as stupid rather than deaf, a view reinforced by the fact that in the past someone could also be 'stupid as a post'. Ears can also be lent, and **lend an ear** is also connected to deafness in the expression 'to lend a deaf ear', meaning to refuse to listen, which is found as early as the fourteenth century. 'To lend an ear' for 'to listen' was already very popular, if not already a cliché, by the time Shakespeare used it in its best-known context: 'Friends, Romans, countrymen, lend me your ears' (*Julius Caesar* (1599) III.2). Despite all the childish jokes made about the Shakespeare quote, the expression is still much used, if getting a bit old-fashioned, both in the form 'lend an ear' and in forms echoing Shakespeare's. One can also have an **ear to the ground**, an expression that conjures up images of old Westerns where a character jumps off his horse, lies down and places an ear to the ground. If he was a really good tracker or scout, he would tell his companions exactly how many horses were following and how far away they were. The character doing this was often a Native American, for it is a technique they were credited with having developed. It is from this that the expression 'to have (or keep) an ear to the ground', for making sure you know what is going on around you, developed in the nineteenth century. The Bible is full of images of deafness representing a refusal to hear. One of the most pleasing, from Psalm 58, describes the wicked, who, compared with the righteous, 'are like the deaf adder that stoppeth her ear; Which will not hearken to the voice of charmers, charming never so wisely'. This became a standard image of the benighted for medieval moralists, and so entered the English language. The expression 'deaf ears' has been in use since the fifteenth century, and **fall on deaf ears** a cliché since the nineteenth. More frequent still at that date was the more active **turn a deaf ear**, made famous in the eighteenth century by Swift's lines, 'They would never hear, / But turn a deaf ear, / As a matter they had no concern in' (*Dingley and Brent*, 1724).

The eyes have also given rise to clichés. In his 1612 play *The White Devil* Webster wrote, 'They that have the yellow jaundice think all objects they look on to be yellow.' This explains the idea behind a **jaundiced eye** or **view**. By the late eighteenth century this idea of jaundiced sight being different from the norm was beginning to be detached from the idea of the actual disease, and so the idea of looking at life with a jaundiced eye, or having a jaundiced view of life, came to mean to be cynical, resentful or bitter. Illness is also behind a **sight for sore eyes**, which conveys the image of something that is such a delight to see, it acts as a cure. Small eyes have a reputation for indicating untrustworthiness, or other undesirable characteristics. This is probably behind **beady eye(d)**. You are unlikely to find 'beady' used in any other context, although technically it can be used to mean 'bead-like'. **More than meets the eye**, a set phrase used to express vague or unformulated doubts, has been popular since the nineteenth century. It is often now reversed in the form: 'There is less in this than meets the eye', a comment supposedly made by the American actress Tallulah Bankhead (1902–68) of one of the plays by the difficult Belgian dramatist Maeterlinck.

The nose only seems to provide **keep your nose clean**, which has been in use since the later nineteenth century, and is the opposite of poking your nose into other people's business, or getting into trouble by nosing around to see what is going on.

The mouth gives us a **kick in the teeth**, which does not seems to have become a cliché until the 1970s, and to **grit your teeth**. Under stress one automatically clenches one's teeth tightly. This can make a grinding noise, similar to that made when a bit of grit has got into food being chewed, hence the latter expression, used to describe such an action since the late eighteenth century. **Dumbing down**, which is more tenuously linked to the mouth, is a fairly recent import from the USA, using the American sense of 'dumb' to mean stupid. Used to lament a perceived lowering of standards, it is, in effect, the modern equivalent of the old codger's lament, **things aren't what they used to be**.

Moving down slightly we come to the **chinless wonder**. 'Chinless' was used in the nineteenth century to imply a lack of character, a firm chin being felt to show firm resolve. While this idea still lurks behind 'chinless wonder', the expression, in use by the 1930s, is mainly used of those who are both dim and privileged, who could also be classified as upper-class twits. The lower part of the face is involved in the **close shave**. This comes from the days of cut-throat razors, the world of Sweeney Todd the demon barber, when a clumsy movement while shaving could result in injury, and be literally a close shave with death. 'Close' is also linked with 'call' and 'thing'. These both come from the world of sport, a **close call** referring to an umpire's decision, a **close thing** to a race result – hence the description of the Battle of Waterloo attributed to (but never actually said by) the Duke of Wellington as 'a damn close-run thing'. A good shave would help you **put a brave face on** things. 'Face' has been used in the sense 'appearance' since the Middle Ages, and 'put a brave face on' was well established by the nineteenth century. Moving downwards just a little brings us to a **pain in the neck**. Used to mean someone irritating, and often shortened to simply 'a pain', this is a polite version of the much lower **pain in the arse** (or 'ass' in the USA), although it could be argued that there is a slight difference in both the meaning of the two expressions and the people about whom you use them, the pain in the neck being more cerebral than that lower down. Both are recorded from the early twentieth century, but are probably older.

Moving yet further down the body, to the chest, we come to the heart. The heart is such a potent symbol in our society, as the seat variously of love, the spirit and life, it comes as no surprise to find it is also potent in language formation. Some of the clichés involving the heart go back to early ideas about its function, and preserve ancient history. The ancients believed, for example, that sorrow or envy were bad for the heart and would eat away at it, each sigh draining blood from the organ. This idea made its way to England and became well established; Shakespeare often refers to it, as in:

Might liquid tears, or heart-offending groans,
Or blood-consuming sighs, recall his life,
I would be blind with weeping, sick with groans,
Look pale as primrose with blood-drinking sighs
                              (*Henry VI, Part 2* (1592), III.2)

Thus we describe people as **broken-hearted** by grief, or say that they **eat their heart out**. The latter used to be a term exclusively for grief or longing, but more recently it has also been used as a cry of triumph when someone else has cause to envy the speaker. Shakespeare also uses **heart of gold**, as do other sixteenth-century writers. This seems to have come into the language as translations of the earlier French *coeur d'or*. The well-known sixteenth-century song, often attributed to Henry VIII (1491–1547) but most probably not by him, says, 'Greensleeves was my heart of gold . . .', which may have helped popularize the turn of phrase. In the past 'heart of gold' was used as a straightforward compliment, but in modern use it is nearly always used as a mitigating factor to balance something less complimentary: '. . . but he has a heart of gold'. The image of the *tart with the heart of gold* is almost an independent cliché. **Heart of stone** (or **stony-hearted**) is also old: Homer's *Odyssey* has: 'Thy heart is even harder than stone'; and the Bible: 'His heart is as firm as a stone; yea, as hard as a piece of the nether millstone' (Job 41:24). More recently Oscar Wilde exploited the expression's cliché status to comment on Dickens's 1841 novel *The Old Curiosity Shop*: 'One must have a heart of stone to read the death of Little Nell without laughing.' **After your own heart** also appears in the Bible: 'The Lord hath sought him a man after his own heart' (1 Samuel 13:14). This expression had been translated into English by 825. If you do something **with a heavy heart** you are again echoing the Bible: 'Heaviness in the heart of man maketh it stoop: but a good word maketh it glad' (Proverbs 12:25). **Heavy-hearted** had appeared by 1400, and 'with a heavy heart' was well established by the seventeenth century. **Your heart's desire** was also well established in the seventeenth century, as was **to your heart's content**. While at first these two expressions were more or less interchangeable, they have since come to be used differently: your heart's desire tends to be something you win or gain, so has an active, striving element to it; your heart's content, usually preceded by 'to', has lost most of its force, and is now little more than a tag with a vague sense of 'as much as you want'. To **have your heart in the right place** is one of those expressions that it does not do to dwell on. Once you start to think about it, it loses all reasonable sense, because of course your heart has to be in the right place – you are literally in dead trouble if not. But here the heart has been so thoroughly identified with feelings or intentions that the idiocy of the literal sense is completely bypassed. The phrase was in use by the 1800s and became a cliché soon after. A different metaphorical use of 'heart' is found in the **heart of the matter**, which has been a cliché since at least the second half of the nineteenth century and is nowadays used with numbing frequency as the headline of articles on heart disease. Yet another sense is found in **hale and hearty**. 'Hale' is a northern dialect variant of 'whole', not found in standard speech outside this set phrase, and in this context means 'sound, fit'. This use of 'hearty' links up with expressions such as a 'hearty meal', although a 'hearty laugh' also relates to old senses of 'hearty', which include 'vigorous', 'heartfelt' and 'merry'. The heart as emotion is again found in two doublets, **hearts and minds** and **heart and soul**. Both are old combinations, but the ways they are used have changed over time. 'Hearts and minds', an expression that covers the emotions and intellect, the subjective and the objective, was pretty clichéd by the seventeenth century, but developed a new form in recent times with the **battle** (or occasionally **war** or **fight**) **for** (also **win** or **lose**) **hearts and minds**, which only seems to have become a cliché in the last few decades. 'Heart and soul', which dates from much the same time as 'hearts and minds', is a much more emotional expression, indicating a total commitment to something, most often, nowadays, love. To **make a clean breast of** something belongs here, for the breast has been used as an alternative for the heart since the earliest records of English. Although the expression has not been found before the eighteenth century, the image calls on earlier material, in particular the ideas of purging and purity associated with Christian confession, and with the action of beating one's breast in remorse. More or less on the same level is the shoulder, and that rather old-fashioned expression, to **stand shoulder to shoulder** with someone, has had a recent revival as part of the language of the WAR ON TERROR (see Chapter 11). **Cut your arm off**, meaning 'eager', is paired with the similar **bite your arm or hand off**, which forms a link to the next section, the hands.

To give someone a **helping hand** has been used since at least the fifteenth century. **Within grasp of** seems to have become a cliché over a hundred years later. The other clichés associated with hands are connected with clothing. **Off the cuff**, although strictly to do with wrists, not hands, fits most conveniently here. This expression for 'seemingly impromptu or unplanned' comes from the habit speakers used to have of writing notes on their shirt cuffs, at which they could take surreptitious glances, thereby being able to speak without a fully prepared script. This could be done in the days when shirts, particularly those worn by after-dinner speakers, were made of stiff cotton heavily starched. Nowadays people may use biro on their hands for the same purpose. It is recorded from the 1930s, but may well be older.

In our society, where gloves are simply optional cold-weather gear and their function purely practical, it is difficult to recapture the intense social significance of gloves in the past. Beautifully embroidered gloves were standard presentation items to visiting monarchs. A number of pairs presented to Elizabeth I have survived, and they are so narrow that it is difficult to imagine that they could ever be worn. Perhaps this was the point. You implied that you believed that the monarch was so refined and had such an aristocratic delicacy that they could wear the impossible. More recently, fine gloves (as opposed to workmen's protective ones) were still an important signal of social rank, and until well into the twentieth century no respectable woman would go out without wearing them. The complex topology involved means that there can scarcely be a more intimate relationship than that between a hand and a glove, hence **hand in glove**. The expression, in use since the first half of the seventeenth century in the form 'hand and glove', is most commonly used of something underhand, but it can also be used simply to suggest a very close co-operation or relationship. To **handle with kid gloves** is more recent. Kid gloves are the softest and finest kind, worn by Victorian ladies in the evening, and rapidly wearing out despite the most careful use. By the middle of the nineteenth century 'kid gloves' was being used to suggest daintiness: 'He was, in fact, a mere kid-glove sportsman,' wrote a reporter scathingly in 1856. By the late nineteenth century 'with kid gloves' was being used to describe delicate negotiations and the handling of difficult problems.

Moving on down to the abdomen we come to the contrasting **lap of luxury** and to **feel gutted**. In the first cliché, yet again we find a very old image in the lap as a place of protection or influence. The Greeks placed the outcome of events *in the lap of the gods*, and we have many expressions such as *to land something in somebody's lap*, meaning to make it their responsibility. The lap is also the place a parent takes a child to comfort and protect it. Thus the lap of luxury is a place where you are protected from the harsher things of life, but by implication also controlled to some extent by your wealth. It has been in use since the beginning of the nineteenth century, and is usually used with an element of disapproval or envy. 'To be or to feel gutted' for 'upset, very disappointed', on the other hand, dates as a cliché only from the late 1980s. Its spread was helped by the way in which footballers took it up to replace the 1970s vogue term SICK AS A PARROT to express their feelings when they lost.

The lower parts of the body are reflected in the expressions 'to give someone a **kick in the pants**' and to **kick butt** or **ass**, both imports, as their language shows, from the USA. 'Kick in the pants' dates from the 1930s, but 'kick butt' is very much more recent, largely replacing the older English equivalent **kick in the arse**. Compare also PAIN IN THE ARSE, above. The legs provide **not a leg to stand on**, which leaves you without anything to support yourself, either monetarily or in an argument. It is first found in the sixteenth century, appropriately enough in Thomas Nashe's *The Unfortunate Traveller* (1594). The opposite image is found in the very recent **has legs** or **will run**, to say that something should work, although most would still class these as slang. If you visit a doctor and have your reflexes tested by being tapped below the knee, then you exhibit a **knee-jerk reaction**, a term that is overused particularly of politicians. You can be **on your knees** in two ways: when begging or praying for something; or when humbled and grovelling, either from physical causes, or, related to the other use, in supplication to a conqueror. In the latter sense to **bring someone to their knees** is also used. Both terms have been in use metaphorically since the nineteenth century, although they existed long before used literally.

If we look at the body as a whole, we find things that **cost an arm and a leg**. An alternative to **cost the earth**, this expression started life in the USA in the middle of the twentieth century. **Bend over backwards** involves even more of the body. Originally a graphic illustration of something that is really difficult and uncomfortable to do, it was first used in the USA in the 1920s, but its effectiveness was rapidly destroyed by overuse. The body as a whole is made up of **flesh and blood**, an expression with two meanings. In the sense 'human, individual' it goes back to the Bible. In the sense 'blood relative' it developed from theories current in the ancient world, going back to at least Galen in the second century AD. It was believed that sexual intercourse involved an actual exchange of blood between the two people involved, so that they literally became of the same blood. This also explains why the Christian Church traditionally bans marriage to any close relative of a deceased spouse, regarding it as incest, a ban enshrined in English law until the end of the nineteenth century. **Bad blood** belongs here, both breeding and ill feeling. In the sense of ill feeling it was certainly well established by the end of the eighteenth century ('ill blood' seems to have been the term used in the seventeenth), and comes from the use of blood as an alternative for the heart as the seat of emotions or feelings. It is more difficult to trace the history of the term in its sense of hereditary bad character. There are some ambiguous uses in the early nineteenth century that could include this sense, and it was certainly used by then in the literal sense of blood that has turned bad, although 'bad blood' is not a medical term we would recognize today. Indeed, 'bad blood' in this sense was used as a euphemism for syphilis well into the twentieth century. It therefore seems highly unlikely that stock-breeders were not using 'bad blood' – at least as an ellipsis for bad bloodline – much earlier.

One of the qualities that these breeders would have looked for in their choice of breeding animals was appearance. The idea of a link between goodness, beauty and truth, and one between ugliness and dishonesty, goes back to the distant past. The ancient Greek word *kallon* meant both beauty and goodness, and hence by implication rightness, truth and associated positive things (which is why Keats can write in the 1820 'Ode to a Grecian Urn': ' "Beauty is truth, truth beauty," – that is all / Ye know on earth, and all ye need to know'). The opposite word, implying wrong, ugly and bad, was *kakos*. This link between ugly and bad appears in later languages and is common in English. As a cliché it gives us **ugly customer** for someone we suspect. The nearest thing to a complementary cliché to this is the ironic **small but perfect(ly formed)**, which seems to have developed in the nineteenth century. The *OED* has an example of 'small but perfect' from 1863. By 1914 Duff Cooper could write to his future wife, Lady Diana, of 'Your two stout lovers, frowning at one another across the hearth rug, while your small, but perfectly formed one kept the party in a roar.' However, this is stretching things, for the true opposite of 'small but perfect' is **built like a tank**. The evolution of this unflattering comparison can be traced in *The Times* archive. In 1955 an advertisement for Nife car batteries started appearing with a headline that read: 'Which battery is built like a Centurion tank?' Here the comparison is literal, for the copy boasts that the battery is made of steel like a Centurion and so can withstand the roughest conditions. By 1963 an article on the German motor industry is telling its readers that 'the passenger cab of a Mercedes is built like a tank', and praises its ability to withstand impact. Then in 1965 a rugby correspondent writes, 'then Stewart, narrowly thwarted, sent Mundy, built like a cruiser tank, crashing over the line for the first try.'

Before we leave the body we should look at the science of medicine. To **take the medicine** obviously reflects the unpleasantness of taking medicine before the later twentieth century. At the time when this expression is first recorded, in the mid nineteenth century, it was common for people to take a 'purging potion' (strong laxative and/or emetic) as part of their general health-maintenance regime. This was known as 'taking a medicine', so when we think of the image behind this expression for doing something unpleasant, we should perhaps think of something much more stomach-churning than simply a dose of cough mixture or an aspirin. To 'take your medicine' is perhaps an idiom rather than a cliché, as is the mysterious 'drug on the market'. The term 'drug' has been used for something that is unwanted since the seventeenth century, but we are not sure why, or even if it is the same word as the medicinal drug. An emerging cliché is the lazy habit of describing something as looking as if it had been done by someone or something **on speed** or **on acid**. HANDING OUT DRUGS LIKE SMARTIES is covered in Chapter 2. Most other medical clichés deal with general health, rather than directly with medicine. So we find terms like **quality of life**. This is a useful expression in medicine and the social sciences which has now become so fashionable that it can be stretched to cover almost anything. Those getting better **feel a different person**, perhaps due to the **caring and sharing** behaviour of those looking after them. The latter has been a cliché since the 1970s, reflecting the vast expansion in the use and meaning of 'caring' in modern social and political use. The expression is now being overtaken in some areas by TOUCHY-FEELY (see Chapter 3). One medical cliché that does not bear much thought is **infectious laughter** and similar uses of infectious – of the sort found in the *Independent* on 3 September 2004: 'He's highly charismatic, with an infectious personality; you find you just can't take your eyes off him', which makes it sound as if the personality is some hideous growth that grabs your attention. 'Infectious' for 'catching emotions' has been in use since at least the start of the seventeenth century, when it is used of grief, but is not recorded of laughter until the nineteenth century. We can also note, using the tenuous link of the breathing in of laughter, the **oxygen of publicity**, which owes its cliché status to a speech by Margaret Thatcher made on 15 July 1985, when she said, 'We must try to find ways to starve the terrorist and the hijacker of the oxygen of publicity on which they depend'; and **with bated breath** (increasingly frequently appearing as 'baited breath'), which is yet another example of a cliché keeping alive obsolete words, for 'bated' is a short form of 'abated' meaning 'reduced'. This too is a quote, from Shakespeare's *Merchant of Venice* (1596–8), Act I, scene 3, which has the lines: 'Shall I bend low and, in a bondman's key, / With bated breath and whisp'ring humbleness, / Say . . .'

The Mind

If we look now at what goes on in the brain, we come to the clichés of thought, feeling and madness. The word 'minded' for thought or intention has recently come to the fore. As a combining form, '. . . -minded', it started to be popular back in the nineteenth century, with forms such as 'peace-minded'. In the 1920s it became very fashionable, with odd combinations such as 'radio-minded' and 'air-minded' (the latter meaning interested in planes and their development). What is more recent is the clichéd use of **I am minded to . . .** This is not a new form – the *OED* has it from the fifteenth century – but it has been increasingly used since the late 1990s in Parliament and official pronouncements. Cynics might say it has become a euphemistic way of saying, 'I am going to do this, but know that not everyone will like it, so I will pretend that I am still open to argument.' Other clichés using the word 'mind' include **mindset** (recorded from the 1930s, although it did not start to become fashionable until the 1970s); **mind over matter**, in use since at least the early nineteenth century (although the concept is old, for Virgil, who lived 70–19 BC, uses a similar expression, which translates as 'mind moves matter', in his *Aeneid*); and **the mind boggles**. To 'boggle', which probably comes from the type of mischievous spirit called a bogle, originally meant to shy at something like a startled horse, an apt description of what happens when you do not want to think about something. As used today, the expression is largely a development of the second half of the twentieth century. An overused term for original thinking is to **think outside the box**. This comes from a puzzle used by psychologists and others to test lateral thinking, which involves being asked to join nine dots, drawn inside a box, with four lines. No mention is made of the box in the instruction, but most people will try to join the dots without crossing the lines that form the box. This is impossible: the only way to complete the puzzle is to extend the lines outside the box. The expression came into use in the 1970s. There have been occasions when to think outside the box has been conflated with OUT OF THE LOOP (see above, under 'Technology') to give the crossbred, and nonsensical, 'to think outside the loop'.

If we turn now to the emotional aspects of the mind, we find the **emotional rollercoaster** (the rollercoaster is first recorded in 1888; 'emotional rollercoaster' starts cropping up in *The Times* from the early 1970s), no doubt caused by **bad vibes**, that archetypical term of the psychedelic sixties. **Emotional intelligence** and **emotional quotient** are fast catching up as clichés. Another cliché that sounds as if it might be from the sixties, but seems actually to be from the eighties, is **feel-good factor**. It was at first used to explain the political and economic phenomena of the times, but now is generally used to suggest general added satisfaction. This **added benefit** (an alternative to **value added**) is often a **figment of the imagination**. This expression, in use since the mid nineteenth century, can take on a wide range of meanings. While it is often used as little more than an emphatic way of saying 'imaginary', it can also be used to convey ideas as diverse as wishful thinking, or a polite way of saying 'lie'. Although it has not yet reached cliché status, I suspect that 'experimenter effect', a term from psychology to describe the way in which the mere fact of being observed affects the results of an experiment, is poised to become an alternative.

Insanity has its own group of clichés. **'I'm mad, I am'** has in itself become a clichéd boast of those proud of their allegedly unconventional behaviour. The root sense of 'rage' is madness rather than anger. This means that the now rather dated **all the rage** belongs in this group. Surprisingly this expression goes back to at least 1785, when it was listed among other fashionable phrases, including **the thing**, used much as we do today. We regularly use a whole range of expressions connected with insanity or extreme emotion for something that is fashionable, many of which are also earlier than one might expect: we have a **craze for** something (recorded 1813) or are **crazy about** it (1779), are **mad for** it (1670), or **wild about** it ('wild to' 1797; 'wild about' 1868). To balance all this, one needs a **reality check**, a 1930s development from the USA.

Sex

And finally we get to the sex promised in the chapter title. Appearance is, of course, an important element in attracting a partner. Appraisals of a woman's appearance by men can range from the crude – **don't get many of those to the pound**; **legs up to her armpits**, both twentieth century – to the poetic – a **vision of beauty**, a more grandiose but no less sentimental version of PRETTY AS A PICTURE (see Chapter 5). Sir Walter Scott was using 'beautiful vision' by 1823, and Benjamin Jowett, in his 1894 translation of Plato's *Republic*, has 'Yes, and the most ridiculous thing of all will be the sight of women naked in the palaestra, exercising with the men, especially when they are no longer young; they certainly will not be a vision of beauty, any more than the enthusiastic old men who in spite of wrinkles and ugliness continue to frequent the gymnasia.' **Drop-dead gorgeous**, although generally used of females, is one of the few such descriptions that can be used of either sex. The use of 'drop dead' to emphasize 'gorgeous' is related to the use of TO DIE FOR (see Chapter 18). **Tall, dark and handsome** has long been found as a combination, and by the 1870s or 1880s was beginning to be used as a clichéd description of the ideal hero, what would in the past have been described as 'the answer to a maiden's prayer' (an expression now so quaint that it has dropped out of the list of clichés). However, 'tall, dark and handsome' really took off in the early years of the twentieth century, and was the title of a song in 1928 and the title of a 1941 film. It is now rarely used except as a conscious cliché, except in the poorest of romantic novels. Someone attractive to one person may seem to another to have **dubious charms**. While this is not confined to appearance and the opposite sex, the expression, in use by at least the Edwardian period, is most often used in this way. Despite the cliché that **gentlemen prefer blondes** (a companion cliché to BLONDE BOMBSHELL; see Chapter 5), some may include among dubious charms those of the **bottle blonde**. *Gentlemen Prefer Blondes* was the title of a 1925 comic novel by Anita Loos, the sequel to which was called *But Gentlemen Marry Brunettes*.

Just as clichés of physical description can be split into the crude and polite, so too can terms for the relationship between the sexes. In the realms of the romantic or euphemistic come terms such as the **fair sex**. In use since the seventeenth century, this cliché, originally meant as a compliment, is now not only hopelessly old-fashioned, but usually downright offensive, particularly when used in combination with, or with the implication of, the **weaker sex**. The latter dates back to the same period, although the even more offensive, but now obsolescent, **weaker vessel** goes back to the Bible. (One must, however, remember that the **female of the species is more dangerous than the male** – a quotation cliché from a Kipling poem.) Someone who would like to consider themselves **footloose and fancy free** and to believe that they and their **significant other** are **just good friends** may find that it is **just one of those things** and they are caught up in a **whirlwind romance**. 'Footloose and fancy free' combines an American nineteenth-century coinage, 'footloose' – the opposite of hobbled, tied down – with 'fancy', used to mean 'love, amorous inclination' since 1559. Although 'fancy' in this sense is marked as obsolete in the dictionaries, it surely still survives as a verb in the sense 'to find sexually attractive'. 'Significant other' is one of the many terms adopted to deal with the fact that the social signalling of relationships has changed in the last fifty years. With married women no longer automatically adopting their husband's surname, and many couples choosing not to marry, there has been a struggle to find terms that convey, for example when introducing people, the relationship between them in an efficient and socially acceptable way. 'Significant other' is one of the more saccharine solutions. The term first appeared in psychology for a person who has a marked influence on another, particularly on a child, but was being adopted for sexual partner by the 1970s. 'Just good friends' is a long-standing journalist's cliché, in use since at least the 1920s to indicate a lack of sexual relationship (although often with a **nudge nudge** implication – a term which took off with the 1969 Monty Python sketch). 'Just one of those things' became popular in the 1930s and got a tremendous boost as a term for relationships from the Cole Porter song 'Just One of those Things' (written 1935, but not a big hit until 1941). The song's popularity was assured by its being used in at least six films. 'Whirlwind romance' is another journalistic cliché dating from the mid twentieth century (balanced by **Marry in haste, repent at leisure**, a proverb dating from at least the seventeenth century, well before the days of easy divorce; although Diogenes Laertius, who lived around AD 200–250, claims in his *Lives of the Philosophers* that when asked if a man should marry, the great fifth-century BC Athenian philosopher Socrates replied, 'Whichever you do, you will repent it'). A similar term is **swept off your feet**, in use by the beginning of the twentieth century. Perhaps the primmest term for relationships with the opposite sex is my **lady wife**. The use of the word 'lady' is full of dangers nowadays, both on grounds of political correctness and as a class marker. To some it is as offensive as the FAIR or WEAKER SEX (see above), marking the speaker as outdatedly sexist. Expressions such as **ladies first** or **the lady of the house** are seen as vulgarisms (although 'Is the lady of the house at home?' is used as a conscious cliché to mark the door-to-door salesman). 'Lady wife' is even more complicated, for while it is used as a conscious cliché to indicate working-class attempts at elegance or chivalry, it is also used to indicate stereotypes of the retired colonel type, from its use in the services. In addition, it conjures up memories of the old music-hall cliché joke **that's no lady, that's my wife**.

The classic clichéd chat-up line is **Do you come here often?** Nowadays, this is a conscious cliché, used to imitate the desperate, embarrassed attempt of a tongue-tied youth to find some way of opening a conversation with a girl. It became a catch-phrase after being used on *The Goon Show* in the 1950s, in which case the correct response is **only in the mating season**. This exchange can still be heard. Nearly as corny for the aspirant seducer is **my wife doesn't understand me**. Its history has not been traced, but it is by no means recent, and has probably been in use for at least the whole of the twentieth century. Eric Partridge describes it in his *Catchphrases* as 'prob[ably] almost immemorial, both in Britain and the US'. The reluctant girl may get out of a date by saying that she is **washing her hair** at the suggested time, a polite fiction usually found as a conscious cliché. A female wishing to seduce a male may be **dressed to kill**. This is a surprisingly old cliché, 'kill' in the sense of 'make a conquest' being well established by the early eighteenth century, and the full 'dressed to kill' being well established by the early nineteenth century. Modern journalists like to pun on the literal and figurative uses of the expression. She could be described by the rather old-fashioned as a **sex kitten**, a cliché of the 1950s which now seems dated because the helpless image of the kitten is no longer as admired in women. It was particularly associated with the French actress Brigitte Bardot, and then with actresses of similar looks. Blended with the earlier BLONDE BOMBSHELL (Chapter 5), the expression produced the term **sex bomb**, used from the 1960s. In order to seduce she might **slip** or **change into something more comfortable,** a conscious cliché from the world of film, used as the words of the vamp before reappearing in something seductive (and often very uncomfortable-looking), usually a negligée. The line appeared in various forms in various films, most famously spoken by Jean Harlow in her 1930 film *Hell's Angels* (written by Howard

Estabrook and Harry Behn), 'Would you be shocked if I changed into something more comfortable?' If she is successful, the man may become more serious and say **let me take you away from all this**, another cliché of film. The following exchange between a robot frog and Miss Piggy in a 1976 episode of *The Muppets* has become something of a catchphrase in its own right, and more or less sums up the status of MARRIAGE MADE IN HEAVEN (for which, see Chapter 6): 'Yeah. Look, let me take you away from all this. Aaah, a marriage made in heaven! A frog and a pig. We can have bouncing baby figs!' However, if the apparent seducer is actually a **muck-raking** journalist (found from the beginning of the twentieth century) he may claim he **made his excuses and left**, an expression coined by Duncan Webb, the chief crime reporter of the *People* in the 1950s. The female equivalent is the **kiss and tell** story. Although this is a cliché of modern journalism, which has developed the variant **kiss and sell** from the large amounts of money that have been made from selling salacious information to the media, the actual expression is an old one. In his *Burlesque* of 1675 Charles Cotton wrote, 'And if he needs must kiss and tell, I'll kick him headlong into Hell', and a few years later William Congreve was writing, 'Oh fie Miss, you must not kiss and tell' (*Love for Love*, 1695). A brave man will, like the Duke of Wellington, say **publish and be damned**. There is some doubt as to whether Wellington really said this in reply to a former mistress who tried to get him to pay her money to leave their relationship out of her autobiography. Nowadays the 'damned' element often refers not to a curse from the person written about, but to public reaction to the published work.

Once we get down to the real business of sex, as the **actress said to the bishop** (Eric Partridge says of this: 'Certainly in RAF use *c.*1944–7, but prob[ably] going back to Edwardian days; only very slightly ob[solete] by 1975, it is likely to outlive us all'), we come to a number of different clichés for activities **between the sheets**. As a term for sexual activity this expression has been in use since Shakespeare's day. In fact Shakespeare was rather fond of using 'sheets' in this way, doing so at least seven times, for example when Iago expresses his suspicions that Othello has seduced his wife, Emilia, with the words: 'And it is thought abroad that 'twixt my sheets / He has done my office' (I.3). Men seem keen to have their performance endorsed, even if they are merely **sowing their wild oats**. This expression is found from the middle of the sixteenth century, and is summed up in a quote of 1576 that writes of 'That wilful and unruly age, which lacketh ripeness and discretion, and (as we say) hath not sowed all their wild oates.' Modern herbicides, like modern spermicides, have gone a long way to removing the problem of wild oats, but in the past they could be a real problem in farmers' fields, representing an unwanted, intrusive crop, rather than useful, desired grain. **Did you feel the earth move?** (often found as **Did the earth move for you?**) is an adaptation of Ernest Hemingway's 'Did thee feel the earth move?' in the big sex scene in his 1940 novel of the Spanish civil war, *For Whom the Bell Tolls* (filmed 1943), and this rather pretentious expression soon became a humorous way of referring to the intensity of sexual reaction. And why, incidentally, do so many Americans seem incapable of getting the use of 'thee' and 'thou' right? Less poetic is **How was it for you?** Both these are rarely found used today except as jokes. A much less considerate lover is implied by **lie back and think of England**. This cliché has a somewhat clouded history. In the form 'close your eyes and think of England' it seems to have been a late nineteenth-century catchphrase, not particularly associated with sexual intercourse, but with doing anything unpleasant. The story that one of her ladies-in-waiting said it to Queen Victoria on her wedding night has no known foundation. A diary entry by Lady Hillingdon (1857–1940) for 1912 is sometimes cited as a source, but it is far more likely that she was already using an established expression when she wrote, 'I am happy now that Charles calls on my bedchamber less frequently than of old. As it is, I now endure but two calls a week and when I hear his steps outside my door I lie down on my bed, close my eyes, open my legs and think of England.' The expression is used not just of unwanted sex, but also of rape, euphemistically known as a **fate worse than death**. The latter cliché, also used in the past as a general term for a fall from sexual grace, dates from the early nineteenth century and grew in use with that century's obsession with female 'purity'. With the more balanced views of the twentieth century it became more and more difficult to use seriously and it is now often used in non-sexual contexts. One who does fall may be **left holding the baby**. The sense 'left with something unwanted' seems to have developed in business circles at the start of the twentieth century to describe someone left holding shares that cannot be sold at a profit. The old-fashioned parent might have told the **fallen woman** to **never darken my door again**. This is only ever used now as a conscious cliché to evoke the image of the stern Victorian father casting off the errant child, an image summed up in Alfred, Lord Tennyson's poem 'Dora' (1842): 'You shall pack / And never darken my doors again.' The earliest recorded use is by Benjamin Franklin, who said in an entirely sex-free context of someone who had taken offence, 'I am afraid she would resent it so as never to darken my door again' (*Busy-body*, 1729); but from the way he uses it, it was obviously already well established. 'To darken a door' by itself was used in the past simply to mean 'enter'.

The old-fashioned antithesis to the fallen woman is the **blushing bride**. This goes back to at least the eighteenth century, and reflects the modesty and purity expected in an innocent bride, for she is blushing not only because she is the centre of attention, but because marriage inevitably leads to bed. Modern mores being what they are, it is not surprising that this cliché is in decline. If she really is the innocent expected by traditionalists (who should be described as 'puritan', not as is so often mistakenly done as 'prurient', which means, to quote the *OED*, 'given to the indulgence of lewd ideas', the opposite of what is intended), she may be in need of guidance. *Everything You Always Wanted to Know about Sex, but Were Afraid to Ask* was a sex guide written by David Reuben and published in 1969. In 1972 Woody Allen used it for the title of one of his films. He had purchased the right to use the title from Reuben, but the two works have nothing else in common. The title soon became a formula phrase: **everything you've always wanted to know about . . . but were afraid to ask**, widely used by advertisers. Another sex manual, *The Joy of Sex*, a best-selling book by Alex Comfort published in 1972, gives us the formula **the joy of . . .**, a cliché of headlines and book titles. Comfort in turn based the title on earlier instructional books such as *The Joy of Cooking* (1932). The word 'sex' also features in the clichés **sex, lies and videotape,** the title of a 1989 film, which is very popular with headline writers, and much alluded to whenever newspaper stories break involving scandal and secret recordings; and **sex and drugs and rock and roll**. This cliché of rock as rebellion and the lifestyle that goes with it comes from the title of a 1977 song performed and written by Ian Dury and the Blockheads, correctly written, for purists, 'Sex & Drugs & Rock & Roll'. After a while the blushing bride may find that the **honeymoon is over**. 'Honeymoon' has been used in a transferred sense for a period of goodwill or especial friendliness since the sixteenth century. 'The honeymoon is over' is found used literally in *The Times* as early as 1786, when the writer of a letter to the editor leaps to the defence of 'sluttish wives' who had been attacked by a previous writer for not dressing smartly, saying, 'it is but too often the case with the generality of husbands, when they have gained the heart and affections of a deserving female, and when after the honeymoon is over, that they treat them with so much indifference, and merely as a sort of upper servants, that a woman of any spirit can never brook.' The letter is signed 'A Sluttish Wife'. The first case I can find of it being used in the modern sense is in a political speech of 1894. An unsuccessful marriage might then turn into a **love–hate relationship**. Love and hate have been contrasted probably since the words first appeared in English, but as a psychological term, now diluted by overuse, it is first found in English in 1925, in a translation of Sigmund Freud's *Collected Papers*.

The **love that dare not speak its name** (from the line 'I am the love that dare not speak its name' in Lord Alfred Douglas's 1896 poem 'Two Loves'; because of Douglas's role in the trial of Oscar Wilde, the line is often misattributed to Wilde) seems to suffer from stereotypes rather than clichés. The use of 'pink' for homosexual, as in the **pink pound**, is overused, but serves a useful function in identifying a target market. In the 1920s 'lavender' was the colour used to indicate homosexuality, but since the 1970s 'pink' has predominated. It is said to come from the use of a pink triangle sewn on to the uniform of homosexuals interned by the Nazis. There are a few related turns of phrase, such as *camp as a row of tents*, that approach cliché status, but overall, given the high and eloquent profile of homosexuals today, the language has gained few clichés from this section of society.

Finally, a group of sex-related clichés that do not fit easily into any narrative, but need dealing with. **Born and bred** belongs here because there is no birth without sex. This alliterative expression has been in use since the fourteenth century, and by 1542 Nicholas Udall, headmaster of Eton and the first known Englishman to write a comedy, could use the elaboration: 'In the same Isle born, bred and brought up'. In modern times it is mainly used in contexts of xenophobia or unthinking patriotism, whether local or national – try adding terms such as 'a Yorkshireman' or 'an Englishman' after it. More obviously sexual are the **dirty mac brigade** and **dirty old man**. Dirty old men (DOMs) – those who enjoy pornography or chasing younger women – are traditionally thought of as wearing dirty mackintoshes. There is a basis of truth in this, for accounts of places such as the Windmill Theatre, famous for its nude shows in the Second World War, by the comedians who cut their teeth there, describe the way in which the DOMs who used to sit through show after show, gradually moving forward until they reached the front row, always wore a long coat of some kind, or at least kept a newspaper on their laps, so no one could see what they were doing with their hands. From this tradition 'dirty mac' has come to be an alternative for 'dirty old man', and from that has come to represent something that is seedy or degrading. **Don't do anything I wouldn't do** is used as a jocular comment to anyone going somewhere to enjoy themselves, particularly if there is a possibility of sex being involved. It seems to date from around 1900 – it was certainly in use by the First World War – and was particularly popular as a catchphrase said to those going on leave from the forces in the Second World War. An alternative is **be good – and if you can't be good, be careful**, which dates from about the same time, having been the title of an American popular song of 1907.

16. Bible and Religion

It is hard to remember in our modern, secular and multicultural society quite how soaked in the language of religion people used to be. This applies not only to the more distant past, but to times within living memory. Throughout my schooldays at a Church of England school, for instance, I sat through two full services every school day, and was expected to attend church every Sunday. Everything in these services was drawn from the Authorized Version of the Bible and the Book of Common Prayer (all biblical quotes given here and throughout the book are from these texts). Given this saturation, which would have been typical of school life for hundreds of years, it is not surprising that the English language is full of echoes from these texts. In addition, each day of the Church year has its prescribed lessons, one each from the Old and New Testaments at Morning Prayer and another pair for Evening Prayer. These lessons would, of course, be the parts of the Bible that were most heard by church-goers, and when clichés are drawn from them the relevant dates of the lessons are given in brackets. Not all the biblical quotes and allusions that have given rise to clichés are listed here; others fit more comfortably in other chapters. However, the majority are here, and give us an interesting insight into the books and stories in the Bible that were most important to people. The clichés also give ample illustration of the way in which a set phrase can stay indefinitely in the language once it has been established, with people quite happy to use sixteenth-century vocabulary and turns of phrase that they would never dream of using otherwise.

Some of the biblical clichés are what we might call 'general', either because they allude to the Bible or because they are found in a number of places. **Gospel truth** is an example of the first type. It was used in a literal sense to mean 'the word of God' from at least the seventeenth century. By the nineteenth it had developed into a cliché simply meaning 'honestly, truly'. In twentieth-century film and television it developed further into a cliché for worried, and usually dishonest, working-class people trying to convince 'their betters' of their honesty. Similarly, anyone wanting to sound like a vicar in the media was likely to use the phrase 'and it **came to pass**'. This expression, found throughout the Bible, is perhaps best known from Luke 2:1, the opening of the Christmas story: 'And it came to pass in those days, and there went out a decree from Caesar Augustus, that all the world should be taxed.' It was well established in the language by the sixteenth century, and a cliché by the eighteenth. **Gird up your loins** is an expression to encourage effort, although it is now rather old-fashioned. It occurs a number of times in the Old Testament, most notably in the form 'Gird up now thy loins like a man' (Job 38:3; Evening Prayer, 13 July). The expression reflects the simply cut, loose and flowing long garments of the time, when doing anything physically demanding involved using a girdle or belt to keep your clothes from tripping you up. The expression was already being used figuratively when St Paul wrote, 'Gird up the loins of thy mind' (1 Peter 1:13; Morning Prayer, 27 November). **Manna from heaven** refers to the episode in Exodus when the Children of Israel, stuck without resources in the desert, are miraculously sent manna to keep them from starvation, but the expression as we use it seems to be an adaptation of 'He rained down manna also upon them for to eat: and gave them food from heaven' in Psalm 78:25 in the version used in the Book of Common Prayer. There are two expressions that look as if they should be traceable to a religious quotation, but are not. **Trials and tribulations** occurs nowhere in this form in either the King James Bible or the Book of Common Prayer (although each word is found individually), while **without let or hindrance** is a legal set phrase that is most prominently found in the preamble to the

British passport, 'Her Britannic Majesty's Secretary of State requests and requires . . . all those whom it may concern to allow the bearer to pass freely without let or hindrance . . .' 'Let' here is an otherwise near-obsolete word meaning 'prevention, stopping'. It survives in the let in tennis, which occurs when the net prevents the clean passing of the ball. 'To let' in this sense was still common in Shakespeare's day, hence Hamlet's otherwise incomprehensible comment to the friends who try to stop him following his father's ghost: 'Unhand me, gentlemen. By heaven, I'll make a ghost of him that lets me' (Act I, scene 5). Its decline is a fine example of the rule that no two words that sound alike and have possibly confusing meanings can happily co-exist in a language (see further at STEM THE TIDE, Chapter 11).

If we turn to direct quotes from the Bible, Matthew is the outright winner in the popularity stakes. This is the longest and fullest of the Gospels, and still, to some extent, the one that people know best. To **hide your light under a bushel** comes from Matthew 5:14–15, where Jesus tells his followers to be open about their beliefs: 'Ye are the light of the world. A city that is set on a hill cannot be hid. Neither do men light a candle, and put it under a bushel, but on a candlestick; and it giveth light unto all that are in the house. Let your light so shine before men.' Bushel, here, is a container with a volume large enough to hold a bushel (eight pints). The passage has been used as an image in English since the sixteenth century, but the actual wording we now use seems to be nineteenth century. Next comes **not a jot or tittle**. This is found in the same chapter (read at Morning Prayer, January 8; Evening Prayer, 11 July), verse 18, where Jesus says: 'Till heaven and earth pass, one jot or tittle shall in no wise pass from the law, till all be fulfilled.' It has been in use since the Middle Ages, although it was mainly restricted to religious contexts until the sixteenth century. 'Jot' is the old form of the word 'iota', the Greek letter 'i', and tittle is an old word for an accent or mark such as the dot over the 'i', so both represent the smallest marks possible. Next comes

left hand doesn't know what the right is doing. This is
found in Matthew 6:3 (read at services the next day), when Jesus
says, 'When thou doest alms, let not thy left hand know what
thy right hand doeth: that thine alms may be in secret.' In
other words, **do good by stealth**. Modern adaptations of the
expression are used ironically to mean that someone is unco-
ordinated, or else to indicate that different parts of an organization don't know what each other are doing. A formula phrase
from Matthew 26:52 (Morning Prayer, 17 February; Evening
Prayer, 19 August) is **those who live by the . . . die by the
. . .** which is based on 'All they that take the sword shall perish
with the sword.' It was adapted as a variable saying, most often
as 'They who live by the sword shall die by the sword', and this
has become a common formula. Indeed the pattern was set as
early as 1601, when we find: 'Those that live by blood: in blood
they die.' The punishment for those who live by the sword is
probably to be **cast into outer darkness**. In chapter 8:12
(Morning Prayer, 13 January; Evening Prayer, 16 July) Matthew
writes, 'But the children of the kingdom shall be cast out into
outer darkness: there shall be weeping and gnashing of teeth.'
He repeats the exact words from 'cast' to 'teeth' twice more
(chapters 22 and 25). The variant **wailing and gnashing of
teeth** comes from yet another similar passage in chapter 13.
Outer darkness here is the equivalent of hell, the state of being
cut off from the Light of God. It has been used since the
nineteenth century to mean being a social outcast, someone
rejected, or similar. You may want to **wash your hands of**
such people. This comes from Matthew 27:24 (Morning Prayer,
20 February; Evening Prayer, 21 August), which tells how the
Roman governor of Judea, Pontius Pilate, offered to release
Jesus, but when the crowd demanded the release of Barabbas
instead, he 'washed his hands before the multitude, saying I am
innocent of the blood of this just person'. The expression has
been used since the sixteenth century, and by the eighteenth
was a cliché that could be used of trivial things without obvious

reference to the original circumstances. On a lighter note, **out of the mouths of babes and sucklings** is a rather sentimental comment used today to comment on some cute or inadvertently pertinent saying by a child, but originally it had a far more devout meaning, the original being: 'Out of the mouths of babes and sucklings hast thou perfected praise' (Matthew 21:16; Morning Prayer, 6 February; Evening Prayer, 8 August). This in turn derives from an earlier line in the Old Testament: 'Out of the mouths of babes and sucklings hast thou ordained strength' (Psalm 8:2). From Matthew 5:13 (Morning Prayer, 7 January; Evening Prayer, 10 July) comes the expression **salt of the earth**: 'Ye are the salt of the earth: but if the salt have lost his savour, wherewith shall it be salted?' The expression has been used in the language since Anglo-Saxon times, but really took off as a cliché in the nineteenth century. Then it was used to mean someone of great worthiness and reliability, but in current use its meaning has changed, perhaps under the influence of the idea of 'earthiness', and now tends to have strong class markers, implying someone who may not be well educated or have obvious middle-class trappings, but is nevertheless thoroughly reliable – sometimes, indeed, not far from the Victorian cliché of working-class respectability POOR BUT HONEST, but otherwise a ROUGH DIAMOND (for both, see Chapter 9). Another cliché from Matthew connected with earth is to **shake the dust from your feet**. This is an allusion to Jesus' instructions to his disciples: 'Whosoever shall not receive you, nor hear your words, when ye depart out of that house or city, shake off the dust of your feet' (Matthew 10:14; Morning Prayer, 17 January; Evening Prayer, 21 July), in other words, eradicate all associations with them. The expression has been used for leaving, usually indignantly, since the eighteenth century. Fanny Burney wrote in 1782: 'I then paid off my lodging, and "shaking the dust from my feet", bid a long adieu to London.' In Matthew 7:6 (Morning Prayer, 11 January; Evening Prayer, 14 July) Jesus says, 'Give not that which is holy unto the dogs, neither **cast** ye your **pearls**

before swine, lest they trample them under their feet', the pearls here being **pearls of wisdom**, or at least of the holy word. From this the expression has come to mean to offer things you value to people who will not appreciate them, a use found from at least the seventeenth century, and a cliché by the nineteenth. The same chapter (verse 14) gives us **straight and narrow**. 'Strait' was the original form here, being an old word for narrow, with the expression coming from: 'Strait is the gate, and narrow is the way, which leadeth unto life' (Morning Prayer, 12 January; Evening Prayer, 15 July) – meaning that it is easy to wander off the narrow path to eternal life. In sixteenth-century writing the use of coupled synonyms was a much admired elegancy. In more modern writing 'strait' and 'narrow' together are likely to be seen as tautology, and with the loss of 'strait' except as a narrow sea and in the set phrase **straitened circumstances** (eighteenth century), it is not unreasonable to have substituted 'straight', which alters the image but not its meaning. In both forms the words were a set pairing by the sixteenth century, but the expression 'the straight and narrow' for a socially acceptable way of living has not yet been found before the 1830s. Finally, a **sign of the times** is from Jesus' words to the Pharisees: 'O ye hypocrites, ye can discern the face of the sky; but can ye not discern the signs of the times?' (Matthew 16:2; Morning Prayer, 29 January; Evening Prayer, 31 July).

Second only to Matthew as a source come the various epistles of St Paul. Again, this is not particularly surprising. Paul, an early and zealous convert to Christianity, was the major voice in transforming it from a Jewish sect to a world religion. His epistles are the major guide on how to lead a Christian life in practical detail, and as such were prominent in church as well as in the home. His influence still lingers. For example, he is the source of **the forces** or **powers of darkness**. This cliché for the devil, the **Prince of Darkness**, or evil in general, is found in Colossians 1:13 (Morning Prayer, 11 October; Evening Prayer, 2 April), where thanks are given to God 'who hath delivered us from the power of darkness'. 'Powers of darkness' is recorded in English from the fourteenth century, and was a commonplace of religious writings from the seventeenth century, reaching cliché status by at least the nineteenth. The use of 'forces' rather than 'powers' seems to have come from the common expression **forces of evil**, which was in use by 1862. These combinations are still bearing fruit, particularly in America, where the same rhetoric can be found currently used about the dark forces behind terrorism and members of the **axis of evil**. Both preachers and politicians can be said disparagingly to **hold forth**. This comes from Philippians 2:16 (Morning Prayer, 8 October; Evening Prayer, 25 April), where Christians are told that they should go through the world 'Holding forth the word of life'. From this the expression came to be used for delivering a sermon or bearing witness to the Word of God. Since people who are sermonizing tend to speak both at length and somewhat obsessively, it is easy to see how the modern senses of 'to hold forth' developed. This had happened by the eighteenth century, but since 'hold forth' could still be used at the time for 'hold out, present' some rather incongruous uses, to the modern ear, can be found, such as Robert Burns's 'In plain braid Scots hold forth a plain braid story' (*Brigs of Ayr*, 1787). The Epistle to the Romans gives us three clichés. **Hope against hope** comes from: 'Who against hope believed in hope that he might become the father of many nations' (Romans 4:18; Morning Prayer, 4 August; Evening Prayer, 20 February). **The powers that be**, a grandiloquent alternative for 'they' when complaining about those in charge, although often used ironically, comes from Paul's pronouncement 'The powers that be are ordained by God' and that everyone who ignores this is damned (Romans 13:1; Morning Prayer, 16 August; Evening Prayer, March 4), and **wages of sin** from Romans 6:23 (Morning Prayer, 6 August; Evening Prayer, 22 February). The full quote is 'The wages of sin is death', and the peculiar grammar is because 'wages' was originally a singular noun, but because it ends in 's' has come to be treated as plural. Perhaps because of the uncomfortable grammar, the whole form is now rarely found. The **inner man** is one of those clichés that radically change the original meaning of the coiner. St Paul says that Christ 'would grant you, according to the riches of his glory, to be strengthened with might by his Spirit in the inner man' (Ephesians 3:16; Morning Prayer, 2 October; Evening Prayer, 19 April). The expression has been used in English of the soul, mind or spiritual part of man since about the year 1000, but since the late eighteenth century has been used humorously to mean the stomach. **Labour of love** has also drifted from its original sense of a charitable deed. The expression 'your works of faith and labours of love' occurs at both 1 Thessalonians 1:3 (Morning Prayer, 6 October; Evening Prayer, 4 May) and Hebrews 6:10 (Morning Prayer, November 12; Evening Prayer, 30 May). In a **thorn in the flesh** or **side** St Paul is picking up a passage from Judges 2:3, where God tells the Israelites not to ally themselves to the people of their new land for 'they shall become as thorns in your sides'. In 2 Corinthians 12:7 (Morning Prayer, 20 September; Evening Prayer, 8 April) Paul says, 'there was given me a thorn in the flesh, the messenger of Satan to buffet me.' The version with 'flesh' is the more popular in the UK, that with 'side' in the USA. One final echo from Paul is found in **charity begins at home**. 'Charity' is a difficult word. While most modern users limit it to the idea of giving money to help the needy, the Latin word it is based on had a very different meaning. *Caritas* meant 'dearness, love based on respect (as opposed to sexual attraction)' as well as 'expensiveness', much in the way that we use 'dear' for both senses in English. 'Charity' was thus the word chosen in the King James Bible for 'Christian love', and many of our sayings containing the word 'charity' originally used it in this sense, including 'charity begins at home'. One aspect of Christian love is the giving of alms to the poor, so that this sense of charity has all along existed alongside the other, and it is not surprising that the two have become confused. Both ideas are found in the First Epistle to Timothy (read at Evening Prayer in the middle of May, at Morning Prayer over several days in October), in the instruction, 'But if any provide not for his own, and specially for those of his own house, he hath denied the faith, and is worse than an infidel' and in the instruction that children should 'learn first to shew piety at home'. Forms of the saying are found from the fourteenth century, and by the early seventeenth were well-enough known for Francis Beaumont and John Fletcher to write, 'Charity and beating begins at home' (*Wit without Money*).

Isaiah is the most popular Old Testament source. Once again the text plays an important part in readings through the church year, for his writings were regarded as important foreshadowings of the coming of Christ, and no doubt the influence of his writings is helped by the wonderful language and vivid images with which his prophecies were made. Not all these quotes are obviously religious. A **drop in the bucket**, for example, comes from Isaiah 40:12 (the lesson for Morning Prayer on 11 December, and Evensong on the first Sunday after Christmas), where we are told God 'hath measured the waters in the hollow of his hand . . . and weighed the mountains in scales, and the hills in a balance . . . Behold, the nations are as a drop of a bucket, and are counted as the small dust of the balance.' A **drop in the ocean**, a more emphatic version of 'drop in the bucket', was well established by the end of the eighteenth century. Isaiah 3 gives us two clichés: the **staff of life** for bread, or whatever else serves as the local staple (because it *supports* life), an allusion to 'the stay and the staff, the whole stay of bread' (Isaiah 3:1) and in use in English by the 1630s; and to **grind the faces of the poor**, from Isaiah 3:15: 'What mean ye that ye beat my people to pieces and grind the faces of the poor?' This now has a rather old-fashioned ring to it, but together with the use of 'grinding' to mean 'oppressive, wearing' has helped give rise to expressions such as **grindingly poor** and **in grinding poverty**. Isaiah 3 is read at Morning Prayer on 20 November, the feast of King Edmund, the martyred Anglo-Saxon king who gave his name to Bury St Edmunds. Those who hypocritically **pay lip service** to something may also act **holier than thou**. The former comes from Isaiah 29:13, 'This people draw near me with their mouth, and with their lips do honour me, but have removed their heart far from me', a passage that is echoed at Matthew 15:8 and which is read at Evening Prayer on 6 December. The latter comes from Isaiah 65:5, which attacks those who have the attitude 'Stand by thyself, come not near to me; for I am holier than thou', and is read at Evening Prayer on 30 November, the Feast of St Andrew, and again exactly one month later. There may be **no peace for the wicked** ('There is no peace, saith the Lord, unto the wicked', Isaiah 48:22; Evening Prayer, 16 December; the phrase has been used since the later nineteenth century), but the good may choose to turn their **swords into ploughshares**, which comes from Isaiah's great vision of a time of peace, when people 'shall beat their swords into ploughshares, and their spears into pruninghooks' (2:4, read at Evening Prayer on 19 November and more importantly at Evensong on the first Sunday in Advent). This expression was much used in the period of Russian and American disarmament in the 1990s when news stories showed the metal of armaments being recycled into domestic products, although this powerful image, beautiful until dulled by overuse, has been popular for a long time.

Daniel, that romantic collection of miracles and dreams, comes next in popularity. The Book of Daniel tells us how the king, Nebuchadnezzar, has dreamed a disturbing dream which, come the morning, he can no longer remember. Rather unreasonably, he insists that his magicians and astrologers not only interpret the dream, but tell him what it was in the first place. Only Daniel can perform this task, and he tells the king:

Thou, O king, sawest, and behold a great image . . . This image's head was of fine gold, his breast and his arms of silver, his belly and his thighs of brass, his legs of iron, his feet part of iron and part of clay. Thou sawest till that a stone was cut out without hands, which smote the image upon his feet that were of iron and clay, and brake them to pieces. Then was the iron, the clay, the brass, the silver, and the gold, broken to pieces together, and became like the chaff of the summer threshing-floors. (2:31–5)

Daniel interprets this dream to represent a decline in the quality of kings, until the dynasty is swept away. The whole thing is summed up in the expression **feet of clay**, in use by the beginning of the nineteenth century in the general sense of an underlying weakness. Nebuchadnezzar's successor, Belshazzar, profanes the looted golden vessels of the Temple of Jerusalem, by using them to drink from at a feast (Daniel 5). As a warning of the consequences of this impiety a hand appears and writes the words '*mene, mene, tekel, upharsin*' on the wall. When Daniel is called on to interpret this **writing on the wall**, he interprets the word '*tekel*' as 'Thou art weighed in the balances [from which we get **weighed in the balance**] and art found wanting', and '*mene*' as 'God has numbered thy kingdom, and finished it.' This latter seems to have become combined with expressions such as 'the number of thy days' (Exodus 23:26) to produce his **days are numbered**. The scene of the writing on the wall was the inspiration for Edward Fitzgerald's much-quoted lines 'The moving finger writes; and having writ, / Moves on' (*Rubáiyát of Omar Khayyám* 1859), and the two are sometimes confused. These stories from Daniel are read in church over morning and evening prayers in the middle of September.

No other books of the Old Testament have been quite as influential on the language as Daniel and Isaiah. Genesis gives us 'Ye shall eat **the fat of the land**' (45:18; Morning Prayer, 31 January; Evensong, the fourth Sunday in Lent) and the **land of Nod**. This nursery term for going to sleep was a pretty feeble joke when Jonathan Swift used it in the 1730s in his *Polite Conversation*, and it has not improved with repetition. In Genesis

4:16 (Morning Prayer, 4 January) Cain is exiled to the Land of Nod after he kills Abel. Since you *nod off* when you go to sleep, this became a punning way to say you were going to sleep. The same story of the ultimate in sibling rivalry gives us to **raise Cain**. This expression must have been well established by the 1840s, when the St Louis *Daily Pennant* published the dreadful riddle, typical of Victorian humour, 'Why have we every reason to believe that Adam and Eve were both rowdies? Because . . . they both raised Cain.' Cain, son of Adam and Eve, was the first murderer and a social outcast, he and his descendants bearing the mark of Cain after he murdered his brother, Abel. Thus 'to raise Cain' was to behave in a way that Cain might have done: to make a disturbance, be noisy, *cry blue murder*.

Exodus gives us **an eye for an eye**. Exodus 21:24 says, 'And if any mischief follow, then thou shall give life for life, eye for eye, tooth for tooth, hand for hand, foot for foot, burning for burning, wound for wound, stripe for stripe.' The form 'eye for an eye', used to indicate retaliation in kind, sits more comfortably on the English tongue. It is one of the few biblical clichés that is not one of the prescribed lessons.

The next book is Leviticus, which gives us **stumbling block**. Its rather odd grammar – normally it would mean a block that stumbles – comes from the fact that it is a translation. Leviticus 19:13 orders, 'Thou shalt not curse the deaf, nor put a stumbling block before the blind' (Morning Prayer, 29 February). It has been used figuratively since the sixteenth century.

The life of King David gives us two clichés: the term **David and Goliath** for the defeat of something big by someone much less powerful – a favourite of sporting journalists – comes from the way in which David, while still a mere shepherd-boy, uses his sling to kill the champion of the Philistines, the giant Goliath of Gath (1 Samuel 17, the story being read over Morning and Evening Prayer on 26 April). **How are the mighty fallen** is from David's beautiful lament for the deaths of Saul and Jonathan:

The beauty of Israel is slain upon thy high places: how are the mighty fallen! Tell it not in Gath, publish it not in the streets of Askelon, lest the daughters of the Philistines rejoice . . . I am distressed for thee, my brother Jonathan: very pleasant hast thou been unto me: thy love to me was wonderful, passing the love of women. How are the mighty fallen, and the weapons of war perished! (2 Samuel 1; Evening Prayer, 3 May)

As a cliché it is usually used as a statement of grim satisfaction that someone has got their comeuppance, what is known by that German vogue word **schadenfreude**. The latter is a cliché of the intellectually pretentious, and is formed from the German words for 'harm' and 'joy'.

Job gives us the **root of the matter**: 'Why persecute him, seeing the root of the matter is found in me?' (Job 19:28, Evening Prayer, 7 July), while Psalms gives us **deep calling unto deep,** based on the words of Psalm 42:7: 'Deep calleth unto deep'. The latter has been in use since at least the middle of the nineteenth century, and was regarded as pompous even then. If you make a **rod for your own back** (most often used of the way other people raise their children) you are echoing Proverbs 26:3: 'A whip for the horse, a bridle for the ass, and a rod for the fool's back' (Evening Prayer, July 29); and if you feel those people are at the **tender mercies** of their brats you echo Proverbs 12:10: 'A righteous man regardeth the life of his beast: but the tender mercies of the wicked are cruel' (Morning Prayer, 23 July). Ezekiel's vision of the Valley of Dry Bones (Ezekiel 37; Morning Prayer, 12–13 September) is the probable source of **dry as a bone**. Hosea 8:7 (Morning Prayer, 24 September) gives us: 'They have sown the wind and they shall **reap the whirlwind**', while **root and branch** adapts Malachi 4:1: 'For, behold, the day cometh, that shall burn as an oven; and all the proud, yea, and all that do wickedly, shall be stubble: and the day that cometh shall burn them up, saith the Lord of hosts, that it shall leave them neither root nor branch', and has been in regular use since the seventeenth century. Although Malachi is rather an obscure book of the Bible, this particular passage is read as one of the more prominent lessons – at Evening Prayer on 24 June. This is not only St John the Baptist's Day, a day that was often picked for important national gatherings such as troop musterings, as well as being a Quarter Day, when debts were due to be paid, but is also one of the Ember days, days set apart for fasting and prayer. All these events would encourage church attendance on this day, so the lesson would have been heard by many.

While St Matthew's Gospel dominates clichés from the New Testament, Luke and John provide two each. From Luke we get **tidings of joy**, an expression based on the message of the angels to the shepherds in the Christmas story: 'Behold, I bring you good tidings of great joy, which shall be to all people. For unto you is born this day in the city of David a Saviour, which is Christ the Lord' (2:10–11; read at Morning Prayer on 26 March, the day after the Feast of the Annunciation, when Mary was told she was pregnant, and Evening Prayer on 25 September, and prominent in many Christmas services). For modern users the principal source is probably the Christmas carol 'God Rest You Merry, Gentlemen', with its chorus, 'Tidings of comfort and joy', based on Luke. The other is **good Samaritan**, from the parable in Luke 10 (Morning Prayer, 11 April; Evening Prayer, 12 October), which tells the story of how a man was mugged on the road to Jerusalem and left half-dead on the roadside. Two people, including a priest, **passed by on the other side** when they saw him lying there, but a Samaritan who came past went to help him, tended his wounds, took him to an inn, and the next day left money with the inn-keeper, telling him to spend what was necessary. Jesus told this story in answer to the question 'Who is my neighbour?' after he had instructed his followers to love their neighbours. The point of the story was that the Samaritans were traditional enemies of the Jews. Because of this, 'good Samaritan' has been used to mean a good neighbour, but nowadays is usually used to mean someone who helps someone in trouble. In recent years use of the expression has been given a new twist by Mrs Thatcher's comment in defence of her policies, said during a television interview in 1989, 'No one would remember the Good Samaritan if he'd only had good intentions. He had money as well.' St John 8:7 (Morning Prayer, 23 May; Evening Prayer, 23 November) tells the story of the woman taken in adultery. Jesus is asked what should be done with the woman, since the law of Moses says that she should be stoned. He replies, 'He that is without sin among you, let him first cast a stone at her.' Since none of her accusers can claim to be without sin, they slink away, leaving her unharmed, and giving us the expression to **cast the first stone**. John 15:13 (Morning Prayer, 4 June; Evening Prayer, 6 December) also gives us '**Greater love hath no man** than this, that a man lay down his life for his friends.' It is used as a moving and straightforward quotation on memorials and in similar situations, but nowadays, when it is used in general writing, it is nearly always with irony, as in the Cabinet minister who quipped of Chris Patten, then the Secretary of State, 'Greater love hath no man than that he lays down his jokes for his Prime Minister' (*Independent*, 13 October 1989).

The Song of Solomon, that great work of erotic literature (in its true sense) is, unsurprisingly, not used for lessons in church, but has always been read for its beautiful images. In another example of a clichéd phrase travelling far from its original sense, **ivory tower** comes from 7:4, where the beloved is told, 'Thy neck is as a tower of ivory.' This became a standard image of beauty in medieval literature – Chaucer, for instance, uses it of the heroine of his *Book of the Duchess* – and it was widely used as a symbol of the Virgin Mary. However, the image associated with an ivory tower changed radically after 1837 when Sainte-Beuve used it to describe the French poet Alfred de Vigny 'in his ivory tower', and it came to mean a privileged seclusion, sheltered from the realities of the harsh world outside. It is now used particularly of academics, perhaps under the influence of some loose association with **dreaming spires**, a description of Oxford used by Matthew Arnold in his 1866 poem 'Thyrsis'.

Given that hymns are sung so frequently at church, one might expect they too would be a rich source of clichés, but only a handful are derived from them. To **move in a mysterious way** is from a 1779 hymn written by William Cowper which starts, 'God moves in a mysterious way / His wonders to perform'. The cliché from the hymn that everyone knows, '**All Things Bright and Beautiful**', was written by the Irish poet Mrs Cecil Alexander and published in 1848. Its lines 'The rich man in his castle, / The poor man at his gate, / God made them high or lowly, / And ordered their estate' are much-quoted as representative of VICTORIAN VALUES (see Chapter 14). She was also responsible for such well-known hymns as 'There is a Green Hill Far Away' and the carol 'Once in Royal David's City'. But the line that everyone knows is **all creatures great and small**, which really took off with the books of the vet James Herriot. In 1974 *All Creatures Great and Small* was used as the title of a film based on his autobiographical books, and the success of this led to a television series with the same title, which ran from 1978 to 1990. What is now called 'Herriot Country' has a takeaway called 'All Pizzas Great and Small'. **Pie in the sky** comes from the 1911 satirical song 'The Preacher and the Slave', written as a parody of the sort of hymns put out by the Salvation Army: the slave is promised, if he works hard and is subservient, 'You will eat, bye and bye, in the glorious land above the sky! Work and pray, live on hay, you'll get pie in the sky when you die.' It was written by Joe Hill, unionist and leader of the International Workers of the World, as part of their campaign to improve working conditions. For a similar sentiment see JAM TOMORROW (Chapter 7). Hymns also appear in the modern cliché for unity **singing off the same hymnsheet**, which is sometimes secularized to 'on (or from) the same page'.

The Book of Common Prayer does much better. **For better or worse** comes from the words of the Marriage Service: 'for better, for worse, for richer, for poorer, in sickness and in health'. However, it was already well established in the language when the Book of Common Prayer was compiled, in 1549. Something very similar is found in Old English, and Chaucer's friend the poet John Gower used it in about 1390 in a form that suggests it was already a set phrase: 'For bet, for wers, for ought, for noght, Sche passeth nevere fro my thought' ['For better, for worse, for anything, for nothing, She is never out of my thoughts']; it is even found in an earlier version of the marriage service from *c.*1403 in the form 'to hald and to have at bed and at borde, for fayrer for layther [lit. 'lother' = 'more troublesome (circumstances)'], for better for wers . . . til ded us depart'. The Book of Common Prayer has probably kept alive the word 'bounden' – an old past participle of the verb 'to bind' – found in the set phrase **bounden duty**. A bounden duty is literally one you are kept bound to by legal or moral ties. The expression dates from the sixteenth century, and can be found in the Communion Service, which has both 'It is very meet, right and our bounden duty, that we should at all times, and in all places, give thanks unto thee O Lord' and 'We beseech thee to accept this our bounden duty and service.' Similarly, the expression **tower of strength** – an old-fashioned way of saying 'strong tower', and used to describe people since the fourteenth century – was well established by the sixteenth century when it was used in the Book of Common Prayer ('O lord . . . Be unto them a tower of strength'), and by Shakespeare. Despite this, commentators credit Tennyson's 1853 'Ode on the Death of the Duke of Wellington' with establishing the expression as a cliché for someone who is a great support: 'O fallen at length, that tower of strength / Which stood four-square to all the winds that blew', although surely Tennyson got it from these earlier sources.

Finally, in the field of Christian texts, two saints make the grade. The fourth-century St Jerome hits the jackpot with the first recorded use of the ultimate cliché – to **avoid like the plague** – when he advised his readers to 'Avoid as you would the plague a clergyman who is also a man of business.' This seems to be one of the phrases that most readily spring to people's minds when clichés are mentioned. Certainly, anyone writing on clichés will lose count of the number of times people crack the joke about avoiding clichés like the plague. St Ambrose (339–97) answered a query from St Augustine with another popular cliché that few would think was the work of one of the church fathers. When St Augustine wrote to ask which Church rite he should follow, St Ambrose replied, '**When in Rome, do as the Romans do**' (*Si fueris Romae, Romano vivito more*); in other words, Augustine was advised to follow the local practice.

General invocations based on God and vaguely Christian religion abound, and can range from the general assertion that someone does not have a **God-given right** to do what they want even if they think they do, to the downright peculiar, such as Diego Maradona's assertion that the hand-ball that won him and the Argentinians the football World Cup in 1986 was the **hand of God**. This previously respectable theological term quickly became a catchphrase and was even adopted as the title of a football fanzine. Some such expressions are still closely connected to religion, such as the description of someone as a **pillar of the church** because they *support* the church and *uphold* what it stands for (compare TOWER OF STRENGTH above). This has been used since the fourteenth century, with another version, **pillar of society**, a more modern adaptation to our more secular society. Another such is **sanctity of marriage**, used nowadays as a rallying cry by the illiberal and those without the imagination to put themselves in another's place. **Happy-clappy**, a fairly recent introduction used to describe a type of evangelical Christianity involving enthusiasm and upbeat music, is spreading to describe a similar approach to life in general, as an alternative to TOUCHY-FEELY (see Chapter 3).

Another group of clichés takes religious words and turns them into something purely secular. Thus **icon**, which once had the primary meaning of a religious image, is now used loosely to mean anything admired, in terms such as 'fashion icon' or 'gay icon', while buildings can be **iconic**. The spread of this fashionable use has no doubt been helped by the use of 'icon' for the little symbols on computer screens, although the use of the term for a cultural symbol, dating from the mid twentieth century, precedes the computing sense introduced in the 1980s. One might expect that it would **put the fear of God into** people to use the ultimate symbol of Christianity, crucifixion, loosely in everyday speech, but **crucify** in the sense of 'torment, distress' appears surprisingly early, and in 1621 it is used to mean 'torment mentally', in Robert Burton's *Anatomy of Melancholy*: 'As great trouble as to perfect the motion of Mars and Mercury, which so crucifies our astronomers.' Here Burton is playing on words, for the English term 'crux' for an intellectual difficulty, something that is difficult to interpret, is also the Latin word for 'cross', the same word that is the origin of crucify. This academic use would have helped spread the use of 'crucify' outside a church context, although the very loose use, as in 'the team was crucified by the other side', is comparatively modern. Similarly, **saving grace** is a theological term, used of the grace of God that allows sinning humans to reach heaven, which has been in use since the sixteenth century. But by the nineteenth century the term had started to be used for a redeeming quality in someone that is felt to compensate for other faults. The position of **guiding light** is less clear-cut. This expression for a leader or example could come directly from the idea of a lighthouse, beacon or similar light being used to guide people through the night, but early uses of this image were often theological. Looser usage increased in the 1960s, when the Conservative Chancellor of the Exchequer, Selwyn Lloyd, used the term of guidelines attempting to curb pay-rises.

More sloppy uses of religious concepts are used by the sentimental, who talk of things being **blessings in disguise** (from the mid eighteenth century); or, even worse, use that ghastly recent interjection **bless!** Such people may also be **thankful for small mercies** and possibly even talk of people being dressed up in their **Sunday best**. More common still is the misuse of the word 'miracle', either in set phrases such as a **miracle of modern engineering** or, for example, in speaking unthinkingly of a **miraculous escape** when what is really meant is 'lucky'. Describing something as the **Holy Grail**, as in 'the Holy Grail of market research', can barely be described as Christian, and this mythical object searched for by the Knights of King Arthur's Round Table (the source of the overused **quest**) has its origins in Celtic rather than Christian mythology.

There is surprisingly little reference to individual sects among clichés, the one exception being the jocular **Is the Pope a Catholic?** This highly colloquial rhetorical question has spawned a whole variety of similar formula phrases, of which **Does a bear shit in the woods?** is the commonest. These range from the pretty obvious, such as **Does a fish like to swim?** or **Do kangaroos hop?** via variants such as **Does the Pope have a balcony?** to the splendour of **Does Dolly Parton sleep on her back?**

The Devil

Having dealt with the domain of the Church, it would be unfair not to look at that of the Devil. A recent addition to the list of clichés has been the formula phrase 'the . . . from hell', most commonly **neighbours from hell**, who might also be described as the **Devil incarnate**. 'Incarnate' is another example of a rare word preserved in everyday speech by a cliché. The insult 'A son of perdition, and a devil incarnate' is found in 1395, and the term has been used as a general insult ever since. To have **hell to pay**, meaning 'serious consequences', goes back to the eighteenth century, from the idea that the sinner will pay for his actions when he becomes a **lost soul** (used in a non-religious sense by the nineteenth century). Of course many of these people could be described by the old-fashioned **devil may care**, from an old exclamation meaning 'the devil can see to it!' which came into use in the eighteenth century – or they may find themselves caught **between the Devil and the deep blue sea**. This expression for being caught between two evils has been in use since the seventeenth century, but without the 'blue', which is a twentieth-century addition. More literary types might describe it as being caught between **Scylla and Charybdis**, from the monster and the whirlpool that made the strait between mainland Italy and Sicily so risky, according to ancient stories (most notably Homer's *Odyssey*). A more colloquial alternative is **between a rock and a hard place**, which may contain echoes of Scylla and Charybdis, and which, despite only becoming widely current in the last twenty-five years, was being discussed by American academics as early as 1921. For all the threat presented by the Devil it is worth remembering that **hell hath no fury like a woman scorned**. This is the popular version of William Congreve's lines from his 1697 play *The Mourning Bride*: 'Heav'n has no rage, like love to hatred turn'd, / Nor Hell a fury like a woman scorn'd.' Usually appearing in a truncated form, 'Hell has no fury . . .', it is also much parodied and used as a formula phrase. In his *Dictionary of Catchphrases* (1977) Eric Partridge records a twentieth-century version as 'Hell has no fury like a woman's corns.'

Other religions

Other religions have made their way into the language, usually, as is so often the case when complex ideas are absorbed into popular culture, in a distorted form. **New Age** is the most recent of these. Originally used by self-designated New Agers for an approach to life that emphasized the spiritual and natural, this has been taken up to describe anything vaguely **alternative** and has been ruthlessly exploited by advertisers. True New Agers, with their affection for meditation, may be accused of **navel gazing**. The image of someone who is turned in on themselves, unable to see things in terms of the outside world, and hence parochial or escapist, being like a mystic contemplating his own navel has been around since the early part of the twentieth century. The term 'navel contemplating' is earlier than the shorter 'navel gazing', and is derived from one of the practices of a religious sect (members of which were called by the magnificent name 'Omphalopsychics') who achieved a trance state by gazing at their navels and were described as 'navel contemplators' in the mid nineteenth century. Another modern Western interest gives us **the sound of one hand clapping**, the clichéd Zen conundrum meant as an aid to meditation, often found used to indicate mysticism in general. This sort of conundrum is presumably also behind the **sound of silence**, well known as the title of a 1966 Simon and Garfunkel song. Idol-worshipping pagans in general give us to **put someone on a pedestal**, found from the mid nineteenth century (although the idea is inherent in the denouement of Shakespeare's *Winter's Tale* (1610–11)). Woody Allen, in his monologue *I Had a Rough Marriage* (1964), played on the expression when he said, 'It was partially my fault that we got divorced . . . I tended to place my wife under a pedestal.' The idea of multiple layers of heaven is found in the ancient world and was carried over into the Jewish and Muslim cosmologies. One classical interpretation of the universe claimed that there were seven spheres around the earth, corresponding to the seven then-known planets, with the highest, the **seventh heaven**, the abode of bliss. In a literal sense the seventh and highest level as a reward for the good life appears in Chaucer's work. In a figurative sense it is used in the same way as *paradise* or *bliss*, for a state of great happiness, from the early nineteenth century.

17. Good and Bad, True and False, Success and Failure

Good

It is a cliché of literary criticism that it is very much easier to write well and interestingly about vice than virtue and that the good are not as interesting as the bad. The most interesting character in Milton's *Paradise Lost* (1667) is notoriously Lucifer. Among the Victorian novelists, who were so often keen to write about virtuous women, only Mrs Gaskell was regularly successful in making her good women convincing and interesting. Dickens was outstandingly bad, at least to most modern readers, at writing about good women. The same difficulty seems to affect the English language in general. We have many more terms for wrongdoing than for goodness. Alongside this, there is a greater range of clichés for the concrete aspects of vice or virtue than for the more abstract.

A good person might be described as **one in a million**. A straightforward use of the expression is found as early as 1685 in a work called *Sir Courtly Nice* by the Restoration playwright and early American colonizer John Crowne, where a character comes out with the comment, 'Not one Lady in a Million, whose breath I can endure.' However, the expression is not used in order to praise something until the nineteenth century. Other terms of goodness are half-hearted at best. Thus **short and sweet**, in use since the first part of the sixteenth century, and often, even then, used ironically, is qualified praise at best. There is the **virtuous circle**, but this is a much later formation based on the more frequent **vicious circle**. The virtuous circle appears in the middle of the twentieth century. The vicious circle comes originally from logic and is first found in 1793 as a term for a circular argument (one where each element depends on another, rather than consisting of a straight line of reasoning). It was being used in the modern sense of a series of linked events that act upon each other to make a situation worse, by the 1830s.

Those looking for greater evidence of virtue may be described by the cynical as living in a **fool's paradise**, an expression that has been in the language since the fifteenth century.

Bad

Terms for bad or evil can include dramatic descriptions such as the **heart of darkness**, which comes from the title of Joseph Conrad's 1902 novel, an account of human corruption and exploitation in Africa. The title of the book draws on associations with both the *dark continent* and the PRINCE OF DARKNESS (see Chapter 16). Nowadays it tends to be used loosely to mean a hidden evil. The sentiment behind the **lesser of two evils** goes back to the ancient world. It was obviously well known by the fourth century BC when Aristotle wrote in his *Nichomachean Ethics*: 'We must as a second-best course, it is said, take the least of two evils.' It is also found in Roman writing, and from there was passed on to the medieval world, Chaucer writing *c.*1385, 'Of harmes two the less is for to choose', and the fifteenth-century theologian Thomas à Kempis, 'Of the two evils the lesser is always to be chosen.' Other clichés, however, focus on doing harm, usually criminal, to other people. While the simple expression **dirty tricks** has been around since the later part of the nineteenth century, the special sense of underhand activity designed to discredit someone dates only from the mid twentieth century, when it was CIA slang for covert intelligence operations, the CIA itself getting the nickname 'The Department of Dirty Tricks'. An alternative term for this sort of behaviour is to **do the dirty on**. In the past the **hardened criminal** (often the opposite of the class once known as the DESERVING POOR (see Chapter 9), a term prominent in the nineteenth century, but now ousted by **political correctness**) might have a **partner in crime**, to **put the bite**, **heat** or **squeeze** on someone. 'Hardened' has been used in the sense 'obdurate, set on a course' since the fourteenth century, and has been linked to criminals as a cliché since at least the middle of the nineteenth century. Slang terms for putting pressure on people are the product of the world of the Prohibition gangster in the USA, dating from the 1920s and 1930s. 'Squeeze', however, in a more general sense of 'put pressure on' dates from at least the beginning of the early eighteenth century. They may commit a **heinous crime**, which has been a set phrase since the end of the sixteenth century, and was used regularly in political and forensic writing through to the eighteenth century. Nowadays 'heinous' is rarely found outside formal writing except in this combination, and many people would be hard-pressed to give a firm definition of it, let alone choose which is the preferred pronunciation. It comes from the same root as the word 'hateful'. After the crime the police may **round up the usual suspects**. This comes from a line in the 1942 film *Casablanca* when Louis, the collaborating French police chief, says 'Major Strasser has been shot. Round up the usual suspects' (see further on *Casablanca* at BEGINNING OF A BEAUTIFUL FRIENDSHIP, Chapter 5). A 1995 film *The Usual Suspects* increased use of the expression. The optimistic hope that these people get their **just deserts**. 'Deserts', in the sense 'what you deserve', is obsolete outside the world of hymns, except in this set phrase. The expression has been in use since at least the early nineteenth century.

Truth and Falsehood

Yet again, the bad dominates the good statistically with these terms. Even those clichés that deal with the truth carry with them an element of doubt. The **unvarnished truth**, for example, is linked to the idea that there is also a varnished truth – something that has been worked on and embellished. The first recorded use in any sense of 'unvarnished' is Shakespeare's 'I will a round, unvarnish'd tale deliver, / Of my whole course of love' (*Othello* (1602–4), I.3), and we probably owe our use of the word to mean 'plain, direct' to this. The linking of truth to unvarnished was established by the nineteenth century. The hand placed on the heart has long been a sign of sincerity and pledging your word, the heart, as we saw in Chapter 15, being thought of as the seat of life and the emotions. The children's oath 'Cross my heart and hope to die' is a relic of this. **Hand on heart** was also used by Shakespeare, but again is seen, at least today, as PROTESTING TOO MUCH (Shakespeare again; see Chapter 7), although it is probably more trustworthy than that favourite of politicians, **the truth of the matter**. The latter brings to the hearer's mind the idea either that the speaker has not told the truth up until now, or that at best he has been **economical with the truth**. The current fashion for using this expression to mean 'being evasive', or more frequently simply 'lying', is due to a statement made by Sir Robert Armstrong in the Supreme Court, New South Wales, during the Spycatcher case in 1986, when the government was trying to stop the publication of a book by a former member of MI5: '[The letter] contains a misleading impression, not a lie. It was being economical with the truth.' However, Sir Robert was not being original in his use of this phrase. Edmund Burke, in *Two Letters on Proposals for Peace* (1796), has: 'Falsehoods and delusion are allowed in no case whatsoever: But, as in the exercise of all the virtues, there is economy of truth' and the expression is also used by Samuel Pepys and Mark Twain among others. In fact, 'economy of truth' is an old theological term that originally meant 'presenting doctrine in a way that suits the hearer', but which in the nineteenth century was nearly as much of a cliché, and used in the same way, as 'economical with the truth' is today. Much worse is the **deliberate falsehood**. In use since the nineteenth century, the phrase avoids the speaker having to use the word 'lie', but gives the accused no chance of claiming that their misinformation was a slip of the tongue. This may explain its popularity with politicians. Worse still is the **bare-faced**, **bald-faced** or **bold-faced liar** or **lie**. There is a lot of debate about these three forms of the expression. 'Bare-faced' and 'bold-faced' are both terms used by Shakespeare to mean impudence. 'Bald-faced' is recorded not much later in a literal sense, of animals with hairless faces, but is not recorded of lies or liars until the middle of the twentieth century. The form 'bald-faced liar' seems to have appeared in the USA as an alternative for 'bare-faced', and it is the preferred form there, with 'bare-faced' the more common in British English.

Success and Failure

The positive aspects of this group of expressions do rather better than in the other groups, although the muted or negative still dominate. The successful, those who have achieved their **dearest wish**, will find themselves **highly acclaimed** and with a **host of friends**. If you **make it big** you can expect the **red carpet** to be rolled out for you. 'Make it big' is a comparatively recent Americanism, not recorded until the second half of the twentieth century. It seems to have pulled together two early senses of the verb 'to make'. One, common from the early seventeenth century, is usually found in the form 'to be made', meaning to be rich or established in a career. It is first found in 1614: 'If riches be that that makes men happy (according to the foolish phrase men use when such things befall one "O he is made!")'. The other started life in the same century, as a nautical expression for to travel a certain distance, then to reach a place, and from that, to achieve a goal. A red carpet is traditionally rolled out for honoured guests to walk on – one, for instance, was laid out for Queen Victoria when she visited the Bank of

Ireland in Dublin in 1849. By the 1930s the expression was being
used to mean to be given special attention or treatment.

A significant number of clichés deal with the struggle to
succeed or the battle to avoid failure – the **make or break**
situation. This expression originally meant that you would either
be 'made' (see MAKE IT BIG, above) or be a **broken man**,
depending on the outcome. 'Make or break' has been in use
since the nineteenth century. Attempts to do your best are
reflected in terms such as to the **best of my abilities** (nineteenth
century) or the more depressing DESPITE MY BEST EFFORTS (see
Chapter 14) or **valiant effort**. The similar **level best** has been
said to have originated in the California gold fields in the nineteenth century. People panning for gold would shake the matter
in the pans until it was level, the better to spot the fragments of
gold. Although the phrase certainly seems to have originated in
the USA in the mid nineteenth century, this explanation sounds
very like folk etymology, and is unlikely to be true. To avoid
failure you may **move heaven and earth** to **keep your head
above water**. The first of these dates from the eighteenth
century. The second, like to GRASP AT STRAWS (see Chapter 6),
uses the image of a drowning person struggling to survive. It has
been used of someone threatened with being drowned by their
debts or other financial worries since the early eighteenth century, but its use for someone at risk of being *overwhelmed* by
work or responsibilities is more recent. Your efforts may, of
course, **pale into insignificance** (early twentieth century, with
'pale' used in the same way as 'fade' might be) before an **overwhelming response** – used as a common response to in-
efficiency, implying that an organization is about to *drown* under
the *flood* demand. The opposite reaction is to take a **sledgehammer to crack a nut**. This expression has been in use since
the middle of the nineteenth century, with 'sledgehammer to
kill a gnat' an early alternative. 'Sledge' in this sense is a very old
word, in the language since the earliest records, used to describe
a heavy hammer that needs two hands to use, particularly one

used by a blacksmith. Its distant ancestor is related to the verb 'to slay'.

These attempts to **hold back the tide** may **end in failure**, even when faced with the bullying **failure is not an option**. Legend tells us that King Canute of England (*c.*995–1035), tired of the outrageous flattery of his courtiers, tried to show them his own limitations and his awareness of them by demonstrating that he could not hold back the tide. Canute has been badly treated by popular culture, which refers to him as if he was really trying to contain the uncontainable and get the sea to obey him. The expression is sometimes found in the alliterative **turn back the tide**. **Abject failure**, where 'abject' is used in the sense 'total' rather than its original sense of 'degrading', may lead to **abject poverty**, which is degrading. At the very best you may have to give an **abject apology**. This may be **rejected out of hand**. 'Out of hand' is an old turn of phrase, dating from the Middle Ages, meaning 'immediately'. Although you are unlikely to meet it in this sense today, other than combined with 'reject', I have been unable to find an example of this combination before the 1890s. Perhaps the most banal expression of failure was uttered in May 2003, when Donald Rumsfeld is said to have commented of the **sorry state** of affairs in Iraq, '**Stuff happens**.'

A final cliché that can be used of success or failure is the **no-win** or **win-win situation**. 'No-win' has been a cliché since the 1960s. Overused in books on business, negotiating and interpersonal relationships, as the climate has changed from a macho, confrontational style of business to a more consensus-based style, 'no-win', a type of confrontation where neither side gets what they want, has been replaced by 'win-win'. In modern business theory, as Gerard Nierenberg, president of the Negotiation Institute, put it in the *Wall Street Journal* in 1987, 'In a successful negotiation, everybody wins.' 'No-win' has spread to have a more general sense of 'a loser', while 'win-win' has started to be used of personal relationships.

18. Life and Death

In this pessimistic world, where **nothing is certain except death and taxes** (an adaptation of Benjamin Franklin's 'In this world nothing can be said to be certain, except death and taxes', used in a letter of 1783, but the idea was by no means new when he wrote it), it is perhaps not surprising that clichés involving ideas of death are far more common than those dealing with life. Even those that do deal with life often imply death within them. This is obvious in clichés such as a **matter of life or death**. Although it can be used literally, the expression is usually used with a degree of hyperbole. The first recorded instance in the *OED* is a comment by Charles Dickens, in 1837, about its being a matter of life and death to get hold of a manuscript. Quite how far ironic or exaggerated use has gone can be seen from the famous Bill Shankley quote of 1981: 'Some people think football is a matter of life and death . . . I can assure them it is much more serious than that', a quote which is itself well on the way to the status of cliché. A similar dilution is currently going on with the expressions **life-threatening** and **sell your life dear**, and has already happened with **vital**, which originally meant 'concerning life, essential for life'. A threat of loss of life is also to be found in 'to do something **for dear life**', whether it be 'run', 'cling' or 'hold on'. The 'dear' in 'for dear life' is one of those cases where a set phrase has preserved a usage that would otherwise seem odd or outdated, and means 'dear to you'. It came into use in the nineteenth century, when 'to ride for dear life' was a common usage. Death is yet again hovering in the background in **(in) the land of the living**, for it is used in contrast to the DEAR DEPARTED (see below) who have **gone before**. This elaborate way of saying 'alive' is a quotation from Jeremiah (11:19): 'But I was like a lamb or an ox that is brought to the slaughter; and I knew not that they had devised devices against me, saying Let us . . . cut him off from the land of the living, that his name may be no more remembered.' The same again applies to someone who has lived to a **ripe old age**, a comment that is usually only made after the person is dead. Even the positive **springtime of life**, indicating the hopeful beginning of things, is usually found as 'cut off in the springtime of life', meaning an early death. And when you get a NEW LEASE OF LIFE (see Chapter 12) a previous decline is implied.

There are, however, some positive images connected with life. A **picture of health**, which was probably already well established when Jane Austen used the expression in *Emma* (1815), is one such, although it does not contain the word 'live'. There are the modern journalistic clichés to **build** or **make a decent** or **new life** and to **build your life around** something. The tolerant LIVE AND LET LIVE (see Chapter 6) now has its negative counterpoint in **live and let die** (the title of a 1973 Bond film). References to **life's rich tapestry** or **fabric** are heavily weighted for older people by memories of the satiric use of the similar **life's rich pageant** in the comic monologues of Arthur Marshall (1910–89). More ambiguous is to **live life in the fast lane**, which dates from the final quarter of the twentieth century, and which promises to END IN TEARS (see Chapter 1). The unpleasant, slangy **get a life** (from the 1980s) was once restricted to schoolchildren, but has moved more and more into the mainstream without losing its juvenile sentiments. **Life's too short** for many things. This cliché of the stressed-out later twentieth century is most famously exemplified in Shirley Conran's 1975 book *Superwoman*, which contains: 'OUR MOTTO: Life is too short to stuff a mushroom.'

A link between life and death is **in the throes of**, although not many would recognize it as such. Throes were originally intense or violent pains, particularly those of birth and death (and **death throes**, the most clichéd of all, is still used). It started to be used figuratively at the end of the seventeenth century.

If clichés involving life seem rather negative, those that deal with the recently dead do their best to avoid mentioning the fact. The world of grief and condolence is full of euphemisms for 'dead' or 'death'. Many of these euphemisms employ the idea of movement or travel to replace 'die', and of course, at the same time, suggest that the **dear departed** who has **departed this life** has GONE TO A BETTER PLACE (see Chapter 7, under Shakespeare). Of 'departed this life', which has been in use since the sixteenth century, the **late great** Eric Partridge writes in his 1940 *Dictionary of Clichés*, 'it began as a euphemism, became a genteelism, and is now a stupidity.' ('Late great' sounds modern from its use in the music industry, but it was a favourite expression of Samuel Pepys's, and is first recorded in 1656.) **Dead and gone** goes back to the Middle Ages, while **late lamented**, **gone but not forgotten** and **not lost but gone before** are gravestone clichés from the Victorian period, a time when society could have an unhealthy relationship with death. 'Not Lost but Gone Before' was the title of a poem by Caroline Norton (1808–77), in which she wrote:

> For death and life, in ceaseless strife,
> Beat wild on the world's shore,
> And all our calm is in that balm –
> Not lost but gone before.

This in turn was probably inspired by the writing of the third-century St Cyprian, who said, 'Our brethren who have been freed from the world by the summons of the Lord should not be mourned, since we know that they are not lost but sent before.' More quotation is to be found in **rest in peace**, a translation of the Latin *Requiescat in pace* from the Requiem mass, and the source of the letters RIP on gravestones; and in **dust to dust**, taken from the words said at the interment in the Burial of the Dead from The Book of Common Prayer: 'Earth to earth, ashes to ashes, dust to dust.' It too has been a cliché since the mid nineteenth century. **Vale of tears** is not quite a quotation from the Bible, but an echo of biblical passages such as Psalm 23's 'Yea though I walk through the valley of the shadow of death, I will fear no evil.' This is picked up by an unknown eleventh-century author (various names have been attached to the work) who wrote a hymn to the Virgin Mary beginning, '*Salve, regina, mater misericordiae*' ('Hail, holy queen, mother of mercy'). In this work those praying are described as '*gementes et flentes In hac lacrimarum valle*' ('mourning and weeping in this vale of tears'). 'Vale of tears' was a very popular expression as early as the seventeenth century, while the magnificent alternative 'weeping-dale' is found in about 1400.

We are as uncomfortable speaking plainly of the point or cause of death as of the dead. We come out with platitudes such as 'she had her **whole life** or **future ahead of** or **before** her' (of course she did, as does everyone) or talk in a rather dated way of someone **coming to an untimely end** (in use since the sixteenth century). Going out of fashion is **in extremis**. In Latin this literally means 'in the furthest reaches'. In English it is used to mean 'at the point of death'. More recently, as it has become less common in its original sense, it has come to be used to mean 'in great difficulties'. A more homely image for one about to **pass on to the other side** is **at death's door**. This has been in use since at least the sixteenth century, and picks up on the imagery found when speaking of the gates of heaven or hell, which is very old indeed. There is also the **dying breath** or **dying gasp**. These seem to have become clichés by the nineteenth century, if not in the previous century. **Gone to a watery grave** is yet another euphemism. This term for drowning probably uses the poetic form 'watery' rather than the more normal 'wet' not just to soften the sense, but because it also elevates the sentiment, for 'watery grave' is a quote from Shakespeare's play *Pericles* (*c*.1607–8). A number of other clichés describe actual causes of death, but when they are not euphemisms they shy away from the reality of death by being used figuratively rather than literally. One of the more recent of these is **killing fields**. This entered the language in a very grim form, as an expression for a place of mass execution via the 1984 film about genocide in Cambodia called *The Killing Fields*. This story of an American journalist caught up in the horror of the events under the Khmer Rouge in the 1970s was written by Bruce Robinson, based on an article by Sidney Schanberg about his experiences. The actual title was taken from a comment made by an American diplomat in 1980 about Cambodia. It is now used to refer to the killing of both humans and animals, being particularly popular for headlines about such things as seal culls, but is usually greatly debased from the horrors of its origin. Rather older is **death by a thousand cuts**. This unpleasant Chinese method of execution, the details of which were highly mythologized in the West, was officially banned in 1905, but entered the language in the 1960s thanks to an entry in the *Quotations of Chairman Mao* (better known as *The Little Red Book*). Mao wrote, ' "He who is not afraid of death by a thousand cuts dares to unhorse the emperor" – this is the indomitable spirit needed in our struggle to build socialism and communism.' At the time this work was almost obligatory reading for a certain type of revolutionary student in the West, and thus the phrase became assimilated. It has become a cliché of commentators on financial cuts and cuts to public services. Older still is the origin of the **kiss of death**, usually linked to the Judas kiss, the kiss Judas Iscariot gave to Jesus to identify him to the officials who had come to arrest him. However, the expression is not recorded in the *OED* until 1948. Not only is this very late for a first use of a Christian image, but it is one year after the appearance of a film called *Kiss of Death*. In this film a criminal who informs on his colleagues is hunted down by a psychopathic member of the gang and murdered. It is probably this, rather than any real tradition, that lies behind the Hollywood convention of a kiss that marks a Mafioso as doomed. The expression has a further film and criminal association that boosted its use, in the lyrics of the highly successful theme song of the James Bond film *Gold-finger* (1964). Stronger biblical associations are found in **like a lamb to the slaughter**, which is a direct quote from the Book of Jeremiah (51:39), where the prophet announces God's plans for Babylon: 'I will bring them down like lambs to the slaughter.' Similar images occur elsewhere in the Bible: Psalm 44 has 'We are counted as sheep for the slaughter'; and Acts 8:32, quoting Isaiah 53:7, has 'He was led as a sheep to the slaughter; and like a lamb dumb before his shearer, so opened he not his mouth.' While 'sheep' is sometimes found, Jeremiah's 'lamb' is the more popular expression, probably because the latter is a more emotive image and gives a greater sense of innocence.

Not all clichés involving death are mealy-mouthed euph-emism. A good number are used metaphorically and often with black humour. To **dig your own grave**, meaning to get your-self in even deeper trouble, is one such. The earliest quotation I have been able to find in *The Times* dates from 1787, but as it is used there as a joke it was obviously well established by then, which is confirmed by the number of times the expression is used in slightly later articles. The supposedly hilarious account in which it is found illustrates how much more robust attitudes to death were in the past:

The occurrence of a circumstance a few days ago at Clerkenwell Church, viz. the sudden death of a ringer, whilst he with the others was ringing the dead-peal of a deceased brother is something similar to the sexton, who some years ago unintentionally dug his own grave, the ground falling in upon him, and he afterwards being interred there; for as the one dug his own grave, the other may be said to have rung his own knell.

The Times can also help us with the evolution of **dead and buried**. How it came to be used as a simple emphatic can be seen in such literal uses as that found in an article of 1785: 'Dupre is since dead and his dangerous secret lies buried with him.' **Dead and done with** was the more common expression in the nineteenth century, with the balance tipped in favour of 'dead and buried' in the twentieth.

Deep six is a slang term for 'to bury, dispose of' that attracted particular attention in 1973 when it was claimed at the Watergate hearings that someone had been instructed to 'deep six' vital incriminating documents which had been thrown into the Potomac river. It is an American expression which came into use in the 1920s, and may have gained greater currency from being the title of a 1958 war film. Its origin is usually traced to a claimed rule that the dead must be buried at sea in at least six fathoms of water, but it is interesting that although it is indeed used to mean 'bury at sea, drown', in the first recorded use in the *OED* it means 'a grave', which would link it with the idea of **six feet under** (recorded 1942 in the *OED*, although a report in *The Times* of the Glasgow Poison Case of 1857 quotes someone as saying, 'I wish I was six feet underground'). Even more flippant is **dead as a dodo**. Surprisingly, the *OED* has only one citation for this expression, and that as recently as 1960, although *The Times* database shows it was well used in the 1950s. This suggests that it took the twentieth century's concern over extinction before the attractions of the alliteration were strong enough to rival the earlier **dead as a doornail**, which goes back to the fourteenth century, and uses the doornail as an example of something that is totally lifeless. American English has the options of **dead as a mackerel** or the earlier **dead as a herring**, the latter in use in England in the seventeenth century. These show the tendency of clichés to preserve otherwise obsolete vocabulary, for the doornail is a large-headed nail used to stud medieval doors, and an item unlikely to be found in your local DIY store, while the dead herring refers to the salted fish that was preserved over long periods in the days before refrigeration, and was quite evidently long dead. Equally flippant is **dead but**

won't lie down (*c.*1910), for someone who refuses to give up. It is generally used when such behaviour is not felt to be heroic, but goes beyond what is reasonable. At best it is an acknowledgement of doggedness. It has been used since the beginning of the twentieth century. If you combine this with stupidity you might be described as **dead from the neck up**, while if you are deeply asleep you may be **dead to the world**. The latter, however, has come a long way from its origin. The original sense (still to be found in specialist writing) was a description of someone who had entered a religious life, leaving all worldly things behind. This sense was given prominence by Wordsworth, who wrote of 'A few Monks, a stern society, / Dead to the world and scorning earth-born joys' ('Cuckoo at Laverna', 1837). The expression was already being used more generally in the later eighteenth century to mean something excluded from normal life. The modern sense developed in the later nineteenth century. Another in this group is **death warmed up**, used as a jocular way of describing someone who looks ill, which dates from the Second World War. Also from the Second World War is **gone for a Burton**. This was originally RAF slang for someone who had died on duty, coined at a time when the life expectancy of aircrew was terrifyingly short, but was later modified to mean 'lost, broken, missing'. The origin of the expression has been hotly debated. The two front-running theories are either that the 'Burton' referred to is the tailoring chain, in which case there is a possible link to THE FULL MONTY (see Chapter 5); or, slightly in the lead as a source, that it refers to going for a Burton ale. While these expressions are humorous ways of referring to **grim reality** (another nineteenth-century cliché), **spinning in your grave** is never anything but jocular. The idea that the dead are made restless by the transgressions of the living, which must be the idea that ultimately lies behind the cliché, goes back to the ancient world and is probably best known in English from the appearance of the ghost of Hamlet's father. 'Spinning' is a modern, emphatic variation on the mid nineteenth-century **turning in his grave**.

We move even further from the realities of death when we speak of something being **the final** or **last** or **another nail in the coffin**, meaning something that contributes to the end of something else. It dates from at least the late eighteenth century, and was at one time a slang term for alcoholic drink. **Dead men's shoes** was a cliché from the nineteenth century, but was in use much earlier. In its original form, **to wait for dead men's shoes**, it meant to wait for an inheritance, but it now tends to be used of promotion, particularly due to retirement.

People who go willingly to their deaths are represented by the heroic **do or die**, an expression that has been used to encourage enthusiasts towards brainless self-immolation since at least the eighteenth century. That current use is often ironic is a reflection of modern society. While in the process of such histrionics the doer may find themselves on their **last legs** or at their **last gasp**. Both these expressions originally meant 'close to death', but are now also used to mean 'near exhaustion' or 'at one's limit' in some way. 'Last legs' goes back to at least the late sixteenth century, the idea being that you are *on your feet* for the last time, and 'last gasp' is recorded only a little later. To **take your life in your hands**, while it can still be used literally, rarely means more than 'scary', and often no more than 'needs a bit of care'.

Another group of clichés use the word 'dead', but are such dead metaphors that the sense of death has itself died. **Dead in the water**, for a ship that is not moving, found from the mid nineteenth century, is one such; the **dead of night**, popular in Shakespeare's day (he uses it several times), is another. 'Deadly', used in **deadly earnest**, has gone the way of 'terrible' and 'awful', and lost all sense of its original meaning. This is an old development – in 1660 Samuel Pepys could write in his *Diary*, 'A deadly drinker he is, and grown exceedingly fat.' And there is now no sense of a deed that deserves recording by the erection of a monument after the doer has died in **monumental effort**, which seems to have acquired its diluted sense by the middle of the nineteenth century. A recent addition to this list is **to die for**, meaning merely 'desirable'.

At least two clichés are to do with events after death. One is **post-mortem**, which from the late 1960s has been increasingly used to describe any kind of investigation. The other is an ancient term. To **rise from the ashes** refers to the legend of the phoenix. The myth of the phoenix is widely found in the ancient world, and was taken up by early Christianity as an image of the Resurrection. It is said that only one phoenix at a time is alive. When its time comes to die it flies to Egypt, where it builds a nest from precious, sweet-smelling woods, settles in it and bursts into flames. A new bird is born, which rises from its parent's ashes in all its beauty. Once again the image has been steadily debased, and what was a telling image of rebirth is now most often encountered as a headline attached to a report of some minor fire.

Bring closure to, a highly overused cliché of very little real meaning derived from Gestalt psychology, is used of both death and disaster. Like death, accidents seem to bring out clichés. They provide us with a way of responding when we do not want to think about events. Perhaps the most irritating of the clichés associated with things going wrong is the self-satisfied **accident waiting to happen** (sometimes found as **a tragedy** or **a disaster** rather than 'accident'). What makes this so annoying is that its use implies one of two things: either that the smug user had foreseen the accident and thinks others should have done so (in which case why did they not do something themselves to prevent it?), or else that 'they', whoever that may be, must be held to account for someone else's idiocy. The term is a favourite of journalists, alongside expressions such as **disastrous turn of events** and **tragic accident**. The companion cliché to an accident waiting to happen is **death trap**, defined by the *OED* as 'applied to any place or structure which is unhealthy or danger-ous without its being suspected, and is thus a trap for the lives of the unwary'. This term is so familiar that we use it without thinking, but if you do stop to think about it, it is a rather strange construction. After all, it should logically mean something to trap death. It therefore comes as no surprise that the first quotation containing it comes from poetry, from Robert Browning's 1835 'Paracelsus': 'This murky, loathsome Death-trap, this slaughter-house.' Both Browning's liking for stretching grammar, and the fact that it is poetry, account for the peculiarity of the term. Another hidden quotation can be found in **the dread hand**, which appears in William Blake's 'The Tiger' (1794), a poem about the creative power of the Divinity:

> And what shoulder, and what art,
> Could twist the sinews of thy heart?
> And when thy heart began to beat,
> What dread hand? And what dread feet?

Our use of 'the dread hand of' – to mean not just something that is feared, but something that will blight what it touches – has wandered far from the original use, and it is a fine example of the way in which obsolete words are preserved in clichés. Another example is 'dire', which originally meant 'evil' or 'portentous' but is rarely used nowadays except in a trivialized sense (as in 'the food was dire'); exceptions are **dire necessity**, **dire emergency** and **dire consequences**. These became set phrases in the nineteenth century, and it is their overuse that led to the weakened modern use of the word. The other cliché containing 'dire' is **in dire straits**. Here we have two obsolete words linked together, for 'straits' meaning 'difficulties' (derived from the sense 'narrow' via the sense of being in a tight place) is now at best archaic outside this one use (the only other time this sense comes up is in the equally clichéd STRAITENED CIRCUM-STANCES; see Chapter 16). It is therefore all the more surprising that this seems to be a relatively modern expression, and one totally ignored by the *OED*. Use has been heavily affected by the success of the band of the same name, since they had their first hits in the late 1970s. In all accidents people **come to grief**. This expression for 'to meet with disaster or mishap', 'to fail', has been a cliché since the mid nineteenth century. The construction is rather odd, and presumably indicates 'to arrive at a state of grief'.

Doom merchants – developed from **doom and gloom** in the twentieth century, given currency by the pessimistic leprechaun in *Finian's Rainbow* (original stage production 1947, film 1968) – will remind us that **accidents do happen**, also found as 'Accidents will occur in the best-regulated families' in Charles Dickens's *David Copperfield* (1849–50), a variation on an expression that was becoming a cliché at the time, although it had been around for about a hundred years beforehand. It is also found as 'accidents will happen' and 'accidents can happen'. In order to make people **safe and sound** (from the Middle Ages), it may be necessary to take **drastic action, measures** or **powers**, such as those taken recently in the **interests of national security** in the course of the so-called WAR ON TERROR (see Chapter 11). 'Drastic' was originally a medical word, meaning powerful or vigorous, and 'a drastic purge' would, for instance, be a strong laxative. The use of 'drastic' to mean something approaching 'desperate' as well as 'strong' is a mid twentieth-century development, although the sense 'vigorous' is found from the early nineteenth century. Many would claim that such action was **too little too late**, a cliché that appeared at the start of the twentieth century in the form 'too little and too late', with the snappier, shortened form beginning to replace it around the middle of the century. This might result in our being on a **slippery slope** (figurative use from at least the mid nineteenth century) to an **unmitigated disaster** (nineteenth-century cliché) which will **wreak havoc** and bring us all to **rack and ruin**. This is a fine collection of words rarely found outside these set terms. 'Mitigate', meaning to soften or alleviate, came into the language in the Middle Ages (with 'unmitigated' first recorded from Shakespeare in 1599) and suffers from a modern confusion with 'militate', which has a near opposite meaning. 'Wreak' is an archaic term related to 'wreck'. It has been used to mean 'to inflict something or do something in vengeance' since the end of the Middle Ages, but the combination of the two words 'wreak' and 'havoc', used as an alternative to **cause chaos**, seems to date only from the nineteenth century. The only other context you are likely to find the word used in nowadays is the rare **wreak vengeance** (see further Chapter 11). The 'rack' of 'rack and ruin' is a re-spelling of 'wreak' found from the sixteenth century. The opposite of the slippery slope is of course to come **back from the brink** (the earliest citation I have found is early twentieth century, but it is probably older). Failure to come back from the brink may mean that a **dream come true** develops into a **dream turned to a nightmare**. These are both journalistic clichés of the mid twentieth century. 'Dream' in the sense of 'aspiration' is largely a twentieth-century development, with terms such as the AMERICAN DREAM (see Chapter 14) dating from the 1930s, *dreamboat*, for someone attractive, from the 1940s and DREAM TICKET (see Chapter 24) from 1960, although the much earlier DREAMS OF AVARICE (see Chapter 9) can come close to this sense. By the 1960s 'dream come true' was well-enough established as a cliché for 'dream turned to a nightmare' to develop from it. Such a failure will be a **blow**, perhaps even a **body blow** (from the world of boxing, recorded literally from the late eighteenth century and figuratively from the early twentieth), which may **blight someone's life**. But readers will be spared the **gory details**, a set phrase that sometimes retains its original connection with blood, but has also been extended to apply to the details of anything unpleasant. It does not seem to have been used before the twentieth century. When things go wrong they may nowadays be ascribed to a **system failure**, which obscures the fact that people have been involved, and may be at fault: very convenient for those wishing to cover up or excuse the mess they have made, who are likely to add that such things must **never be allowed to happen again**.

To finish on a more cheerful note ('cheerful note' was originally a nineteenth-century journalist's cliché describing birdsong or music, which was being used figuratively by the end of that century), if you only feel a bit grumpy, you might be described as having got out of the **wrong side of the bed**. This comes from an ancient superstition, going back to Roman times, that to get out of bed on the left-hand side, or left foot first, is unlucky. However, to get out on the right side, or backwards, if done without premeditation, is lucky. Allusions to these beliefs are recorded in English from the sixteenth century, but as a cliché for being in a bad mood it dates from the nineteenth century. To **move** or **rearrange the deckchairs on the** **Titanic** is nowadays nearly always used with a certain degree of jocularity, but came into use in a more serious context, possibly inspired by a comment recorded in the *Washington Post* on 16 May 1976: 'After losing five of the last six primaries, President Ford's campaign manager, Rogers Morton, was asked if he plans any change in strategy. Said Morton: "I'm not going to rearrange the furniture on the deck of the Titanic."' The idea may not have originated with Morton.

19. Hot and Cold

The need to regulate temperature comes second only to food and drink as a basic survival need for humans. As a result it is also closely connected with our social customs and interactions. We love an open fire in the winter, even if it is only an inefficient flame-effect gas fire and we have more than adequate central heating. On cold days we invite people to come into the warmth of the home, or for a nice hot cup of tea. In summer we invite people round for a cooling drink. It is therefore not surprising that figurative language is full of hot and cold, warm and cool. Only a small proportion of these count as clichés: the majority lie in the realm of idiom or dead metaphor. It is noticeable that those clichés that use the extremes of hot and cold as imagery tend to have negative associations – typically we go hot and cold all over with horror; the exceptions are to do with warming food and drink, and the use of 'hot' itself in a slangy sense of music and sex. The moderate **comfort zone** (twentieth century) of warm and cool generally denotes good things, although the word 'tepid' has bad connotations.

If we act **in the heat of the moment (**a cliché by the mid nineteenth century**)** we are acting in an uncontrolled **hot-blooded** way (first recorded in Shakespeare). To **put the heat on** someone is an expression from underworld American slang of the 1930s (when 'turn the heat on' was more common). Originally 'the heat' in this sense was pursuit of a criminal by the police, but it has expanded to cover any kind of unpleasant pressure. Your actions may have been caused by the discomfort of a **sweltering hot** day, or because you had a **consuming passion** for something. The latter term does not seem to have come into common use until the late nineteenth or early twentieth century, but it was a cliché by the second decade of the twentieth century, and a great favourite of Edgar Rice Burroughs, for example in the cliché-ridden 'Time and again did Numa charge – sudden, vicious charges – but the lithe, active tormentor always managed to elude him and with such insolent ease that the lion forgot even his great hunger in the consuming passion of his rage, leaving his meat for considerable spaces of time in vain efforts to catch his enemy' (*Jungle Tales of Tarzan*, 1919). Nowadays 'consuming passion' is often found used by journalists with a pun on 'consumerism'. An alternative cliché is **burning desire**. This is a set phrase, common since the eighteenth century. Alternatively the hot blood may have been caused by something **hotly contested**. This is most commonly found linked with a sporting match or an election. If something goes wrong it may become **a hot potato** – something that is embarrassing or difficult to deal with, something you want to get rid of. The expression was well established by the middle of the nineteenth century, when it was often used in the form 'drop like a hot potato'. Nowadays it is often used as 'pass on like a hot potato', or qualified as in 'a political hot potato'. To understand the image we should probably be thinking in terms of potatoes baked in their jackets, which were sold as street food in the nineteenth century, or ones baked in the ashes of a hot fire. This links 'hot potato' with PULL SOMEONE'S CHESTNUTS OUT OF THE FIRE (see Chapter 6). In the past, 'hot brick' was used as frequently as 'hot potato', but it is now comparatively rare, although it is found as a jargon term for a charged battery for electronic equipment. There is one expression, perhaps more idiom than cliché, that does use 'hot' in a positive sense, and that is **to sell like hot cakes**. This uses the positive associations of heat and food discussed above, and the sense of 'hot' to mean anything that sells well, as in **hot property**.

For more positive images we have to turn down the heat a little. We have warm feelings for people we like, and give strangers a **warm welcome**, a set phrase that dates from at least the eighteenth century, and is the opposite of giving them a COLD SHOULDER (see below). We describe friendly people as 'warm-hearted' and say that certain actions **warm the cockles of your heart**. The cockles of people's hearts have been being warmed since the seventeenth century, but no one is really sure why. Some say it is because the heart is vaguely the same shape as a cockle shell; others that the zoological name for a cockle is *cardium*, which comes from the Greek for 'heart', again because of its shape; still others that it refers to the Latin name for the heart's ventricles, *cochleae cordis* (literally snail shells of the heart). This last seems the most likely, as it would give an image of warmth that goes right down to the component parts of the heart, and could have started life as one of those academic puns of the sort that lies behind the elbow's funny bone being at the end of the humerus. The use of 'warm' is comparatively recent (nineteenth century); previously people said that something 'rejoiced' or 'delighted' or similar the cockles of their hearts.

There are various views on where the expression **to get cold feet** comes from. It has been suggested, for example, that it comes from an old Italian proverb, *avegh minga frecc i pee*, which literally means to have cold feet, and was quoted by Ben Jonson in the seventeenth century; however, this means to be without money, broke. Although it has been argued that being without money is something that would make you lose your nerve, and that the one comes from the other, this ignores the fact that to have cold feet in the modern sense is not recorded before the end of the nineteenth century, and then in America. Admittedly, nineteenth-century Italian immigrants could have brought the proverb with them, but it seems unlikely. It is not necessary to look for such a complicated history. Anyone who has experienced really cold feet knows that the discomfort is enough, to use a related image, to dampen your ardour (the original sense of ardour is 'heat'), and make you want to give up and go home.

A **cold-blooded** human has nothing to do with reptiles or animals that are cold-blooded. Instead it goes back to the ancient theory of the four humours, and their qualities of hot, cold, dry and wet. If your physiology was out of balance and you were too hot, you acted rashly, in a hot-blooded way. If it was too cold, you were overly calm and rational. Emotions heated the blood, which cooled down with calmness. As a writer of 1619 put it: 'When the heate of that lust and lustinesse is past . . . they come againe unto their cold blood.' The same idea is found in French, in the expression *sang-froid*, which literally means 'cold blood'. The cold-blooded and **in cold blood** go back to Shakespeare's day. **Cold-hearted** is a companion image, coming from the same idea of emotion being hot and lack of emotion cold. The similar *cold fish* is an extension to the literally cold-blooded, a fish being both cold and unable to express emotion. This expression dates only from the 1940s, while both cold heart and cold-hearted are also first recorded in Shakespeare.

There are two terms for rejection based on 'cold'. If you are **left out in the cold** you experience the opposite of being given a WARM WELCOME (see above). The expression has been in use figuratively since the middle of the nineteenth century. John Le Carré's 1963 spy novel *The Spy Who Came in from the Cold*, where 'the cold' referred to the communist Eastern Bloc, echoing the term 'Cold War', gave a new twist to the old saying, one that is often used by headline writers. To be given the **cold shoulder** implies active rejection, rather than the more passive sense of 'left out in the cold'. There is a story that can be found in a number of reference books that 'the cold shoulder' comes from welcome guests in the distant past being given hot food, but unwelcome ones merely given meat from a cold shoulder of mutton. However, there is nothing other than imagination to support this fanciful view. It would appear to be a Scotticism introduced to the general public (or possibly invented) by Sir Walter Scott. It first appears in 1816 in his novel *The Antiquary*: 'The Countess's dislike didna gang farther at first than just showing o' the cauld shouther'; and then reappears eight years later in more accessible form in *St Ronan's Well*: 'I must tip him the could shoulder, or he will be pestering me eternally.' Scott is one of those writers who were once very much read and had a great influence on the language, and there can be little doubt that we owe the term to him. This may be **cold comfort** for those looking for more romantic explanations. This term for inadequate consolation is an old one, the earliest example coming from the fourteenth-century poem 'Patience', where the anonymous author says of Jonah in the whale's belly: 'Lord, cold was his comfort, and his care huge.' Contemporary use of the expression is affected by the enormous success of Stella Gibbons's 1932 novel *Cold Comfort Farm*, which satirized the craze for novels of grim country life, such as those of Mary Webb.

The only positive use of chillier words is the ubiquitous use of COOL (see Chapter 24) as a term of approval. For some teenagers, indeed, this seems to be the commonest four-letter word in their vocabulary. But even then 'cool' can be negative or at the best ambiguous. A **cool customer** can be a term of approval of, say, someone who defuses a bomb without turning a hair. But it can also be used of an unrepentant shoplifter or someone who queue-jumps without embarrassment, as well as describing someone who is unenthusiastic – the opposite of warm.

20. Time

As well as those clichés that are based on units of time, we have those in which time itself appears. Something that is **lost in the mists of time** belongs in the **dim and distant past**. Time has been described as obscured by mist since the early eighteenth century, although the first recorded instance, 'And who see clearly thro' the Mists of Time, / Those puzling Glooms where busy Mortals stray', from a 1701 poem by one M. Chudliegh, is so paradoxical as to suggest that the phrase was already well established. 'Dim and distant past' was in use in the late nine-teenth century. Alternative terms for a time too long ago to locate are **time immemorial** and **time out of mind**. Strictly speaking 'time immemorial' is any time before 1199, this being the date set in 1275 as the time before which no one could remember, and therefore no legal cases could deal with events before that date. 'Time out of mind', recorded from the fifteenth century, is just the plain English version of the same thing, 'immemorial' being literally 'beyond memory or recall'. The obliterating forces of time are also found in the formula phrase **the . . . that time forgot**, which is based on the title of the 1924 science fiction novel *The Land that Time Forgot* by Edgar Rice Burroughs. Something enduring will stand the **test of time**, an expression that is recorded from the early nineteenth century, but which does not seem to have become a cliché until the early twentieth. An alternative is **tried and tested**. The right time may be when the **time is ripe**. The image here is of a situation gradually developing like a ripening fruit, until the moment when it is ready for action to be taken. It became common in the nineteenth century, probably from Shakespeare's 'When the time is ripe . . . I'll steal to Glendower and Lord

Mortimer' (*Henry IV, Part I* (1597), I.3). The history of **in the nick of time** is rather obscure. 'Nick' is ultimately the same word as that meaning a small cut or notch, and is used to mean 'the exact moment' in the simple form 'the nick' from 1577 ('nick of time' is dated 1674). Quite how this meaning evolved is not clear, but 'nick' has a wide variety of other meanings, many of them now obsolete, including a mark that shows you how far to wind or tighten something like a lute string, from which the expression 'to the nick' evolved, meaning 'just so', and another sense of 'the exact point aimed at', which are both in the same semantic area.

Other clichés involve time on a large scale. To **turn the clock back** or **back the clock**, used since the middle of the nineteenth century, is nearly always negative for understandable reasons. **Before the dawn of time** or **history** is also nineteenth century and has often been used in book titles. 'Dawn of history' seems to have been more frequently used in the past than 'dawn of time', but 'time' is now the commoner. This is also the time of the **dinosaur**. As a term for something old or obsolete this is a twentieth-century expression, particularly common in the combination 'dinosaur of rock'. 'Yore', meaning 'a long time ago, in times past', survived as an archaism until the nineteenth century, but is now found only in the set phrase **in days of yore**. This is recorded from the seventeenth century, but only came to be used frequently and loosely in the nineteenth century, often as an alternative for the formal storytelling setting **long ago and far away**. The **end of an era** is a popular cliché with journalists and speech-makers. This expression is perfectly useful if the writer really is speaking of an era, but it is often used to speak of the end of a sports career, or simply of the presence of somebody in a particular place, in which case it is a ridiculously grandiose term. An alternative cliché in these contexts is to speak of a **Golden Age**. The idea of a Golden Age, when things were perfect, or at least better, goes back to the ancient Greeks, whose Golden Age was a time when men and gods mixed together, and there was no evil – the Greek equivalent of the time before the Fall. 'In that golden age . . . they . . . ate roots for bread and fruits for flesh,' wrote Lord North in 1557, in one of the earliest recorded uses in English. The term was later used to describe the writings of a group of Latin authors, those who wrote between the times of Cicero and Ovid being considered the finest authors, those of the Golden Age, with the next generation of writers belonging to the Silver Age. Now it is applied to the best or finest period of anything, often very loosely, although it is nice to see a conscious reference to the description of those Latin authors in the much cited 'golden age of children's literature'. The opposite extreme to the Golden Age is **the end of civilization as we know it**. This was a Hollywood cliché for a great disaster, in use from the 1930s. Most notably, in Orson Welles's and Joseph Mankiewicz's great film *Citizen Kane* (1941) a possible world war was described as 'A project which would mean the end of civilization as we now know it.' This set phrase has now developed into a formula phrase.

When looking at clichés based on the way we divide up time on a human scale, we find that they tend to concentrate on the shorter units of time. Years do give us **a few years down the line**, a recent cliché, and an unnecessarily complicated way of saying 'later', as well as the equally redundant **years of age**, which adds nothing to 'years' or 'years old'. Even worse is the falsely jocular so many **years young**. The week as a unit has only produced the recent and ugly **24/7**. Days are much more productive. The day starts with a **false dawn**, referring to a phenomenon found in some parts of the world where there is a brief lightening of the dark about an hour before dawn, known as either the false dawn or false sunrise, a translation of an Arabic phrase. This has only come to be used to mean 'a cause of hope that comes to nothing' in the second half of the twentieth century. The related **light dawned** is one of a whole set of images linking perception with the idea of light, ranging from the cartoonists' use of a light bulb to indicate understanding or a *bright idea*, to things coming to you in a *blinding flash*. 'The light dawned' seems to have come into use about 1800, and was well established by 1874 when L. Carr wrote, 'A light dawned through the thick opacity of his brain.' **Late in the day** (from around the 1800s, meaning simply 'late', or 'too late') we are AT THE END OF THE DAY, which, like WHEN ALL IS SAID AND DONE, is a filler (see Chapter 23 for both), waffle used to try to give importance to a statement. These can nearly always be left out without significant change to the sense of the sentence, as can **as surely as night follows day**. Despite the fact that this expression for the inevitable is not recorded in the *OED*, the comparison is an old one. Polonius' famous lecture to his son Laertes on how to behave (*Hamlet* (1601), I.3) ends with:

> This above all: to thine own self be true,
> And it must follow, as the night the day,
> Thou canst not then be false to any man.

From the way Polonius talks in clichés throughout the play, we may guess that the idea was not original even then. **Those were the days** is not recorded before the early twentieth century. Its use was reinforced by the success of a song with that title sung by Mary Hopkins in 1968. The similar **glory days** is not recorded until the middle of the century. It is now often used as a variant of expressions such as *the best days of your life*. Finally we have the platitudinous **It's not every day that you see that**, and **early days**, used as a catch-all to explain why something has not worked. The latter is often used as an excuse or in expressions such as 'Oh well, it's early days yet', to reassure.

Moving down to the hour brings us the **eleventh hour** and **their finest hour**, both of them quotations. The first is from the Bible, Matthew 20. This tells the parable in which the doctrine of grace is explained in a story of the labourers in the lord's vineyard who were all paid the same for their work whether they had been working all day, or had only started in the eleventh hour – the last hour of the Roman working day. This brought the expression into the language from the earliest records. The expression was given further resonance in the twentieth century when at the end of the First World War the Armistice was signed on the eleventh hour of the eleventh day in the eleventh month of 1918, the desire for neat numbers overriding any consideration of the fate of those who got killed while the fighting went on until the hour was reached. The rise in popularity of 'their finest hour' can probably be traced to the speech Winston Churchill made on 18 June 1940, in which he said that the Battle of Britain was about to begin and that the fate of Western civilization hung on the result. He concluded: 'Let us therefore brace ourselves to do our duty, and so bear ourselves that, if the British Commonwealth and its Empire lasts for a thousand years, men will say, "This was their finest hour."' Although Churchill's words were unlikely to have been original to him, their fame led to 'finest hour' being adopted as a cliché. Initially the words' significance was too well remembered for them to be used lightly, but nowadays they are often used ironically, while the meaning has changed from 'time of greatest heroism' to 'moment of triumph'.

Finally, we come to a 'moment', a word that at various times has indicated different lengths of time, including a fortieth of an hour and a unit of 3.5 seconds, but which is now often used as a synonym for a second. The **defining moment** has been a cliché since the 1980s. An article published in the *Independent* on 5 August 1998 catalogued the rise of the term as represented on the newspaper's database, from 62 examples in 1993, to 411 in 1997, and 302 in just the first five months of 1997. The same article also pointed out that WATERSHED (see Chapter 21) was an even more popular term. Sometimes one is lucky enough to find a blend of the two:

It is difficult to pinpoint the exact moment at which British education went into decline, so lengthy and inexorable has the process been. But the replacement of O-levels by GCSE in 1988 was a defining water-shed. (*Daily Mail*, 27 August 1998)

One could perhaps claim that in the 1980s and 1990s 'defining moment' was the cliché **of the moment**, or that it caught the **mood of the moment**, a sub-cliché of the former. These expressions tend to be used by those writing about fashion or in a particularly fey style. They do, however, avoid that fashionable alternative, **zeitgeist** (literally, in German, 'the spirit of the time').

21. Nature

Such is the British nation's love of animals (itself a well-established cliché) that expressions relating to them need their own chapter. This section deals only with the plant world and the larger aspects of nature, the planet earth, including its geography and geology, and the weather.

Plants

In the English psyche, when it comes to flowers the **best** or **pick of the bunch** (*The Times* archive has 'best' from 1836, 'pick' from 1873) is the **English rose**. The rose is, of course, the symbol of England, so it is not surprising that the pale rosy complexion typically found in our northern climes should be dubbed 'English rose'. However, it did not become a cliché until the middle of the twentieth century. The probable source of the English rose as a cliché dates from 1902 and the enormous success of Basil Hood's opera *Merrie England*. The hit song of this was 'Dan Cupid Hath a Garden', which opens:

> Dan Cupid hath a garden
> Where women are the flow'rs . . .
> And Oh! the sweetest blossom
> That in the garden grows,
> The fairest Queen, it is, I ween,
> The perfect English rose.

It is a linguistic curiosity that although we have had roses of many different colours growing in our gardens for centuries, and indeed a variety of colours can be found in the native wild rose, and despite the strong associations of the deep-red rose with love, the primary colour associated with roses is pink. This is not just an English cultural tradition. In many languages, including French and German, the word for pink is the same as that for rose. Perhaps this is because among the wild roses found in Europe the most striking is the dog rose (see Chapter 22 for the significance of 'dog' in the name). This comes in a variety of shades of pink, and sometimes the petals shade from pink to white, making it also the most suitable rose for the origin of the perfect English rose complexion. In English we have a shade called rose pink, but are unusual in also having pink as a separate word from rose. In its turn 'pink' is a linguistic curiosity. The word for the colour, not found before the later seventeenth century, comes from the flower named 'pink', from the genus *Dianthus* which comes in a variety of shades from red to white, but is commonly pink, particularly in its wild forms. The origin of the flower name is obscure. There are various theories about where it came from, but the one I like best is that it is linked to the fringed edges of the petals of many varieties. There was an old verb 'to pink', meaning, among other things, to edge with decorative work (a sense still found in the dressmaker's pinking shears, used to put a zigzag edge on cloth to stop it fraying). Since the petals looked pinked the word was transferred to the flower, and the colour name then taken from the flower. The history of the colour is further obscured by the fact that the word 'pink' was also given to a yellow pigment, usually qualified by being called Dutch pink or English pink. Extraordinarily the two terms survived side by side, for a long time, so that one finds nineteenth-century colour suppliers advertising their supplies of English, Dutch and rose pink (only the last being something we would recognize as pink). As a final digression on the colour pink, recent research has shown that more and more people, particularly the young, are identifying pink as an independent colour, and not as 'a pale red, sometimes with a slight purple tinge' as the *OED* has it, or as a mixture of red and white. A further cliché involving roses is found in **everything's coming up roses**, an expression coined by Stephen Sondheim for his 1958 musical *Gypsy* (based on the life of Gypsy Rose Lee) which was firmly fixed in the language within ten years – so much so that the *OED* has yet to recognize its origin. Sondheim's own definition of the meaning is 'things are going to get better than ever'. The rapid acceptance of the phrase may owe something to the fact that **everything in the garden is lovely** (or **rosy**), used to much the same effect, was already established as a cliché. This came from a song popularized by the music-hall singer Marie Lloyd in the first decades of the twentieth century. 'Everything's coming up roses' is sometimes found as a formula phrase, and sometimes shortened to **everything's roses**. These in turn may owe part of their acceptance to Robert Browning's 1855 poem 'The Patriot', which contains the line, 'It was roses, roses all the way'; this would once have qualified as a cliché but is now out of fashion. 'It's **not all roses**' is also less used than it was in the past. The sentimental **rosy-cheeked**, which is one of the rare instances where the rose does indicate the colour red, is more difficult to classify. One can hardly say it is not a cliché – it is too objectionable – but perhaps we should put it in a special class of obsolescent cliché. Rosy-cheeked, or even worse **apple-cheeked**, were favourite terms in the nineteenth century. Dickens, in his 1848 novel *Dombey and Son*, managed to get the full set with 'a plump, rosy-cheeked . . . apple-faced young woman', a description it does not do to think too much about. Although these two expressions are used of country people of both sexes and all ages, they are chiefly associated with young girls, or with words such as 'tots', 'cherubs' or other saccharine terms. It is difficult to classify 'rosy-cheeked' as a simple cliché because it is now mainly used only in a historical context. Tastes and ideas of beauty have changed. Rosy cheeks belong to an era when the attractive rich were delicately light-skinned, because they could afford to stay indoors. The urban poor might also be pale – but would be expected to be (in clichéd terms) skinny from poverty and unhealthily pale, perhaps from anaemia. Country folk would be expected to be leathery skinned from exposure to the sun all year. Thus to be reasonably round-cheeked from a good, healthy diet, with a good high colour, particularly in the young, would be valued as a sign of health and relative prosperity.

Put all these roses together and you will no doubt get that favourite of the plant catalogue, a **riot of colour**. The expression has been in use since at least the 1890s, but was used in different contexts in the past. A piece in *The Times* in 1891, for example, praises the French Impressionists for the riot of colour in their art. Probably the abuse of the expression as an unthinking term for a garden does not date from much earlier than the 1960s. Of course, gardens may be spoilt by disease, and then your **hopes are blighted**. 'Blighted' in the sense of 'ruined, spoilt' is found from the mid nineteenth century, but the *OED* does not record 'blighted hopes' at all, although an article in *The Times* in 1916 describes hopes of peace between the Germans and English as blighted.

Surprisingly, edible plants have given us few clichés, the only one I can think of being the **carrot and stick**, and this really belongs with the donkey who is both being punished with the stick and chasing the incentive of the carrot. The use of carrot as an inducement has not been found before 1895 and the full carrot and stick only from 1916. No one really seems to know where the expression comes from. The *OED* writes of 'the proverbial method of tempting a donkey to move by dangling a carrot before it', but there is no proverb. Others have suggested its origin may lie in a cartoon. It is certainly a popular image with cartoonists, and perhaps a trawl through nineteenth-century copies of *Punch* would come up with an answer. What is clear is that the expression has lost much of its bite with the years. Early uses make it clear that in its own way the carrot is as cruel as the stick, for the donkey is never going to reach it. This seems to have been lost in modern usage.

Only two other clichés remain that deal with types of plants. **Neck of the woods** was originally a term for a narrow, neck-shaped stretch of woodland. However, in the period that the frontier of America was being settled the concept of a piece of wood in an open area was reversed, and by the 1830s 'neck of the woods' was being used for a settlement cut out of wooded country. From there it came to be used for any remote area, and then applied more generally to mean region or neighbourhood. The other cliché is (**to get back to**) **grass roots**. This has been current since the beginning of the twentieth century. The companion phrase is 'to do something **from the ground up**' and the expressions can be blended in the form 'from the grass roots up'. While 'grass roots' is often used to mean 'at the most basic level, the fundamental', it also has a specifically political use, to mean 'the rank and file of an organization'. Some uses of the expression are influenced by the ideas behind **back to your roots**. This use of 'roots' to mean your background, where you have ties, also only developed in the twentieth century, although expressions such as to **put down roots** seem to be older. What exactly is meant by these roots has rarely been precisely defined, and 'back to your roots' is often used in an almost mystic sense, promising self-discovery or redemption.

Two final clichés deal with things going wrong with plants. Unseasonable frost will **nip in the bud**, and plants will fail to grow or flower. In use since the sixteenth century, it is famously part of the standard illustration of the mixed metaphor, attributed to the Irish politician Sir Boyle Roche (1743–1807): 'Mr Speaker, I smell a rat; I see him forming in the air and darkening the sky; but I'll nip him in the bud.' At the end of the year plants may **run to seed**, which may be a good thing if you want the seeds, but is a disaster for those trying to keep a garden looking good. Plants that have run to seed end up looking **seedy**. 'Run to seed' has been recorded figuratively since the middle of the nineteenth century, but may well be older, as 'seedy' is found as early as 1739.

The earth

If we turn from the ground and the plants that grow in it to the earth as a whole we find the idea that an event can be **earth-shattering**, an overblown term that goes with **cataclysmic** and the infuriating current buzzword, also based on earthquakes, **epicentre** (infuriating because the word does not mean some emphatic form of centre, but the point in the earth underneath the quake). Interestingly, the first occurrence of the term 'earth-shattering' in *The Times* is as the title of a film released in 1956. This seems to be about the time the term became a cliché, and there may be a connection, although the film has sunk so thoroughly from view that I have been unable to find out anything about it. The study of earthquakes is called seismology, and the adjective from this, particularly in the form **seismic shift**, has been enthusiastically taken up by those no longer satisfied by simple words like 'large'. This use of 'seismic' emerged in the 1960s, and was sufficiently threadbare fifteen to twenty years later for **tectonic shift** to be added to the list of clichés. Companion clichés to these are DID THE EARTH MOVE? (see Chapter 15), and **abyss**, used figuratively since the early seventeenth century and most frequently found as a cliché in forms such as **(hanging) over** or **looking into the abyss**, or as an **abyss of despair**, or **an abyss opening before your feet**. Other clichés that work on a global scale are **old as the hills**, an image reflecting the immensity of geological time, and which dates from the beginning of the nineteenth century, and **poles apart**. In the middle of the nineteenth century this is found in the full form of 'as wide as the poles apart', with the abbreviated form appearing right at the end of the century.

Weather

As one would expect from a society obsessed with weather, we have a number of clichés derived from it. Although a number of frequently used expressions are taken from good weather, such as having a **sunny disposition** (about the only time you are likely to meet 'disposition' in this sense), the over-quoted **sunny side of the street** (from the 1930 song, lyrics by Dorothy Fields), the nauseating **little ray of sunshin**e or the dubious **fair-weather friend** (eighteenth century), the majority, as again is to be expected, reflect bad weather. If you are in disgrace, you may be **under a cloud**, which goes back to the fifteenth century and qualifies as a cliché from the eighteenth century at the latest. One step worse is when **dark clouds hang over**, an image of much heavier rain, if not thunder, than is implied by 'under a cloud'. This expression dates from the 1730s. About a hundred years later, **bolt from the blue** appears. Here the image is one of unexpected events, for while dark clouds predict thunder and lightning, lightning from clear, blue skies is a real surprise. 'The blue' has been used to signify the sky since at least the eighteenth century – John Wesley, in one of his translations of the Psalms, writes of 'the ethereal blue'. However, the shorter version, **out of the blue**, does not seem to have come into use until the twentieth century, although 'out of the clear sky' is late nineteenth. Rain clouds are also implicated in the slangy **rain on your parade**. This Americanism for spoiling someone's fun has been in use since about 1900 in the USA, but only became fashionable in the UK in the late twentieth century, although the more emphatic *to piss on someone's parade*, which echoes *it's pissing down*, is found by 1984. Another Americanism, to TAKE A RAIN CHECK, is covered in Chapter 4, while a recent arrival is **perfect storm**, popularized by the film *The Perfect Storm* of 2000. Uses of this expression can descend into bathos, as in the following from the *Independent* of 12 May 2004: ' "I have been in this industry for nearly 20 years and I have never seen all of these things come together at one time. It's a perfect storm," Lynda Utterbeck, the executive director of the National Ice Cream Retailers Association, told reporter . . .', with reference to ice cream sales over the summer. All this rain may lead to rivers in full flow, which can turn into floods **as fast** or **quick as lightning** or even **like greased lightning**.

If you have managed to **weather the storm** (in use since the sixteenth century, a cliché by the nineteenth) you may be in for a spell of cold weather, which gives us two opposing groups of clichés. Those of a positive bent may dream of a **white Christmas**. Although the expression dates from the middle of the nineteenth century, and Charles Dickens was extolling the joys of a snowy Christmas in his *Pickwick Papers* (1837), the clichéd use of 'white Christmas' dates from the immensely successful song written by Irving Berlin in 1942. Dickens's ideas of Christmas seem to come from the reality of his youth, when winters were particularly cold. Nowadays heavy snow at Christmas is common in many parts of the USA, where the song was written, but it is now very rare in most of the UK. However, such is the force of the song, Hollywood images and the traditional scenes found on Christmas cards, that the connection between snow and Christmas is very strong indeed, a cause of great disappointment for many children. The more pessimistic view of cold gives us **thin ice** to skate on dangerously (the earliest example I have found, from 1844, takes the form 'dancing on thin ice'), **icy tones** of voice and the **icy grip** of winter or fear. This last has been a cliché of journalism from at least the late nineteenth century. Finally, a mass of ice will give you an iceberg, and the overused **tip of the iceberg**. Amazingly, the *OED* does not record this expression until 1969, although the user does describe it as a 'well-known metaphor', and even *The Times* archive does not have it before 1963.

Ice leads us to water, and water to **making waves**. This image, which like the tip of the iceberg is only recorded from the 1960s, picks up on the metaphorical use of a choppy sea and on the image of ROCKING THE BOAT (see Chapter 11), which is recorded some thirty years earlier. Yet another watery image that looks old, but is not recorded before the 1960s, is **water under the bridge**. In North America the water is more likely to have gone **over the dam** than under the bridge. But although the expression has not been recorded until fairly recently, the idea of time and events flowing on like water is old, going back at least to the comment of the sixth-century BC Greek philosopher Heraclitus, 'You can't step twice into the same river.' Earlier than 'water under the bridge' is the use of **watershed** to mean a turning point. A watershed is literally the place on a mountain that divides two different river systems, water flowing off in more than one direction. As a cliché its use may ultimately go back to Longfellow, a source of many unconscious quotes, who wrote in an 1878 poem called 'Kéramos': 'Midnight! The outpost of advancing day! . . . The watershed of Time, from which the streams of Yesterday and To-morrow take their way.'

There is a tenuous link from water, via the word 'gulf', to our next cliché, the **yawning gulf** or **gap**. After our run of 1960s material, the background to this is reassuringly old, for the idea of a chasm being like the earth yawning goes back in English at least as far as King Alfred's translation of Orosius in the ninth century, and 'yawning gulf' is found in this sense in Edmund Spenser's *Faerie Queen* (1590). 'Yawning' was being used figuratively by the end of the eighteenth century, but these set phrases seem only to date from the twentieth century.

22. Animals

Horses

The animal inspiring by far the most clichés in English is the horse. Given the importance of horses as transport and beasts of burden over the centuries, it is hardly surprising that English contains dozens of everyday expressions relating to horses. We have proverbs advising against such things as looking at a gift horse in the mouth; we feel we could eat a horse; we describe something dependable as a workhorse (or disparagingly as an old workhorse); and we give someone a leg-up. All these are perfectly respectable English idioms, but mainly relate to horses in general or horses used for riding. There are surprisingly few clichés linked with working farm horses, perhaps a reflection of the different influences of the different classes of society on the English language. The most obvious cliché from the working horse is to **die in harness**, used to mean to die when still employed, usually with the implication that the job was one held for a long time, or particularly liked. Even this has a muddled history. It is often claimed that Shakespeare used the expression, but when Macbeth says, 'At least we'll die with harness on our back' (V.5), Shakespeare is using 'harness' in an old sense, to mean 'armour'. The other, horse-related sense of 'in harness' was common in the nineteenth century, used to mean 'in work', and the current expression developed from this. There was some overlap in usage of the two expressions, for, as we have seen, Shakespeare's plays have extended the use of expressions well beyond their usual time-span. Thus in 1849 *The Times* reviews a volumes of verse on Scottish history, and quotes lines that rejoice in the fact that a soldier 'died in harness for his king' – a use of the Shakespearean sense. However, the next year we find an obituary for the Prime Minister, Sir Robert Peel, extolling him for having 'died "in harness"' – the first time the current usage is found in the paper. Why does 'to die in harness' irritate, while expressions like 'eat a horse', although trite, do not? It could be the mixed ancestry that marked it out in the past as an uncomfortable expression; but more probably it is a combination of the unpleasantness of the image of an animal worked until it drops and the sententiousness already found in Peel's obituary that makes it so unwelcome. A different kind of harnessed horse is found in to **drive a coach and horses through**, an image that may once have been telling, but which is now muddied by unfamiliarity. The early forms of this expression usually use the term 'a coach and six', that is to say a really large coach which would need a correspondingly large space to drive through. In the early sixteenth century Thomas Otway, in his play *The Atheist*, wrote, 'Is there not a hole in my belly, that you may turn a coach-and-six in?' 'Big enough to turn a coach and six in' survived in dialect until at least the late nineteenth century. The expression we use stems from a comment made about 1672 by Sir Stephen Rice (1637–1715), Chief Baron of the Exchequer. We are told: 'This man was often heard to say, before he came to be a judge, That he would drive a Coach and Six horses through the Act of Settlement.' Thereafter, 'drive a coach and horses through' seems to have been restricted to destroying laws or parliamentary bills until it gained a more general use in the twentieth century. If you do not want to drive, you may find you have to **hold your horses**. This expression, meaning to wait, calm down, developed in the first part of the nineteenth century in the USA and still has an American ring to it. A similar idea is found in the term 'rein in', used metaphorically to mean 'restrain'. While this hardly counts as a cliché it is well on its way to being a dead metaphor, as is shown by the frequency with which it appears in the papers in the spelling 'reign in' or even 'rain in'. The problem here, of course, is that 'rein', as a verb, has never been particularly common, and the spelling is therefore unfamiliar. A final cliché from harnessed animals is to **kick against the pricks**. The image here is of a horse that rebels when it feels the pricking of spurs, or oxen the goad, and it is a surprisingly ancient image. Versions are found in classical Greek and Latin, and the version we use came into English from the Bible, from the passage in the Acts of the Apostles (9:5) when Saul, on his way to Damascus to persecute the Christians, has a vision of Jesus and converts to Christianity, afterwards taking the name Paul. In his vision 'The Lord said, I am Jesus whom thou persecutest: it is hard for thee to kick against the pricks.' The expression was originally used to mean resisting authority to your own harm, but nowadays it is used more generally to mean to be recalcitrant, rebellious, or just plain difficult. It is frequently found with a play on the sexual or insulting use of 'prick'.

If we turn to ridden horses, just as you can die in harness, so you can **die with your boots on**. The image conjured up by this expression has changed radically over the centuries. Today the primary image is one associated with cowboy films and hard-living men who spend their time on horseback, wanting to die in action. Back in the late seventeenth century, when a good death was one where you died from old age or at least in your bed with plenty of time to prepare for the next life, and would thus die with your boots off, 'to die with your boots or shoes on' was a slang expression meaning 'to be hanged', which could also be used to mean 'to die suddenly and unexpectedly'. Grose's *Dictionary of the Vulgar Tongue* of 1785, a wonderful book and a primary source of early slang, has the entry: 'You will die the death of a trooper's horse, that is with your shoes on, a jocular method of telling any one he will be hanged.' The expression later came to mean to die in battle. The Wild West associations had developed by 1873, when Joaquin Miller published *Life Among the Modocs*, his description of life among the Native Americans and in mining camps of Northern California in the 1850s. This book, which blends fact and fiction, contains the line: 'If you keep on slinging your six-shooter around loose . . . you will . . . die with your boots on.' From this developed the sense 'to die while actively occupied', a sense that coincides with to DIE IN HARNESS (see above). Another cliché sometimes associated with the Wild West and horses is to **hit the ground running**. There have been various attempts to explain the origin of this cliché. Some say that it comes from the American Pony Express dispatch riders changing horses on the run; others have linked it to rodeo riders getting out of the way of broncos that have bucked them off, or hobos jumping off trains in order to avoid being caught. However, there *is* evidence that it was advice given to paratroopers in the Second World War. Now that the latest edition of the *OED* has covered the expression, we can at least get a better idea of its history. The first recorded use, from an Ohio newspaper of 1895, certainly has a Western ring to it – 'The bullet went under me. I knew he had five more cartridges, so I hit the ground running and squatted low down when his gun barked a second time' – but there is no Pony Express link here, and the context suggests it may already have been a well-established expression usable in many contexts. The expression is used of hobos in the *OED's* second quote, from 1935: 'The bum dropped off while the train was still travelling at a good speed . . . He . . . swung down from the ladder at the end of the baggage car and hit the ground running. It took him a dozen paces to check his speed.' In the 1960s it began to be used as a business cliché for going straight into a new task at full speed (ignoring the implication that this means doing it without investigation or considering actions in depth) and was firmly estabished by the 1970s. It went on to become a favourite with the Reagan administration in the 1980s, reflecting that regime's fixation with John Wayne heroics and Hollywood clichés. Similar hard riding is found in **to ride roughshod over something**. If a horse is going to travel over slippery terrain it can be roughshod – shod with the nails left projecting to give the horse a better grip on the ground. In the past, cavalry horses would also have been shod in this way, not only to prevent them slipping and disrupting a charge, but also to inflict more damage on the enemy as they rode over them, and this unpleasant practice is where the cliché comes from. The expression is found literally from the seventeenth century, with the metaphorical use found from the early nineteenth.

The racing horse has been a much more fruitful source of clichés than the working one. Horse racing for money is recorded in England as far back as the twelfth century, but as we know it today has its origins in the reign of Charles II (1660–85), although most of the clichés that developed from it are much later. A pretty obvious example is **horses for courses**, derived from the idea that you must select the horse to suit the track it is running on. The expression was in use literally in racing circles by the late nineteenth century, but only came into use metaphorically by the 1960s, since when it has come to be a largely meaningless filler, used by those who want to seem knowing without doing much thinking. If you are lucky, your chosen horse may be running on the **inside track**, that is, on the inside of the curve of the racecourse, which gives it a certain advantage. The literal use of this is first recorded by the *OED* in 1857, and it is already in figurative use in *The Times* by 1863 (an example missed by the *OED*, which cites its first such use as appearing in 1867). It rapidly became a business cliché. A similar business cliché is **fast track**, which was originally a US term for a dry and hard, and therefore fast, racetrack (recorded 1934) and became a cliché by the 1960s. This should not be confused with that tedious boast of LIVING LIFE IN THE FAST LANE (see Chapter 13), which comes, of course, from driving. Another term associated with riding at speed is **neck or nothing**, meaning to risk all or 'go flat out' to achieve something. This rather old-fashioned cliché has an obscure history, dating from the late seventeenth century.

The actual process of a horse race has been another rich source of clichés. Nowadays races begin from starting boxes, but early courses were less sophisticated and a scratch would be made in the earth to indicate the starting line; it is this custom that is one of the sources of **up to scratch**. Because of the handicapping system, some horses would be given a **head start** and placed in front of the scratch. Those with a better record would have to **start from scratch**. In fact, a number of sports used the term 'scratch' for a line made in the ground, the earliest recorded use, in the late eighteenth century, being for cricket. The modern sense of 'up to scratch' was firmly established by the mid nineteenth century. Alongside horse racing a prime candidate for the main source of this expression is early boxing matches, when a scratch would be made in the centre of the boxing ring before the start of a fight. When a fighter was knocked down he was given a thirty-second count and then had to make his own way to the scratch if the fight was to go on. If he could not do this, he was not up to scratch and had lost the match. But to return to horses. The race was often started by holding up something easily seen and then dropping it. This object might be a handkerchief, but just as often was a hat. This is probably the origin of the expression **at the drop of a hat**, a cliché that developed in America in the middle of the nineteenth century. Since the contestants would spring into action as soon as the signal was given, it came to mean 'immediately, instantly'. Near the end of the race the horses are likely to come into **the home straight** or **stretch** (the former the norm in the UK, the latter in the USA). This had become a cliché by the mid nineteenth century, so that we find the following rather incongruous image in an American newspaper of 1864: 'Already we see the slave States . . . on the home-stretch to become free.' Finally, the leader might **win hands down**. Although some might think this is an image from poker, it actually comes from horse racing. A jockey who can see he is well ahead of the field will relax his hold on the reins and let his hands drop, allowing the horse to ease up. The expression has been used for 'to win easily' since the middle of the nineteenth century.

For many, the whole point of horse racing is the betting, and this too has produced clichés. That favourite of businessmen and wage negotiators, **across the board**, comes from the USA, where it refers to the noticeboard at racetracks showing the odds on a horse to come first, second or third, and an across-the-board bet is one that places equal amounts on these three outcomes. It became a cliché in the USA in the 1950s, and in England by the 1960s. Before placing a bet, you will want to know the horse's **track record** – how the animal has performed in the past on any particular track. This was transferred to mean people's achievements about the middle of the twentieth century. It is currently very popular business jargon, where it often seems to mean nothing more than experience. Of course, your calculations may be put out by someone running a **dark horse**. This cliché, for someone or something with hidden qualities, has been used since the first part of the nineteenth century to describe a horse about which little is known. The general political use, for someone who is unexpectedly elected, is used in the USA in a more specialized sense. There it means someone who is not an official candidate, but who is chosen as a compromise when voters cannot agree on who to select from those who have put themselves forward. As a result of a dark horse the favourite may be **out of the running**, with no chance of winning, an expression that has been used of things other than horses since the second half of the nineteenth century.

A final handful of miscellaneous horse-related clichés gives us the following. To **put through your paces** comes originally from demonstrating a horse's abilities, but has now moved so far from the original image that it is frequently used of cars. To **lock the stable door after the horse has gone** started life as a proverb which appears in a wide variety of forms such as 'It's no use shutting (locking or bolting) the stable (or barn) door after the horse has fled (or bolted or gone)'. All mean to take action after the damage is done, or do TOO LITTLE TOO LATE (see Chapter 18). Until at least the nineteenth century the proverb frequently came in the form of advice about its being no good locking the stable door after the horse is stolen. It shows how resistant to modernization both proverbs and clichés are that this has not been updated to reflect the frequency of car thefts we find in modern society. Another cliché that has survived long after it has ceased to have connection with everyday life is 'to get on your HIGH HORSE', for which see Chapter 3. A very different type of obsolete horse is found in the **stalking horse**. This creature could originally be some other kind of animal, such as an ox, but as hunters frequently use horses, they came to predominate. As birds or other game would not run from an apparently harmless animal, a hunter could use the cover provided by it to get close to the game before shooting it. Recorded literally from the early sixteenth century, it became a very popular image in the seventeenth century (Shakespeare writes, 'He uses his folly like a stalking-horse and under the presentation of that he shoots his wit' (*As You Like It* (1599), IV.3)), and soon became a cliché used of duplicitous politicians, clerics or foreign machinations in general. Since the 1980s the expression has taken on a special political meaning, of someone who stands for the leadership only to provoke an election and let a stronger candidate win.

An important consideration when dealing with all these trained animals is not to **frighten the horses**. In the days when horses were the main source of transport, frightened horses were a real physical danger in the streets, and everyone would have been brought up to take care not to frighten them. A hangover from this can still be seen today in the exaggerated care some drivers take to slow down when overtaking riders. The famous actress Mrs Patrick Campbell (1865–1940) is supposed to have said, 'It doesn't matter what you do in the bedroom as long as you don't do it in the street and frighten the horses', and the fame of this quotation has no doubt added to the associations the expression has. At all costs, you do not want the horses running wild. To say that **wild horses wouldn't** get you to do something alludes to the barbarian custom of punishing people by having them dragged along or apart by wild horses. This punishment is referred to in English as early as the mid thirteenth century, when deserving to be drawn by wild horses is one of the insults hurled between the comically quarrelling Owl and the Nightingale in the poem of that name. In the nineteenth century this was turned into the expression 'wild horses wouldn't draw . . .' with the more modern 'drag' probably being substituted in the twentieth century. Over time the idea of punishment has become diluted and has been replaced with a vague idea of reluctance to do something, played on by the inestimable P. G. Wodehouse, who wrote, 'There was a time when you had to employ wild horses to drag me from London, and they had to spit on their hands and make a special effort' (*Sunset at Blandings*, 1977).

Dogs and other domestic animals

After the horse the next most prominent domesticated animal is the dog. Although the obvious cliché about this animal is that he is **man's best friend**, it may come as a shock to our senti- mental age that in the past the dog was seen as a symbol of inferiority. This is because the dog was thought of as subservient – think of the cringing of a dog before a cross owner – and from that developed the general idea of inferiority – hence such expressions as 'doggy-paddle' for undeveloped swimming, 'a dog's breakfast' for a mess, the use of 'dog' in the names of inedible plants such as dog daisy and dog rose, and sayings such as 'it isn't fit for a dog'. One cliché that is an expression of inferiority is the **dog's chance**. The first usage of this I have been able to find is in *The Times* in 1900 (a couple of years earlier than the quotation in the *OED*), but it must have been well established before then, for *The Times* is quoting a judge speaking in court saying, 'How could it be said to be untrue to say that the company never had a dog's chance of success?' and a judge of the Queen's Bench would not have been using language that was in any way unconventional in such a context. While it is tempting to link the expression to an obscure seventeenth-century usage of 'dog's chance' as a translation of the Roman term *canicula* (literally 'little bitch') for the lowest score in dice, the gap in the record is too long to be able to do this.

Dog eat dog looks like another disparaging comment on a dog's behaviour, but in fact it was originally quite the opposite, for it is a corruption of a proverb, found in the first century BC in Latin, and in English from the sixteenth century, that 'dog does not eat dog'. 'Dog eat dog' is not found until the twentieth century, and presumably represents a situation where the LAW OF THE JUNGLE (see below) has taken charge, and dog does now eat dog. **Every dog has his day**, a popular proverb since the sixteenth century, used as a rather depressing form of encouragement, or claim that something will go right at least once, balances both 'dog eat dog' and **it's a dog's life**. This reflects a very ancient idea of the low quality of life normal for a dog – after all, the Greeks, in the fifth century BC, called one school of philosophers 'cynics' from the Greek word *kynikos* for dog-like, because they rejected the trappings of civilization, and, they thought, lived like dogs. 'A dog's life' has been used in English for a hard life since the sixteenth century, although it does not seem to have become a cliché until the nineteenth century. However, dogs' lives have become so much better in the modern world that the term is now often used ironically, to describe a life of comfort. The same upbeat idea is found in **there's life in the old dog yet**. The term 'old dog', meaning someone experienced or well versed in something, has been used since the sixteenth century (and is the reason you **cannot teach an old dog new tricks** – even to **jump through hoops**; performing animals have been doing this in the UK since at least the eighteenth century, but the metaphorical use is twentieth century). However, alongside this, the sense of 'dog' for 'a despicable person' has drifted into a friendly insult or term of reproof in much the same way that 'terrible' or 'awesome' have become diluted. This explains the rather jovial or raffish feeling associated with 'there's life in the old dog yet', well enough established to be used as the title of an article in the *New Sporting Magazine* in February 1840. Note the obsolescent sense given to 'yet', indicating 'still', very different from the sense contained in a sentence such as 'He has not done it yet.'

Dogged determination is a rather more ambiguous cliché. Is it positive or negative in implication? Nowadays it seems to depend on context. Yet again an obsolete or obsolescent word (terms like 'dogged persistence' are still sometimes found) is preserved. 'Dogged' by itself is an old adjective, in the past used to mean 'dog-like', both in the sense of 'faithful hound' and 'cur', with 'dogged appetite' an old term for bulimia, but it is now obsolete in these senses. 'Dogged determination' does not feature in the *OED*, but it seems to have come into vogue in the 1830s, very much in a disparaging sense, being associated with words like 'sullen' and 'ferocious', and thus very much in the 'cur' sense of dogged. The image is of the sort of dog that will not let go once it has got a hold of something, and the change from condemnatory to sometimes approving meanings seems to reflect a change in attitudes to getting what you want. The opposite of the dog that will not let go is the one whose **bark is worse than his bite**. The Latin version of this saying goes back to the first century AD, and the concept at least goes back to the seventeenth century in English, although the actual wording is not found until the nineteenth century. As might be expected from a saying that is inspired by the behaviour of a household pet, while it can be used to imply ineffectiveness, it is often used quite affectionately. However, **dogs of war** certainly have a bite. This term comes initially from Shakespeare's *Julius Caesar* (1599), where Mark Antony, standing over Caesar's body, prophesies the civil war that will split Rome and says, 'Caesar's spirit ranging for revenge . . . shall . . . Cry "Havoc!" and let slip the dogs of war / That this foul deed shall smell above the earth / With carrion men, groaning for burial' (III.1). The term 'dogs of war' was familiar enough in the nineteenth century for a writer in 1842 to play on it in a popular novel with the threat to 'let slip the dogs of law on him', but this sort of use is still very much an allusion to Shakespeare. It really only took off as a clichéd term for 'mercenaries' after the success of Frederick Forsyth's 1974 novel *The Dogs of War* (filmed in 1980) about a mercenary's attempt to take over an African country.

A cliché that seems to be on the way out is **the dog's bollocks**. This term for 'the best, excellent' was much used by the British magazine *Viz* (based in the north of England) in the late 1980s, and became immensely popular for a while. Despite the fact that 'bollocks' is usually a derogatory term, 'dog's bollocks' probably came to mean 'outstanding' because that is what a dog's bollocks are (presumably there was originally some expression, now lost, such as 'stands out like a dog's bollocks'). In 1993 the Wychwood Brewery produced an outstanding real ale called the Dog's Bollocks, which introduced the phrase to a new audience. The expression grew steadily in use, even being used in advertising, but looks to be falling out of fashion equally rapidly. One problem is that it is often shortened to **the bollocks**, leading to confusion between 'It's the bollocks' (good), and 'It's bollocks' (bad). In part its popularity probably stems from being a naughty alternative to older terms such as THE BEE'S KNEES (see below), a view supported by such jocular variants as 'the pooch's privates' and 'the mutt's nuts'.

Finally among the dogs we come to **the curious incident of the dog in the night-time**. This is a quote from Sir Arthur Conan Doyle's short story 'Silver Blaze', published in 1894 as the first story in the collection *The Memoirs of Sherlock Holmes*. The relevant passage runs:

'Is there any other point to which you would wish to draw my attention?'

'To the curious incident of the dog in the night-time.'

'The dog did nothing in the night-time.'

'That was the curious incident,' remarked Sherlock Holmes.

In his usual infuriating manner, Holmes says no more about it until the end of the story, when he explains that the fact that the dog did not bark showed him that the theft he is investigating must have been an inside job, as the dog must have known the thief. 'Dog in the night-time' has long been well used, but it moved firmly into the category of clichés after the **runaway success** (another horse cliché) of Mark Haddon's book *The Curious Incident of the Dog in the Night-Time* (2003).

Cats are another popular pet, and if they are too pampered, they become **fat cats**. This expression developed about 1920, according to that great commentator on the American language H. L. Mencken, who says 'fat cat' originally meant 'a rich man willing to make a heavy contribution to a party campaign fund'. The *OED's* first quote is from 1928, and their citations show that the term was being used for a financial supporter right up until the 1960s, the same decade that the modern sense of wealthy (and implicitly overpaid) businessman developed. Although there are plenty of other expressions that include cats – 'cat got your tongue', 'the cat that got the cream', 'to fight like cat and dog', 'to rain cats and dogs' – the only other one that really qualifies as a cliché is to **rub the wrong way**. This comes from the effect of stroking a pet against the natural lie of its hair, and a cat is the most obvious candidate. It has been in use since at least the middle of the nineteenth century.

There is one further exception, which might be called a clichéd habit of speech that originally encompassed a whole range of animals. For some unexplained reason, a fashion arose in 1920s America, that age of flappers, wild spending and fashionable excess, for ever wilder ways of saying 'excellent' in terms of parts of animals. Cats were prominent in this. Something good could be the **cat's meow**, the **cat's whiskers** or the **cat's pyjamas**. But it could also be the flea's or monkey's eyebrows,

the canary's tusks, the elephant's adenoids, the bullfrog's beard
or the **bee's knees**. Of these only the bee's knees, the cat's
whiskers and the cat's pyjamas passed into general speech and
still survive, although in restricted use.

Farm animals in general have not given many clichés to the
language. One that at first looks as if it should be linked to horses
is **buck the trend**. Although the most familiar use of the term
'buck' is to describe the action of a horse trying to unseat its
rider (originally the term was 'buckjump' from the way a running
deer moves) in this cliché the word 'buck' is an alternative form
of the verb 'butt', which is found in English dialect and was
taken to America where it flourished. From describing cows and
other animals butting each other, the sense came to be used of
humans pushing against both physical and intangible things and
thence for resistance in general. The expression to be **at the
end of your tether** (or **rope** in North America) is an obvious
domestic animal image, for a tethered animal in that position
has gone as far as it can and can carry on no further. 'Tether'
had come to mean 'the limit of what you are able to do' by
1579, when we are told, 'Men must not passe their tedder', but
'end of your tether' is not recorded until 1809.

The extremes of life and death are also found in clichés from
domestic animals. There was a time, particularly before the shire
horse was bred, that the ox was the standard draft animal, being
used to pull ploughs and heavy wagons. Oxen were therefore bred
for size and strength as well as docility (hence **strong as an ox** and
the once popular **dull as an ox**). Their size and solidity led to the
expression to drop **like a felled ox**. At the other end of the life
cycle is **wet behind the ears**, referring to an animal that is so
newborn it is not yet fully dry. The FEMALE OF THE SPECIES (see
Chapter 15) gives us the **sacred cow**. Cows are sacred in the
Hindu religion, and the British in India coined the term 'sacred
cow' for the animals that are left to roam unmolested. By 1910
the expression had been transferred to an institution, idea or
person considered above criticism or change.

Finally among domesticated animals we turn to hens. In the 1920s scientists observed that hens have a social system whereby any hen can and will peck at any hen less dominant than it is, but not at those more dominant. In this way they establish and maintain a social hierarchy. The scientists called this the **pecking order**. The term seems to have been used of human behaviour almost from the start. **Chickens** also **come home to roost**. The origin of this expression is a proverb which says that curses, like chickens, come home to roost. It is found as early as Chaucer, who used it of birds in general, but the form with chickens only appears in 1810. The opposite is to **fly the coop**, a predominantly American expression recorded only from the start of the twentieth century.

Wild Animals

If we turn to the world of hunting we find the expression **fair game**. The *OED*'s first citation for this as an expression for a legitimate target in the abstract sense dates from 1801, but it is certainly much older than this. *The Times* has a quote from 1785, but it was obviously well established by then. Indeed, it is used twice the next year, and it should probably be regarded as already a cliché by the late eighteenth century. In the past there was a companion expression, 'forbidden game', referring to contexts where hunting an animal was forbidden, either because it was out of season, or because you had no right to hunt it. Fair game is game that can be hunted. Nowadays 'fair game' can also have a strong sexual connotation, not surprising when you consider the other sexual associations of the word 'game'. Fox hunting gives us **run to earth**, which has been used figuratively since the middle of the nineteenth century. Go out and shoot rabbits, and you may find your target is **not a happy bunny**. This is a fairly recently arrived ironic way of talking about people with problems or who are upset, a contrast between the Disneyesque image of the happy bunny and the grim reality he or she has to face. **Not a happy camper** is an earlier alternative.

The romantic vision of nature we have developed from watching cosy nature documentaries is contradicted by the clichés that developed in the past. We find **nature red in tooth and claw**, nowadays used as an alternative for DOG EAT DOG (see above), but which in its original form, in Alfred, Lord Tennyson's *In Memoriam* (1850), had a slightly different sense:

> Man . . . Who trusted God was love indeed
> And love Creation's final law –
> Though Nature, red in tooth and claw
> With ravine, shrieked against his creed.

A similar idea is found in the cliché **it's a jungle out there**. 'Jungle' was established as a term applied to something non-vegetable by 1859, when Thomas Carlyle writes of a 'jungle of red tape', and the concept of the **law of the jungle** was established by Rudyard Kipling in *The Jungle Book* of 1894. By the first decade of the twentieth century 'jungle' was given an urban context as a place where the homeless lived. **Asphalt jungle**, meaning the city as a jungle, dates from 1920, but was made better known when W. R. Burnett used it for a book title in 1949. **Blackboard jungle** became a well-known expression for a difficult or out-of-control school when it was used as the title of a film in 1955, based on the novel of the same title by Evan Hunter published the previous year. The popularity of **concrete jungle** also comes from film, having been used as the American title of a 1960 British film released as *The Criminal*. These expressions have also been the source of many journalistic formula phrases, and now almost anything can be a jungle. More *rending and tearing* in the natural world is found in **feeding frenzy**, a term for sharks who can home in to a food source in large numbers and become so aggressive that they attack each other. The expression only came into English in the early 1970s, and has recently been transferred to the behaviour of people competing frantically for something, particularly in the media. All this aggression may cause you to **turn tail**, an image in use since the sixteenth century. It probably comes from the way many prey animals use their raised tails as warning signals when in flight. If an attacked animal succeeds in running away it may retreat to **lick its wounds**. The earliest examples of the clichéd use of this that I have been able to find are from the 1930s, but it seems unlikely that it was not used before this.

A more focused threat from wild animals is found in **keep the wolf from the door**. Wolves have long been a symbol of hunger – 'ravening' is used almost only of wolves – and 'to keep the wolf from the door' originally meant to keep starvation away, although it is used more generally now. The expression is found as early as the 1470s. More fierce behaviour is found in **the lion's share**. This comes from one of Aesop's *Fables*, which tells the story of how a group of animals – the exact membership of the group varies from version to version – went hunting. When they had caught their prey the lion used his size and strength to keep the whole of the kill for himself. Thus, the term should strictly speaking be used to mean all of something, not, as it is, most of it. However, as it has been used as we use it today since the eighteenth century, it is a bit late to quibble. Another individual animal that gets a bad press is the **snake in the grass**. Snakes hidden in grass are difficult to spot, and may not be seen until trodden on. This image for something deceitful was used by Virgil in his *Eclogues* of about 38 BC, and occurs again in Dante's *Inferno*. By the seventeenth century it was well-enough known in England to be used as the title of a book. Behind these images lie important religious myths. Greeks would have been familiar with the story of Orpheus and Eurydice, where Orpheus loses his beloved wife to the bite of a snake she treads on when she does not notice it in the undergrowth. Orpheus' subsequent visit to the land of the dead to try and retrieve her probably had deep religious significance for those initiated into the mysteries of Orphic religion. Even more obviously, the temptation of Eve by the serpent in the Garden of Eden is a fundamental story in Judaism, Christianity and Islam.

In contrast with such antiquity, the **elephant in the room** is probably the most recent animal-based cliché. This expression, for something that is unignorable but not mentioned, seems to have been quite well established in the early 1980s in America, when it was used in a poem by Terry Kettering which appeared in *Bereavement* magazine in 1981. The long poem begins:

> There's an elephant in the room.
> It is large and squatting, so it is hard to get around it.
> Yet we squeeze by with, 'How are you?' and 'I'm fine,' and a
> thousand other
> forms of trivial chatter. We talk about the weather. We talk about work.
> We talk about everything else, except the elephant in the room.

This was reproduced elsewhere and became widely known, becoming particularly associated with the problems of alcoholism. Although 'elephant in the room' is the commonest form, it is also found in forms such as **elephant in the living room**, **elephant in the corner**, **elephant on the dinner table** and even, perhaps because of the alcohol associations, 'the pink elephant in the corner'. In addition the 900-pound gorilla found in jokes (Where does a 900-pound gorilla sleep? Where he likes) and used in the past for someone or some organization that throws its weight about is beginning to muscle in on the elephant's territory, as is the rhinoceros.

Since elephants are so strongly associated with mice in popular imagination (there is no truth in the idea that they are afraid of them) this seems a good point to introduce **Are you a man or a mouse?** Although its impact has been weakened by frequent comic use in mouse-based cartoons, it is still to be found used in all seriousness, even if more rarely than in the past. The expression was a popular one in the sixteenth century, but then carried the implication of success or failure rather than timidity, and this continued through to the nineteenth century. The idea of the mouse element being like Robert Burns's 'wee . . . tim'rous beastie' seems to be a modern one, even though the idea of a mouse as a symbol of timidity goes back to the Middle Ages. While dealing with vermin, we should perhaps consider **come out of the woodwork**. The expression, which is not recorded before the 1960s, has an opposite, to **crawl back into the woodwork**. Two things are striking about its use. The first is that the 1960s seems rather late for popular use of 'woodwork' as a term for something made of wood rather than the craft of working with wood (as in school woodwork classes). This may either be a case of the more unusual use sticking in people's minds, which often leads to something becoming a cliché, or else indicates that the expression has been around much longer than our records suggest. The *OED*'s first example is from 1964, but in the same year 'It Crawled Out of the Woodwork' was used as a title in the television science fiction series *The Outer Limits*, which suggests it was well established by then. The second point is that we never know what it is that crawls out of the woodwork. Is it a reference to mice and rats? Are we talking of the destruction of **house and home** by woodworm, termites or similar?

Before we leave the mammals, there is one rather more positive description left – the **eager beaver**. This is an American cliché that reached the UK by the 1940s. The beaver had been held up as an example of hard work and industry as it built its dams and lodges since the eighteenth century, but the rhyming 'eager' only seems to have been attached to it in the twentieth century. The expression is still primarily American. When it was first introduced it was quite strongly disparaging – Elaine Dundy wrote in 1958 of 'the Eager-Beaver-Culture-Vulture with the list ten yards long, who *just* manages to get it all crossed off before she collapses of aesthetic indigestion each night' – but nowadays it is mainly used in headlines, to advertise commercial products or as mild sarcasm. This is probably in part because our attitude to eagerness has changed.

Birds

Birds have given us one of the clichés that are cited most often if someone is asked for an example of a cliché, and this despite the fact that it is rarely used in real life, but only as typical football-speak. **Sick as a parrot** was, indeed, prominent in the 1970s and 1980s. **Sick as a dog**, or even 'sick as a horse', is the much older equivalent (in use from the 1700s). Various suggestions have been made as to the origin of the sick parrot: from a dialect 'sick as a peat' (pronounced pee-at), meaning feeling heavy, to a seventeenth-century expression, 'melancholy as a sick parrot', but no one has ever come up with a convincing answer, and it remains a linguistic oddity. It is, however, worth noting that its rise to prominence coincided with the popularity of the Monty Python Dead Parrot sketch (discussed in Chapter 5).

The eagle is traditionally the king of the birds. Or at least he was, according to one tradition, until the wren tricked him out of the role (see EVERY LITTLE HELPS, Chapter 6). The eagle has, of course, long been a symbol of empire, used as such by the Romans, Napoleon, the Austro-Hungarian Empire and the Russian Tsars. One of the things it is admired for is its keen sight, for it was anciently held to have the sharpest eyesight of all birds. Hence the expression **eagle-eyed**. Another legend about the eagle says that when its sight grows dull with age it flies up towards the sun, and, by using its unique ability to stare at the sun, it burns away all the cloudiness of age. This story has been known and referred to for as long as we have written records of English. However, eagle eye(d) has only been a cliché since the early nineteenth century. The twentieth century added two more eagle clichés to the language. The first human-carrying lunar module to land on the moon was called 'Eagle'.

When its pilot, Neil Armstrong, touched down in 1969 he told Houston, **The Eagle has landed**. This became a catchphrase, used when putting something tricky in place, or as a cry of achievement. The expression was further popularized when it was used, for a totally unrelated reason, as the title of a 1975 novel by Jack Higgins (filmed in 1976), after which it became a formula phrase, used by headline writers. It should not be confused with **where eagles dare**, also used as a formula phrase, the title of a 1967 novel by Alistair MacLean. The **legal eagle** counts as a cliché not just because it is a staple of headlines and unthinking prose, but because it is really rather meaningless. The term, which came into use in the mid twentieth century in America, is simply a silly term for a lawyer, the eagle element not implying clear-sightedness or any other additional meaning, but just being there for the rhyme. Indeed, so meaningless is it, that the term 'legal beagle' – presenting a very different image for anyone who cared to stop to think – was at one time a serious rival. The similarly rhyming couple **culture vulture**, cited above under EAGER BEAVER, which also dates from the middle of the twentieth century, when such formations were in vogue, is a much more interesting case. The image of the vulture, with its reputation for voraciousness and for feeding on dead corpses, is an integral part of the use of this image to condemn an overeager but undiscriminating pursuer of things that 'should' be seen. However, this condemning use has now been much diluted, and a search on the Internet shows that it is now standard to use it in a neutral or approving way – thereby moving it into the realm of the thoughtless cliché.

There are few other birds that the British public recognizes enough to use in clichés. Pigeons occur in **put** (or **set**) **the cat among the pigeons**. Since pigeons were once much more familiar as domestic animals or pets than they are today, the image is probably that of a cat scattering a flock of pigeons in a farmyard or similar. The expression's history is obscure, and although it sounds old, the earliest example I have been able to find is from 1914. The cuckoo, so easily identified by its call, gives us the newspaper cliché of the **first cuckoo of spring**. At one time *The Times*, then the paper of record, really did print letters reporting the first hearing of the cuckoo. The cuckoo itself has been a symbol of the coming of warmer weather since the beginnings of English literature. The best-known early example is the thirteenth-century lyric, usually rendered in modern English, 'Summer is a-coming in. Loud now sing cuckoo!', although this rather distorts the original, where the Middle English *is icumen* means 'has come' rather than 'is coming'. Even older in origin than this is **cloud cuckoo land**. This is the nineteenth-century translation of the Greek *Nephelococcygia*, formed from the Greek for 'cloud' and 'cuckoo', and coined by the Greek dramatist Aristophanes for his play *The Birds*, first performed in 414 BC. He gave the name to a city built by the birds in the clouds in order to separate them from the evils of mankind. Aristophanes, as ever, uses his fantasy to satirize Athens and the Athenians. We, however, use the expression in a rather different way from the original. Usually found in the form 'living in cloud cuckoo land', and used to indicate that a person is the opposite of someone who has their **feet firmly on the ground**, the expression belongs with 'head in the air' and 'castle in the air'. The only other birds that seem to be found in cliché are waterbirds. So we have the **sitting duck**, one that is an easy target for someone with a gun, and will swiftly become a **dead duck**, although no true sportsman would take any pride in shooting his target other than on the wing; hence the disparaging tone that these expressions often involve. The figurative use of 'sitting duck' dates from the middle of the twentieth century. 'Dead duck' is a shortening of an old saying, 'never waste powder on a dead duck', that is, do not waste effort on a hopeless case. The expression, which originated in the USA, has been in use since the early nineteenth century. A **lame duck** has a much more confused origin, and has also limped off in two different directions. In the UK it belongs with those other financial animals of the stock exchange, the bull and the bear. A 'lame duck' started off as someone who could not meet their obligations on settling-up day and had to default, and is found in this sense as early as 1761. It is presumably from this that the sense of a company that needed to be bailed out by the government developed. On the other side of the Atlantic the term developed the sense of a politician who has failed to get elected or is not eligible to be re-elected (from 1861). It is now most often used, in a further development of this sense, of an administration that is nearing the end of its life. It is in this sense that it has become a cliché, in that it is often used unthinkingly, and the term is being applied earlier and earlier in an administration's life. Thus Tony Blair was described as a lame duck as soon as he announced he would not be standing in the next election (although this died out as the wait for his final resignation grew longer), and George Bush Jnr was a lame duck to some commentators almost as soon as he was re-elected. The **ugly duckling** comes from the Hans Christian Andersen story of the cygnet hatched with a brood of ducklings that was a social outcast because it was so ugly and ungainly, but finally turned into a beautiful swan. This was translated into English in 1869 and was established in less than twenty years as a term for a child (and later a project) that looked unpromising, but had hidden talents or virtues.

There may not be many clichés that refer to specific birds, but there are a good handful that refer to birds in general – not surprising when for many people the majority of birds come under the general classification of 'small brown bird'. The flocks of anonymous birds give us the proverb **birds of a feather flock together**. This has been used since the sixteenth century in English, although similar sentiments are found as far back as Homer. The shortened form, 'birds of a feather', has only been really popular since the nineteenth century. 'Of a feather' here means 'of the same species'. Slightly more individuality is seen in the infuriating expression **a little bird told me**. The origin of this expression seems to go back to the Bible (Ecclesiastes 10:20): 'Curse not the king . . . for a bird of the air shall carry the voice, and that which hath wings shall tell the matter.' The concept was current in the Middle Ages – when, for example, Christian propaganda against Mohammed claimed he was a renegade priest who fooled people into thinking he had a direct line to God by training a bird to fly down to his shoulder to take a nut he had hidden in his ear, telling witnesses that it was whispering God's word in his ear – but the actual expression is not found until the sixteenth century, and did not become a cliché until the twentieth. A single bird is also found in the **early bird who catches the worm**. This proverb has been in use since the seventeenth century, to mean that the person who gets somewhere first will have an advantage. However, nowadays you are more likely to come across 'early bird' used by itself simply as a clichéd term for an early riser or early booker. Early Bird was the name given to the first commercial communications satellite, launched 6 April 1965.

Birds' nests are generally seen as places of warmth and security. They give us that comfortable word 'nestle', and that desirable thing, a **nest egg** (a curious term – originally the artificial egg you put in a hen's nest to induce her to continue to lay after you have taken her real eggs for yourself; then a decoy or an inducement. Presumably it then moved from a bribe to money put aside for retirement, then to money saved for any reason). It is therefore rather surprising to find that the clichés based on nests are anything but pleasant. If you **feather your own nest** you do so dishonestly, at someone else's expense (linked therefore to the NEST EGG). To **foul your (own) nest** is a very early image in English. In 'The Owl and the Nightingale', one of the very earliest poems to have survived from the period when English literature re-emerged after the Norman Conquest, one of the insults hurled at the owl by the nightingale is that it literally lets its young foul their own nest; the obsolete proverb 'It is an ill bird that fouls its own nest' is also medieval. Much less unpleasant is an **empty nest**. This expression, used to describe the feelings of parents whose children have all left home, seems to have been coined in the 1970s. It is not surprising it is so recent, as it is not long since it was quite usual for children to live at home until they got married. The image of the home and family as a nest is an old one. Shakespeare has Macduff say, when he hears Macbeth has been responsible for the deaths of his wife and children:

> All my pretty ones?
> Did you say all? O hell-kite. All?
> What! All my pretty chickens and their dam,
> **At one fell swoop**? (IV.3)

'At one fell swoop' is an interesting example of the way in which a really effective phrase can catch the public's attention, only to be overused. In this case 'fell' means 'evil, deadly', but in context Shakespeare is able to exploit the echo we get in our minds of the sense 'fall', to make the image of a bird taking its prey more vivid. That the expression has become a cliché, and is used unthinkingly, can be demonstrated by the way in which 'fell', now obsolescent, is often corrupted by users into words such as 'foul'. But to return to our empty nest. We are quite likely to say of the children who have left that the **birds have flown the nest**, quite possibly set up in their own homes with the help of money from their parents' nest egg. 'Empty nest' itself is also now undergoing a change. As the old get younger, or at least more vigorous for their years, **empty nesters** are beginning to seem not so much abandoned as liberated by their children leaving home. It is beginning to be seen as a time when they can enjoy life without having to make sacrifices for their adult children. In the USA they may even join the retirees who follow the sun south in mobile homes in the winter, and become **snowbirds**.

Insects

Moving down the scale of animals, we come to insects. Bees are important in the imagery of our culture. They are seen as busy and as examples of providence, unlike the careless grasshopper, which makes no provision against the winter. Around them you will find a **hive of industry**. Hives have been used figuratively to mean 'places swarming with busy occupants' since the early seventeenth century, although I have not found the actual wording 'hive of industry' before 1830, and it is not recorded in the *OED* before 1863. The downside of bees is the way they buzz round and round, reflected in the expression to have a **bee in your bonnet**. This has been a cliché since the eighteenth century, and in use for even longer. The image behind it is that the ideas that obsess the person buzz round in their heads like a bee caught in headgear.

Other irritating insects are found in **with a flea in your ear**, which originated in French, and has been in steady use since about 1430. The imagery is that of the words of a *stinging reproof* hurting the ears as the biting of a flea would. If you have **no flies on** you, you are active, alert and know what is going on, like the livelier cows in a field on which the flies do not settle, choosing the dull, sluggish ones instead. The expression is recorded from the mid nineteenth century in both the USA and Australia (which suggests it was in use by immigrants from the UK, but is unrecorded there). By 1900 it was so well established in the USA that there was a Salvation Army hymn entitled 'There Are No Flies on Jesus', which contained the immortal lines 'There may be flies on you and me, / But there are no flies on Jesus', something to give pause to anyone who thinks HAPPY-CLAPPY evangelism (see Chapter 16) is something new.

23. Fillers

Fillers and buzzwords, dealt with in the next chapter, are the groups of expressions that the general public would most readily identify as clichés. We hear fillers **day in and day out** (nineteenth century) from politicians, particularly when they are being interviewed on the radio. From the writer's point of view such phrases are difficult to deal with, as they do not fall easily into groups. This is because they are essentially meaningless in their entirety or at the very least employ redundant words. Their role in speech is not communication, but either to evade it or, to interpret their use more charitably, to give the speaker time to scramble together his arguments without letting go of the conversation.

Gaining time being one of the objects of the exercise, it is not surprising that time forms an element in some of these fillers. In 2004 members of the Plain English Campaign voted on what they thought were the most irritating expressions in English. **At this moment in time** came in as the most irritating, with **at the end of the day** second. Both of these became very popular with politicians and trade unionists in the 1970s, along with **in this day and age**. All have been roundly condemned for many years, and all are merely waffling ways of saying 'now'. 'At the end of the day' is also used to try to give importance to a statement, and belongs with **when all is said and done** (an expression dating from the sixteenth century), and **in the final analysis**, which was adopted from the French *en dernière analyse* in the nineteenth century. It was originally used in serious logic, usually in the form 'last analysis', and only became a cliché in the mid twentieth century. **Happy days** is the filler of fillers, usually said with a sigh, when the speaker can think of no other thing to say, but feels too embarrassed not to give some response.

Another group of these fillers deals with place. **Here and now** (using both these terms is redundant: 'here' or 'now' would usually do just as well as both) is the commonest, along with **neither here nor there**, which has been in use since the sixteenth century. With **here, there and everywhere** it is, of course, unnecessary to use 'here' and 'there' if you are using 'everywhere', but that did not stop Shakespeare using the expression at least twice, nor Christopher Marlowe before him. **Hither and thither** or **yon** is a highly archaic way of saying the same thing with the same redundancy. Despite this, this expression has been recorded for as long as English has, the first instance being in an Old English gloss to a Latin text, dated to about AD 725. 'Hither and yon', which sounds rather fey to English ears, is the preferred form in the USA, and is also found in English dialect from the eighteenth century. Neither shows any sign of going out of fashion, despite their long histories. **In the midst of** is another archaism, 'midst' being otherwise unused outside poetry. The expression is a genuine medieval one, but as used in modern English means the same as 'in the middle of', or even just 'in'. **Far and away** has been common since the nineteenth century, but **far and wide** is another expression that goes back to the beginning of the language. **First and foremost** is a doublet that has been around since the later fifteenth century, but only became a cliché in the mid nineteenth century, while **first things first** is not recorded before the nineteenth century. **Dizzy heights**, used figuratively, first appears in *The Times* in 1843, while **dizzying heights** cannot be found there until 1976, and does not appear at all in the *OED*. One cliché of place that may not be instantly recognizable by all is **by and large**. In the days of square-rigged ships, 'by' meant to sail within six points of the wind, and 'large' to sail with the wind pretty much at right angles to the course of the ship. An order to the steersman to sail 'by and large', therefore, was a vague one, indicating a range of possible directions – the sort of order that is difficult to understand without first-hand knowledge of square-riggers; presumably **you had to be there** (a cliché that usefully saves the speaker the effort of finding the necessary words). From being a nautical term, 'by and large' was adopted in the seventeenth century to mean 'all ways' and from that to mean 'on the whole'. It has now lost all connection with sailing.

Another group of these fillers deal with truth, although in practice they induce immediate doubt, at least in the more cynical. **Believe it or not** is an obvious example. Although it is usually no more than a verbal tic, introducing the element of doubt merely encourages it. In the USA the expression was made more current by the long-running (from 1929 to the present) syndicated newspaper column written and illustrated by Robert Ripley (1893–1949) and his successors, which dealt with STRANGE BUT TRUE information (see Chapter 8), while in London *Believe It or Not* was the title of a show that ran from 1939 to 1940. The similar **Would you believe it?** seems to be the older of the two expressions, having been used since at least 1776. Although when they started life in the seventeenth century, expressions such as **the fact of the matter** or **as a matter of fact** had a legal or semi-legal sense, 'the fact of the matter' has been a mere filler, rarely adding anything to what is said, since at least the middle of the nineteenth century. Of 'as a matter of fact', Eric Partridge, in his *Dictionary of Clichés*, says, 'Usually the prelude to a lie – or, at best, an evasion.' The same can often be said of the related **and that's a fact** and of **truth to tell** or **to tell the truth**. These have been used for emphasis or as fillers since the mid fourteenth century. The opposite of this usage is when people correct themselves with **No, I tell a lie**. Although **make no mistake** is designed to add emphasis, this is often a filler cliché. It has been in use since the nineteenth century. Since **pure and simple** is often linked to 'truth' (Shakespeare writes of **the simple truth**) we can cover it here. It was in use by the middle of the sixteenth century, but does not seem to have become a cliché until the nineteenth century, when it was very common. Oscar Wilde put it in its place when he wrote, 'The truth is rarely pure, and never simple' (*The Importance of Being Earnest*, 1895). A related phrase is **pure genius**, which is again old – Dryden used it in the seventeenth century – but has only been a cliché since the twentieth century. Wilde's comment applies to it equally well. **In the truest sense of the word** is one of those clichés designed to puzzle those who like to consider the literal sense of what is said. A cliché since the later nineteenth century, it evolved from earlier, philosophical uses, where 'true' and 'truest' were seriously debated comparisons. **In a very real sense** performs a similar role. **Well and truly** is also a nineteenth-century cliché. **Not as such** was probably originally legal jargon of the nineteenth century, but is now largely used as a filler or as obfuscation, as a weaselly way of saying 'no', and is often interpreted as the opposite of the truth, a downright lie.

Related to clichés of truth are those based on logic and the formal presentation of arguments. Most of these have been dealt with elsewhere, but the fillers are covered here. They mostly moved into general speech from the debates of the law courts and parliament (a process that is still going on), and the majority are first recorded from the nineteenth century, although this may be because that is when records first became widely available; further research may find earlier examples. They often have an aura of reasonableness, while actually being waffle. You can use fillers when setting up an argument to suggest (frequently spuriously) that your view is a logical one. One such is **it goes without saying**, which implies that you do not need to support your views with evidence. It has been common since the later nineteenth century, and is a literal translation of the French *cela va sans dire*, which explains the odd grammar. The next step is to say **having said that**, as if the truth of your statement is proved. **Needless to say** is an alternative. You can present an impression of careful wisdom, again without evidence, with **all**

things considered, a less formal equivalent of AFTER DUE CONSIDERATION (see Chapter 12), or sum up with **all in all** or more rarely with **the long and the short of it**, which has been in use since the seventeenth century, as has **each and every**. **Suffice it to say** belongs with this set, and has been well used since the eighteenth century, with similar forms going back as far as the fourteenth. There are numerous fillers that give a spurious authority to the speaker's views: **mark my words**, a cliché since the nineteenth century, is one of these. Others include **just for the record**, common since the 1950s; **too numerous to mention**, a cliché from the nineteenth century which can also be a lazy excuse for not knowing your facts; **without fear of contradiction**; **all things being equal**; and **face (the) facts**, rarely used without the implication that while the speaker can see the reality of the situation, and is prepared to deal with it, the person being spoken to or of is either incapable of understanding the reality, or too emotionally involved to do so. The facts can be blurred by **as it were** (a cliché since the eighteenth century), and **be that as it may**, the main virtue of which is to allow pedants to feel that they are using a subjunctive. You can cast doubt on your opponent with **far be it from me**, which has been in use since the fourteenth century and a cliché since the eighteenth. This has the advantage of pretending modesty or discretion, while actually meaning the opposite of its words. You can accuse someone of **gross exaggeration** or **overstatement** (for some reason these are always gross rather than great) or deflect attention from a winning point with **that's a good question**. **Last but not least** is a depressing thing to hear from many speakers, as you know very well that you are not really at the end of what they are going to say.

The remaining filler clichés do not really fit into any clear groupings and can only be listed. The majority belong to the more formal levels of language. These include the following, in no particular order. **The sum of human (happiness)** is a cliché of the nineteenth century, although similar expressions are found earlier. **Every last one** has been a cliché since at least the 1930s. **Lo and behold** is only recorded from the beginning of the nineteenth century, although the two words are both found separately very much earlier. **Man and boy** has been used so much in caricatures of a certain type of elderly man that it is now rarely used other than as a conscious cliché. The tone was set by the first recorded, and best-known use, in Shakespeare's *Hamlet* (1601) when the comic gravedigger tells Hamlet, 'I have been Sexton here, man and boy, thirty years' (V.1). **With might and main** is a lasting monument to the power of alliteration in English. 'Main', in the sense of physical force, has been obsolete since the sixteenth century, except in this phrase. 'Might and main' is first found as a set phrase in Old English poetry, which depended on alliteration. It occurs in *Beowulf*, one of our oldest recorded poems, and has been in regular use ever since. **Heighten the awareness** is modern bureaucratic-speak for the simpler 'make more aware', used to make it sound more official. **(Come) thick and fast** is a term from the early eighteenth century, an alternative to Robert Burns's FAST AND FURIOUS (see Chapter 7). **With a vengeance**, from the seventeenth century, on the face of it a strange expression, originally meant 'with a curse'. **Without more** or **further ado** employs another word, ado, an archaic word for work or bother, that is obsolete except in these set phrases. These have been in use since the fourteenth century. **Deafening silence**, when first introduced sometime in the 1960s, must have seemed a striking paradox, but rapidly degenerated into a cliché. In the past the expression **eloquent silence** would have been used in the same way, but 'deafening' is now more often found. **The same ilk**, or **of that ilk**, is an expression from the world of heraldry and the aristocracy. In Scotland, in particular, the surname or title of a landholder is often the same as the name of the lands he holds. 'Ilk' means 'same', and 'of that ilk' is used to avoid repetition of title and name, so that 'Sir Iain Moncreiffe of that Ilk' is a handier, more elegant way of saying 'Sir Iain Moncreiffe of

Moncreiffe'. However, since the late eighteenth century 'that ilk' has been understood to mean 'kind, sort, set' and used in a general way, despite the fact that 'the same ilk' is technically a repetition. **Je ne sais quoi**, a French expression, literally 'I don't know what', has been a clichéd way of expressing an indefinable quality, that special extra something, since about the 1880s. Nowadays it sounds rather dated, and is associated with affectation of the **Pretentious, moi?** (a quote from *Fawlty Towers*) sort. Others of this sort include **little did he know**, **bigger and better**, **over and done with** and **tried and tested**, while two that are particularly detested are **literally** and **needs no introduction**. 'Literally' was originally used to emphasize that what has been stated is not figurative, but it is now increasingly used for mere emphasis, sometimes with ridiculous effect. Although this is often deplored as a modern trend, the word has been used in this way since at least the middle of the nineteenth century. 'Needs no introduction' is a particularly pompous-sounding introduction formula, loved by chairpersons through the land. Nor is it very encouraging for the person being introduced, for it carries the subtext 'You probably don't know who this person is, so I'm going to tell you about them.'

Expressions with a more conversational tone include **the thinking man's** or **woman's** something-or-other. The most famous example, probably the source of the expression as a cliché, is the comment attributed to Frank Muir that 'Joan Bakewell is the thinking man's crumpet.' **Bear with me (for just) a moment** is an ungainly way of asking someone to wait, which is being used with increasing frequency (what are we to bear, and why 'with'?). **Let me just say** or **tell you** is a modern usage which adds nothing except a warning that you are about to hear something boring or an arrant self-justification. **Spreading like weeds** is a figurative expression that can be effective, but is increasingly used to create inappropriate images, such as a recent claim that 'chain stores are spreading like weeds'. More informal still is **don't know what hit you**. In origin this refers to someone being killed, shot so effectively that they literally do not know what hit them before they die. This use is recorded from the 1920s, and its use to mean 'taken by surprise' or 'overwhelmed' is recorded from the 1960s. Still more informal is **better than a slap in the face with a wet fish**. This is only the most popular of the 'better than . . .' formulas, indicating that something is better than nothing. Others include **better than a dig in the eye with a blunt stick** and **better than a kick in the pants** (or in Canada **in the ass with a frozen boot**). The wet fish version, at one time much used by low comedians, seems to come from the USA. These expressions have been common since the 1920s, but probably originated in the late nineteenth century. If **between you and me**, or **between you, me and the bedpost**, **lamppost** or **gatepost**, have a rather dated feel, that is not surprising, for they are old. The simple term 'between you and me' for 'in confidence' has been recorded since 1588, when it appeared in the endearingly modern-sounding sentiment: 'This I tell you between you and me, but I would have it go no further.' The more elaborate forms are clichés of the nineteenth century. Dickens used 'Between you and me and the post' in *Nicholas Nickleby* (1838), and a Mrs Royal wrote in 1830 in *Letters from Alabama*, in a way that can still make purists wince, 'Between you and I and the bed post, I begin to think it all a plot of the priests.' **That would be telling** belongs with WAIT AND SEE (see Chapter 14) and A LITTLE BIRD TOLD ME (see Chapter 22), all clichés used to convey superior knowledge and to infuriate the person on the receiving end. In the form **that's telling** it goes back to the eighteenth century. Modern slang has thrown up **as good as it gets**; **but hey, that doesn't mean we can't . . .**; **makes . . . what it is**; and **tell me about it**, an exclamation that means the opposite of what it appears to. It is a modern expression, which has largely replaced the earlier **You're telling me!**, current from the 1920s in the USA, and a decade later in the UK. Older than it might seem at first is the sentiment behind the

inelegant **that was then, this is now**, for although the form is
new, the idea is not. It is found in the Latin tag *tempora mutantur,
et nos mutamur in illis*, 'times change and we change with them',
attributed to the Emperor Lothar I (795–855).

24. Buzzwords

By buzzwords I mean those fashionable expressions, often jargon, which are used, in the inimitable words of the *OED*, 'more to impress than inform'. Curiously, although they are associated with fashion, and can also be described as vogue phrases, they can also be quite long-lasting in their vogue, often behaving like that cliché of fashion writers, the **well-made basic**, rather than as fripperies of fashion, although some terms do indeed come and go with the speed of a sixteen-year-old **fashion victim**'s **must-have** item. I have largely ignored these fly-by-nights, as they may well have come and gone by the time this book is in your hands. I have also largely ignored single words, such as the stomach-turning BLESS! (see Chapter 16), except where they fit naturally into the flow. Instead I have concentrated on those that aim to impress, or that work alongside fillers to allow people to run on automatic and let the words pour out without really needing to think about what they are saying. Along with fillers and the jargon of politicians, these buzzwords are among the terms people most readily identify as clichés, but they present me with one great problem. While the other chapters of this book have presented some sort of theme, and it has been possible to link the clichés together, however tenuously, I have been unable to find any common threads to link buzzwords together other than the fact that they are buzzwords, and have been reduced to dealing with these words alphabetically. The length of this list is reduced by the fact that many have already been dealt with in other chapters, where they have found their natural homes.

At the beginning of the alphabet we find **address the issue**, a pompous way of saying 'deal with the problem'. This is comparatively recent. The first instance of the expression in *The Times* comes from 1976, setting the tone of future use by saying a government committee had 'failed to address the central issue'. From this rather formal context the expression has now spread to everyday contexts. One step up from 'address the issue' is **grapple with the issue** or **problem**. The next word, **agenda**, belongs in the same context. Used loosely instead of 'plans', 'concerns' or 'intentions', it is a very popular word at the moment, on its own or in combinations such as **hidden agenda**, and **secret agenda**. Another term that is used to try to boost the level of importance of a statement is the ubiquitous **-based**. This has its origin in technical terms such as 'evidence-based medicine', 'project-based learning' and even 'home-based working', and while these expressions may not be very elegant, they are **valid** (to use another buzzword) uses of jargon. The word becomes objectionable when it is overused and instead of making communication more effective, simply obscures. Such uses can be found everywhere. A few examples skimmed off the Internet are: 'Join the Conversation in Beliefnet's Pagan & Earth-Based Communities'; 'not all data need be parcel-based'; and 'Outcomes-Based Evaluation for Nonprofit Organizations'. The suffix **-centric** seems to be following hard on the heels of '-based'. **Customer-centric** is the most common, but the forms are multiplying – recent examples include human-centric, music-centric, citizen-centric, book-centric, gay-centric, project-centric, patient-centric and parcel-centric. **Blue-sky** has a surprisingly long and complex history, and uses are no doubt influenced by **the sky's the limit**. 'Blue-sky' started out at the end of the nineteenth century as a term for something cheerful or hopeful, although it soon acquired more sinister connotations in the form 'blue-sky stock', for worthless stock which conmen would sell to over-optimistic buyers. The sense of 'hopeful' evolved into the idea of doing something not for any planned end, but in the hope of good coming from it, which gave us the rather charming concept of 'blue-sky research'. However, this has now mutated into an evil twin of a verb, so that we get such horrors as 'Let's blue-sky it' as a jargon term for 'Let's think about it'. The sort of person who would say this might well also use the expression **braindump** for passing on a large amount of information, often in a hurried or slipshod way. This started out as a technical term. In computing one 'dumps' or transfers a large file from one computer to another; if it is data this is a 'braindump'. The formula phrase **the . . . of choice**, meaning 'preferred, chosen', also seems to have developed in the world of science, particularly medicine, the earliest quote found, from the *British Journal of Urology*, in 1938, being fairly typical of the sort of linguistic environment it comes from: 'Epididymectomy is the operation of choice in tuberculous emididymitis.' It may have passed into general speech via the expression 'drug of choice'. The construction '. . . of choice' is not a natural one in English, which may have helped to make it more memorable and attractive to a certain type of speaker.

We now come to that paradoxically perennial buzzword, **cool**. While the word remains constantly in use, the way in which it is used does change. In the sense of 'calm, relaxed', the opposite of 'heated', the word has a long history, going back to one of our earliest Anglo-Saxon poems, *Beowulf*. **Cool as a cucumber** was well established by 1615, when Beaumont and Fletcher wrote of 'young maids as cold as cucumbers', obviously playing on the usual sense and giving it a sexual twist. **Cool, calm and collected** dates from at least the nineteenth century. It is easy to see how the sense of 'relaxed, calm' could come to be a term of approval. This is first recorded in the 1880s in Black American slang, 'that's cool' being the earliest form. By the 1940s 'cool jazz' was well established, bringing the word to a wider audience. The expression **stay cool** is prominent in Leonard Bernstein's *West Side Story* of 1957, where it is obviously considered typical New York teen slang. Nowadays, 'cool' has largely gone back to its original sense of general approval, with youngsters using **that's cool** or **I'm cool** as a general term of agreement or approval, although 'cool' still also keeps the previously dominant sense of a certain attitude to life. One expression that has now died out is the much derided **Cool Britannia**. When this expression was used by the Labour Party in the 1990s it acquired instant cliché status and instant inbuilt redundancy. However, the expression has a far longer history than just as a political slogan. The politicians picked it up from the name of a strawberry-and-chocolate-flavoured ice cream produced by the firm of Ben and Jerry in 1996, which they stopped manufacturing in June 1998 after the expression became politicized, not wanting to get involved in controversy. But the expression goes back further still, to the last time that Britain was the place for cool youngsters, in the 1960s. Then, Vivian Stanshall wrote the following lyrics for the Bonzo Dog Doo Dah Band, recorded in 1968: 'Cool Britannia / Britannia take a trip / Britons ever, / Ever, ever, ever shall be hip.' Although some have questioned a connection between the two uses, this ignores the cult status the band had in Tony Blair's Oxford days. We finish the letter C with **credibility**. This poor, unfortunate word had a dismal start, first appearing in 1594 in Richard Hooker's *Of the lawes of ecclesiasticall politie* in the nearly incomprehensible statement: 'Sith the ground of credit is the credibility of things credited; and things are made credible either by the known condition and quality of the utterer, or by the manifest likelihood of truth which they have in themselves.' The modern use began to appear in the 1960s when credibility was much used of the effectiveness of the nuclear deterrent, and also in the term 'credibility gap', the gap between what is said in official statements and what people believe. Considering the lack of trust in official statements nowadays, it is surprising that this term is not more used today. Since the 1960s, 'credibility' has become ever more widely and loosely used. The following appears in a recent edition of the *Independent*: 'Godard's legendarily difficult art gives the festival a lot of serious intellectual credibility', which looks like a serious attempt to beat the record for the number of buzzwords that can be fitted into one sentence.

D brings us to **dream team** or **ticket**. 'Dream ticket' is an expression coined in 1960 to describe the candidacy of Richard Nixon and Nelson Rockefeller for President and Vice-President of the United States, the idea being that they represented the perfect team to appeal to the electorate. From then it was applied to other such political teams, and more recently the idea of 'ticket' has developed beyond the use of 'list of candidates' in the original coinage, to a more general sense, 'an opportunity to do something or go somewhere'. 'Dream team' seems to have developed out of 'dream ticket', the attraction being the rhyme, while the sense is not greatly changed.

Jumping forward to the letter I, **impunity** may be a word to look out for, as it is cropping up increasingly, misused to mean 'without compunction', rather than 'without punishment'. 'Led' is a word that is increasingly being used as a combining form. **Market-led**, and in the current fear of terrorism **intelligence-led**, are probably the commonest, but the form has spread widely in officialese so that one finds uses such as: a patient-led NHS; enhancement-led institutional review; Persona-led Heuristic Inspection; practice-led commissioning; and community-led infrastructure. **It makes you think** is a catchphrase cliché, current from the 1920s, popular from the 1930s, and often indicating a singular lack of thought on the part of the speaker, as do some of the previous citations. Also in the Ms is the mindless and irritating **mind how you go**, an impertinence when used by a complete stranger as an alternative to the now declining HAVE A NICE DAY (see Chapter 3). For some reason I find the shop assistant's **there you go** even more infuriating, probably because it seems totally meaningless – where is 'there', and what or who is 'going'?

Moving on to the second half of the alphabet, **never a dull moment** originated in the 1880s, but took on an ironic tone in the Second World War when it became a naval catchphrase used in times of danger or frantic activity. 'The new . . .' is a formula phrase best known from **. . . is the new rock and roll**. As it is a journalistic vogue phrase dating from the early 1990s, it is a mystery why a term so dated as 'rock and roll' is used. Variants on the formula abound, particularly **. . . is the new black**. The urge to **pick some low-hanging fruit** for 'to take the easy option' is, however, recent. 'Low-hanging fruit' for, to quote the *OED*, 'the most readily accomplished of a set of tasks, measures, or goals' has not been recorded before 1990, but it is rapidly spreading. **Proactive** was not coined until the 1930s, and is rare before the 1970s. In form it is the opposite of 'reactive' and means dealing with a situation by controlling what happens through your actions rather than by reacting to what has already happened. At first it was used mainly in fields like psychology and the social sciences, but it has now got into the hands of those dealing with marketing, business studies and advertising, and is beginning to be little more than an emphatic form of 'active' (when it means anything). Fortunately, use seems to be on the decline from a peak in the 1990s. We now move on to another formula phrase, **. . . puts the . . . into . . .** The earliest example of this formula I have come across is in the writings of the American newspaper columnist Don Marquis. He wrote a series of 'poems' supposedly by a cockroach called Archy, the reincarnation of a *vers libre* poet. The only way a cockroach can type is to hurl himself headfirst on to a typewriter's keys one at a time, which means he cannot operate the shift key. 'archy interviews a pharaoh' was first published in book form in *Archy and Mehitabel* in 1927, when Prohibition was still in force in the USA. The Pharaoh tells Archy that he has spent the last four thousand years dreaming of beer:

> my reverend juicelessness
> this is a beerless country
> says i
> well well said the royal

desiccation
my political opponents back home
always maintained
that i would wind up in hell
and it seems they had the right dope
and with these hopeless words
the unfortunate residuum
gave a great cough of despair
and turned to dust and debris
right in my face
it being the only time
i ever actually saw anybody
put the cough
into sarcophagus

At its best this formula can be witty, as in Marquis's example and expressions such as 'puts the angst into gangster' or 'puts the mock into democracy', or at least vaguely amusing: 'puts the bad into troubadour', 'puts the vice into room service'. But it is often clumsily or unimaginatively used, and is certainly overused. At its clumsiest we find advertisements such as 'What puts the "special" in specialty tea?', while some seem to have missed the point, as in 'Unique store puts the hip in hop'. 'Fun' seems to be the word most commonly played on, and I have found the formula used of dysfunctional, fundamentalism (very common), fundraising and funeral (the last an advertisement for a computer game).

Real and **reality** are clearly overused. It has almost become a separate cliché to ask what reality television has to do with reality. Less obvious is the overuse of expressions such as **with real passion**, **in real life** and **the realities of life**, not to mention the juvenile GET REAL (see Chapter 3). **To have resonance** is a cliché that I am reluctant to write too much about, as I am well aware that I have used 'resonance' a number of times in this book, although not, I hope, in too clichéd a way. The use of the word **serious** to mean 'worthy of respect, substantial' became a cliché in the 1980s, particularly in the form **serious money**, although similar uses can be traced for about a hundred years. 'Serious money' was used to sum up the whole of the yuppie culture when Caryl Churchill used it as the title of her 1987 play.

We can finish up this by-no-means exhaustive list of buzz-words with four Ws. **We are not amused** is a catchphrase cliché derived from a story that Queen Victoria made the comment either when an equerry told an improper story within her hearing, or in response to catching someone doing an imitation of her. Victoria denied ever having said it, and it is most probably apocryphal, which is why it is not listed in Chapter 7. **Well**, used instead of 'very', is a vulgarism that has become very fashionable, but which usually makes the user look stupid. **Worked a charm**, like its companion **worked like magic** (often just shortened to **Magic!**), implies that something went really well, as if the people involved were bewitched. The expression dates back to the nineteenth century, but 'Magic!' as an exclamation did not become prominent until the 1970s.

Bibliography

Allen, Robert, *Allen's English Phrases* (Penguin, 2006)

Alt.usage.English, available online at http://alt-usage-english.org/ index.shtml

Ammer, Christine, *Have a Nice Day – No Problem* (Plume, 1992)

Apperson, G. L. (ed.), *Wordsworth Dictionary of Proverbs* (Wordsworth, 1993)

Augarde, Tony (ed.), *The Oxford Dictionary of Modern Quotations* (Oxford University Press, 1991)

Ayto, John and Ian Crofton, *Brewer's Dictionary of Modern Phrase and Fable* (Weidenfeld & Nicolson, 2006)

British National Corpus, available online at http://www.natcorp. ox.ac.uk

Cresswell, Julia, *The Penguin Dictionary of Clichés* (Penguin, 2000)

Deutscher, Guy, *The Unfolding of Language* (Heinemann, 2005)

Dictionary of National Biography, available online at http://www. oxforddnb.com/ and free via many county library websites

Double-tongued Word Wrester, available online at http://www. doubletongued.org/

Early Modern English Dictionaries Database, available online at http:// www.chass.utoronto.ca/english/emed/emedd.html

Green, Jonathan, *Jargon* (Routledge, 1987)

Hendrickson, Robert, *The Facts on File Encyclopedia of Word and Phrase Origins* (Facts on File, 1987)

Kirkpatrick, Betty, *Clichés* (Bloomsbury, 1996)

Knowles, Elizabeth (ed.), *The Oxford Dictionary of Twentieth-Century Quotations* (Oxford University Press, 1998)

Language Hat, available online at http://www.languagehat.com/

Language Log, available online at http://itre.cis.upenn.edu/~myl/ languagelog/

Lowe, Leslie, *Music Master Directory of Popular Music* (1975; Waterlow, 1986)

Mencken, H. L., *The American Language* (1921), available online at http://www.bartleby.com

Oxford English Dictionary (OED), available online at http://www.oed.com and free via many county library websites

Oxford Reference Online, available at http://www.oxfordreference.com/pages and free via many library websites

Partington, Angela (ed.), *The Oxford Dictionary of Quotations*, 4th edn (Oxford University Press, 1992)

Partridge, Eric, *A Dictionary of Clichés* (1940; Routledge, 1978)

Partridge, Eric, ed. Paul Beale, *A Dictionary of Catch Phrases from the Sixteenth Century to the Present Day* (1977; Routledge, 1985)

Phrase Finder, available online at http://www.phrases.org.uk/index.html

Project Gutenberg, available online at http://www.gutenberg.org/

Quinion, Michael, *Port Out and Starboard Home and other Language Myths* (Penguin, 2004)

Rees, Nigel, *A Word in Your Shell-like* (Collins, 2004)

Rees, Nigel, *Dictionary of Clichés* (Cassell, 1996)

Rogers, James, *Dictionary of Clichés* (Ballantine, 1985)

Shapiro, Fred R., *Yale Dictionary of Quotations* (Yale University Press, 2006)

Simpson, John, *The Concise Oxford Dictionary of Proverbs* (Oxford University Press, 1982)

Speake, Jennifer, *Oxford Dictionary of Proverbs* (Oxford University Press, 2004); available online via Oxford Reference Online

Spiegl, Fritz, '*A Game of Two Halves, Brian*' (Harpercollins, 1996)

The Times Digital Archive, available online at http://www.galeuk.com/times/ and free via many library websites

Wikipedia, available online at http://en.wikipedia.org/

Word Detective, available online at http://www.word-detective.com/backidx.html

World Wide Words, available online at http://www.worldwidewords.org/

Index

Acknowledgements

My thanks to Guy Deutscher for permission to quote from *The Unfolding of Language* (Heinemann, 2005); to Professor Mark Harrison and Richard Brown for advice on 'to bite the bullet'; to the Bothy Vineyard, Frilford Heath, Oxfordshire, for help with 'sour grapes'; and to Boyd Tonkin of the *Independent* for putting me right on 'power without responsibility' in his review of my *Penguin Dictionary of Clichés*.

In some cases I have been unable to trace or contact the copyright holder. If notified the publisher will be pleased to rectify any errors or omissions at the earliest opportunity.